The Fugitive's Properties

STEPHEN M. BEST

The Fugitive's Properties

LAW AND THE POETICS OF POSSESSION

THE UNIVERSITY OF CHICAGO PRESS • CHICAGO AND LONDON

Stephen M. Best is associate professor of English at the University of California, Berkeley.

The University of Chicago Press, Chicago 60637

The University of Chicago Press, Ltd., London

© 2004 by Stephen Michael Best

All rights reserved. Published 2004

Printed in the United States of America

13 12 11 10 09 08 07 06 05 04   1 2 3 4 5

ISBN: 0-226-04433-5 (cloth)

ISBN: 0-226-04434-3 (paper)

Library of Congress Cataloging-in-Publication Data

Best, Stephen Michael.

   The fugitive's properties : law and the poetics of possession /
   Stephen M. Best

       p.   cm.

   Includes bibliographical references (p.   ) and index.

   ISBN 0-226-04433-5 (cloth : alk. paper)—ISBN 0-226-04434-3 (pbk. :
   alk. paper)

       1. American literature—19th century—History and criticism.

   2. Slavery in literature.   3. Fugitive slaves—Legal status, laws, etc.—United States.

   4. Stowe, Harriet Beecher, 1811–1896. Uncle Tom's cabin.   5. Law and literature—

   History—19th century.   6. African Americans in literature.   7. Fugitive slaves in literature.

   8. Property in literature.   9. Race in literature.   I. Title.

PS217 .S55 B47 2004

810.9′3552—dc22

                                                         2003016071

♾ The paper used in this publication meets the minimum requirements of the American National
Standard for Information Sciences—Permanence of Paper for Printed Library Materials,
ANSI Z39.48-1992.

To Alan and Monica Best and in memory of Michael Rogin

CONTENTS

ILLUSTRATIONS

DEBTS

Economies are always without bounds, and debts without terminus. I may appear to corrupt the bond of friendship, then, when I characterize it as, variously, a structure of economy (and thus limitless) and debt (and thus infinite). Yet I would be just as much in error were I to fail to acknowledge the wealth of interests in this particular authorial enterprise — an error perhaps inexcusable in a book that is in part about debt. A just accounting begins at Williams College, where David Lionel Smith, in a manner that would propel me toward advanced study, provided sober and persistent encouragement of serious intellectual pursuit. At Penn, Houston A. Baker Jr., Eric Cheyfitz, and Lynda Hart were always available when guidance, readings, bibliographies, and other academic goods often taken for granted were in need. A special word of immense gratitude goes to Houston for unparalleled measures of support and his unswerving commitment to mentoring. Regina Austin, Herman Beavers, Margreta deGrazia, Farah Griffin, Manthia Diawara, John Richetti, John Roberts, and Peter Stallybrass also proved wonderful teachers and mentors.

Many brilliant and generous minds have encouraged me at pivotal moments not to shy away from hard thinking and have left me wonderfully disoriented and not quite sure whether my text (or my thoughts in general) offered a map or the geography in need of mapping: Lauren Berlant, Claudia Brett, Victoria Shane Cook, Michele Frank, Farah Griffin, Jay Grossman, Susan Harding, Martin Hilton, Glen Ligon, Mark Lleydorf, Charles Lofton, Crystal Lucky, Jeff Masten, Jason Miller, José Muñoz, Tim Murphy, Arnold Rampersad, Paul Rogers, Craig Smith, Antonio Viego, and Tobias Woolf.

The new vistas opened up to me by my colleagues and friends at Berkeley have been perhaps the most striking. I thank Elizabeth Abel, Mitch Breitweiser, Judith Butler, Carol Clover, Catherine Gallagher, Kevis Goodman, Saidiya Hartman, Tom Lacquer, Colleen Lye, D. A. Miller, Chris Nealon, Sam Otter, Beth Pittenger, Robert Post, Michael Rogin, Kaja Silverman, and Ula Taylor for their commitment to ideas in general and to mine in particular. I am also thankful for the stimulus and research support of Hoang Phan and Thy Phu.

In 1997 I had the opportunity to spend a semester in dialogue with other scholars as part of the "Histories of the Future" research seminar at the Humanities Research Institute (University of California, Irvine). In 1998–99, I was extended a similar opportunity by the Doreen Townsend Center for the Humanities at Berkeley. My thinking on these matters came to a head in 2003 when I had the opportunity to collaborate with Saidiya on the organization of the Mellon Foundation Sawyer Seminar/HRI research seminar "Redress in Law, Literature, and Social Thought"; a more rigorous, generous, and committed group of friends I cannot imagine. This book was written with the research support of Madeline Matz, Zoran Sinobad, and other librarians at the Library of Congress and the Schomburg Center of the New York Public Library. It was also written with the financial support of the Hellman Family Faculty Fund and numerous fellowships from the Committee on Research at Berkeley. Audiences at Johns Hopkins University, the Tate Britain, Birkbeck School of Law—University of London, University of California, Santa Cruz, University of California, San Diego, Stanford University, and Boalt Hall (Berkeley) provided productive dialogue and sent me along fruitful pathways. I am grateful to my colleagues at the Aspen Institute seminar "Law and Society" (2003) for their engagement, criticism, and support and grateful, too, to my editor at the University of Chicago Press, Alan Thomas, for his.

To Judith Jackson Fossett and Clayton Fossett, and my sisters Lisa and Nat, I own an inestimable debt of gratitude. The debt shall be repaid, but— puzzlingly—life, in this case, seems too short a term.

The Slave's Two Bodies

> Slaves were held *pro nullis: pro mortuis: pro quadrupedibus.* They had no head
> in state, no name, title or register: they were not capable of being injured . . . nor
> were they proper objects of cognation or affinity, but of *quasi-cognation* only:
> they could be sold, transferred, or pawned as goods or personal estate.
> JOHN TAYLOR, *Elements of the Civil Law* (1755)

> Slaves, though moveable by their nature, are considered as immoveable by the
> operation of law.
> WILLIAM GOODELL, *The American Slave Code* (1853)

Harriet Beecher Stowe receives no end of criticism when she suggests, in
the closing pages of *Uncle Tom's Cabin* (1852), that in answer to "the struggle
between abolitionist and colonizationist" the best thing those Americans
touched by the emancipatory spirit could do for the country's slaves is to
"assist them in their passage to th[e] shores" of Africa.[1] For Stowe to make
such a proposal at midcentury is, at the very least, to revive a political
scheme logistically infeasible since the demise of the American Colonization Society in the 1830s. For her to appease "abolitionist and colonizationist" in this way is, at its worst, secretly to traffic in faulty etymologies,
for it equates the "abolition" of slavery (defined as "the act of . . . putting an
end to" something [*Oxford English Dictionary,* 2d ed.]) with the "abolition" of slaves (defined, somewhat differently, as "a putting out of memory"
[*Oxford English Dictionary,* 2d ed.]). Stowe has it that the "effort at *repa-
ration* for the wrongs that the American nation has brought" on members
of "an ignorant, inexperienced, half-barbarized race" comes, logically, in
the form of repatriation—the least morally costly option for those "American Christian[s who] owe . . . the African race" (625–26, emphasis mine).

Yet Stowe's equation of slavery with slaves divulges a rather keen insight—that slavery as a system of exchange has perhaps progressed so far as
to be linked inextricably to its object of exchange. For sure, there could be

1

no slavery without slaves. But it may be the case that the latter is so thoroughly symbolic of the former—so exhaustively a "property" of it—that abolition requires annulment of them both (not only the form of slavery but the slaves themselves). Slavery may necessitate colonization, according to this line of thought. And in specific regard to this scheme, Stowe's husband would confess in a telling remark to John P. Jewett, the book's publisher, "I should have supposed . . . she couldn't find any place else to come out at."[2] Slavery threatens to live on in its commodity; its commodity has a life of its own. Or, in this instance, in what amounts to the same thing, the commodity celebrates its becoming human in the slave.[3] "This accursed system," Stowe complains, has been spurred on by the Fugitive Slave Law of 1850 and has made it such that anyone, North or South, can "trade the souls and bodies of men as an equivalent to money, in their mercantile dealings" (624). Slavery threatens to leave, in perpetuity, its unique scandal of value. The slave has become a money form.[4]

But the crime of slavery is doubly resonant for Stowe. The violation marked by slavery is certainly biblical in scope, for it takes God's original "nontransferable" property and makes it exchangeable: "That soul immortal, once bought with blood and anguish by the Son of God, when the earth shook, and the rocks rent, and the graves were opened, can be sold, leased, mortgaged, exchanged for groceries or dry goods, to suit the phases of trade, or the fancy of the purchaser" (467). Yet the events of 1850 go even further—turning "the souls and bodies of men" into expressions of "money," into exemplars of exchange. The slave becomes a model of symbolization and figuration. And contrary to Stowe's description of George Shelby as bearer of the "indubitable signs [arguably, his whiteness], which showed too plainly that the man could *not* become a thing," the slaves in her text seem increasingly to purvey slavery's "indubitable signs" of ownership—the traces and markings of blackness. Stowe implicitly maintains that a system of property relations indicated by yet hidden beneath the figure of blackness has two enduring effects on both property and figuration. The first is to secure a system that could only be "abolished" once the figures were "pu[t] out of memory." The second is to create a unique species of "living property"—an everyday animism that cuts across the founding difference between persons and property and that, by turns, violates liberal standards of sovereign possession (standards in which the first thing one owns is oneself). It is these violations that, in effect, lead Aunt Chloe to lament, in response to Uncle Tom's sale, that "thar's wrong about it *somewhar* . . . I can't jest make out whar 't is, but thar's wrong somewhar, I'm *clar* o' that" (164). Stowe fears that Americans may never again be able to make "clar" the distinction between persons and property. This fear animates her further panic that there may be an afterlife to slavery.

Stowe is not alone in this regard, for there are others who, spurred by similar religious belief, push just as aggressively the claim to slavery's effect on the mortal and the immortal, on the finitude of fleshly existence and the immutable within time. William Goodell, confrere in the antislavery struggle and author of *The American Slave Code—Its Theory and Practice; Its Distinctive Features Shown by Its Statutes, Judicial Decisions, and Illustrative Facts* (1853), descries the law of slavery for extending the tentacles of property rights "not merely to the body, but to the soul."[5] The honesty or piety or benevolence of a man "is a commodity in the market!" complains Goodell—and, what is more, members of the same religious sect, vouching for their property's character, "buy and sell [slaves] on the basis of these recommendations" (18, 28). He saves his most stinging rebuke for those "free citizens and professed Christians of the North" who, for all their moral hand wringing, still speak of "the slaveholder's 'rights of property'" and of reparations for the slaves' emancipation (27). This claim of property in slaves, he warns, "both in theory and practice, as defined by legislation and jurisprudence, as defended by theologians and as sanctioned by ecclesiastical bodies, as carried out into every-day practice by the pious and by the profane, is manifestly and notoriously a claim, not only to the bodies and the physical energies of the slave, but also to his immortal soul, his human intelligence, his moral powers, and even (in the case of a pious slave) to his Christian graces and virtues" (27). With ironic zeal, Goodell seals his case: "This is proved by the fact, that the body of the slave without his soul would be a dead carcase [*sic*] of no value" (27). Slavery, an effect of mortal hubris, encroaches on the sacrosanct precincts of God the Father, for the legal relation of master and slave "challenges as 'goods' and 'chattels personal' . . . the immortal soul of man, the image of the invisible Creator, the temple of the Holy Spirit, the purchase of a Redeemer's blood" (28). Yet quickly and curiously, what Goodell gives with one hand ("defended by theologians and . . . sanctioned by ecclesiastical bodies") he takes with the other: "The statement is no rhetorical flourish; it is no mere logical inference; it is no metaphysical subtlety; it is no empty abstraction. It is no obsolete or inoperative fiction of the law. It is a veritable matter-of-fact reality, acted out every day wherever and whenever a negro or anyone else is claimed as an American slave" (28).

I would charge otherwise, that "metaphysical subtlety" and "fiction of . . . law" are incapable of such capricious effacement, that each is an exigency of the slave as an intelligible form. Another way to put the point is to say that the slave has "two bodies" recognized by law—the first mortal and the second ("considered as immoveable by the operation of law," conceived as an object of "estate") implicitly immortal. As it was often suggested, the slave was an object of property as well as a subject of sentiment. The coeval slave was in every way both a reinterpretation of theological niceties and, springing from such pretenses, a patent "fiction of the law."[6] Goodell concedes as much when he states that "the claim of property in slaves . . . is manifestly and notoriously a claim, not only to the bodies and the physical energies of the slave, but also to his immortal soul"; and, for evidence of the "metaphysical subtlety" or "fiction of the law" that could permit of such a legal outrage, he might well have taken a closer look at a text he himself excavates extensively for the fundaments of American slave law—Sir William Blackstone's *Commentaries on the Laws of England.*[7]

In book 1 ("Of the Rights of Persons"), chapter 7 ("Of the King's Prerogative") of his *Commentaries,* Blackstone offers a gloss of the fiction of the king's two bodies. The king's royal "character" (or "dignity," as he puts it) consists of three "attributes of a great and transcendent nature," which when taken together lead his subjects "to consider him in the light of a superior being" (241). These attributes are "sovereignty" ("no suit or action can be brought against the king . . . because no court can have jurisdiction over him"), "absolute perfection" ("The king can do no wrong"), and "perpetuity" (or "absolute immortality") (242–49). This last Blackstone describes as follows:

> The law ascribes to him, in his political capacity, an absolute immortality. The king never dies. Henry, Edward, or George may die; but the king survives them all. For immediately upon the decease of the reigning prince in his natural capacity, his kingship or imperial dignity, by act of law, without any *interregnum* or interval, is vested at once in his heir; who is, *co instanti* king to all intents and purposes. And so tender is the law of supposing even a possibility of his death, that his natural dissolution is generally called his *demise; demisso regis, vel coronae:* an expression which signifies merely a transfer of property; for, as is observed in [Edmund] Plowden['s *Commentaries or Reports*], when we say the demise of the crown we mean only that, in consequence of the disunion of the king's natural body from his body politic, the kingdom is transferred or demised to his successor; and so the royal dignity remains perpetual.

The king is, in short, two persons in one, a natural king and a supernatural king, a "body natural" and a "body politic" (as Plowden himself drew the distinction prior to Blackstone). "King" is a *persona mixta*. While the king's terrestrial, natural body is mortal and finite, subject to cycles of regeneration and corruption, his royal body stands above and incorporates the natural bodies of both the king himself and his subjects. This sublime, immaterial, sacred body outlives the natural body and thus provides the kingdom with its immortality, with its necessary omnipotence and continuity through time; kingship is "without any *interregnum*." "King is a Name of Continuance," witnessed one sixteenth-century English jurist—or, as another fashioned, in the celebrated case of the *Duchy of Lancaster* (1562):

> Although he [the king] has, or takes, the land in his natural Body, yet to this natural Body is conjoined his Body politic, which contains his royal Estate and Dignity; and the Body politic includes the Body natural, but the Body natural is the lesser, and with this the Body politic is consolidated. So that he has a Body natural, adorned and invested with the Estate and Dignity royal; and he has not a Body natural distinct and divided by itself from the Office and Dignity royal, but a Body natural and a Body politic together indivisible; and these two Bodies are incorporated in one Person, and make one Body and not divers, that is the Body corporate in the Body natural, *et e contra* the Body natural in the Body corporate. So that the Body natural, by this conjunction of the Body politic to it (which Body politic contains the Office, Government, and Majesty royal) is magnified, and by the said Consolidation hath in it the Body politic.[8]

In his memorable study of the fiction of the king's two bodies, Ernst Kantorowicz holds that the doctrine of "twin-born majesty" (medieval in origin) provides early-modern adherents with a heuristic fiction that satisfies the necessities of law and the state; that, with regard to both, it signifies "the Immutable within Time" (*King's Two Bodies,* 8). Kingship conceived as a body politic temporarily incarnated in a king of flesh weds mortality to immortality, individuality to indivisibility ("a Body natural and a Body politic together indivisible; and these two Bodies are incorporated in one Person"), and visibility to invisibility ("[the king's] Body politic is a Body that cannot be seen or handled").[9] Subordinating the first term in these pairs to the second, the mystic fiction of kingship preserves the regime's continuity through time. The language of the king's two bodies identifies the realm's

mystical incorporation with its unique incarnation; and, as a distinctly theological inheritance, kingship restores something of the mystical "body" of
Christ. Confusing the distinctions between body and office, person and
law, Kantorowicz advances, monarchical jurisprudence manages to harmo-
nize modern law with ancient theological doctrine; it casuistically draws
into alignment the personal with the more impersonal concepts of government (or, as Claude Lefort clarifies, for reasons of the fiction's confusion of
love between man and God with that between man and king "love is put 'in
the place of law' ").[10]

What is more, the king is a king not because his natural body possesses
some unique material or mystical substance but because his subjects treat
him like one. The king is a symbolic function, the unique incarnation of a
network of social relations. Within the penumbra of the king's *corpus mys-
ticum,* "there lies an unconscious representation of a society embodied in a
king ... [one] whose members are so captivated by the image of a body that
they project onto it their own union"; "king" is an "image of the people"
and "regime" a shaping (*mise-en-forme*) of human coexistence.[11] The mysteries of monarchical incarnation inhabit the inner shadows of this architecture of projections and reflections—mysteries mocked when the English legal historian Frederic W. Maitland styles the twinned king a being
"*par*sonified," and confesses that he would "not know where to look ... in
the whole series of our law books for so marvelous a display of metaphysical—or we might say metaphysiological—nonsense."[12]

Maitland and Goodel seem, curiously, to understate and overstate their
respective cases. Maitland's confession can be styled agnostic, the ostensibly searching survey of a legal historian who, certainly aware of recent fervor over property in persons, throws a blind eye to the gothic legal architectures that protected the practice—the "metaphysiology" captured, for
example, in John Taylor's reference to "objects of . . . *quasi-cognation,*"
which, strictly put, protects essentially meaningless relations of partial
propinquity, incomplete consanguinity.[13] Goodell, in contrast, appears to
overstate the irrelevance of jurisprudential mystifications to the nineteenth-
century law of property, specifically those "metaphysiological" formulations that protect rights in "chattel personal" and the property status of the
fugitive slave. The king's twinned embodiment satisfies a necessary function of monarchical law and the state, one that exists in a twofold structure
of doubling and projection—of a supernatural body incarnated in a natural body, a "society" given shape by a carnal body. I would argue that the
secular jurisprudence of nineteenth-century America both needs a similar

structure of embodiment and finds a correlate persona in the chattel slave. Legal agnosticism (Maitland) and moral hyperbole (Goodell) suggest just that, as each struggles in its own way to save secular jurisprudence from the undertow of mystical embodiment.

Certainly it is the case that, to the thinkers responsible for America's revolutionary birth, modern democracy marks the final "demise" of the king's mystical incorporation, the final rejection of the royal "body politic" along with its ancillary metaphysics. The American revolutionaries who set the stage for later constitutional disputes rejected the loyalist claim that the Crown was the "supreme legislative head" and the subjects the "members" of the body politic: "There is [a] distinction for which no truly natural or religious reason can be assigned, and that is, the distinction of men into kings and subjects."[14] These same partisans in the royalist debate articulate their rejection (free the state from royal prerogative and identify it with the rule of law) through an imagined decapitation of the body politic that actualizes a democratic "image of the people"—as in Thomas Paine's *Common Sense* (1776), where regicide occurs on *tête*'s substitution by text:

> Yet that we may not appear to be defective even in earthly honours, let a day be solemnly set a part for proclaiming the Charter; let it be brought forth placed on the Divine Law, the Word of God; *let a crown be placed thereon*, by which the world may know, that so far as we approve of monarchy, that in America the law is king. For as in absolute governments the King is law, so in free countries the law ought to be king; and there ought to be no other. But lest any ill use should afterwards arise, let the Crown at the conclusion of the ceremony be demolished, and scattered among the people whose right it is. (434; emphasis mine)

As I said, revolutionary textuality substitutes for corporeal regicide, and the rule of law for royal license and prescription. Yet, the tendency even here for kingly metaphor ("the law is king") and "the Crown" to endure, most acutely in the latter's dissolution into an array of distinct and individual democratic "rights," speaks to the persistence of the symbolic operation of kingship in secular doctrines of the law—specifically, to necessities of incarnation and abstraction, corporeality and representation betrayed by that generation's vocabulary (current to our own) of the law and the state, of "incorporation" and "sovereignty," of "body politic" and "head of state," as well as that lexicon of "immortality" and "individuality" that signifies the dual unity of the corporation (this last of which I will address shortly).

I would go a step further and argue that Paine's persistent corporeality gives answer to a difficulty common to modern democracy—how to make immanent a social body that is no longer embodied in the figure of the prince. I would argue, following Lefort, that absent a kingly idol in which the social might find itself embodied, "certain schemata of organization and representation survive thanks to the displacement and transference on to new entities of the image of the body and of its double nature . . . of a mediation between visible and invisible, between the eternal and the temporal" (249). And, what is more, there seem several formations within nineteenth-century American jurisprudence that, despite efforts at a secular legal code free from the metaphysical subtleties and existential absurdities of monarchical embodiment, indicate some evidence of the displacement and transference of which Lefort speaks. I refer here to the moral, political, and metaphysical debate over slave property (more often a debate over the slave's personhood) and to the equally metaphysical discussion among legal scholars of the ontology of the corporation's "personality."

Abolitionists in the nineteenth-century debate over slavery decried the institution for confusing the boundaries between property and persons—limits held sacrosanct by measures of theology, philosophy, or physics. In the liberal formulation attributed to John Locke, the only warranted exception (and it structured the larger categorical pieties) was the property right one had in one's own labor. It was Locke's theory that every man had a single "*Property* in his own *Person*," that the "*Labour* of his Body, and the *Work* of his Hands . . . are properly his." [15] Locke's reasoning proved central to a structure of thought in which, as C. B. Macpherson clarifies, "the nature of ownership . . . was read back into the nature of the individual"—proved fundamental to the concept of "possessive individualism," where "the human essence is freedom from dependence on the wills of others, and freedom is a function of possession." [16] Partisans on either side of the slavery debate faced the self-evident existential absurdity and moral contradiction that one person can be a simple extension of the will of another. And while some, ignoring such absurdities, asserted that slaves were "chattels personal" (that the owner not only had a right to the slave's services but also possessed total control over his person), others demurred, reimagining the slave as a form of "realty" (or "freehold property," in which the owner had a right to the slave's services only). [17] In the face of abolitionist assaults, many of slavery's apologists narrowed their claims to property rights in slaves to a claim to their labor, and a right to labor for the most part warranted a further right to obedience:

Properly speaking . . . the slave himself is not property but his labour is. . . . We own the labour of the slave and this cannot be done without keeping the person performing the labour, thus owned, in bondage.[18]

(FRANCIS LIEBER, 1849)

The right to such work is all the ownership which any one man can rightfully have in another; and this is all which any slaveholder of the South needs to claim. . . . [We lay claim to] a right to the labor and lawful obedience of the slave.[19]

(ALBERT TAYLOR BLEDSOE, 1856)

The person of the slave is not property, no matter what the fictions of law may say; but the right to his labor is property, and may be transferred like any other property.[20]

(E. N. ELLIOT, 1860)

This perception that slavery's "bundle of rights" attached to the slave's labor and not his or her body even finds echo in the Fugitive Slave Law of 1850, which holds, in short, "that when *a person held to service or labor in any State* or Territory of the United States has heretofore or shall hereafter escape into another State or Territory of the United States, the person or persons to whom such service or labor may be due, or his, her, or their agent or attorney . . . may pursue and reclaim such fugitive person . . . with proof . . . by affidavit . . . of the identity of *the person whose service or labor is claimed to be due as aforesaid. . . .*" The law's figuration of the fugitive as pilfered property and indebted person, object of property and subject of contract, bears distinct consequences for the practice of jurisprudence and for legal and aesthetic representation (as I will argue in chap. 1). It satisfies, however, our inaugural concerns. The fugitive is, in short, two persons in one, and as a matter of nineteenth-century jurisprudence and legal procedure, few forms of legal personhood rival the fugitive for its ability to incite a crisis in (and provisional resolution of) the tenets and practices of the law.

Few, that is, save for the doctrine that "a corporation is a person," which provokes questions of the corporation's ontology (of the grounds of its intelligibility) and of what the law means by "person." What is the corporate entity? Is it a "natural" person in the sense in which that descriptive is commonly used—rational and willing, feeling and moral—or is it an "artificial" person, a mere creation of the state? If the latter, is that creation "imaginary" and "fictitious," or is an act that looks to be a creation merely one of legal recognition, the conferring of a purely legalistic meaning on a "real" presence? Is the corporation even a "person," or is it a "personification" of some entity that preexists the law? And what of its intangibility and invisibility—how could it be both real and invisible? Familiarly, some chose the route of agnosticism, making an end run around these metaphysical and logical subtleties by insisting on the materiality of their metaphors. Any corporation formed out of the union of natural persons is, according to this "reality theory" of corporate personality, a new real person, a real corporate "organism." Paddling about in the extremes of anthropomorphism, advocates of this theory maintain that the corporate organism is, like its constituent members, an "animal" possessed of "organs . . . with a will and with senses": "A *universitas* [or corporate body] . . . is a living organism and a real person, with body and members and a will of its own."[21]

Reality soon gives place to fiction, as the theory of corporate personality that achieves orthodox status in American jurisprudence (a theory codified in American law in the U.S. Supreme Court case of *Dartmouth v. Woodward* [1819]) approaches these conceptual nuances without fear of succumbing to mystificatory nonsense. The legal historian Arthur W. Machen paraphrases this theory as follows: "A corporation is a fictitious, artificial person, composed of natural persons, created by the State, existing in contemplation of law, invisible, soulless, immortal."[22] In the original, an opinion crafted by Chief Justice John Marshall, the theory reads in full:

A corporation is an artificial being, invisible, intangible, and existing only in contemplation of law. Being the mere creature of law, it possesses only those properties that the charter of its creation confers on it, either expressly, or as incidental to its very existence. These are such as are supposed best calculated to effect the object for which it was created. Among the most important are immortality, and, if the expression may be allowed, individuality; properties, by which a perpetual succession of many persons are considered as the same, and may act as a single individual. They enable a corporation to manage its own affairs, and to hold property, without the perplexing intricacies, the hazardous and endless necessity, or perpetual conveyances for the purpose of transmitting it from hand to hand. It is chiefly for the purpose of clothing bodies of men, in succession, with these qualities and capacities, that corporations were invented, and are in use. By these means, a perpetual succession of individuals is capable of acting for the promotion of the particular object, like one immortal being. But this being does not share in the civil government of the country, unless that be the purpose for which it was created. Its immortality no more confers on it political power, or a political character, than immortality would confer such power or character on a natural person.[23]

The corporation is, like kingship, "without any *interregnum.*" Even so, Machen stamps this theory a "*congeries* of self-contradictory terms," correcting for its confusion of material with imaginary quantities:

> A corporation cannot possibly be both an artificial person and an imaginary or fictitious person. That which is artificial is real, and not imaginary: an artificial lake is not an imaginary lake. . . . So a corporation cannot be at the same time "created by the state" and fictitious. If a corporation is "created," it is real, and therefore cannot be a purely fictitious body having no existence except in the legal imagination. Moreover, a corporation cannot possibly be imaginary or fictitious and also composed of natural persons. Neither in mathematics nor in philosophy nor in law can the sum of several actual, rational quantities produce an imaginary quantity.[24]

In Machen's correction, a corporation is a real entity distinct from its constituent members and resistant to the vicissitudes of time in the same way that a bundle of sticks (or a "bundle of rights") and, doctrinally, the "One Catholic and Apostolic Church" are—remove or add a stick and you do not destroy "the identity of the bundle," remove or add a member and "the Church is the same church to-day as in the days of our Lord" (259). In recognizing the corporate entity the law is merely recognizing an "objective fact" (260)—that the corporation is a person to the extent that it responds to the laws commands, that it possesses a personality that lies not in the possession of rights but "in subjection to liabilities [and duties]" (in its attentiveness to "thou-shalt-not's" [260, 263–64]). This emphasis on the law's obeisance before an objective presence explains in part John Dewey's assertion that "'person' signifies what law makes it signify," which act of attribution can only occur with the assist of those "non-legal concepts" that buttress the corporation's objectivity and intelligibility ("considerations popular, historical, political, moral, philosophical, metaphysical and, in connection with the latter, theological" [655]).

The corporation is neither an imaginary fiction nor a natural person, in Machen's view. It is, rather, a "personification," for "although corporate personality is a fiction, the entity that is personified is not fiction. The union of the members is no fiction. The acting as if they were one person is no mere metaphor. In a word although corporate personality is a fiction, yet it is a fiction founded upon fact" (266). As such, Machen takes pains to elaborate, the unevenness of corporate personality—part fact and part fiction, an "immortal [and transcendent] being" composed entirely of "natural persons," an invisible entity incarnated in "a perpetual succession of many persons"—follows the wayward itineraries of the slave in courts of law. What is true for the corporation had been, for all legal purposes from Machen's vantage, also true for the slave: "Although the law of the Southern States declared with emphasis that slaves were not persons, and deprived them of many of the rights usually enjoyed by persons, nevertheless it left them subject to legal duties. For instance, if a slave committed murder, he could be hanged. When the law declared that a slave was not a person, it meant merely that *he was to be treated for some purposes as if he were not a person*" (264, emphasis mine).

Legal scholars often refer to this juridical caprice as the law's "dual invocation of humanity and interest"—statutory law's complex deployments of consent, intentionality, and will, as well as its subtle figurations of abstraction, fancy, and fact. The evident whimsy of the law's exercise of its personifying powers warrants a consideration of the most important corporation case of the nineteenth century, *Santa Clara v. Southern Pacific Railroad* (1885).[25] In that case, the U.S. Supreme Court extends to corporations the legal status of "person" within the meaning of the Fourteenth Amendment to the Constitution: endowing corporations with the rights and privileges, duties and liabilities that the Constitution ascribes to the agents of contractual liberty (the "due process" protection of citizens against deprivation of life, liberty, or property by the state, and the guarantee of "equal protection of the laws," both of which were intended to extend a formal equality to the recently freed slaves). This extension through the figure of the "person" of the rights presumptive of citizenship makes it possible for new as well as old forms of wealth to be protected against state infringement so long as courts of any rank are persuaded to treat them as property. Yet, in *Santa Clara,* as before, the invocation of received form subordinates metaphysical amplification and abstruse argumentation to an agnostic real politik. In the words of John Norton Pomeroy, lawyer for the Southern Pacific Railroad, "whatever be the legal nature of a corporation as an artificial, metaphysical being, separate and distinct from the individual members . . . in applying the fundamental guaranties of the constitution . . . *these metaphysical and technical notions must give way to the reality.* . . . For the purpose of protecting rights, the property of all business and trading corporations is the property of the individual corporators. . . . There is no real distinction between artificial persons or corporations, and natural persons."[26]

The modern corporation owes much to the recently emancipated, as many scholars have pointed out, but the Fourteenth Amendment is not the origin of its debt; for, as still others have shown, the personhood of the emancipated was no novel legal form born of legislative magic, and paradoxically owed much to the *persona mixta* of the enslaved. The emancipated, Saidiya Hartman argues, while formally free, were no less assuredly trapped within a circuit of bondage. The personhood enshrined in both legislative enactment and legal primer was burdened with debt, duty, and other entanglements of conscience and accountability—all as proper repayment for a freedom purchased with the human and fiduciary expenditures of war. "Put your trust in God, and bend your back joyfully and hopefully to the burden," cautioned one of the freed's more avuncular counselors. While emancipation extended "freedman's privileges" it also shackled the emancipated with "freedman's duties" (in this same adviser's words), which paradox "engendered an anomalous condition betwixt and between slavery and freedom."[27] Slavery finds itself chiasmatically mirrored in freedom—the enslaved's occasional criminal liability reflected in the freedman's wounded and guilty conscience. And while this structure of accountability makes us wonder what (if any) transformation of the "person" was wrought by emancipation, a certain cynicism should also make us wonder how far back into the archives of law *Santa Clara*'s "person" ought properly to lead us. *Santa Clara* provides evidence yet again that "'person' signifies what law makes it signify"—that, by offering yet another complex engendering of the form of the person, the law is capable uninterruptedly to wed property to personhood, legal agnosticism to theological catechism, and mortality to immortality (capable, finally, to keep alive the "confused intermixture[s]" [Dewey, 658] of an antebellum marketplace). The case's uncertain footing in emancipatory enactment gives hint of Dewey's larger suspicion that the notion of personality constantly undergoes "chameleon-like change" in western culture, "a change [that] has never, moreover, effected complete replacement of an earlier by a later idea" (658). My own initial proposal was that slavery threatened to leave, in perpetuity, its unique scandal of value; and it seems that, considering this potential for "chameleon-like change," considering, too, that revolution (even that which would dispense with the institution of slavery) promises to remain largely inefficacious at the level of the semiotic, Harriet Beecher Stowe has every cause for concern.

FUGITIVE PROPERTY

In *The Fugitive's Properties*, I take Dewey's view of form in history (of form as a dialectic of continuity and change) as axiomatic—as an axiom key to my wider assertion that within the text of the law there is an afterlife of slavery. As a general matter, I engage these questions of slavery here as matters of aesthetic and legal representation—as an aesthetics of legal representation—and route these concerns through the historical frame of transformations in the conception of property, the latter of which were wrought by both the struggle to achieve the slaves' emancipation and the effort to define property rights in an expanding market in intangible assets. What incites the various arguments of *The Fugitive's Properties* is a curiously fictive and abstract transformation in turn-of-the-century American jurisprudence: the emergence of intellectual property rights in one's countenance, vocal style, ideas and thoughts, literary expressions, and other aspects of personality, which together gain legal ascendancy in the wake of the introduction of numerous mechanically reproductive devices. The invention and patent of the photographic camera (1839) and phonograph (1877) raised concern for a property right in one's "personal appearance, sayings, and acts," curiosity for the extent to which one has a "right to be let alone" (*Pavesich v. New England Life Insurance Co.* [1905]; *Robertson v. Rochester Folding Box Co.* [1902]). In subsequent decades, plaintiffs demanded a property right in their singing style on account of the voice's wireless communication and phonic reproduction (*Gardella v. Log Cabin Products, Inc.* [1937]). Similarly, the introduction of the motion picture camera (1892) stimulated a great deal of consternation over the reach of copyrights in dramatic and literary material (*Kalem Co. v. Harper Bros.* [1911]; *London v. Biograph Co.* [1916]). With the introduction of these and other technologies, parties sought to secure property rights in heretofore inalienable aspects of their personhood: their visual image, ideas, facial expressions, and even vocal style.

I take it as a given that these diverse claims in the sphere of intellectual property formed a single orbit in an expanding universe of property. The expansion to which I refer is one that many legal scholars and historians of capitalism claim came about in the shift from antebellum ideas of property as tangible parcels with clear boundaries (an idea modeled on landed property) to notions of property as abstract, intangible, or, as it was often put, a mere "bundle of rights." Plaintiffs demanded a code of law sufficiently elaborated to protect the pursuit of intangible value, one adequately capacious to include within its purview a right to a reasonable return on investment in intangible assets. The object of the law's solicitation was no longer (as it was under common law) absolute dominion over things but, rather, abstract ideas of individual expectations of stable market value and profit; and, with this shift, the law subordinated received protections against arbitrary power and trespass to the more important interest of encouraging marketability. Absent any thing into which property rights could be imagined to inhere, late-nineteenth-century American analytical jurisprudence perpetuated this ephemeralization and abstraction of property through the resurrection of theories of legal code attributed, in the main, to Jeremy Bentham (especially to his *Introduction to the Principles of Morals and Legislation* [1789]). Under the guise of Bentham, John Austin, and others, late-nineteenth-century jurists reconceived property as a scheme of jural correlatives in which one person's "right" to property necessarily implied another's "duty," one person's "power" in property entailed an added "liability" (or responsibility), and one person's "immunity" or freedom from the legal control of another correlated with the latter's powerlessness or "disability." Jurists concluded, in short, that the legal relations of property are between people and not, as had earlier been thought, between people and things. The law ensures the obstinacy and constancy of property (the expected calculability and profitability of investments and assets) by emphasizing property law's requisite constraints on conduct, by policing the domain of hardships.

The overall drift of the law to relativize rights and foreground duties, to demonstrate the complementarity of powers and hardships, of immunities and disabilities bears unique consequences for an intellectual property law that seeks to protect forms of personhood as property (e.g., voice, ideas, countenance). In the argument that unfolds over the forthcoming pages, turn-of-the-century intellectual property law leaves behind the question of the "nature" of the property protected under grants of copyright—a question that had plagued Anglo-American case law and legal treatise from the moment of the passage of the Statute of Anne in 1710. The law takes up, in its stead, market logics and the conception of property as relations of equity, credit extension, indebtedness, and contractual obligation.

The relation of master and slave is implicated in this Benthamite shift, as is slavery, in general, in the wider transformations in nineteenth-century property law. One of the core arguments I make in this book is that this shift of the law's gaze toward duties, obligations, and burdens—this vision of property as a matter of conduct, as a variable of personhood—comes into focus in nineteenth-century courts prima facie as the law of chattel slavery, specifically the law pertaining to fugitive slave persons. I propose that the alienation of human properties, such as labor from the person, becomes a legal conceit once abolition takes place and that this alienation of various "properties" of the person finds resonance in intellectual property law in the late nineteenth century and continues into the twentieth. The issues of personhood and property that slavery elaborates and the issues emanating from the emerging law on intellectual property are part of a fundamental historical continuity in the life of the United States in which the idea of personhood is increasingly subject to the domain of property. Slavery is not simply an antebellum institution that the United States has surpassed but a particular historical *form* of an ongoing crisis involving the subjection of personhood to property. In *The Fugitive's Properties* I thus attempt to provide an account of slavery jurisprudence and intellectual property law, as well as other legal constructions, in relation to the changing form of the commodity relation (the relation between persons and things and the conception of persons as things). Each chapter tracks changes and permutations that happen within the commodity form during the latter half of the nineteenth century, focusing on slavery in those instances not in order to arrive at a blueprint or original cause for subsequent forms of the commodity relation but to provide a way of asking questions about the social specificity of the person-property relation as the law tries to come to terms with new configurations of that relation and, in turn, generates new forms for that relation.

The idea for this book sprang from my belief that slave law and intellectual property law, as two spheres eccentric to the law of real property and emphatic about property's extension into the fleeting and evanescent, help to redefine the very essence of property in nineteenth-century America. To give this idea legs, as it were, I chose as my governing form the "fugitive," which in slave law names the runaway slave who is competing parts pilfered property and indebted person, and in intellectual property law captures those emergent forms of property given occasion by new technologies of mechanical reproduction, such as voice, countenance, and ideas and thoughts. I chose, too, as my governing thematic, the expressive similarities and structural connections between fugitive persons and fugitive personhood. The law assigned to deal with the former bore as its primary burden the codification of property that, paradoxically, behaved like a person—"thinking property," in Aristotle's memorable formulation. What is more, it lived up to that responsibility by way of a structure of reasoning and imagining capable to wed the incommensurables of an owner's willful dispossession and his slave's indebtedness, of domination and intentionality. The law of fugitive personhood, similarly, when faced with a phonograph that enabled the reproduction of the human voice or a photographic camera with which one could abscond with the visage of another, faced,

too, property's vacillation between embodiment and abstraction, corporeality and ideality. In their distinct ways, slave law and intellectual property
law face (and achieve compelling resolutions of) the paradox of the commodity form; whose value, in exchange, as Marx theorized, appears neither
entirely material and within reach nor entirely ideal and elusive but fugacious (and a tantalizingly absent presence) in that we know it exists yet "we
don't know 'where to have it.' " [28]

Or perhaps the problem is that it can be had everywhere, and that is the
source of Stowe's expressed fear. I began with that fear—that anyone can
"trade the souls and bodies of men as an equivalent to money"—in part because it wed this paradox of the commodity form to a certain panic at the
very conception of the human (panic at the law's threatened violations of the
soul); but what really deserves emphasis here is Stowe's alarm at the fugitive's promotion to the status of universal equivalent. For it is this turn in
Stowe's thought that suggests that the fugitive is implicated in broader
transformations in commercial law and culture. The law's purpose with regards to the fugitive, as Stowe appears to see, is to manage the slave's coeval
status as material property and willing self; but that purpose, as she also appears to see, has evolved in the direction of managing the relation between
the alienable (property) and the inalienable (the self) as a simple function
of the abstraction implicit in property, as a rigorous arithmetic of fungible
units. Some fluctuating measure of "souls" plus some fluctuating measure
of "bodies" yields "an equivalent to money." In this sense, the problem of
the fugitive in law and society, as Stowe perhaps could show but could not
see, is the problem of transcendent abstraction. Guyora Binder and Robert
Weisberg describe this problem as it relates to the development of American legal forms in the nineteenth century, specifically the rise of commercial
formalism: "Money became a more abstracted symbol that could float
above property and contracts, though it could always be reduced to those
things when necessary. . . . The abstraction of property and contract into
money had a 'shattering effect' on contract law. Legislatures resisted the ne-
gotiability of private money out of fear of losing control of the money supply. Thus, law in a capitalist society controlled the meaning of social and
contractual relations by controlling the ability of inscriptions of debt and
value to float free of their origins, to achieve transcendent abstraction." [29]
Legal forms mediate between the commitments of contract and the errantry
of monetary values. The fugitive (as much a legal "form" as any other) is a
figure for these untethered "inscriptions of debt and value," for this drift of
value in the marketplace.

Marxist and critical legal theorists have for long observed that one of the achievements of nineteenth-century jurisprudence was the transformation of American law into an instrument of capitalism independent of the preferences of capitalist actors.[30] Legal forms, by midcentury, they argue, achieve "relative autonomy," which term refers to the ability of the law to "exhibit power independent of or in opposition to the will of individual capitalists or even the capitalist 'class' and yet at the same time also articulate the systemic requirements of capitalism" (Binder and Weisberg, 526). Perhaps the clearest expression of the relative autonomy of legal form from the will of actors is the "formal equality" granted to both individuals and inanimate entities such as corporations, an equality contradicted by felt political, economic, and cultural inequalities. This relative autonomy of legal form, according to Isaac Balbus, results from a "homology" between legal form and commodity form. Again, Binder and Weisberg: "At the political level, individuals are 'homologized' into the abstract identity of equal 'citizens' in order to make political and economic representation of their 'interests' possible. Indeed, humans become their 'interests,' ceasing to act like social beings, but instead merely inviting commodity-like negotiations with others' interests. . . . Individuals and inanimate enterprises then become mutually commensurable and negotiable on the plain [*sic*] of interests" (527). Stowe understood the Fugitive Slave Law of 1850 to have this equalizing effect at the level of interest, understood it to draw legal form and commodity form intimately into alignment. Southern slave owners and speculators in the slave market; "good citizens" and opponents of the Fugitive Slave Law; "the sons of the free states" and magistrates, police, and other agents of Northern states—all were made "citizens" through the instrument of the Bill of Rights. However, they were turned into commensurate "interests" by the Fugitive Slave Law, a document of market and federation that recast political relations between citizen and state as economic relations between creditors and debtors.[31] The fugitive, as Stowe suspected, and as I want rigorously to argue in *The Fugitive's Properties,* thus played a pivotal role in the rise of commercial formalism in American law.

The Fugitive's Properties is divided into three parts, each of which takes up a particular text as especially pivotal or salient to the question of the "fugitive"—to the law's express homology between legal form and commodity form and the problem of transcendent abstraction. Those texts are *Dred Scott v. Sandford* (1857), *Uncle Tom's Cabin* (1852), and *Plessy v. Ferguson* (1896).

The first part of this study, *Caveat Emptor,* considers a legal wrinkle in the nineteenth-century drama of "possessive individualism," a problem of that economy that, in the wake of emancipation, instructs, disciplines, and intervenes in the legal consideration of personhood as property—the impediment, simply, as William James remarks, "that between what a man calls *me* and what he simply calls *mine* the line is difficult to draw."[32] These pages take up in particular the topic of "fugitive sound," of sound's evanescence and the troubling fugacity of voice. Here I am interested to engage a number of issues clustered around the phonograph and the application of the law of intellectual property to acoustic phenomena, paying particular attention to the correspondence of shifting conceptions of property with the reproduction of the human voice. Invention and law intersect as the latter extends copyright grants in published musical scores to cover voice. Extensions of this sort, I argue, require legal scrutiny of the fungibility of voice—that is, some consideration of voice as either an inalienable aspect of personhood or an alienable property within the market. What interests me here is the tendency, with regards to both impersonation and mechanical reproduction, to conceive of emergent properties such as voice not as material things but as the mere effect of that nimbus of motives that typically fall beneath the sign of the "person"—that is, promise, reciprocity, obligation, indebtedness. Property becomes a matter of rights and duties, powers and hardships (so, e.g., the right to one's voice as property is a correlate of others' duties to neither imitate nor surreptitiously record it).

Scrutiny of this sort—of the exchangeability of an aspect of personhood heretofore deemed inalienable—stimulates the specter of slavery and fears of the specious circulation of personhood as a market commodity. In a sequence of readings, I link the legal hermeneutics through which abstract property is transformed into fabulations of will and consent to a long tradition of positivist jurisprudence, one that includes within its orbit both Hobbes's *Leviathan* and the Supreme Court's decision in *Dred Scott v. Sandford*. I see the positivist proclivity to valorize the "original intent" of the Constitution and the "plain meaning" of its words—the *autopoesis* that permits the legal text, in common parlance, to "speak for itself"—as integral to the unfolding protection at midcentury of fugitive property. Without this ascription of will to the text itself, I argue, a more important circuit of motives would have failed to have achieved apprehension under law—the perception of Dred Scott not as stolen property but as fugitive *person*, a consenting subject who not only partook (if obliquely) of the "popular will" and "consent" that gave rise to the Constitution itself as a legal instrument but a subject who was also indebted, for, as a fugitive, he had reneged on the promise to deliver his labor to both market and master. Opprobrious theft assumes the form of hoarded gift; the gift the slave makes of himself absolves the theft of his property in himself. With regards to fugitive forms of property, the law's *autopoesis* represents a hermeneutic of the gift.

The second section of the book, *Pro Bono Publico,* takes up the late-nineteenth-century moral charge that the emerging speculative economy's financial abstractions were instruments of overexpropriation (and thus threats to the public interest). Here I take Harriet Beecher Stowe's *Uncle Tom's Cabin* as the literary correlate to a midcentury logic of speculative economy, part of a legal universe in which the book's adaptation is imagined to be a kind of translation, and, relatedly, speculation is imagined to be a kind of literary work. Stowe's minstrel characters personify the inconstancy and volatility, pretense and counterfeit, passion and subjective affect of the speculative forms of valuation that characterize the period's credit economy. Through the text's minstrel accents—in particular, the punning of minstrel dialect and the parody of the cakewalk foregrounded in its adaptations—a relationship is established between the fugacity of meaning in racial punning and the peculiar fecundity of capitalist inflation and speculation. In this chapter I discuss the long tradition of *Uncle Tom's Cabin's* adaptation on stage and screen, uncovering what I call a "social text of fugitivity": legal and literary discourses in which figurations of the fugitive (as errant and inconstant) shape economic transactions and the representation of speculative value. What interests me in this regard are, on the one hand, legal cases that function as aesthetic instruments, engendering a type of social character who is the embodiment of ambivalence about capitalism's mechanisms of valuation and profit and, on the other, literary texts that play a role in the fashioning of a new concept of the self, one that answers to the problems of affect in valuation, incertitude in the market, and deferral in the world of credit.

In the third section of the book, *Sine Qua Non,* I maintain my earlier focus on the consubstantiality of aesthetics and economics (on the intimacies of invention and law) but emphasize, in this instance, a set of homologies between early film form and legal logic. Of particular interest are the filigreed and multiple connections between, on the one hand, a set of early silent films produced at the turn of the century, in which the effort to document motion yields an explicit renunciation of narrative time and the most rudimentary narrative interest in beginnings, middles, and endings (in the nonidentity of past, present, and future) and, on the other, the thematic and logical echoes of these narrative concerns in *Plessy v. Ferguson* (1896), the U.S. Supreme Court case that establishes the constitutionality of "separate-but-equal" racial accommodations in the public sphere—that is, the case that assures continuity and identity between racial segregation and the Fourteenth Amendment's guarantee of "equal protection of the laws."

With regards to this last, of particular interest is the use, by courts and counselors alike, of the counterfactual form (defined as those if-then statements and contrary-to-fact speculations that allow a court to adjudicate harm, injury, and causation, to infer what would have been the case if some event, which actually happened, had not happened). The counterfactual is often invoked to determine if the experiences of blacks and whites are "equal" for the purposes of the law in dispute. The form finds echo in a sequence of early silent films (often called "trick films") in which blacks and whites are made to trade places. Because they obey similar principles of operation and transvaluation, film form and legal text lead me to wonder: What risks lie where lawyers on either side of the debate over racial segregation and constitutional "equal protection" suspend the pragmatic adjudication of injury for the suppositional equivalencies and ontological uncertainties of the counterfactual form (as when jurists and commentators on racial segregation muse, "Suppose, for a moment, the tables turned")? This final section of *The Fugitive's Properties* adumbrates some of the logical and cognitive constraints of "formal equality"—specifically, the peculiar fact that Jim Crow segregation developed in the shadow of a doctrine of equality and not as its antithesis.

THE AGENCY OF FORM

From fugitive persons to fugitive personhood, errant characters to errant value, the "exchanges" of the market to the "equivalence" between blacks and whites in equal protection law: my method in *The Fugitive's Properties* is analogical and interdisciplinary (aggressively so in each regard). It is therefore important, before turning to the specifics of my readings, to offer a few words on the book's method—a method of "fugitive cuts" (as I prefer to call it).

My reading practice throughout this book is wanton, taking the idea of the fugitive both as historical substance and structure of my various arguments and as model for the text's rhetorical and intellectual strategy. Weaving in and out of my main texts—*Dred Scott v. Sandford, Uncle Tom's Cabin, Plessy v. Ferguson*—my readings move back and forth in time and laterally in topic and in theory in an effort to chart a nineteenth-century crisis (as in turning point) in the conception of property. These exploratory sorties are guided more by analogy than by chronology, more by associative logics than by a conventional expository unfolding of historical causes; but the signposts in each case are the very legal forms and logics that inhabit the text of the law itself (i.e., personification, metaphor, counterfactualism). What I seek to uncover in each reading are hybrid formations or constellations based on the perception of resemblance between ostensibly disjunct discourses (e.g., law, economics, literary, and other media of cultural production)—constellations that are anathema to a great deal of recent literary and legal scholarship.[33]

It has become something of a commonplace within literary theory and legal historiography to distinguish analogy from causality, symbolic resonance from historical continuity. In social and cultural histories based on analogy, the argument goes, the lines of authority run from present to past, and events in the past warrant scrutiny because they resemble events in the present, while in those based on historical continuity and explanation (of how our present circumstances came about) the lines run from the past to the present and follow "a particular irreplaceable causal chain," as Steven Knapp observes.[34] The problem for revisionist criticism is that these two relations appear insufficient on their own to sustain the writing (if not rewriting) of history: "If the past is merely a source of analogies, particular past events may provide models for present action but are in principle expendable; they can all be replaced by analogies borrowed from other traditions or from fiction. If the past is merely a source of explanations, it may well be irreplaceable (there is no other way to explain how we got where we are), but ancestral actions of the greatest explanatory interest may express values remote from any we can now embrace" (117). But as Knapp goes on to observe, much revisionist criticism (whether literary or legal) bears an affinity for historical phenomena that appear to combine analogy (or symbolic resonance) and causality (or explanatory uniqueness)—phenomena that exemplify the coincidence "of continuity, which connects past and present via historical sequences, and analogy, which connects past and present via a property common to both" (115). This coincidence between analogy and causality is one of the principal aims of *The Political Unconscious*, for example; for Jameson (like Althusserians generally) is averse to the division "between antiquarianism [historical continuity] and modernizing 'relevance' and projection [analogy]."[35] The methods Knapp applies to the identity between past and present I would extend to include forms of identity between discourses—in the specific instance in question, fugitive persons and fugitive personhood; for the latter relation (deployed in the text of the law itself), while it seems to call out for the critical distinction of analogy from causality, in fact poses the possibility of a coincidence between symbolic resonance and explanatory uniqueness and, thus, sets the conditions for an alternative history of nineteenth-century law and property.

The Fugitive's Properties is "revisionist" as Knapp here conceives that intellectual project, and my own sensibilities are "New Historicist" as I understand the interpretive regimens and goals of that field.[36] There are two interpretive predilections that I share with New Historicists that, in light of my earlier comments regarding analogy and causality, require mention. First, New Historicists tend to invoke history through anecdotes and to use "the method of Luminous Detail" (as two of its principal practitioners, following Ezra Pound, have put it) to produce a tear, or aporetic opening, in traditional historical discourse.[37] Second, they tend to draw formal analogies or topographic homologies between discrete discourses—what Stephen Greenblatt has called a "negotiation" between discourses, "a set of reciprocities and exchanges, one set among many others, through which we can understand how it happens each discourse achieves some of its independent force and charge."[38] This last inclination is important to both New Historicism and *The Fugitive's Properties*, not least because, by the terms of the field's (as well as the book's) reading practice, seeing the resemblance between literary texts and the cultural system is the first step in plumbing the historical integuments between ostensibly incommensurate discourses. Critics of New Historicism thus often question the status of cause within the field's preferred forms, particularly the forms of the anecdote, the analogical resemblance, and the homological correspondence. These same critics often charge that New Historicists perform amazing contortions in order to avoid asserting causality.[39] In addition, with respect to race, some scholars of African-American literary criticism contend that this avoidance of causation bears particular consequences that cannot be ignored. These critics have found New Historicists insufficiently concerned with race as a vector of power, blind to the dynamics of the social, and uninformed about the coercive force of American institutions and the law in the experience of black people. *The Fugitive's Properties* intends to bridge this gulf between African-American literary criticism and New Historicism.

Key to this goal is a reconception of the analogy/causality distinction. That distinction, though common in much contemporary criticism, is an unprofitable one from the vantage of my method. In much legal history, there is only one type of causality relevant to legal method: the causality implied by the appeal to precedent and enshrined in the phrase "*X* judge cited *Y* case." This mechanism of causation, which often goes by the term "intentionality," presumes an individual (or, at best, personifiable) origin and takes the accessibility of psychological states as not only necessary but inevitable. My argument is that analogy can itself function as a kind of causality; for, in nineteenth-century property disputes, courts often contend with novel forms of property through recourse to analogy (e.g., What good historically protected by law does the emergent and disputed one resemble? What is it "like"?). Here is how the scholar and jurist Oliver Wendell Holmes Jr., put the matter (language to which I will return in the next chapter): "Suppose that a code were made and expressed in language sanctioned by the assent of courts, or tested by the scrutiny of a committee of lawyers. New cases will arise which will elude the most carefully constructed formula. The common law, proceeding, as we have pointed out, by a series of successive approximations—by a continual reconciliation of cases—is prepared for this, and simply modifies the form of its rule."[40] Emergent properties require a structure of identity—a structure achieved through the pragmatic manipulation of form. By their very nature (i.e., beyond the intentionality of the judge), legal analogies place constraints on outcomes (so, e.g., a legal metaphor provides both a speculative possibility [tenor] and a specific embodiment, or limitation on the breadth of possibilities [vehicle]); and that means that form bears a type of causality. Form precedes logic in the law; analogy is a prelude to what is often characterized as "the substance of the law." In short, analogy proffers a type of causality, and New Historicist method a "causality" more subtle than is often implied by that term.

This subtler form of causality I would describe as "the agency of form" and would locate its precursor in one of Aristotle's conceptions of cause. In book 2 of the *Physics,* Aristotle offers four types of cause, four ways to conceive (as he puts it) "the why of things"—the matter, the end, the mover, and the form.[41] Matter is a cause in the way that "the bronze is a cause of the statue, and the silver, of the cup"; and an end is a cause in the sense that it provides the objective "for the sake of which" another activity is engaged, as in "walking . . . for the sake of health" (194b.25–26, 194b.34–35). More familiar to the legal imagination is the causation derived from one who acts, or "that from which change or coming to rest first begins" (194b.30). For example, "the father is the cause of the baby . . . [in the sense that] that which acts is a cause of that which is acted on, and that which brings about a change is a cause of that which is being changed" (194b.30–33). Least likely to fit any legal definition of causation is the mode of attribution Aristotle assigns to form. A type of causation can be attributed to "the form or the pattern" of something—to what he describes as "the formula of the essence" and which he clarifies with the example of mathematics, which can be said to locate causation in "the definition of a straight line or of commensurability or of something else" (194b.27, 198a.18–19). Causation inheres within form when a culture finds within it space to constrain expectations, to organize uses, to channel meaningful purposes. In this regard, Aristotle could be expected to answer the question "why is the glass a glass?" with the protean response "for reasons attributable both to the glassmaker and to the form 'glass.'"

Form and causation. Analogy and homology. The homology between legal form and commodity form. Aristotle offers a way of answering a question operative in the pages of *The Fugitive's Properties:* How do we read the commodity form? He moves us several steps closer to answering the more difficult question of the book: How does the "form" in the commodity form generate social phenomena in ways that are neither mechanical (historical causality) nor fully contingent (analogy)? When I ask, What is the generative power of form? I am not asking the conventional question, What does form cause?—although the question does fit one of the Aristotelian definitions of "cause." It is more a question of what form produces, what form generates; and, because I do not believe that a logic of the commodity can answer that question in advance, I consider the various specific ways that the person-property relation is restaged and recast throughout the late nineteenth and early twentieth centuries. In *The Fugitive's Properties* I offer a vision of the historical agency of form, a model of causation that rivals modes often imputed to human subjects as agents of history. My hope is that out of patience—yours for me, and mine for my texts—I will persuade you of precisely why, in a culture whose history has often followed the fugacious wanderings of fickle racial imperative, our forms should and do matter.

Caveat Emptor

How long, then, shall we stand off from such ringing moral questions as these on the flimsy plea that they have a political value, and, scrutinizing the Constitution, keep saying, "Is it so nominated in the bond? I cannot find it; 'tis not in the bond."

GEORGE WASHINGTON CABLE, "THE FREEDMAN'S CASE IN EQUITY" (1884)

CHAPTER ONE

Fugitive Sound

FUNGIBLE PERSONHOOD, EVANESCENT PROPERTY

La propriété c'est le vol!
PIERRE JOSEPH PROUDHON, *Qu'est-ce Que la Propriété?* (1840)

The several essential features of the phonograph demonstrate the following as *faits accomplis:* the captivity of all manner of sound-waves heretofore designated as "fugitive," and their permanent retention.
THOMAS ALVA EDISON, *The Phonograph and Its Future* (1878)

THEFT AND GIFT

As a matter of practice, nineteenth-century American jurisprudence was overwhelmingly "economic" in focus — economic, not as Aristotle defined it in the *Politics,* as the wise production and distribution (*nemesis*) of household (*oikos*) for the common welfare of all but, rather, as has been offered by Michel Foucault, citing the somewhat narrower suggestion of Guillaume de la Perrière, "the right disposition of things, arranged so as to lead to a convenient end."[1] No adequation need obtain here between "common welfare" and "convenient end[s]"; for, in nineteenth-century America, economy almost certainly corresponds to the latter, that is, to a wealth and property arranged toward the ends of private interest, even in matters of public law. Perhaps no stronger evidence can be marshaled in support of this proposition than one simple development in property law: the jurist's responsibility to determine the correct disposal of "things" within property disputes often entails the added determination of the nature of things themselves (a determination disproportionately in the interest of those who, seeking accommodation of their heretofore invisible "property," make claim to a deserved judicial "scrutiny"). These expanded legal prerogatives were especially in evidence during the latter half of the century, for, with the tremendous and dynamic industrialization and commercialization of American culture at the century's close, state and federal courts were asked to accommodate increasingly evanescent, immaterial, and novel forms of wealth and ownership. They obliged on most occasions.

In the case of *Brett v. Ebel* (1898), the court respected the plaintiff's claim that, by making a covenant on the sale of his business not to solicit his old customers for his new business, he managed successfully to transfer to the purchaser the goodwill he had previously accrued among those customers — that is, a reputation and standing of that business among its frequent patrons said to be a transferable measure of the business's going value, said to be a property in itself. The transfer of property was complete, the court maintained, even though no object had changed hands, only the probability that the old customers would resort to the old place of business.[2] Similar recognitions accrued in the case of *Peabody v. Norfolk* (1868), where the Massachusetts Supreme Court affirmed a property right in silence — a property right, to be specific, in secrets. Peabody, who had given certain trade secrets to Norfolk, his employee, under the promise that Norfolk would not divulge those secrets to others, filed the case to enforce adherence to the promise. The court held, in recognition of Norfolk's agreement to a binding confidence, that "a secret art is a legal subject of property."[3] Words spoken once never to be spoken again were secure subjects of property in the eyes of the law. And in the case of *Chicago Board of Trade v. Christie Grain and Stock Company* (1905), the U.S. Supreme Court permitted members of the board to sell and trade the subtle price differences between lots of agricultural produce through a contracted intermediary, the Western Union Telegraph Company. Undersold farmers decried the board's "trading for differences" — this investment of money in anticipation of the direction of fluctuation of exchange values, this valorization of inference — as the legal renunciation of trade in consumable commodities and, in turn, the endorsement and embrace of an unscrupulous trade in "phantom cotton," "spectral hogs," and "wind wheat."[4] Yet, importantly, the Court's move expanded the scope of agricultural property from the goods themselves to prices and information about those goods, and, furthermore, this recognition of prices as property confirmed, as well, the postbellum transformation of America's market economy into a credit economy, where traffic in goods found itself largely subordinate to traffic in

capital.[5] Finally, in what is perhaps the U.S. Supreme Court's most celebrated decision on these matters, the case of *Santa Clara v. Southern
Pacific Railroad* (1883), the Court extended to corporations the legal status
of "person" within the meaning of the Fifth and Fourteenth Amendments to
the Constitution; and, by endowing corporations with the rights and privileges the Constitution ascribes to the agents of contractual liberty (the
"due process" protection of citizens against deprivation of life, liberty, or
property by the state and "equal protection" of the laws), the Court made it
possible for new as well as old forms of wealth to be protected against state
infringement so long as courts of any rank were persuaded to treat them as
property.[6] In a move that came to characterize transformations in American
jurisprudence as a whole, the creation of immaterial and incorporeal forms
of property turned, with dazzling legal maneuvering, on the personification
of another of the law's constructs, the corporation.[7]

Lines of thinking afforded the greatest legitimacy in American law at the
end of the nineteenth century apparently ran contrary to the judicial designs of antebellum legal culture. At the beginning of the century, legal
fictions pictured property, ideally, as absolute dominion over "things," as
the right to a tangible parcel with clear boundaries.[8] William Blackstone is
the jurist largely responsible for the popularization of this fiction, for, in his
Commentaries on the Laws of England (1765–69), that well-known com-
pendium of received statute, he takes property, or in his words, "hereditaments" ("whatsoever may be inherited"), to encompass all things "as con-
tradistinguished from persons."[9] Landed property is this legal compass's
due north, and trespass the essence of legal interference with property
rights.[10] Courts perceived the concept of property to rest inevitably in the
nature of things, and thus a certain "objectness" provided the premise from
which ownership could be deduced with certainty ("New Property,"
328–29). At the Civil War's end, the perceived inevitability and deductive
certainty between things and rights in Blackstone's common law no longer
obtained. One could then find "right" in the absence of any "thing." The
protection of value rather than things so broadened the purview of property law that the new property seemed capable of embracing every valuable
interest known to the law. "The basic problem of legal thinkers after the
Civil War," Morton Horwitz explains, "[is] how to articulate a conception
of property that could accommodate the tremendous expansion in the va-
riety of forms of ownership spawned by a dynamic industrial society."[11]
New fictions of property began to creep into the constitutional interpretations given by state and federal courts, fictions that firmly managed to en-

sconce themselves into Supreme Court doctrine. The Supreme Court expanded property "to include the pursuit, and therefore the legal protection, of intangible value, or earning power—that is, the right to a reasonable return on investment in intangible assets (for example, 'goodwill')."[12] The Court firmed up this transition in the first *Minnesota Rate Case,* in 1890, when it changed the definition of property from physical things perceived to have some use value to the exchange value of anything.[13] The pivotal words initially were provided by Justice Noah H. Swayne, in his dissent in the *Slaughterhouse Cases,* in 1873, and read, simply, "property is everything which has exchangeable value."[14]

I will return to these words presently. Suffice to say that theft or "takings" (even the mere interference with another's property, which was formerly considered trespass and invasion) now included any action that reduced the market value of property. Divorced from concrete physical objects, the definition of property came increasingly to turn on abstract ideas of individual expectations of stable market values. The new property, as every species of valuable right and interest, threatened to engulf all legal relations. In the words of Horwitz, "American courts [came] as close as they . . . ever had to saying that one had a property right to an unchanging world."[15] In a legal revolution shepherded by Federalists (such as James Kent) and Republicans (such as Joseph Story) alike, the law responded to the demands of entrepreneurs not only to protect property against interference but to promote its marketability. Entrepreneurs expected and received, under the new jurisprudential dispensation, a law "sufficiently elaborated and uniform to make the consequences of business decisions highly predictable."[16] Jeremy Bentham would capture this prognostics of the law of property in the early decades of the eighteenth century: "Property is nothing but the basis of expectation . . . consist[ing] in an established expectation, in the persuasion of being able to draw such and such advantage from the thing possessed."[17] All inference and immateriality, prognostics and predictability, promise and obligation, property lost reference to actual goods and use values and, arguably, acquired the characteristics of a set of "instruments" and securities central to an emerging speculative market capitalism: of contracts or "options" that granted the "privilege" to buy (a "call") or sell (a "put") a commodity at a future date; of hedges for and against the anticipated price of a commodity ("futures"), which either overvalued (selling "long") or undervalued (selling "short") the commodity in question; of the setting of a floor and ceiling to rates of return on the wager either that future rates would exceed the established limits (a "straddle") or remain comfortably nestled within their confines (a "collar"). Within an emerging market of infinite abstraction, interminable speculation and miraculous profits, property served as a synonym for certainty, and property law became a means of proscribing actions in such a way that the future remained consistent with current calculations. In essence, property was a species of pathetic fallacy, a personification of individual "interests" by way of the fabulation of specific "outcomes"—in short, a formalization of a way of thinking about future actions, a means of substantializing acts as a form of property.

The Court's metamorphoses resulted in nothing short of the liquidification of property ("the conversion of capital from fixed tangibles into fluid intangibles" [*Corporate Reconstruction,* 50])—ironically, a textualization of property in which it became so much a function of the *lex scripta* (statute law, written law) as to make it nearly impossible to say "market" without also saying "the law," "possession" without also invoking "property," "things" without also calling to mind the difference between things and the "signs" of things. Historian of capitalism Martin Sklar has chosen an apt analogy to describe this critical state of the law:

> In proportion as market relations mature, the law displaces religion, just as the courts displace the church, and lawyers and judges, the clergy. . . . There can be no modern capitalist market . . . apart from the complex development and the certainty of the law. The law is the Latin of the market, just as the language of money and price is the Vulgate. . . . The modern capitalist market without the law is as little feasible as the church without religion. The courts are the church, the law the canon of everyday life, jurisprudence the theology. (*Corporate Reconstruction,* 86–87)

The expectation of stable market value. The property right to an unchanging world. The certainty of the law. The importance of the "letter of the law," its significance as a reservoir of certainty, intensified as the law's perceived need to conceive of property in terms of bounded, tangible land began to wane. In short, the ephemeralization of property was met by the incarnation of the word. Again Sklar: "Certainty, here, does not mean changeless rigidity, but a consistency of logic and reasoning, which, though rooted in precedent, may also depart from it in adapting to, or providing for, changing conditions. Certainty means, in other words, a logic . . . that yields a reasonable predictability in both the constancy and the variability of the law" (86–87). Legal certainty, by emphasizing a "consistency of logic and reasoning," not only stresses a finite set of inferential procedures

"rooted in precedent" but also valorizes the law as a system capable of functioning with "mathematical" certainty. By the terms of the fallacy, the legal
forms of this "logic" (borne to market in the argot of equity, credit, debt, liability, contract) work like chemical reactions and mathematical theorems.

Legal certainty, as many nineteenth-century jurists warned, collapses legal causation into scientific causation. In "The Path of the Law," written in
1897, a mere seven years after the Supreme Court's pivotal reconfiguration
of property, Oliver Wendell Holmes cautions against the belief that logic is
the only force at work in the law. "The life of the law has not been logic," he
asserts elsewhere, in one of the more memorable of his many dicta, "it has
been experience." [18] The notion that a given system can be worked out like
mathematics from some general axioms of conduct, he warns, has long presented one of law's greatest fallacies, which fallacy, for him, approaches the
comedic: "[It is] as if [judicial wrangling] meant simply that one side or the
other were not doing their sums right, and, if they would take more trouble,
agreement inevitably would come." (Tellingly, Holmes here strikes a chord
with Harriet Beecher Stowe's condemnation of the "severe, unflinching accuracy of logic" that reigns in antebellum jurisprudence, those "accursed
principle[s of] mathematical accuracy" and "elegant surgical instruments
for the work of dissecting the living human heart.") [19] True, Holmes concedes, the "language of judicial decision is mainly the language of logic,"
but the syntax or form of logic only "*flatter[s]* that longing for certainty and
for repose" common to the law: "But certainty generally is illusion, and repose is not the destiny of man" (181). Holmes concedes that, superordinate
to logic, prediction and prophecy are the business of the law. Most people
long to know, and to know clearly, the circumstances under which they
"run the risk" of encountering the punitive arm of the state (167). The jurist's task is thus to predict "the incidence of the public force" through "the
instrumentality of the courts" (167). Again, Holmes's formulation deserves
citation on account of its simplicity alone: "The prophesies of what the
courts will do in fact, and nothing more pretentious, are what I mean by the
law" (172-73). The forms of the law are in fact merely figures of judgment,
of "a judgement as to the relative worth and importance of competing legislative grounds, often an inarticulate and unconscious judgement, it is
true, and yet the very root and nerve of the whole proceeding" (181). Again,
Holmes cautions, it would be wrong here to confuse legal ideas with moral
ideas. "An inarticulate and unconscious judgement" refers only to the force
of an agreed on set of cultural signs—in his words, "the *preference* of a given
body in a given time and place" (181, emphasis mine). It is here that a prag-

matic jurisprudence dispels moral and principle and appears merely akin to public policy.

Contracts provide the most eloquent expression of the path that leads from a view of the law as the domain of morals and promises and toward a view of contractual agreement as pure semiosis (toward, in short, a reliance conception of contract). Again Holmes:

> We talk about a contract as a meeting of the minds of the parties. . . . Yet nothing is more certain than that parties may be bound by a contract to things which neither of them intended, and when one [of the parties] does not know of the other's assent. . . . The making of a contract depends not on the agreement of two minds in one intention, but on the agreement of two sets of external signs—not on the parties' having *meant* the same thing but on their having *said* the same thing. Furthermore, as the signs may be addressed to one sense or another—to sight or to hearing—on the nature of the sign will depend the moment when the contract is made. If the sign is tangible, for instance, a letter, the contract is made when the letter of acceptance is delivered. (177–78)

Holmes's emphasis on "signs" aside, his critique of the will theory of contract (of the vision of contract as a "meeting of . . . minds") represents a decisive shift toward contract's objectification. His agreement rises to the status of what the law assumes is the customary meaning held by an average, ordinary person; the proverbial "reasonable man." Holmes and other Progressives strive to be able better "to create formal, general theories that would provide uniformity, certainty, and predictability of legal arrangements." What stimulates this drive toward contract's objectification is, of course, the corporate form of personhood itself; for, under corporate employment, the organization held responsibility for its employees' contracts. Obligation remains free of the intent of the parties, and thus the law looks to the reliance of a "reasonable person" so as "to ensure that the rest of the world could rely upon uniform and predictable legal consequences."[20]

Justice Swayne's accent on property as "everything which has exchangeable value" and Justice Holmes's shift in the law's bias from the transparencies of logic to "the nature of the sign" together suggest a line of thinking unfolding, concurrently, in the halls of the University of Geneva: a series of lectures given by Ferdinand de Saussure between 1907 and 1911 that would become, on their publication by his students in 1916, his *Cours de linguistique générale*.[21] It is in these lectures that Saussure offers his central doctrine of the "arbitrariness" of the sign—the thesis of "linguistic

value" that states, in short, that the value or identity of any semantic fragment is not "motivated," for there is no necessary relation of language to the
object world. Rather, Saussure contends, the relation is one of "convention," based on a history of accepted usage and consensus, with values emanating from within a system of differences. We refer, then, to the "arbitrariness" of the sign because the moment of identity in language is only
conceivable as the effect of a play of differences in the "system" of value.
Against the commonsense perception of language as a reflection of the
world, Saussure shows this relation to be fundamentally analogical: on the
one hand is language, with its differential system of making meaning; on
the other is an object world of things that becomes available to human
agency only in terms of the network of signification that language casts on
it. To return to our original concern—property—we might say, in light of
Saussure's intervention, that whether or not novel phenomena and things
may in fact be considered property under law is not a matter one can deduce
from an analysis of an object's "properties," from some assessment of the
nature of property; rather, it is a matter of public policy (of consensus, convention, and agreed on methodological postulates, in short, of "preference"). Antagonistic, interested positions within the market differ little,
then, from the differential positions that determine the semiotic content of
signs. Swayne's pivotal assertion—a worthy precursor to literary theory's
linguistic turn—might then also be read, under interested eyes, as "property is semiosis."

The semiotics of property can be summarized as follows. Novel cases
appear often before the bar that cannot properly be disposed of by invoking
settled rules. These cases introduce an instability that can only be eliminated when enough novel cases have accumulated. As has now been quite
thoroughly settled in the writings on the law, the only way to handle such
novel cases is by analogy, by isolating those aspects that most closely resemble familiar ones to settle on the rule, which is then to be adjusted in
light of the other significant facts in the case. Competing lines of precedent
are available to support various specific results or determinations. These
precedents are themselves quite malleable and lead to efforts to develop
more or less coherently organized complexes of thought and argument.
However, coherence here is not arrived at by strict adherence to logical
consistency; it is, rather, the formalized result of a set of informal associations, subterranean affiliations connected and made "the law" by repeated
association.[22] Holmes's emphasis on property's basis in unspoken preferences ("an inarticulate and unconscious judgement") effectively denies the

claims of the legal system to logical or "mathematical" certainty and emphasizes, in turn, the primacy of property's semiotic attachments. Holmes would himself state, in "Codes, and the Arrangement of the Law" (1870), "Suppose that a code were made and expressed in language sanctioned by the assent of courts, or tested by the scrutiny of a committee of lawyers. New cases will arise that will elude the most carefully constructed formula. The common law, proceeding, as we have pointed out, by a series of successive approximations—by a continual reconciliation of cases—is prepared for this, and simply modifies the form of its rule." [23] Within the legal hermeneutic I have framed here, semantic preference draws a world into existence, adjusts the world so as "better to fit the representation." [24] "The law, in sum, is not some 'reflection' of, or 'superstructure' hovering above, capitalist property and market relations; it is an essential mode of existence and expression of those relations" (*Corporate Reconstruction*, 89).

I would like to pause here to lay out the arc of this chapter, which will consider the cultural significance of this mode of expression as it relates to ongoing questions of property: specifically, the relation of new forms of intangible property to a concern in nineteenth- and early-twentieth-century jurisprudence with the textuality of the law—the link, in short, between property's disputed ontology and legal hermeneutics. I offer first a summary of the changing economic and legal circumstances of the period. Both the cases and the treatises refer to the prognostic nature of the law of property: to the probability that the old customers will resort to the old place; to the expectation that employees will adhere to their promise not to divulge trade secrets; and to an anticipation of stable market values rooted in the assumption that all market actors will deliver on their contractual promises. Each refers as well to the need for the law, in interpreting contracts, to adapt and provide for "changing conditions," to account for novelty. The tendency for emergent forms of property to take the form of actions either encouraged or prescribed (to point, if even obliquely, to intentions) is not an incidental one from the vantage of the law; and, important for my concerns, this tendency betrays the general move in nineteenth-century American jurisprudence for property to absorb, in its expansion, dimensions of life commonly understood as the province of personhood. In this chapter, I will consider property's drift in the direction of the commodification of personhood under the rubric of "property's personification." I will emphasize one particular concern in these unfolding disputes over intangible property: the effort to secure one's voice as property in the face of its mechanical reproduction. This effort marks a significant legal wrinkle in the nine-teenth-century drama of possessive individualism—as I noted in the in-troduction, the impediment, simply, as William James remarks, that "be-tween what a man calls *me* and what he simply calls *mine* the line is difficult to draw."

In addressing the question of voice as property I want to draw into focus a sustained example of the changing form of the commodity relation. I aim to situate the issues surrounding voice and its mechanical reproduction within the context of an ongoing crisis in American jurisprudence—that crisis in which personhood not only appears increasingly subject to the do-main of property but, more specifically, its commodification resonates in the nineteenth-century moral imagination as theft, dispossession, unjust expropriation. Over the latter half of the nineteenth century the notion of the person was at once fragmented into its various attributes, capacities, and "properties," while at the same time new notions of personhood origi-nally compelled by changing economic circumstances came themselves to appear to be the product of a startling (and specious) array of legal maneu-vers. None of this is to my mind unprecedented; but what I will try to do over the coming pages is situate a number of emergent intellectual property concerns as part of a fundamental historical continuity in the life of the United States.

Where it approaches a cultural studies commonplace to admit that new technologies and attendant transformations in the conception of property are the residua of complicated forms of historical change, I will argue more strenuously that slavery provides a particular historical form of the ongoing crisis in which persons are treated as things, and things as persons, one that lends historical depth and contour to the subordination (at century's end) of personality to the property relation. I will maintain, furthermore, and as a matter of literary and legal hermeneutics, that this relation between intel-lectual property law and slave law is not simply an analogy extrinsic to the logics of the law; rather, as analogy on display within the text of the law it-self, it is to my mind a fundament of the law.

Another way to phrase this last concern is as follows. The borrowing of forms and metaphoric transfer are strategies common to legal reasoning, and within property law in particular these strategies find expression in the drawing of analogies between emergent property forms and old ones. This intimacy between property and figuration represents a more general con-cern within nineteenth-century jurisprudence. That is, the problem of clas-sifying and protecting new forms of insubstantial and elusive property is the expression of a problem within American jurisprudence of long and esteemed provenance—the problem of positivism, to be precise, or the contradiction in which various figures of speech (e.g., personification, analogy, metaphor) are deployed within a legal hermeneutic expressly committed to figuration's denial. Positivism shares intellectual affinities with what was often called "originalism" in nineteenth-century constitutional law and what has more recently been described as "strict intentionalism"; and together these intellectual traditions form a legal architecture that, resting on the dichotomy between literal and metaphoric meaning, seeks to purge the law of metaphor on the principle that the law possesses an autonomy independent of the (nonlegal) sphere of the literary. In this drive to preserve both its autonomy and its perspicuity, the law, as Stanley Fish observes, "is continually creating and recreating itself out of the very materials and forces it is obliged, by its very desire to *be* law, to push away."[25]

I would describe this denial as a "metaphoric substitution," meaning to encompass within that phrase the many acts of borrowing, translation, and appropriation that occur in and around the figure of the "fugitive"—the substitution of feature for personhood; the substitution of things for persons; the translation of property (e.g., slaves) into elements of contractual obligation; the appropriation of metaphor for purposes of pragmatic adjudication. Like Fish, I take it as an axiom of legal positivism that these substitutions not only build up over time but also cover over their very operation, so that what is finally (and by definition) taken for granted is the long work of a dissimulated metaphor. What is more, having taken substitution and negation as axiomatic, I will over the course of this chapter move back and forth in time and laterally across topics and discourses—from intellectual property encounters with "fugitive personhood" to antebellum concerns with "fugitive persons"—all in an effort to track not only the specific changes and permutations that happen within the commodity form but the more general and occluded work of dissimulation in the law as well.

In this chapter, my reading practice follows the social and historical peregrinations of form itself, showing how new forms are generated from old formulas, how slavery might be rethought within the emergent terms of intellectual property law, and, in general, how the relation between persons and things, and conceiving persons as things, becomes a varying preoccupation of the law in the aftermath of slavery. I take as my initial concern the troubling ontology of voice as it relates to property's abstraction—a difficulty within copyright law that achieves momentary resolution in Samuel Warren and Louis Brandeis's foundational essay "The Right to Privacy" (1890), in which voice is identified with "the right to be let alone," specifically "the right to one's personality." From here I move back through a range of legal and popular texts—the performances of the virtuoso slave "Blind Tom," the apocryphal tales of Thomas Danforth Rice's rise to prominence on the Jacksonian minstrel stage, as well as the Supreme Court case of *Dred Scott v. Sandford* (1857)—finding in them all some evidence of the necessary cultural labor that attends property's personification.

I take *Dred Scott* to be particularly pivotal and salient to the matters of property and legal textuality at issue in this chapter. The case is most often remembered as a test of the logics of states' rights and sovereignty that come into play following the passage of the Compromise of 1850 (and in particular the Fugitive Slave Law), and one that conclusively severs all links between Americans of African descent and the rights and privileges coincident with federal citizenship. What is less often acknowledged is the case's effect on nineteenth-century legal thought and reasoning. *Dred Scott*, as a number of legal scholars have recently observed, proved essential to the conception of nineteenth-century American jurisprudence that had given new emphasis to interpretation—and particularly to that conception of legal practice guided by the proposition that application of a legal instrument was an effort to realize its "intent." [26] For Whig constitutionalists such as Joseph Story, Francis Lieber, and Abraham Lincoln, intent entailed the manifest design of the Constitution as a legal instrument and was conceived as the law's purpose in giving such an instrument legal effect (so, as just one example, for Lincoln the very presence of a clause eventually abolishing the slave trade suggested that the framers intended to set slavery on the path of, in his words, "ultimate extinction"—a conception of intent as the manifest design of the institutions the founders founded).[27] For "originalists" such as Andrew Jackson, John C. Calhoun, and Roger Taney (author of the "Opinion of the Court" in *Dred Scott*), intent involved the psychological motives of the founders—it was implicated in their very personalities and desires. The "original intent" of the Constitution achieved its force only through the instrument of textual perspicuity, which the originalists accessed through reference to the instrument's language at the time of its ratification and which they would defend rhetorically through reference to "the letter of the law" and the "plain meaning" of its words (the ability of the document, in common parlance, to "speak for itself"). The meaning arrived at by any subsequent court would be an expression, in their view, of the voluntariness, mutuality, and reciprocity—of the "consent" and the exercise of "popular will"—that gave rise to the Constitution itself as a legal instrument.

I will refer to this transfer of will as the "autopoesis" of the legal system and will argue that, without it, a more important circuit of motives would have failed to have achieved apprehension under law—the perception of Dred Scott not as stolen property but as fugitive *person,* a consenting subject who not only partook (if obliquely) of the "popular will" (codified as that identity was in the Constitution's fugitive slave clause) but a subject who was also indebted; for, like the fugitive, he had reneged on the promise to deliver his labor to both market and master. Of particular interest to me are the homologies between the perception of the legal text as self-declaring and of the fugitive as willful property, as an agent of perfidy. *Dred Scott* is, by reason of this homology, symptomatic of greater upheavals in the law, most importantly the transformation of coercion into consent: in which property comes increasingly to appear to be a species of contract; in which property rights and protections against trespass give way to contract's reciprocities of voluntariness, promise, and mutuality; and in which the specter of property's theft is resolved through legal recourse to contract's promise and the logic of the gift.

COPYRIGHT LAW

Of special concern in the nineteenth century's evolving fictions of property are the relations—filigreed, multiple, and sinuous—of modern communications technologies to statutory copyright. A flurry of mechanical reproductive technologies appeared in the latter half of the century: Thomas Edison patented the phonograph in 1877 and the motion picture camera in 1892; Emile Berliner introduced the gramophone in 1887; the Lumière brothers revealed their cinematograph in 1895; and Eadweard Muybridge introduced the zoopraxiscope in the 1870s. Soon thereafter, civil courts began to have to answer to plaintiffs' demands for property rights in their photographic images, published dramatic and literary material, "pictorial illustrations," "graceful movements," facial expressions (in look-alike cases), and vocal "style" and "captured performance" (in sound-alike cases).[28] Edison's phonograph poses particularly vexed questions and some of the greatest challenges to the constitutional protections of the published literary and artistic work of authors and artists.[29] Here I use the term "vexed" advisedly, for, prior to the invention of the phonograph, the human voice circulated in the law (if "circulated" is the correct word) as intensely corporeal and so intimately proximate to the person as to appear legally inseparable from it. What is more, this deep embeddedness of voice raised the added difficulty of determining how the law of intellectual property might be made to apply to the acoustic, which lacks copyright law's perquisite and prerequisite to ownership: writing (or, what amounts to the same thing, a tangible "market in signs"). For my purposes, there are two trajectories in the ever-evolving legal effort to protect sound as property, the first of which begins with Congress's extension of the Constitution's copyright protections to include musical compositions under the act of February 3, 1831, and ends with the early mechanical reproduction case of *White-Smith Music Company v. Apollo Co.* (1908), and the second of which begins with the publication of Samuel Warren and Louis Brandeis's germinal article "The Right to Privacy" (1890), which, because it "enjoys the unique distinction of having initiated and theoretically outlined a new field of jurisprudence," as one commentator put it, has yet to achieve anything approaching a proper denouement.[30] Where the tradition in American jurisprudence that ended in *White-Smith* tended to emphasize the immateriality of sound (appearing antipathetic even to the abstraction implicit in property), the one that began in "The Right to Privacy" read the question of sound's amenability to ownership as a question of alienability, of the embeddedness of "voice" in "person." Together, immateriality and embeddedness form the warp and weft of the legal question of sound as property. Another way of phrasing the matter would be to say that, with regard to sound, property and privacy are flip sides of the same coin; it thus seems appropriate to elaborate sound's currency in the turn-of-the-century marketplace.

As just stated, in the act of February 3, 1831, Congress extended the Constitution's copyright protections of an author's "Writings and Discoveries" (specifically "maps, charts, and books") to include written musical scores. In amendments in the years 1856 and 1859, federal statute further broadened copyright law to include a right of performance, at which point it became possible to consider the activation of written scores as protectable, possible to see performances of a written score as covered by the same law that endowed the score itself with all the characteristics of (and protections that attend) intellectual property. The "performance right," as Jane Gaines notes in her study of intellectual property and popular culture, was construed as broadly as was possible at midcentury, covering both the "theatrical work and the musical composition as performed publically by actors and played by instrumentalists."[31] These amendments freed copyright's protections from the restraint of the written score. The law's allowances can thus be said to anticipate its recognition of mechanical sound recording as a form capable of embrace by copyright, in which unique case the law of copyright would protect a composer's "work" against the infringement of another's unauthorized "copy." However, this vision of prolepsis is itself somewhat limited; for it is not the case that all transformations of the written score constitute "performances" eligible for the revised statutes' protections.

In the case of *White-Smith Music Company v. Apollo Co.* (1908), the composer Adam Geibel pursued legal protection of two musical compositions, "Little Cotton Dolly" and "Kentucky Babe," for which he had secured copyright when he published them in the form of sheet music.[32] He sought the protection of his aesthetic labors against the infringing activities of the Apollo Company, a manufacturer of player pianos. On the matter of whether Apollo's piano rolls infringed against Geibel's scores, the U.S. Supreme Court ruled that in general player pianos ("pianolas," as they were popularly called) performed no activity against which a musical composer might reasonably seek protection. The Constitution's copyright guarantees, the Court reasoned, extended only to those cultural forms that "directly or indirectly" (320) bore the trace of the copyright proprietor's hand (in this case, sheets of music and their activation in live performances). The laws of property in culture dealt only with "the concrete and not with the abstract right of property" (322). Copyright law governed only "the tangible resul[t] of mental conception" (320) and the "copy," which last term, the Court reasoned further, Congress used "in its ordinary sense of indicating reproduction or duplication of the original" (322). Copyrights did not provide for "the protection of the intellectual conception apart from the thing produced" (323). A copy of a book, map, chart, or musical composition presumed the presence of "a written or printed record of it in intelligible notation" (323). Musical tones, the Court admitted—especially those emanating from a mechanism such as the pianola—presented a rather distinct quandary within the legal universe of intellectual property; for sounds acquired through the sense of hearing could not be considered the stock of which reproductions consisted unless via "a strained and artificial meaning" of the term "copy": "Musical tones are not a copy which appeals to the eye. In no sense can musical sounds which reach us through the sense of hearing be said to be copies, as that term is generally understood" (323). Musical compositions existed as (unprotected) intellectual conceptions in the mind of the composer and achieved "expression" by means of some chosen instrument; yet they are vulnerable to piracy and plagiary only once rendered within "intelligible notation." Appeals to the ear were de facto eccentric to copyright's visual prerequisites and, hence, de jure unintelligible as property. Only once music took on the form of writing could it become a "tangible thing" and the copyright proprietor rest assured that he possessed a "concrete . . . right of property." For sure, the majority conceded, the perforated rolls consist of a writing, but that writing failed to meet the standard of intelligibility, since the rolls were "not intended to be read as an ordinary piece of sheet music" (323)—that is, read by other persons. "Conveying no meaning . . . to the eye of even an expert musician . . . these prepared wax cylinders can neither substitute the copyrighted sheets of music nor serve any purpose which is within their scope."[33] In sum, piano rolls were illegible, and their captured sounds not considered property, since they consisted of a writing that was capable of being read only by a machine. Only a lean humanistic construal of intelligibility sustains intellectual property, the majority warned, for "if the broad construction of publishing and copying . . . is to be given to [copyright] statute it would seem equally applicable to the cylinder of a music box . . . the record of a graphophone, or to the pipe organ" (323).

Questions of legibility and intelligibility in *White-Smith* turned on the now-familiar distinction between "copy" and "work." The Court's assertion that piano rolls were not "copies" of any underlying musical compositions echoed the 1831 law's understanding of musical compositions as "written" scores. The Court's analogy between sheet music and piano roll compelled its conclusion that whereas the former was perceived directly by the eye, the latter could only be "read" with the help of a machine (*Contested Culture,* 131). Perforated rolls and phonograph records were texts "illegible" to naked human sight and, thus, were neither "copies" (they had no readership, in a word) nor "works" (they were clearly preceded by and subordinate to compositions for which some "author" had been given a monopoly grant of copyright). So long as these texts were read by machines, the Court held, they could not be considered "copies" of any prior privileged musical composition; nor, by the same token, could they be protected as "works." They were (and would continue to be for the next three-quarters of the century) simply "performances," but ones that, because executed by a machine, were excessive to the largely humanist "performance right" of federal statute.[34]

Justice Holmes, cautious of statute's power to narrow the scope of (if not extinguish) copyright's broad "rational significance" (324), or common-law principles, introduced in his concurrence in *White-Smith* the notion of possession *in vacuo.* The notion of property, he ventures, "starts from a confirmed possession of a tangible object, and consists in the right to exclude others from interference with the more or less free doing with it as one wills" (224). In copyright, he concedes, property approximates "a more abstract expression," since there is not an object in possession to which this right of exclusion can be directed. The right to exclude is in this sense "*in vacuo*": "It restrains the spontaneity of men where, but for it, there would be nothing of any kind to hinder their doing as they saw fit. It is a prohibition of conduct remote from the persons or tangibles of the party having the right" (324). Restraint of "spontaneity" is an "extraordinary right," he adds, and one cautiously extended to those who have "invented some new collocation of visible or audible points,—of lines, colors, sounds, or words" (324). In the vast orbit of property, the right to exclude could be directed toward either "a tangible object" or "a[n] abstract expression." But in copyright, the law focused with unbending rigor on the reproduction of "the specific form . . . the collocation devised [by the author] . . . according to what was its *essence*" (324, emphasis mine). The scores for "Little Cotton Dolly" and "Kentucky Babe" accorded with legal construals of the musical composition as "a collocation of sounds . . . reduced to a tangible expression" (324); but, as such, and in recognition of copyright's "specific[ity]," on translation into the player piano's machine language, the alleged "essence" to musical script was freed from copyright's restraints.

The Court's objective in *White-Smith* was deceptively simple—to contend with an emergent commodity as a form of property by means of the translation of the new commodity into a previously recognized legal form— and the mechanism animated to achieve this end was far from novel, for it did not apply exclusively to the protection of sound but, rather, applied to intellectual property as a whole. The Court seized on the piano roll's perforations, seeing in them the rudiments of all intellectual property (a "writing"). *White-Smith* affirmed this legal fiction in a move that jettisoned "musical tones" and "musical sounds" beyond the reach of copyright; and though a year later copyright allowances and restrictions would extend to cover works reproduced mechanically (the phonograph record and the piano roll), the law still applied in the main to published works, with the effect that the creative "work" brought to bear on the notated "work" "has historically been unseen by copyright law."[35] It is thus the case that *White-Smith*, despite its repeal, secured a special ontology of musical sounds and voices as ephemeral, intangible, unfixed—an impermanence characteristic of all acoustic phenomena, a tendency for sounds to evaporate "as soon as apprehended." The acoustic, Gaines notes, "has never been solid enough for copyright law to recognize" ("Piracy of Identity," 89)—an observation whose astuteness is confirmed both in the holdings in twentieth-century cases regarding sound-alikes ("voice does not function as a trademark or tradename"; "A voice is not copyrightable. The sounds are not 'fixed'"), as well as in the law's surreptitious admission of the scribal into its very conception of the acoustic as vocal "style" (L., *stilus,* a pointed instrument for writing).[36]

At the turn of the century, between the introduction of mechanical reproductive devices and their comprehension at law, voices and other acoustic phenomena had, at best, when unattended by writing, a bleak livelihood in the marketplace. Evidence to this effect appears in the first sound-alike case, *Gardella v. Log Cabin Products Inc.* (1937), in which the Italian actress Tess Gardella, the "voice" of Aunt Jemima, filed suit against her employer's competitor for using a radio jingle imitating her "characterization," which last was embodied in the vocal style she had perfected.[37] Gardella lost. The "unique" and "peculiar" characteristics of her voice—in short, her "style"—were not, by law, copyrightable. This loss proved exemplary. Insubstantial in the extreme, aesthetic labors, like secrets and probabilities, frustrated received codifications of property—frustrated, moreover, the prevailing "pictures" of property. As the legal scholar Carol Rose notes, most framings of property require visible markers that "eradicat[e] . . . the dimension of time" and "giv[e] the impression that time does not matter, that the past will be like the future."[38] Whether one is speaking of walls and fences or of maps and writings, each provide such synoptic, atemporal glimpses of property. Against its legal codification, the acoustic seems inescapably temporal; and the temporal is precisely what is not acknowledged by the fictions of copyright law. It is a central paradox of turn-of-the-century copyright law that, because it operated on the assumption that its reach was only to those properties that were "concrete" and "tangible," the more vigorously it pursued evermore complicated fixes on immaterial things, the more those immaterial things (the acoustic, in this instance) appeared inescapably erosive and ephemeral, transient and perishable. But all was not lost in the effort to protect voice.

In "The Right to Privacy" (1890), Samuel D. Warren and Louis D. Brandeis conceive the common law as a venerable donor of basic legal principles, one that demonstrates its "eternal youth" by its ability to "gro[w] to meet the demands of society" (193). To take just one example, the principle that every individual shall have "full protection in person and in property" is for all intents and purposes "as old as the common law"; but, the essay's authors add, the archaism of the principle neither precludes nor excuses the law from the requirement that it "define anew the exact nature and extent of such protection" (193). The nineteenth-century transformation in the conception of property and correlate expansion in property rights are, taken together, just one test of the common law's resolve to remain ever relevant. As Warren and Brandeis see matters, the common law right to property has matured in three stages. In the first instance, the law gives "remedy only for physical interference with life and property" (193). In short, "full protection in person and property" deters battery. Later (and one is not sure, by their account, when), the law expanded its operative senses of "person" as well as "property," for it came to recognize "man's spiritual nature . . . his feelings and his intellect" as part of the "form[s] of possession—intangible, as well as tangible" protected by his right to property. This advance in the legal protection of the person extended the circumference of property rights to forms of possession increasingly proximate to (and evidently inalienable from) the person. With this move, the common law came to recognize a "legal value to sensations." Warren and Brandeis describe a law that met "the demands of society" as it responded to the "intense intellectual and emotional life, and the heightening of sensations which came with the advance of civilization."[39] "Assault" (or mere attempts to do injury, the putting of another in fear of injury) came to join battery as an interference with the person—the first guarded intangible civil "privileges," the second "physical" properties, and together they ascribed the limit to what the law conceived of as the "person": "Now the right to life has come to mean the right to enjoy life,—the right to be let alone" (193). The enhancement of property and the specification of the person were considerably more intimate, if not de jure identical. The "right to enjoy life" had become (on a nebulous "society's" muted "demand") a right of property. Enjoyment grew out of property. Property begat enjoyment.[40]

The "advance of civilization" and "demands of society" did not, in truth, meet strict legal standards of stare decisis, a weakness that explained, in part, Warren and Brandeis's further clarification that, on account specifically of circumstances precipitated by "recent inventions and business methods," the law needed to solicit "solitude and privacy" as aspects of its protected rights. Novel mechanical devices such as the telephone and the phonograph permitted the surreptitious theft and circulation of "thoughts, emotions, and sensations" or those parts of "the pain, pleasure, and profit of life" that lay in excess of "physical things" (195). These technological innovations, on the one hand, threatened to make good the prediction that "what is whispered in the closet shall be proclaimed from the housetops," while, on the other, the photographic camera and the questionable ethics of "newspaper enterprise" violated the sanctity of personhood with "the unauthorized circulation of portraits of private persons" (195). The "too enterprising press, the photographer, or the possessor of any other modern device for recording or reproducing scenes or sounds" (206) came to possess the privileged and potentially abusive power to abscond with the "words spoken" (199), "casual . . . expression[s]" (207), and "personal appearance, sayings, [and] acts" (213) of any unsuspecting individual. Theft under these circumstances amounted not to trespass against property but to an invasion of solitude and privacy. Warren and Brandeis did not arrive at such distinctions willy-nilly, nor from a blind metaphysical faith or commonsensical investment in the identification of solitude with speech. Respect for precedent (stare decisis) made it necessary for these jurists to distinguish violations of privacy from theft as that term is commonly understood. Respecting precedent, then, three legal domains were applicable to words spoken and usurped by mechanical device: defamation, property, and privacy.

Beginning with the "nature of the instrumen[t]" (197) by which privacy has been invaded, Warren and Brandeis observe that the injury "bears a superficial resemblance" to slander and libel—a class of wrongs covered by laws against defamation. And when they move to consider the remedies offered by the law of defamation, it appears that a violation of privacy is actionable on the grounds that it, like slander or libel, results in "wounded feelings" (197). Unfortunately, the essay's authors warn, the law of defamation rests not on any principle that protects the sanctity of feeling but on the belief that only injuries that damage one's reputation are material and, hence, actionable. In theory, the actions of a press, of a photographer, or of the possessor of any recording device could be considered slanderous or libelous invasions of privacy when taken in the abstract (for each could result in the "unauthorized circulation" [195], "publication and reproduction" [207], or "publicity" [197] of one's words or image). However, it would not necessarily follow, on closer legal scrutiny, that all invasions of privacy should be adjudicated on the grounds established by the law of defamation; for, with regards to the individual whose solitude has been invaded, "the matter published of him, however widely circulated, and however unsuited to publicity, must, in order to be actionable, have a direct tendency to injure him in his intercourse with others, and even if in writing or in print, must subject him to the hatred, ridicule, or contempt of his fellowmen" (197). The jurists had to concede, on these grounds, that an act of slander or libel could be an invasion of privacy, but an invasion of privacy would not necessarily be considered legally slanderous or libelous. What is more, the law of defamation remedied wrongs against (protected the correlative rights of) "honor" (198) and "reputation" (197)—rights that, by a fiction of law, were "in their nature material rather than spiritual" (197). The law, they advance, "recognizes no principle upon which compensation can be granted for mere injury to the *feelings*" (197, emphasis mine). It could brook no protection for the "mental suffering" (198) of a violated privacy. It could take no definitive hold of the "thoughts, emotions, and sensations" usurped by an invasion of privacy.

Thoughts, emotions, and sensations, while inadequate to the protected sphere of one's reputation, might find legal cover, Warren and Brandeis propose, under copyright laws and statutes; for, in statutory copyright (and its companion case law) one finds legal doctrines that appear applicable, in their view, to cases of invasion of privacy. And it was the application of the Constitution's "exclusive Right[s]" language to "Writings," coupled with the tendency for statutory copyright's express monopoly grants to presuppose, in their exclusions, correlate rights in the public domain, that raised difficulties for the application of statutory copyright to "thoughts, emotions . . . sensations" and other aspects of privacy. Anything in excess of specific protections (i.e., anything that is not written or published) fell to the public domain—an arena that obviously (and perhaps painfully so) was not the precinct of a privacy right. Absent support in either the law of defamation's protection of "reputation" or statutory copyright's tooprudent regard for "property," Warren and Brandeis return to the common law's copyright protections, where they find "a more general right to privacy" (198) beneath the right to intellectual property. When menaced by the media, Warren and Brandeis venture, every individual is promised by the common law a right "to be let alone" (205).

The right to privacy approaches a right to property, and this resemblance may suffice in their view as a bulwark against the theft of voice: "It is *like* the right not to be assaulted or beaten, the right not to be imprisoned, the right not to be maliciously prosecuted, the right not to be defamed. In each of these rights, *as indeed in all other rights recognized by law, there inheres the quality of being owned or possessed*—and (as that is the distinguishing attribute of property) there may be some propriety in speaking of those rights as property" (205, emphasis mine). It is difficult, Warren and Brandeis concede, to regard "peace of mind" and "relief" as valuable elements of property "in the common acceptation of that term" (201), for the violations in question do not in every case involve "theft and physical appropriation" (205). The principle that protects "words spoken" from "any . . . modern device for recording or reproducing scenes or sounds" is the same as that which guards personal writings against unauthorized publication (206); and this principle originates in common-law copyright, which secures to each individual the right to determine when and how his or her "thoughts, sentiments, and emotions" shall be communicated to the public:

> The same protection is accorded to a casual letter or an entry in a diary and to the most valuable poem or essay, to a botch or daub and to a masterpiece. In every such case the individual is entitled to decide whether that which is his shall be given to the public. No other has the right to publish his productions in any form, without his consent. This right is wholly independent of the material on which, or the means by which, the thought, sentiment, or emotion is expressed. It may exist independently of any corporeal being, as in words spoken, a song sung, a drama acted . . . . A pantomime acted, a sonata performed, is [*sic*] no less entitled to protection than if each had been reduced to writing. . . . Thoughts, emotions, and sensations. should receive the same protection, whether expressed in writing, or in conduct, in conversation, in attitudes, or in facial expression. (199, 206)

In short, the principle that grounds common-law copyright—the only legal protection for "thoughts, emotions, and sensations"—"is in reality not the principle of private property, but that of an inviolate personality" (205). Common-law copyright provides no means with which to cut the border between the "deliberate expression of thoughts and emotions" that occurs in publication and "the casual and often involuntary expression given to them in the ordinary conduct of life" (207). As this right proves indifferent to the "form" or "corporeal being" of expression, no basis can be found "to restrain publication and reproduction . . . except the right to privacy, as a part of the more general right to the immunity of the person,—the right to one's personality" (207).

Chief among Warren and Brandeis's concerns in "The Right to Privacy," as many have argued and as this last phrase makes readily apparent, is a clarification of the rights (and correlative duties) that attend "personality." Personality gained legal protections on the recognition of the common law principle that the right to property in one's writings (the right to freedom from interference, piracy, and reproduction) was grounded on a more general right to immunity from interference of all types—the right "to be left alone" and "the right to one's personality." Warren and Brandeis wanted to lay the groundwork for a common-law right to privacy—the foundations of a right to a private selfhood that subsequent jurists would recognize as a personal right, not a property right (a right inalienable and nontransferable, not a market-based right that would leave the self in question subject to alienation and transfer). "At issue in the distinction between privacy and property," as Robert Post summarizes the matter, "is the legal conception of the person"—or, phrased with the aim of clarifying that conception, privacy remains intact so long as the "person" resists all those characteristics of "property" coincident with the market. The right to privacy sees a self beyond market exchange. Again Post: "The violation of personality can be prevented by surrounding the personality with *a buffering space* of 'solitude and privacy' to insulate emotions and sensations from the world" (650–51, emphasis mine).

Discovered in the interstices of common-law copyright, the private self is essentially "legible." But, in the eyes of Warren and Brandeis, the private self is akin to a "secret-writing."[41] The "Privacy" essay might therefore be said to fill a vacuum in turn-of-the-century statutory copyright's conception of property, to have exposed the limits of intellectual property doctrine: the jettisoning of the acoustic, by means initiated by "recent inventions," beyond the purview of property law. The legal fundaments Warren and Brandeis uncover in the common law's protection of personal writings subtly undermine the principles that serve as the foundation of statutory copyright—principles maintained so stridently in *White-Smith* that the case seems finally to emancipate the acoustic from the scriptural. The handwritten "person" in "The Right to Privacy" fills in the vacuum exposed in *White-Smith;* for, lodging voice within personality, the former shields "words spoken," "casual . . . expression[s]," and "whisper[s]" from their surreptitious usurpation by "modern device[s] for recording or reproducing . . . sounds": "The common law secures to each individual the right of determining, ordinarily, to what extent his thoughts, sentiments, and emotions shall be communicated to others" (198). Theft under the circumstances elaborated in the "Privacy" essay amounts not to trespass against property but to an unwelcome invasion of that "buffering space" anathema to property by its very definition. This imbrication of voice in personality (as opposed to property) is what I mean by the "deep embeddedness of voice."

In fact, to Warren and Brandeis's claims concerning the inviolability of voice, I would add that their essay's defense of "words spoken" and other forms of orality as privacy's proper domain serves to reinforce a vision of

voice as a veritable marker of identity, what the law refers to as an "inalienable."[42] In general, late-nineteenth-century civil law fears reference to inalienables in market terms (terms such as "exchange," "transfer," and
"alienation") for such reference, as certain commentators on property note,
carries with it the "specter" of slavery (and this because of the institution's
legal demise in 1865).[43] One need only recall here Harriet Beecher Stowe's
earlier conception of slavery as an "*accursed* system" spurred on by the passage of the Fugitive Slave Law of 1850, a system whose law provides evidence of the conspiracy between northern and southern men such as
Daniel Webster and John C. Calhoun, architects of the Compromise of
1850, to, in her words, "trade the souls and bodies of men as an equivalent
to money, in their mercantile dealings."[44] This "*dreadful* commerce" of
legislative fiat, she adds, violates the absolute injunctions of natural law, for
it takes God's original "nontransferable" property and makes it exchangeable: "That soul immortal, once bought with blood and anguish by the Son
of God, when the earth shook, and the rocks rent, and the graves were
opened, can be sold, leased, mortgaged, exchanged for groceries or dry
goods, to suit the phases of trade, or the fancy of the purchaser" (*Uncle
Tom's Cabin,* 467). Stowe has it that it is slaves who are the victims of theft,
prey to a legally sanctioned expropriation of their very personhood that
served, above all, to epitomize the inexorable reach of the nineteenth-
century bourgeois free market.[45] Yet, her tone of sentimental horror not
only colors the pages of her own propagandistic literature but extends even
to the letter of the law, reaching as far as the law of intellectual property.

The alarms rang deafeningly in an early test of the privacy tort, the case
of *Pavesich v. New England Life Insurance Co.,* handed down in 1905. In
Pavesich the Georgia Supreme Court ruled on the matter of the defendant
company's unsanctioned use of the plaintiff's image in a company advertisement. The Court ruled that such usage "brings . . . the individual of ordinary sensibility, to a realization that his liberty has been taken away from
him. . . . He cannot be otherwise than conscious of the fact that he is no
longer free, and that he is in reality a slave, without hope of freedom, held
to service by a merciless master; and if a man of true instincts, or even of ordinary sensibilities, no one can be more conscious of his enthrallment than
he is."[46] Little is lost in the admission that enslavement, here a proxy formation to intellectual property, merely rises to the status of metaphor; but,
it merits reiteration that the enforcement of trope is the very work of the law,
the very means by which intellectual property law extends its reach into domains heretofore beyond the grasp of its sacralizing mark.[47] In *Pavesich,* the

attributes of a person threaten to become property; the plaintiff's "features and form" (219) circulate in advance of their legal recognition as property, in the absence of legal sanction. I want to propose here, as a distillation of this chapter's argument, that mechanical reproduction stimulated the above proxy formation to intellectual property precisely because novel copyright appropriations reeked of specious fiduciary motive, of exploit for economic benefit—reeked, to be precise, of the commodification of attributes previously protected, by law, as inalienable and "personal." Mechanical reproduction, in short, returned civil law to the problem of expropriation and the injurious commodification of personhood. Yet, to the degree to which the specter of an immoral expropriation threatened some of the more treasured principles of copyright, the ultimate goal of intellectual property law would ironically be to embrace something like enslavement, to make use of a cultural tradition that had been able to transform expropriation into legitimate exchange—property into something resembling contract. From the vantage of the speculative economy of late-nineteenth-century America, such a transformation would require nothing short of an alteration of the conditions for the emergence of the instruments of capital—a "miraculous fertility" in which theft became gift, property a version of personhood, and the legal *injuria* of tort a mere trifle in the law of contract.

With this transformation in mind, I want now to explore a cluster of related terms—"person," "personhood," "personification," "impersonation"—terms that, given their resonance with notions of intentionality, self-possession, and willfulness, appear rich figures for the emerging contractual instruments of market capitalism (including the instrument of one's voice). I said earlier that the law contends with novelty—that it recognizes disparate phenomena as property—with the help of analogy, through the isolation of those aspects of a form that most closely resemble familiar ones to settle on the rule, which is then adjusted in light of the other significant facts in the case. I said too that the development of more or less coherently organized complexes of thought and argument were "the formalized result of a set of informal associations, subterranean affiliations connected and made 'the law' by repeated association." With those assertions in mind, and with an eye to the "blindness" of the law later revealed by "The Right to Privacy" (the fragile materiality of the letter and the weakened efficacy of the book as the prevailing metaphor for intellectual property), I want now to turn to a particular example that once again draws slavery and intellectual property into an uneasy alliance; one whose poetics anticipates both the forms of textuality elaborated above and the more complex instances that will interest me before long.

THE HUMAN PHONOGRAPH

On October 7, 1857, a planter by the name of Colonel Bethune displayed his slave Tom (né Thomas Wiggins) through the contracted medium of one Perry H. Oliver at Temperance Hall in Columbus, Georgia. Slavery was itself no stranger to exhibition, finding in the spectacle of auctioning opportunity for speculation and profit. Yet the events of Temperance Hall were nothing short of journalistic gold; for, in all but the most somnolent quarters, what Tom accomplished before pit and circle triggered, by most accounts, decades thereafter, a "furore of excitement." [48] Tom, blind and eight years old, would on his debut gain a reputation nationally as a "wonder of the world" and "marvel of the age" due to his ability to master complicated technical tests of memory and to his musical ability; and his celebrity would continue unabated for more than half a century, first in bond to Colonel Bethune (in form if not in fact) from emancipation until 1887, at which time he was promoted and celebrated as "The Last Slave Set Free by Order of the Supreme Court of the United States." The ambiguous overlap of ownership and obedience in the relation between master and slave would continue till Tom's death in 1908. [49] Long Grabs, correspondent for the Fayetteville (N.C.) *Observer*, filed this dispatch subsequent to an antebellum performance:

> The blind negro Tom has been performing here to a crowded house. He is certainly a wonder. . . . He resembles any ordinary negro boy 13 years old and is perfectly blind and an idiot in everything but music, language, imitation, and perhaps memory. He has never been instructed in music or educated in any way. He learned to play the piano from hearing others, learns airs and tunes from hearing them sung, and can play any piece on first trial as well as the most accomplished performer. . . . A true conception of unaided, blind musical genius . . . [t]his poor blind boy is cursed with but little of human nature; he seems to be an unconscious agent acting as he is acted on, and his mind a vacant receptacle where Nature stores her jewels to recall them at her pleasure. [50]

Grabs understands Tom's performances, in the main, as acts of imitation, as evidence of an intrinsic human capacity for mimicry. He learns "from hearing others" and lacks nearly all human capacities save those of "music, language, imitation, and perhaps memory," giving, on occasion, "inconceivable imitations of the Drum and Fife, Railroad cars, Guitars, etc.," as well as, on others, after only a single hearing, performances of the most difficult musical passages from *Norma, Linda,* and *La Traviata*—"tune for tune, note for note."[51] On Oliver's command, by the account of Rebecca Harding Davis—"Now, Tom, boy, something we like from Verdi"—"harmonies . . . you would have chosen as the purest exponents of passion began to float through the room."[52] Intoxicated by melodies harmonic and sonorous, Davis waxes romantic; but she has clearly seen spectacles of this sort before. Intentionally or not, Davis's reference to a "coal-black" and "repugnant . . . object" (105), with "protruding heels" (105), "ape-jaw" (105), "great blubber lips and shining teeth" (110), and "imbecile character of the face" (which impression was "all you saw when he faced you" [110]), characterizes Tom in a language that no doubt calls to mind the grotesqueries of the minstrel show. And Davis's consorts, "the *débris* of [the] town, the roughs, the boys, school-children" (110), confirm the measure of parity between these musical and minstrel imitations, for it was they who found Tom "nearly as well worth a quarter as the negro-minstrels" (110). But, on recognition of the resemblance between Tom's peculiar blackness and blackface, distrustful eyes trumped exacting ears, and the most cynical assessments followed. Unlike Davis, others allege that Tom's imitations "indicate mnemonic and imitative powers [far more] than a genius for music"; and, as such, he appears more accurately classed "not so much with musicians as with the many persons who . . . achieve astounding feats in the way of arithmetical calculation."[53] "Fidelity," "infallible exactitude," and "*verbatim et literatim*" were often an exposé's necessary (though sometimes damning) descriptives.[54]

A lingering uncertainty dims the Fayetteville correspondent's portrayal of events, however, when, on the matter of the source of Tom's musical ability, an already ticklish commitment to journalistic objectivity takes flight behind the smoke and mirrors of metaphysical speculation: "This poor blind boy . . . seems to be an unconscious agent acting as he is acted on, and his mind a vacant receptacle where Nature stores her jewels to recall them at her pleasure." Spectators sit in wonder at this "genius" who appears, contrarily, as Willa Cather describes, to be a mere "human phonograph, a sort of animated memory, with sound producing powers."[55] It is, Cather avows, "as if the soul of Beethoven had slipped into the body of an idiot" (166), as if behind the cloak of impersonation lie mysteries of identification impossible to solve: "It was a strange sight to see him walk out on stage and with his own lips—and another man's words—introduce himself . . . applaud himself, and apologize, still in the third person, for his lack of courtesy" (166). The veil approaches perfect opacity in the account of another reviewer, who, writing for the Baltimore *Sun* in 1859, candidly gives voice to the bewitching paradox so many clamored to witness: "All preconceived ideas of music as a science, an art or an acquisition were thoroughly baffled, and a new question thrust on us as to what music really is in the economy of nature. Accustomed to regard it as a gift, improved and perfected by cultivation and practice, we here find it perfectly developed in a blind negro boy, and constituting a part of his nature, as much so as the color of his skin."[56] A single question piques the interest of both expert and audience ("not the purest bench of musical criticism before which to bring poor Tom" [*Davis Reader,* 109]): what "magic" propels his artistic performance? Enigmas of origin provide a mystery to value: "There is no Art about him. . . . His instruction comes from a Higher Power, and this, Philosophers are pleased to term, genius. . . . He can, however long or difficult the Piece, imitate it upon hearing it once only. Without understanding a single Rudiment of Written Music. . . . When the veil of darkness was drawn over his eyes, as if to make amends for the infliction upon the poor Negro Boy, a flood of light was poured into his brain, and his mind became an Opera of Beauty, written by the hand of God, in syllables of music, for the delight of the world" (fig. 1). The transfer of the scriptural from composer to deity should strike us as faintly alarming—a ghostly fabulation of Tom's legal dispossession.

Tom's performances placed on display unsettled transformations of sound from forms exchanged between persons (i.e., Beethoven and Tom) to properties circulated between things (i.e., piano and slave). His performance of Beethoven seemed enigmatic and marvelous precisely due to its dual character. On the one hand, Tom's performances were clear acts of imitation, reproductions of sound that reflected exchange between (that required) two performers—the interpersonal reproduction of work for which Verdi and other composers function as original authors and owners. But in the play of presence and absence that was so much a part of Bethune's investment—the "secret thereof" that incites his surplus and the flow of capital—Tom's secondi also appeared as acts of duplication, reproductions of sound that took place through the distinct aid of machines.[57] Tom the machine, the mere "vacant receptacle," duplicated and copied another technological interface, specifically the written score, merely "animating" the written sound notations of an original "author," Verdi. When imitating,

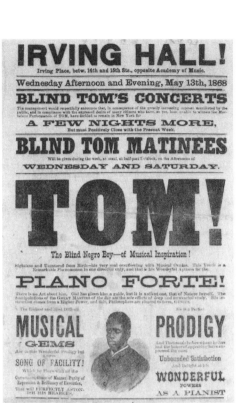

Figure 1. The virtuoso slave "Blind Tom," whose astounding musical abilities made him appear curiously self-possessed and dispossessed. Able to reproduce musical passages with mechanical precision and yet property by the terms of the civil law, he gave off the signs of the phonograph long before its invention. (Photo courtesy Manuscripts, Archives and Rare Books Division, Schomburg Center for Research in Black Culture, New York Public Library, Astor, Lenox and Tilden Foundations [Broadside Collection, SC-CN-99-158])

Tom became, in the act of repetition, a creative human subject, however qualified that creativity and marginal that subjectivity might have been. When duplicating, repetitions made him a mere mimetic contrivance.

The choice between imitation and duplication may seem misguided given that Tom's early career predated by several years the watershed in American inventiveness mentioned in the previous section. The choice may also seem misguided given imitation's and duplication's shared dependence on the scriptural, in the form of a musical composer's "scores," a scribe's "transcriptions," or a printing press's "copies." What astounded in the case of Tom was not that his imitative abilities indicated innate or primordial powers—any notation-literate pianist, even one of the prepubescent sort, could imitate. Davis signals the astonishment effect unique to Tom when she gives account of a challenge, by a musician of considerable braggadocio, who, on claiming that "Tom would fail," "drew out a thick roll of score . . . a Fantasia of his own composition never published" (111). "From the first note to the last," Davis reports, Tom "gave the *secondo* triumphantly" (111). Evident in the challenge, what astounded in the case of Tom was that, perfectly blind, he appeared able to reproduce classical music without making recourse at any time to the scriptural: a "blind boy, who never saw a note of music in his life, plays you the entire work . . . and makes no mistake—not one false register, or slur, or discord, or omission."[58] He short- circuited the literary layer and reproduced by ear alone. Tom's performances skipped the eyes, deemphasized the visual, which (as the very institution of copyright emphasized) constituted the register most would have thought necessary to the reproduction of Western musical form: "We can learn all that great genius can reduce *to rule* and put in *tangible form;* he knows more than that . . . something beyond my comprehension" (*Marvelous Musical Prodigy,* 7).

The spectacle of the virtuoso slave triggered an eye-rubbing uncertainty, a skepticism in the text of objectivity that betrayed maladies of possession of a complexity heretofore unexamined. The romanticism of an "unaided . . . musical genius" on par with "the most accomplished performer" foregrounded interiority in a technology of the letter that valorized an expressive and attentive handedness ("a flood of light was poured into his brain"; "written with the hand of God, in syllables of music").[59] Fascination with the "co-ordination" or "accord" between "the soul, the eye, and the hand" ironically figured an image of chattel as self-possessed.[60] Yet only a romanticism quite complete would fail here as elsewhere to see the specter of a personhood dispossessed, a dispossession captured in reference to a recondite agency ("he seems to be an unconscious agent acting as he is acted on"; "a vacant receptacle where Nature stores her jewels to recall them at her pleasure"), but figured, interestingly, in addition, in Tom's impersonation of another agency ("with his own lips—and another man's words—[he would] introduce himself . . . applaud himself, and apologize, still in the third person, for his lack of courtesy"). On the grounds, then, of an at least formal intimacy between the semiotics of the popular (imitation, duplication) and the rhetoric of the law (persons, property), let it be said in addition that the specter of the virtuoso slave (of self-possessed chattel) participates in a crisis in the conception of property, a turning point, that is, in the legal recognition of property rights in aspects of personhood.[61]

I am being coy here for reasons of getting a lexicon of property onto the page, so let me hasten to make one last observation before moving to assess the broader implications of this racial curiosity. We might note a patent frustration in attempts to cut the border between the aesthetic and the mechanical, labors marred by a language of incomprehension: "All preconceived ideas of music as a science, an art or an acquisition were thoroughly baffled, and a new question thrust upon us as to what music really is in the economy of nature"; "we can learn all that great genius can reduce to rule and put in tangible form; he knows more than that . . . something beyond my comprehension." The popular makes phenomena available for perception in advance of their rationalization and legal codification. Rhetorics of preconceptions "baffled" and of aesthetic forms "beyond . . . comprehension" indicate an instability in the received knowledge of culture and its modes of production—an instability, to be precise, in the perception of the acoustic as property, as an element of market exchange and transfer, as a locus of value. The novelty of piano secondi reproduced "without understanding a single Rudiment of Written Music," is, in fact, the novelty of the mechanical reproduction of sound before its technical achievement—an imagining, in short, of acoustic property (of the acoustic as alienable and commodity) in advance of the phonograph and the application of the law of intellectual property to sound. In sum, what Tom made available for scrutiny, proleptically if obliquely, was the implication of metamorphoses in the acoustic in the received codification of persons and property. Doubly auratic and arithmetic, like the talking commodities of *Das Kapital*, Tom accrued the prophetic and annunciatory signs of a "mechanical reproduction" *avant la lettre.*[62]

You will have detected already some tendencies within my argument— principally, an emphasis on the dynamic between a formalized code of law and a set of informal associations that betray the law's ubiquitous habits of mind. This dynamic deserves to be rephrased in language familiar to the historian of literature and the scholar of intellectual property. To begin, it is taken as a given within legal doctrine that intellectual property "lacks the tangible qualities associated with real property" and that when absent real property's "thingness," "the law must supply alternative concepts to take the place of physical boundaries."[63] The preferred substitute is writing.[64] By the formal associations of the law, by its apparent logic, writing stands as the necessary analogue to all forms of intellectual and aesthetic property. Writing provides the cornerstone to the social construction of authorship and the cultural legitimation of literary property. In the words of the scholar of copyright Mark Rose, the "production of this representation involved . . . the abstraction of the concept of literary property from the physical book and then the presentation of this new, immaterial property as no less fixed and certain than any other kind of property."[65] The work of the law amounts to the work of abstraction. What is more, the rhetorical attempt has long been to build a concept of literary property on the model of heritable, landed estate—a metaphoric labor Rose finds eloquently expressed as early as 1752 in Arthur Murphy's *Gray's-Inn Journal,* whose author notes of the "ancient Patriarchs of Poetry" that "a great part of their possessions [are] let on lease to the moderns," referring variously to Dryden's "hereditary estate" and Pope's "grounds," to a Shakespeare nestled comfortably "upon a cliff" with "possessions very near as extensive as Homer's" and a Milton busily in search of "flowers to transplant into his own Paradise."[66] The metaphoric abstraction of the "book" into the author's "grounds" joins literary property and real estate in an imaginary complex, a counterfactual synthesis of the immaterial and the material that brings the difference before us "through the pretense of overcoming it."[67]

Acoustic phenomena resist such synthesis yet come nearer than any other class of phenomena (nearer, even, than literary property) to what may be called the "metaphysics" of intellectual property; for, intangible and evanescent, sounds typify a whole class of disembodied and immaterial items that, seemingly incapable of clear demarcation, often require the translation of property claims into secondary symbolic systems. Intellectual property doctrine achieves an "objectification of personality" by means of writing, a transformation of this mystified ground of the self into a thing or object whose value is determined by reference to its difference from and similarity to other things and objects within a market.[68] A pivotal moment in this transformation (a moment of the extension of intellectual property doctrine to include new forms of mechanical reproduction) occurs in the case of *Bleistein v. Donaldson Lithographing Company* (1903), a case involving the reproduction of circus posters in which Holmes, writing for the majority, asserts that under copyright the object of the law's solicitation is "personality" as such: "The copy is the personal reaction of an individual upon nature. *Personality always contains something unique.* It expresses its singularity even in handwriting, and a very modest grade of art has in it *something irreducible,* which is one man's alone. That something he may copyright."[69] Odd, this invocation of handwriting in the era of mechanical reproduction. On closer scrutiny, personality evolves in the direction not of objectification but, rather, corporealization. "Personality" gives way to "handwriting." "Handwriting" ripens into "something irreducible." Considerable consequences to the handwritten mark (and the law's ecology of form) follow.

"The order of each man's words is as singular as his countenance"; "a literary work really original, like the human face, will always have some singularities, some lines, some features, to characterize it, and to fix and establish its identity"; "music, it is argued, is intended for the ear as writing is for the eye"; "voice does not function as a trademark or tradename"; "the voice is as distinctive and personal as a face."[70] The law achieves commensurability between disparate things by making a metaphor available for perception, and, then, in denial of the very tropes out of which the law generates its results, asserting that the structure of the metaphor is how the real world works—that the metaphor is in fact a metonymy. The figure is not in fact an aperçu of the real world; rather, it is an apprehension of the language of translation, of the semantic mechanisms of trope. Forgetting and denial are, thus, the cognitive styles that predominate in intellectual property law.[71] In the figure of writing (surrogate to an immaterial sound) the law is in fact making the figural real, largely by reifying metaphoric equivalents into metonymic manipulations of scale. Kenneth Burke has this to say about metonymy in *A Grammar of Motives:*

> Language develops by metaphorical extension, in borrowing words from the realm of the corporeal, visible, tangible and applying them by analogy to the realm of the incorporeal, invisible, and intangible; then in the course of time, the original corporeal reference is forgotten, and only the incorporeal, metaphorical extension survives. . . . Poets regain the original relation, in reverse, by a "metaphorical extension" back from the intangible into a tangible equivalent . . . ; and this "archaicizing" device we call metonymy. . . . The basic "strategy" in metonymy is . . . to convey some incorporeal or intangible state in terms of the corporeal or tangible.[72]

Circa 1900, the law of intellectual property served as a form of reduction, a means to capture an immaterial order within a material index, a strategy, as Karl Marx would put it, of rendering an "unbodily substance" (absurd in his view) in an expressive bodily equivalent.[73] In short, the law's "archaicizing" gestures (to use Burke's awkward term) idealized what Charles Sanders Pierce terms "the index," which he defines as a sign "physically connected with its object."[74]

We might enrich lines of thinking common to the sphere of intellectual property if we rephrase what I have offered thus far in ways that highlight this chapter's central concern — how the law represents the circulation of attributes deemed inalienable and personal as goods within a market. We begin with the recognition that what distinguishes intellectual property from other spheres of the law of property are the specific protocols by which the former manages crisis. Copyright manages crisis — textual indeterminacy, the play of meaning, unauthorized textual iteration — by means of constructions of the "author" as the solitary origin of any given textual event, the enduring "person" in whom rights over a given production can be originally invested.[75] Writing focuses these investments in the person, emerging as property precisely because imagined, in addition, as somehow limned to the person, as uniquely capable to bear the traces and marks of the person (hence, Holmes's valorization of the handwritten mark as an exemplar of personality as such). This modern regime of ownership reduces errant, evanescent phenomena to the enduring outlines of the person.[76]

I want to turn, as promised, from the laws governing fugitive personhood to those governing fugitive persons; and, because what I want to do now is follow out these minute inflections between property and personhood, it seems reasonable to rehearse the previous dimensions of my argument. I began with the proposal that, historically, in turn-of-the-century market culture, rights of possession, investment, and future profit in immaterial forms of wealth gain legal ascendancy in and through the reconception of property as a species of intentionality. Civil law "personifies" the goods and workings of the market, evacuating the concept of property of "thingness" by making it a mere variable of contractual obligation, a codification of fantasized intentions. Plaintiffs win property rights in the probability that old customers will resort to the old place of business; in the reasonable predictability that employees will participate in a "secret art" and not divulge trade secrets to competitors; and in themselves as "artificial persons" endowed with immortal rights heretofore mortal and finite ("properties, by which a perpetual succession of many persons are considered the same, and may act as a single individual").[77] The law of property achieves "certainty and repose" (to recall the words of Justice Holmes) through the fabulation of desired outcomes, the personification of an owner's "interests" (what in rhetoric George Puttenham labels "counterfait in personation"—"if ye wil attribute any humane quality, as reason or speech to . . . insensible things").[78] Civil law ascribes interests and secure intentions to fictive persons when and where no tangible property exists— for example, "fidelity" to the terms of contract, "obligation" to reciprocate in the future. And, in this respect, the words of Michel Foucault prove instructive: "People know what they do . . . ; they frequently know why they do what they do; but what they don't know is what what they do does."[79] Rephrased, we may possess a conception of (and act on) intentions and interests at the local level (the "petty calculations, clashes of wills, [and] meshing of minor interests" that constitute the pragmatics of power [*Michel Foucault*, 188]); however, when the particular becomes abstract, and the miniature magnified, intention assumes the form of a fabulation, and the consequences of interests emerge as mere fictions. Actors calculate, imbue their actions with their interests, but "it does not follow that the broader consequences of these ideal actions are coordinated" (*Michel Foucault*, 187). The words of literary critic Walter Benn Michaels provide an eloquent frame for our concerns: "The desire to personify the economy is the desire to bridge the gap between our actions and the consequences of our actions by imagining a person who does not do what we do but who does what what we do does" (*Gold Standard*, 179).

Yet if armed with the knowledge that the law secures errant property by suffusing it with the interests and intentions of a person and if armed with the further knowledge that the "person" is the very yoke of past volition, current will, and future obligation that fetters errant intellectual properties to an enduring purpose (what Friedrich Nietzsche describes as the "long chain of will" linking "something desired once" and "distant eventualities"), and, given all that we have gathered beneath the sign "property," if we recall our further observation that the circulation of the attributes of the person as goods within the market is the very trigger for suspicion of unjust exchange, of exploitation for economic profit, of unconsenting dispossession—if armed with this knowledge we were to return to the desire to wed action to consequence, the law's ascription of intentions to the market economy grows considerably in complexity.[80] Personification, I propose, in light of the above, is almost always about making abstractions do the dirty work of our desires. The metamorphosis of voice from fugitive sound to property under law—from irrational, unlocalizable, contingent "event" to legally apprehended "thing"—partakes of the personifications rampant throughout turn-of-the-century property law.

At issue in the classification of voice as an element within the domain of intellectual property law are reigning conceptions of the person. The emergence of voice as property is intimately bound up, in this argument, with transformations in the conception of the person. And, given this intimacy of property with persons, the closest legal analogue to the mechanical reproduction of voice (to its commodification and exchange) is the vision of its theft through impersonation (an analogy that is, in part, an answer to the mystery of Blind Tom). Jane Gaines has already made a point of this connection in her own work on voice and intellectual property law: "The body's own sound collection and reproduction apparatus [is] the prototype for the mechanical and electronic record/store/playback functions: listening, remembering, speaking, or singing" (*Contested Culture,* 128–29). What this analogy means, in the context of the specific historical questions at issue in this chapter, is that alongside any analysis of the formal legal protections of voice's mechanical reproduction we must assess analogous visions of personhood's theft—specters of theft that must serve a heuristic function, as analogue and precursor to the pilfering of another's persona through the imitation of his or her voice.

We move, then, to a single example of the law's administration of specious exchange, a case in which the violation of an already suspect property right is reimagined as a species of credit fraud—a transformation of prediction into prodigality and futures into fugitiveness, which reconceives threats to the security of property as the evasions of a guilty, responsible, and obligated person. Constitutional law strikes out against a rationale crafted in the domain of moral philosophy—that a person cannot be property, yet slaves were property, on the principle that, as Immanuel Kant put it, "no one . . . can bind himself by a contract to the kind of dependency through which he ceases to be a person, for he can make a contract only insofar as he is a person."[81] To manage the specter of expropriation, a personhood dispossessed assumes the form of a good promised yet not delivered. The violation of theft, the dispossession of personhood thrown on the market, of inalienables become goods within a market, is reimagined as a breach of contract (figured as errant creditor, fugitive from economic justice). Opprobrious theft assumes the form of hoarded gift, and legal dispossession takes the form of the dispossessed's perfidy, with the final effect of securing exchange in the absence of property, circulation in the absence of goods. I refer, of course, to Dred Scott's challenge to John F. A. Sanford's reasonable expectation of stable market value, which, curiously enough, arrived at America's court of last appeal only months before Colonel Bethune embarked on his errant investment strategy.

THE POETICS OF PROPERTY, 1857: *DRED SCOTT V. SANDFORD*

It was not merely wanderlust but more likely shrewd knowledge of law and politics that led Dred Scott and his wife Harriet to file twin petitions on April 6, 1846, in Missouri circuit court. The Scotts charged Eliza Irene Emerson (widow of army doctor John Emerson, who originally claimed the Scotts as property) with actions of assault and false imprisonment against themselves as free persons—charges that together amounted, under the civil provisions of the time, to a suit for freedom. Their suits, *Dred Scott v. Emerson* and *Harriet v. Emerson,* detailed a decade of intermittent residence in slave territory and on free soil: at Fort Armstrong in the state of Illinois, at Jefferson Barracks in St. Louis, at Fort Jessup in Western Louisiana, and at Fort Snelling, a barracks nestled on the west bank of the Mississippi River in Upper Louisiana, that is, on the border of territory brokered in the Louisiana Purchase ("free" soil according to the terms of the Missouri Compromise).[82] In these inaugural cases, the court returned a verdict for the defendant on a technicality. The Scotts could not prove themselves free persons aggrieved by another's property claim since any evidence of Mrs. Emerson's proprietary rights would have, in slave territory, made them distinctly unfree. Since none of the testimony actually proved Mrs. Emerson's ownership of the Scotts, charges that she had aggressed against free persons could not in fact be adjudicated, while her property rights independent of the material evidence presented in the case were nonetheless preserved. Clearly, on this score, trapped within this paradox, the Scotts were not mollified. They filed an appeal subsequent to the circuit court ruling, which appeal the paired litigants advanced against Emerson and her brother, John F. A. Sanford, who in the interim had been appointed executor of his sister's estate in Missouri.[83] The Scotts won a nominal freedom on appeal on precedents established within Missouri law, whose courts had recently ruled that "a master who took his slave to reside in a state or territory where slavery was prohibited thereby emancipated him."[84]

With a litigious ardor arguably unwarranted by Dred Scott's then modest estimated price of five hundred dollars, Emerson and Sanford took the case to the Missouri Supreme Court, where they were granted a right of

66 CHAPTER ONE

property against Scott.[85] The Supreme Court reversed the appeals court's decision on the grounds of comity (or conflict) of laws, reducing the surfeit of claims and counterclaims to the substantive question of which (and whose) law should have been given precedence: Should Missouri have followed the principle of attachment, which maintained that the grip of southern laws prevailed on the slave when he entered a free state and that, therefore, his status remained unchanged? Or should the Court have followed the doctrine of reversion, which held that a slave taken into a free state obtained a margin of freedom in the sense that his master lost the power to control him but that on return to slave territory the status of slave reattached to him (a difference in law that, as one jurist noted, in dissent in the final suit, "put the liberty of the slave into a parenthesis")?[86] Or, should the Court have followed the model of foot-on-the-soil-of-freedom emancipation, the principle of "once free, forever free" established in the legendary British civil case of *Somerset v. Stewart* (1772)?[87] And, if this last principle was to be respected, could the Court classify the Scotts' five years on land "*sacro sancta civitas* [where liberty always had an asylum]" (*Dred Scott*, 739) as a residence permanent enough to constitute "domicile" or did those years only amount to a temporary residence, a simple "sojourning" with no bearing on their status as slaves (in the words of one court, a "fraudulent shuffling backwards and forwards" between states of an elaborately evacuated liberty)?[88] States, the high court of Missouri argued, bore no intrinsic compulsion to recognize and enforce each others' laws; they should only do so as a matter of judicial discretion and when "controlled by circumstances."[89] Attachment took precedence on appeal. Case closed as a matter of mere sojourning.

While the essential facts in the case remained the same, the state supreme court's decision differed from the earlier rulings in one crucial respect. Handed down on March 22, 1852, the decision issued from the bench in the wake of the tremulous exchanges over slavery and territorial expansion that culminated in the Compromise of 1850 and the passage of the Fugitive Slave Law. Owing to these "circumstances" and to the intermittent yet considerably intense waves of antiabolitionist sentiment they produced, the Court reversed the favorable ruling Scott received from the appeals tribunal. "Times are not now as they were when the former decisions on this subject were made" warned appeals judge William Scott in concurrence (*Scott v. Emerson*, 587). The Scotts and their counsel decided not to file a federal appeal for fear that the U.S. Supreme Court would refuse to review the case on the grounds that it lacked jurisdiction and chose instead to pursue a new legal challenge on the broader and more federally relevant issue of their legal right to sue as citizens of the United States — to claim, in short, capacious rights to contract, sue and be sued, give evidence, and enjoy broad powers of usufruct over both real and personal property.[90] The claim to citizenship rights by a person of African descent struck Roger B. Taney, the Court's principal functionary, not only as spurious and a clear violation both of the letter and spirit of the law but also, from the point of view of a southern Jacksonian Democrat with secessionist sympathies, as downright audacious.

In "plain words — too plain to be misunderstood," asserts the Chief Justice, in the case of *Dred Scott v. Sandford* (1857), the Constitution excludes Negroes, "whether emancipated or not," from the orbit of protections it extends to "citizens" — a category "so well understood" when it "came from the hands of [the] framers" that "no further description or definition was necessary" (*Dred Scott*, 720). Taney's philology is of enviable simplicity: "The words 'people of the United States' and 'citizens' are synonymous terms, and mean the same thing. They both describe the political body, who, according to our republican institutions, form the sovereignty . . . what we familiarly call the 'sovereign people'" (700). The term "'citizen,' as derived from *civitas*," writes Justice Grier in concurrence, "conveys the ideas of connection or identification with the State or government," and rigorously excludes from its orbit "the condition of being private property, the subject of individual power and ownership" (730). The letter of the law moves with deliberate, ineluctable force to exclude property (and, with it, all necessary responsibilities) from the federal government's protective reach. As the majority reason further, while "citizen" signifies in ways that "seem to embrace the whole human family" (702), while the Constitution is unequivocal in its protection of citizens as the fulcra of rights of "individual power and ownership," the document is equally unambiguous in its desire to exclude Negroes from within its protective folds, for when it mentions them — in the three-fifths clause, the fugitive slave clause, and the provision regarding the slave trade — its purpose is to "treat them as property" (709). The Constitution merely codifies practice — the practice of exchange: "No one of that race had ever migrated to the United States voluntarily; all of them had been brought here as articles of merchandise" (703). Taney's opinion (the voice of the majority) illumines the legal inscription and legitimation of this received market practice. The opinion reads:

> The question is simply this: can a negro, whose ancestors were imported into this country and sold as slaves, become a member of the political community formed and brought into existence by the Constitution of the United

States, and as such become entitled to all the rights, and privileges, and immunities, guarantied [*sic*] by that instrument to the citizen. . . . There are two clauses in the Constitution that point directly and specifically to the negro race as a separate class of persons, and show clearly that they were not regarded as a portion of the people or citizens of the government then formed. One of these clauses reserves to each of the thirteen States the right to import slaves until the year 1808, if it thinks proper. And the importation that it thus sanctions was unquestionably of persons of the race of which we are speaking, as the traffic in slaves in the United States had always been confined to them. And by the other provision the States pledge themselves to each other to maintain the right to property of the master, by delivering up to him any slave who may have escaped from his service. . . . The only two provisions which point to them and include them, treat them as property, and make it the duty of the Government to protect it; no other power, in relation to this race, is to be found in the Constitution; and as it is a Government of special, delegated powers, no authority beyond these two provisions can be constitutionally exercised. The Government of the United States has no right to interfere for any purpose but that of protecting the rights of the owner, leaving it altogether with several States to deal with this race, whether emancipated or not, as each State may think justice, humanity, and interests and safety of society require. The States evidently intended to reserve this power exclusively to themselves. (700, 703, 709)

On the contentious matter of federal protections of property the Chief Justice maintains that these protections are minimal, adding, in point of clarification, that property is largely the dominion of the states: "The States evidently intended to reserve this power exclusively to themselves." What is more, obdurate defense of these state powers is justified by the very language of the Constitution, where, in his view, state power trumps federal power. Taney's interpretive certainty on this matter exempts him, in the end, from the necessity of formal judicial rigor, permitting in its stead stress on proslavery inference and proscription of all hints of abolitionist temper:

The powers of the government, and the rights of the citizen under it, are positive and practical regulations plainly written down. The people of the United States have delegated to it certain enumerated powers, and forbidden it to exercise others. It has no power over the person or property of a citizen but what the citizens of the United States have granted. . . . And if the Constitution recognizes the right of property of the master in a slave, and makes no distinction between that description of property and other property owned by a citizen, no tribunal acting under the authority of the United

States, whether it be legislative, executive, or judicial, has a right to draw such a distinction, or deny to it the benefit of the provisions and guarantees which have been provided for the protection of private property against the encroachments of the governments. . . . [The] right of property in a slave is distinctly and expressly affirmed in the Constitution. The right to traffic in it, like an ordinary article of merchandise and property, was guaranteed to the citizens of the United States, in every State that might desire it, for twenty years. And the Government in express terms is pledged to protect it in all future time, if the slave escapes from his owner. This is done in plain words—too plain to be misunderstood. And no word can be found in the Constitution which gives Congress a greater power over slave property, or which entitles property of that kind to less protection than property of any other description. The only power conferred is the power coupled with the duty of guarding the owner of his rights. (720)

There are phrases here familiar to our ears ("rights," "privileges," "enumerated powers"), phrases that capture a good many of American liberalism's most treasured conceits—principally and specifically, the view of federal government as a narrow trust set up by individuals to form a society the point of which is to secure order and protect property. Root source for the framers' view of government as a specially attenuated enterprise are the writings of Baron de Montesquieu, who enjoyed considerable popularity amongst the members of America's Revolutionary generation (though most often among anti-Federalists) for having taken the rule of law to depend on "institutional restraints that prevent governmental agents from oppressing the rest of society" (restraints that would be figured in the textbook of American letters as the "balance of powers").[91] To find evidence of the enormous fascination of this generation with Montesquieu's ideas, one might even direct attention to certain of John Adams's writings (a noted Federalist), writings from a thinker whose entire political thought turns about the issue of the balance of powers. "Power must be opposed to power," Adams carps, in response to Mary Wollstonecraft's *French Revolution*, "force to force, strength to strength, interest to interest, as well as reason to reason, eloquence to eloquence, and passion to passion."[92] Perhaps more than needed to be said. Yet, in *Dred Scott* there are still other phrases that prove more lusciously intriguing to the literary exegete: "plainly written down"; "distinctly and expressly affirmed"; "guaranteed" and "pledged"; "in plain words—too plain to be misunderstood"; and phrases "so well understood" that "no further description or definition was necessary." Lexical ornaments of a classic liberalism, for sure, but those of

us schooled in the lessons of poststructuralism have come to be quite leery
of an alleged perspicuity (familiar with the abiding interests that lurk where
meanings are said to have been set down in words "too plain to be misunderstood"). The political theory to which these words point, if "classic,"
is that of a classic legal positivism; and, a few of the implications of this
rhetoric of antirhetoric for the practice of American jurisprudence bear
consideration.[93]

We begin our discussion of *Dred Scott*, then, with a clarification of terms.
Positivism is a theory of legal interpretation deeply and ironically averse to
interpretation, a mode of textual analysis, as Robert Post has shown, in the
essay "Theories of Constitutional Interpretation," which takes as its principal objective a description of the activities of the judicial branch of government "when constitutional meaning is not problematic."[94] The common, liberal narrative of positive law goes something as follows: the framers
proposed a compact among themselves to limit the power of government in
the form of the Constitution; the people signified their agreement to that
compact by their ratification of the Constitution. From the vantage of positive law, all subsequent interpretation of the Constitution should "be designed to give effect to the terms of that original act of agreement" ("Constitutional Interpretation," 21), and, on the strength of the consent marked
by the text itself, all "relevant inquiry must focus on the *public* understanding of the language when the Constitution was developed."[95] Thus, when
Taney animates the language of conspicuous meanings—"plain words—
too plain to be misunderstood"—he succumbs to a hermeneutic practice that had taken considerable hold on American jurisprudence by the
early nineteenth century, wielding the concession of Federalist and anti-
Federalist jurists alike to respect the sanctity of the Constitution as positive
law, as the concrete manifestation of a "real" social contract.[96] Proponents
of this particular interpretive posture found that the Constitution's authority flowed from this "single [and ostensibly contractual] act of willful self-
regulation" ("Constitutional Interpretation," 21) in which framers and
people become one—"the political community formed and brought into
existence by the Constitution of the United States" (*Dred Scott,* 700). Governmental power became such only, in liberalism's talismanic phrase,
through the "consent of the governed."

Within antebellum debate on the practice of American jurisprudence,
specifically as regards the slavery question, the judiciary was often feared,
and rather publicly so, as a nonresponsible branch of government, as a
body capable to make laws yet not accountable to the people (*Justice Ac-*

cused, 132). It is within this context that interpreters of the Constitution—Taney included—portrayed themselves as merely passive enforcers of the "democratic will," of the "will of the people" ("Constitutional Interpretation," 21), as defenders of a legal methodology whose moral power rested in its principled equation of constitutional authority with a consent "derived from the integrated notions of voluntariness, promise, and mutuality" (*Justice Accused,* 133–34). It is within this context, in short, that Taney and judges of like sentiment idealized the judiciary as that branch of government that applied the will of others, that abnegated all sovereign, law-making qualities. Thus it appears in the normative universe of the *Dred Scott* majority that jurisprudential commitment ranks obedience to authentic meaning above idiosyncratic interpretation—priorities familiarly conceived as the elevation of fidelity to law above the interests of personal, moral impulse.[97] Here, once again, I quote the words of the Chief Justice:

> No one, we presume, supposes that any change in public opinion or feeling in relation to this unfortunate race . . . should induce the court to give to the words of the Constitution a more liberal construction in their favor than they were intended to bear when the instrument was framed and adopted . . . ; but while it remains unaltered, it must be construed now as it was understood at the time of its adoption. It is not only the same in words, but the same in meaning . . . ; and as long as it continues to exist in its present form, it speaks not only in the same words, but with the same meaning and intent with which it spoke when it came from the hands of the framers. . . . Any other rule of construction would abrogate the judicial character of this court, and make it the mere reflex of the popular opinion or passions of the day. (709)

We have here, clearly, an inveterate expression of judicial restraint, where a self-professed helplessness before the letter of the law fits hand in glove with contractual obligation and commitment to the framers' covenant and promise, where the contingencies of interpretation yield to the vox populi, and where the immutable future of a document "framed" subordinates "public" "popular opinion" and the "feeling" and "passions of the day."[98] Years earlier, it is worthy of note, Taney's predecessor on the bench, Chief Justice John Marshall, would abjure in another ruling that, "in considering this question [and all questions before the Court] . . . we must never forget that it is *a constitution* we are expounding"—words of little import in Taney's valorization of the timelessness of the text's original construal.[99]

Restraint, contract, consent, will—terms familiar to any jurist's ear and, certainly, to ears attuned to the timbre of constitutional text. However, we should hear in Taney's arithmetic of judicial restraint ("It is not only the same in words, but the same in meaning") not simply echoes of Adams's and Madison's vaunted "*balance* of powers" but also a vocabulary of quantification and an arithmetic of meaning shared by a diverse majority within America's post-Revolutionary generation. To take one example, Benjamin Franklin advocates, in his *Dissertation on Liberty and Necessity, Pleasure and Pain,* a disciplining of affect to the rigors of mathematical laws: "As the *Desire* of being freed from Uneasiness is equal to the *Uneasiness,* and the *Pleasure* of satisfying the Desire equal to the *Desire,* the *Pleasure* thereby produc'd must necessarily be equal to the *Uneasiness* or *Pain* that produces it: Of three lines, A, B, and C, if A is equal to B, and B to C, C must be equal to A. . . . So many Degrees as one Scale of the Balance descends, so many exactly the other ascends; and one cannot rise or fall without the Fall or Rise of the other: 'Tis impossible to taste of *Pleasure,* without feeling its preceding proportionate *Pain;* or to be sensible to *Pain,* without feeling it's [*sic*] necessary Consequent *Pleasure.*"[100] Political principles, too, in the view of Thomas Paine, are most readily apprehended by means of the figure of arithmetic (by a translation of the juridical into the fractional), even in the political fiction of a parliamentary "check" on monarchical power: "For as the greater weight will always carry up the less, and as all the wheels of a machine are put in motion by one, it only remains to know which power in the constitution has the most weight, for that will govern; and tho' the others, or a part of them, may clog, or, as the phrase is, check the rapidity of its motion, yet so long as they cannot stop it, their endeavours will be ineffectual. The first moving power will at last have its way, and what it wants in speed is supplied by time."[101] Finally, John C. Calhoun, Taney's political ally, would graft figures of systematic and scientific, positive and credible knowledge onto Taney's "letter of the law" (onto Franklin's "proportionate" and "consequent," and onto Paine's common denominator of "the first moving power")—a final and perhaps appropriate confirmation of the objectivist passions that inspired the period's rhetorical impresario: "In order to have a clear and just conception of the nature and object of government, it is indispensable to understand correctly what that constitution or law of our nature is, in which government originates; or, to express it more fully and accurately—that law, without which government would not, and with which, it must necessarily exist. Without this, it is as impossible to lay any solid foundation for the science of government, as it would be to lay one for that of astronomy, without a like understanding of that constitution or law of the material world, according to which the several bodies composing the solar system mutually act on each other, and by which they are kept in their respective spheres."[102]

Taney and Calhoun, Franklin and Paine. All would seem (as Holmes, you recall, would later charge) to be "doing their sums right," to have achieved (again, to recall the words of Stowe) those "accursed principle[s of] mathematical accuracy," those "elegant surgical instruments for the work of dissecting the living human heart." Yet there is in this language implicit allegiance to a genealogy neither framer nor jurist would—at risk of an impressive roster of liberal credentials—be too eager to acknowledge. To the degree to which perspicuity's necessary figure is that of mathematics (to the degree to which legal positivism finds expression in a vocabulary of quantification and contract, mathematics and consent, arithmetic and certainty), the rhetoric of conspicuous meanings points to a source in seventeenth-century political thought—not, as has often been assumed, in the writings of John Locke but in those of Thomas Hobbes and other defenders of absolutism.[103] Consider the following dark paradox of secular law.

The American Revolution and subsequent exertions over constitutional doctrine threw into relief with an unparalleled sharpness the old problem of the origin of law, of the source of the law's authority. To be precise, it was the series of events that transpired in Philadelphia in the weeks leading up to July 4, 1776, that rendered conspicuous the consequences not of revolution per se but of secularization—namely, in the political sphere, the effects on legal doctrine and practice of the emancipation of secular power from the authority of the Church, an emancipation made manifest in the subordination of natural law beneath the dictates of positive law (the former conceived loosely as any absolute injunction taken to emanate from God, nature, or reason, while the latter is more often defined, technically and tautologically, as those norms of artificial law "issued from and institutionally recognized by the existing legal authority").[104] By Hannah Arendt's assessment, it is the rise of European absolutism—the existence, that is, of an absolute sovereign whose will is taken as the source of both power and law—which, paradoxically, can be given the greatest amount of credit where the ramifications of emancipation are concerned; for the absolute monarch is "commonly and rightly credited with having prepared the rise of the nation-state, [and with having been] responsible, by the same token, for the rise of the secular realm with a dignity and a splendour of its own."[105] Such were the concerns of continental revolutionaries, especially the French, who, once unburdened of absolutism as the prevailing structure of the state, translated the universal text of Roman law, the *Corpus juris civilis,* into the Napoleonic code or *Code civil* of 1804 (*Blackwell Dictionary,* 322). Matters were considerably more complicated for the Revolutionary generation in America, for, once its members forswore their allegiance to the Crown, the postcolonies were still confronted with the question of how to establish power—concerned, that is, not with the question of how to limit power, not with the old problem of law and power per se, "but [with] the source of law which would bestow legality on positive, posited laws" (*On Revolution,* 160). Absent earlier sources of foundation such as custom or the exalted position of the monarch, the framers faced like no other revolutionaries the inescapable need for an absolute, specifically, "the need of all positive, man-made laws for an external source to bestow legality on them," an externality that would permit them "to transcend as a 'higher law' the legislative act itself" (*On Revolution,* 161). In one of the ironies of American jurisprudence, the very perspicuity of the legal word—its distinctness, autonomy, and precision, its pragmatic self-sufficiency and arithmetic simplicity—provides just such a source of the absolute.

It is Thomas Hobbes, the first modern political theorist, who, writing in exile from the very revolutionaries who overturned Charles I, limited and reestablished the law's power through a resurrection of the sovereign. The author of *Leviathan* takes with the utmost seriousness a latent disagreement between the members of a modern state: that without a social contract "nature" (a violent, chaotic, and dangerous civil order) rules, and "masterless men" of individuated desires and unsympathetic interests prevail.[106] Such disagreement threatens with inefficiency, at best, and civil war, at worst; and, in Hobbes's thesis, these tacit dangers can only be avoided "by vesting authority in a sovereign whose decisions on matters of law and public business must be taken as final."[107] Hobbes formulates the idea that for the sake of peace and avoidance of civil war an abstract entity called the "state" should exercise all power and be the exclusive object of loyalty (*Blackwell Dictionary,* 394). Subjects vest authority in a specifically personified state—monarch, Leviathan, the commonwealth, or, of late, the legislature—what Hobbes designates, famously, a "*Feigned* or *Artificiall person* . . . that great LEVIATHAN called a common-WEALTH, or STATE, (in latine CIVITAS) which is but an Artificiall Man" (*Leviathan,* 9). Positive law is thus the command of the sovereign, and a sovereign power (whether delegated or not, whether limited or not) is taken as the power to enact one's will (personal or collective) into law (*Justice Accused,* 132), a power that stands in contrast to natural law, or "NATURE (the Art whereby God hath

made and governes the World)" (*Leviathan,* 9). "Hobbes is intent on ruling out traditional justifications of political authority, appeals to the natural
superiority of the ruler and the like. His announcement that all obligations
arise from the individual's actions emphatically slams the door shut on any
such traditional justifications" (*Happy Slaves,* 79). Law reflects the consent
and covenants that created this state authority, hence Hobbes's paradigm
claim on consent theory: "There being no obligation on any man, which
ariseth not from some act of his own" (*Leviathan,* 298). Hobbes derived
political authority from consent for two reasons. First, to free the sovereign,
not to bind him: "Hobbes bound the original democracy that authorized
the sovereign to the acts of the sovereign it had authorized."[108] Second,
Hobbes strove to enable the subjects of the state to feel as though they were
part of the sovereign, "to identify with its actions as if those actions were
their own" (*"Ronald Reagan,"* 300). Unlike John Locke, who argued, like
Plowden, that the state was based on reason (*semblable reason semblable ley*
[what seems to be reasonable seems to be law]), Hobbes relied on fear and
authority.[109]

The code of law reflects the consent and covenants that gave rise to this
state authority and leads to a model of the law as mutual, reciprocal, and
transparent that holds two distinct consequences for the practice of nineteenth-century American jurisprudence. First, there is the matter of the
founding covenant. Since the subjects of the modern state create the sovereign by consenting to have it represent them, they are bound by his acts
("there being no obligation on any man, which ariseth not from some act of
his own"). Authoring the sovereign, we authorize it to act in our names and
transfer a finite set of rights by way of a covenant, by way of a promise.[110]
Second, we promise to maintain a certain state of will toward the sovereign,
and the state of will we are obliged to maintain is a willingness to perform
the covenant. As subjects of the modern state, we may find that we confront
rules we find neither rational nor desirable, but we are not justified to dis-
obey or to interpose our will against the will of the sovereign. On the one
hand, the sovereign acts in every man's name; so the sovereign cannot,
strictly speaking, act unjustly. On the other hand, acts of disobedience on
the part of the subjects of the modern state are automatically unjust, on the
grounds that they violate the covenant made with and by others to obey
(which brings us, finally, to the "letter" of the law).

One of the principal doctrines in *Leviathan* maintains that man's freedom consists in those areas (assumed by Hobbes to be an immense continent) in which the law is silent.[111] The circumference of our liberties

remains quite vast on the promise that we adhere to the "rule of law," which is taken to include only the narrowest construal of obligations (responsibilities to the social contract in the specific instances where certain rights had been transferred to the sovereign). Once again, I quote Hobbes directly: "The use of the Lawes, (which are but Rules Authorized) is not to bind the People from all Voluntary actions; but to direct and keep them in such a motion, as not to hurt themselves by their own impetuous desires, rashness, or indiscretion; as Hedges are set, not to stop Travellers, but to keep them in the way" (*Leviathan,* 176). Care should be taken not to miss the forest for the trees here; for Hobbes's bucolic image veils that principle of legal order of relevance to the practice of nineteenth-century constitutional law. From the principle that law is the command of the sovereign, it follows, Hobbes went on to argue, that the task of jurisprudence is to determine, scientifically and arithmetically, the pedigree and logical coherence of the established legal order, to arrive at an "origin" and a "geometry" of the law: "The Law is more easily understood by few, than many words. For all words, are subject to ambiguity; and therefore multiplication of words in the body of the Law, is multiplication of ambiguity" (*Leviathan,* 177). This geometry, or calculus, of the law could only be arrived at, in Hobbes's view, by means of a purge, essentially an obliteration of all metaphor from legal discourse. Metaphors, he claimed, were an "abuse of Speech" (*Leviathan,* 21). He proffers, further, that they should be "utterly excluded" from "all rigorous search of Truth" since "they openly professe deceipt" (*Leviathan,* 41). Metaphor and other forms of poetic embellishment mystify and deceive and, on these grounds, ought properly to be evacuated from the law. Multiplication of words. Multiplication of ambiguity. Here is where the narrowest construal of the law—legal positivism, faith in the "letter of the law" as metaphor free—appears, ironically, to need the figure of arithmetic, the vocabulary of quantity, and the presumed certainty and predictability of mathematical models.

Hobbes puts metaphor and rhetoric under fire (and elevates the law's "geometry" to a position of preeminence). Mary Poovey has recently proposed that Hobbes valorized the statistical and the numerical, at least partly, because by the time he penned *Leviathan* "the only analytic method considered capable of compelling assent was mathematical demonstration."[112] Hobbes, she continues,

> deemed it politically necessary to use a mode of analysis capable of *compelling* assent, because only a government to which everyone assented could

put an end to what Hobbes viewed as universal chaos. . . . Hobbes con-
tended that mathematical demonstration had the potential to compel assent
because it produced *certain* knowledge; thus mathematical demonstration
was superior to [the] experimental demonstration [advanced by Francis Bacon in *Novum Organum*], which he considered capable of producing only
probable knowledge. . . . Ideally, he believed, the process or reasoning used
in mathematics could be generalized to knowledge production, so that philosophy could become a kind of arithmetic. (104)

Poovey concludes:

> In *Leviathan* arithmetic . . . served an illustrative function; the figure of
> mathematics or arithmetic was holding the *place* of certainty in a world in
> which certainty was no longer available because consensus was no longer
> possible. . . . Quantification functions as an implicit metaphor for social re-
> lations: people interact with each other as if there were a fixed amount of re-
> spect for which everyone vies. . . . Quantification also functions as an inter-
> pretive instrument: by translating incommensurable differences or qualities
> into something that can be quantified, Hobbes renders social relations
> amenable to arithmetic. . . . Translating sociality into numbers allows for a
> level of precision and certainty that could not be attained through narrative
> descriptions or comparisons of incommensurate things. (107–8)

Thus, the figure of mathematics—that reduction of words that yields a reduction of "ambiguity"—provides the mark of consent, the evidence of assent, the triumph of positive law, the grounds of contractualism. "Into
[Hobbes's] machine went the likes of envy and fear and anxiety and pain
and murder [i.e., the incommensurate elements of Poovey's 'sociality'], out
came sovereignty and positive law; out came motions and magnitudes,
sense and behavior, liberty and necessity" (*Pride and Solace,* 63).

My plotted summary of *Leviathan* and the notion of sovereignty could
appear to suggest that Hobbes's resurrection of sovereign authority blindly
valorized the rigor and retribution of feudal power. Such is not the case;
and the reasons are strictly historical. Taken in the context of England's
constitutional crisis, Hobbes's regard for the monarchy is arguably inspired
by the consideration "that the office of the monarch provided an external
framework of order within which the commercial interests of the middle
class could be pursued."[113] Grounded in the theory of the founding contract, the mutual pledge of ruler and subjects, sovereignty serves as a defense of consent, covenant, and good faith—as a formalization of the special

relationships idealized in defenses of market capital (i.e., obligation, reciprocity, trust, solidarity, like-mindedness, and mutual aid). Hobbes, as others have noted, "may be seen as the first competent advocate of the claims and aspirations of the rising Protestant middle class" (*Hobbes and America,* 55), and, furthermore, his *Leviathan* may be seen as the *Summa theologica* of a commercial Protestantism in which the liberal-democratic valorization of the absolute will of the individual is assumed to be a mere formalization of the temperaments of market capitalism. The "person," in *Leviathan,* is the very expression of these myriad principles of mutuality and reciprocity — the reification to which we assent as members of the body politic:

> A PERSON, is he, whose words or actions are considered, either as his own, or as representing the words or actions of an other man, or of any other thing to whom they are attributed, whether Truly or by Fiction. When they are considered as his owne, then is he called a *Naturall Person:* And when they are considered as representing the words and actions of an other, then is he a *Feigned* or *Artificiall person.* . . . Of Persons Artificiall, some have their words and actions *Owned* by those whom they represent. And then the Person is the *Actor;* and he that owneth his words and actions, is the AUTHOR: In which case the Actor acteth by Authority. For that which in speaking of goods and possessions, is called an *Owner,* and in latine *Dominus* . . . ; speaking of Actions, is called Author. And as the Right of possession, is called Dominion; so the right of doing any Action, is called AUTHORITY.[114]

We have here, in one of the most oft-cited passages from *Leviathan,* the substance of a "geometry." Complex declensions of "person" serve as a ruse of transparency. Repetition banishes all possibility of deception and duplicity from the domain of civil society. In the culture of an emergent capitalism (a culture in which predictions of value and exchange correlate with idealizations of credit extension such as trust, like-mindedness, fidelity, and reciprocity), metaphoric deception gives expression to civil disobedience; and mystification proves a violation of the mutuality, solidarity, and trust assumed within a regime of consent and obligation. Quantification, to recall Poovey, holds the place of certainty or, better, transparency, reducing apparently incommensurate differences to the common denominator of the "person."

Hobbes's emphasis on the source of law (on the authority of, and our necessary obligation to the law) arguably situates him as the intellectual progenitor of the discipline of legal governance called legal positivism — a secular legal tradition that accepts the metaphysical belief in the unity or homogeneity of the legal order as a system of rules. Focused primarily on the source of law, on the code or the common law, positivist doctrine closes up the legal order into a habitus "unified by no more cogent principle than reference to the library of legal texts, statutes, and reports" (*Blackwell Dictionary*, 323), into a systematics or "geometry" of the law motivated by no more persuasive concept than the *autopoesis* of the legal system. In nineteenth-century American analytical jurisprudence, courts began to articulate a doctrinal posture that took the content of the law as axiomatic. In turn, jurists were free to concern themselves solely with the arrangement of "the sources and institutions of the legal system into a formally defined normative order or 'rule of law'" (*Blackwell Dictionary*, 327). As Taney's own moves make evident, the study and practice of law focused with a renewed vigor on the study of the text and nothing but the text—a text, again, importantly, ostensibly purged of metaphor and arithmetical in its workings. In doctrinal terms, the "letter of the law" dominated all legal cases. Thus, conditions were with the self-referential text as they were with the warrantless sovereign: "The notion of an absolute source of law, inherited from the classical tradition and translated into jurisprudential theories of the sovereignty of the legislature or of the people, remained and to some degree remains in place: *in the theory of law the king had yet to be beheaded*" (*Blackwell Dictionary*, 323, emphasis mine).[115]

It bears consideration, in light of the above, that the "plain words" of the constitutional provisions in dispute in the case of *Dred Scott v. Sandford* did not treat, as Taney would have it, "the negro race," or "the master," or "slave property." The letter of the law referred only (and assiduously) to "persons."[116] Not one of the provisions that seems on first glance to deal with "free inhabitants" and their enslaved brethren manages, on closer scrutiny, as Taney would aver with regard to the enslaved, to "point to them and include them, [and] treat them as property." In the clause regarding representation and taxation, the language of the article refers, simply, to two types of person: "free Persons" (who could be of either European or African descent) and "other Persons."[117] Representation and taxes were to be computed by adding to the whole of the former "three-fifths" of the latter. The clause refers, therefore, to two ratios of person and reflects the governing belief that, on the assumption that productive labor was the best rule for ascertaining wealth (and, by extension, taxation), population should serve as an index of property, value, and representation. It follows, then, that reference to "other persons" in a document that speaks only of "persons" does not necessarily give formal recognition and legitimacy to the treatment of slaves as property, a central supposition of Taney's opinion. What is more, the compromise formulation certainly does not assert in line with the accuracy required by law, or by a legal "geometry," that a slave was 60 percent human and 40 percent property—does not do so with anything like the certainty Taney's "plain words—too plain to be misunderstood" would appear either to assume or to mandate. As measures of value and wealth, the focal points for taxes and representation, slaves were no more treated as property than were free persons.[118] The clause only incorporated a differential estimate of the slave's wealth-producing capacity as a person— reflecting, by that estimate, the widespread and largely accurate belief, long championed by utilitarian political economists such as Adam Smith, "in the relative inefficiency of slave labor" as against free labor (*Dred Scott Case*, 352–54).[119]

Similarly, the slave trade clause states only that "the Migration or Importation of such Persons as any of the States now existing shall think proper to admit, shall not be prohibited by the Congress prior to the Year one thousand eight hundred and eight, but a Tax or duty may be imposed on such Importation, not exceeding ten dollars for each Persons." Certainly, the rhetoric permits a continuation of the slave trade but, again, as in the previous clause, with a force of law wanting relative to Taney's potent "traffic . . . guaranteed." And, though the clause is unique in its reflection of the property-holding aspect of slavery, it references ownership obliquely and with an inscrutability that, before the exigencies at midcentury, would seem almost to call out for Taney's substitution of "merchandise and property" for "persons."

Taney achieves a revision of similar import in his reading of the remaining constitutional provision regarding slaves and slavery. This last provision, the fugitive-from-labor clause of Article 4 of the Constitution, reads as follows: "No Person held to Service in one State, under the Laws thereof, escaping into another, shall, in Consequence of any Law or Regulation therein, be discharged from such Service or Labor, but shall be delivered up on Claim of the Party to whom such Service or Labour may be due." Here the figuration of the fugitive as debtor should strike us as faintly alarming. The clause seems almost to repudiate the ownership of persons by reference to the fugitive's debt (debt's disparities create debtors, not property; indebtedness produces subjects, persons perceived by law as capable of reciprocity, as liable for fiduciary inequalities and responsible for their just compensation). Yet, paradoxically, by the same token, the fabrication of the enslaved as indebted preserves property; for, if in this instance to be a slave is to be a debtor, if the very condition of servitude is indebtedness (in short, to the degree to which there are no slaves who are not also debtors), then the volition signified by the term "debt" is in suspension— by the law's own accounting, paradoxically present and absent.[120] By express provision in the Constitution, the "person held to service or labour" appears so fully commensurate with the "debtor" as to make the latter's willfulness, liability, and obligation nothing less than the pure projection of legal rhetoric.

The law needs to embrace two incommensurables. In the hand of humanity rests the "fugitive" slave, who, like his or her legal analogue (the fugitive who flees from justice), willfully eludes obligation. Yet in the hand of interest lies the slave or person who, by definition, has done nothing to incur his or her debt, since there is no slave in advance of liability who can will a debt: property in personhood *tout court*. The figuration of the fugitive as debtor produces a willful subject against the express legal nullification of willfulness. To be precise, it projects a willful subject when the will-less is in suspension, fabulates a subject not owned when the owned escapes (to use the language of the common law) "absolute dominion," fantasizes a person at the precise moment when the security of property is subject to greatest question. On the evidence of the fugitive slave clause, ownership of slave property assumes an indebtedness of persons in which past volition and present liability, a careless will and a current obligation, occupy the same juridical "moment," a reciprocity that, within the constitutional rhetoric of property in persons, appears knotted in the very category "fugitive." Debt allows intimacy between the ideational antinomies of property and persons, allows the former comfortably to fold in on and embrace the latter. Debt makes property appear in the form of personhood and translates ownership into obedience with all the effectiveness expected of legal rhetoric. The constitutional clause regarding fugitive slaves fashions a shadow market world in which slaves serve as the subjects and not the objects of exchange—legal specters of contractual personhood that figure the agon of slavery's economies, aporia captured in P. J. Proudhon's impetuous yet canny assertion, "La propriété c'est le vol!" whose pun evokes both pelf and peregrination. To summarize, then, the clauses in question: all three treat slaves as "persons"; none uses the words "property," "slavery," "negroes," or any other of the institution's grammatical commonplaces; and, in each, a specific form of personhood serves as a euphemism for "slave." No express affirmation of slavery as a property right appears in the Constitution, only the most highly mediated reference to occult bonds of obligation and obedience between persons.[121] There are further consequences, however, to the figuration of the fugitive as one who has reneged on a promise to provide his labor; for the temporality of debt suggests a "to-be-givenness" with unique effects on the legal status of slave property.

As the anthropologist Marcel Mauss proposed in his pathbreaking work "Essai sur le don," in societies absent the rudiments of modern market capitalism—"pure individual contract, the money market, sale proper, fixed price, and weighed and coined money"—principles and practices of exchange are enacted by means of a traffic in gifts.[122] Mauss's essay, a speculation on the origins of modern contract (and on the inseparability of credit from contract), proposes that giving, receiving, and reciprocating gifts expresses, affirms, and in fact creates a social link between the participants, a "special relationship of trust, solidarity, and mutual aid" that Mauss would call, following A. R. Radcliff-Brown, the production of "friendly feeling."[123] Gift exchange is peculiarly affective, retaining residues of desire and passion, emotional and spiritual content—what Lewis Hyde calls "uneconomic" feeling—a content long eschewed by the formalized and reified structures of modern legal contract.[124] This peculiarly sensational exchange mingles "sentiments and persons," "personalities and things" in a way, Mauss adds, that "necessarily implies the notion of credit" (35)—that is to say, like-mindedness and credibility, reputation and indebtedness. In gift, that is, we find guilt, in hospitality humiliation, moral inequalities that are the densely social equivalent of contract's telescoped fiduciary imbalances. Traffic in gifts evidences the quasi-delict origins of modern contract: "The mere fact of having the thing [the gift of a more venerable persona] puts the *accipiens* in a condition of quasi-culpability (*damnatus, nexus, aere observatus*), of spiritual inferiority, moral inequality (*magister, minister*) *vis-à-vis* the donor, the *tradens*" (51). Gift, in other words, instantiates an obligation to reciprocate, and, in its presupposition of friendliness, hospitality, and generosity (the moral and fiduciary economy of credit extension known as "fidelity" or "trust" or "good faith"), it presumes, also, the deferral of that obligation into the future.[125] Generosity begets humility, in Mauss's thinking, the endless and ungainly reciprocity of interest: "We must always return more than we receive; the return is always bigger and more costly" (63).

It is here, at the nexus of credit and interest, gift and exchange, that we arrive back at the original terms of our discussion—property and contract. For, whereas Mauss applies his anthropology to cultures absent the rudiments of capitalist exchange, there is an implicit (and largely analogous) hiatus in all contractual exchange, a lacuna in the texture of all contractual obligation that has been noted by the literary critic Brook Thomas: "Promises are especially important in establishing commitments to those beyond our immediate circle of friends and family. Indeed, distance seems to be a vital part of the dynamic of promising, since a promise is almost always evoked when delivery on an obligation involves a delay. Promises, therefore, are ideally suited for the transfer of goods that are *absent in either time or space*" (*American Literary Realism,* 30, emphasis mine). We might extend Mauss's insights into the passional (or, correlatively, Thomas's insights into promise's delay) to cover violation of (caesuras and crises in) the principles and norms of market exchange, apply them to crises in equity, contract, and liability—apply them, that is, to slavery.

To return to the terms and concerns of *Dred Scott,* indebtedness is the ruse of consent, an alibi in which the slave's obligation screens the Constitution's sanction of the expropriation of labor, in which liability masks the protocols of injury (the Scotts' charge of "assault and false imprisonment"), and in which the gift the slave makes of himself absolves the theft of his property in himself. I said earlier, with regards to the rising importance of positivism in nineteenth-century American jurisprudence, that governmental power becomes such only through the "consent of the governed." We might now qualify this last with the proviso "both slave and free." Taney's affirmation of the citizen as a subject of consent and the slave as a subject of debt (a difference of degree, not of kind) confirms another one of classical liberalism's foundational maxim of government: *Multitudo juris consense et utilitatis communione fociata* [A multitude of people united together by a communion of interests, and common laws to which they *all* submit with *one* accord].[126] We might conclude, too, on the evidence of this fabulated consent, that the fugitive is a marker of *autopoesis* in *Dred Scott*'s machinery of jurisprudence. The fugitive is positivism's persona—and, when Stanley Fish defines the doctrine of formalism as "the thesis that one can write sentences of such precision and simplicity that their meanings leap off the page in a way no one—no matter what his or her situation or point of view—can ignore," he captures with his own precision and simplicity the sleight of hand effected by Taney's particular figuration of the fugitive as a subject of will and consent.[127] In sum, we have in the letter of the law a reification of will, a fabulation of the passional based on faith in a mutual affection between masters and slaves (an affect often celebrated by writers as distinct as George Fitzhugh and Mary Boykin Chesnutt).[128] Indebtedness presents a theodicy that provides moral justification for enslavement—a translation of usurpation into the slave's gift and of theft into the slave's willful dispossession.[129]

I am moving in the direction of linking the *autopoesis* of positivist hermeneutics to the circuit of motives that limn master to slave, and in that regard the argument I am making here is informed by the propositions Eric Cheyfitz offers in his own study of the material and metaphysical modalities of the term "property" in the West, *The Poetics of Imperialism: Translation and Colonization from "The Tempest" to "Tarzan."*[130] When the term "negro" replaces "three-fifths of other persons," and "the slave escape[d]" "persons . . . whose labor may be due," the situation in *Dred Scott* approaches that described by Henry Peacham, tellingly, as "this excellent Art of translating," which art or technique is characterized by fellow rhetoricians as the root (L., *ars [artis]*, root) of all rhetoric.[131] In *The Arcadian Rhetoric,* Abraham Fraunce provides a definition of "trope," this "Grammaticall rule" of all poesis, in language that, with peculiar resonances, captures the multiplicities of Taney's interpretive labor in *Dred Scott:* "A trope or turning is when a word is turned from his naturall signification, to some other, so convenientlie, as that it seeme rather willinglie ledd, than driven by force to that other signification."[132] Or, again, in George Puttenham's *The Arte of English Poesie,* where *metaphora,* "or the Figure of transporte," is described as follows: "Single words have their sense and understanding altered and figured many wayes, to wit, by transport, abuse, crosse-naming, new naming, change of name. This will seeme very darke to you. . . . There is a kind of *wresting* [emphasis mine] of a single word from his owne right signification, to another not so naturall, but yet of some affinitie or conveniencie with it."[133] Following Cheyfitz, I would draw your attention to these rhetoricians' use of the terms "seeme" and "wresting" to describe acts of translation. The rhetoric of reversal in their accounts of poesis evokes the violence of all metaphoric displacement, or translation, the coercive reversal that is all rhetoric; and, on account of the ambivalence of Fraunce's "seeme" or Puttenham's "wresting," we can attribute to the eloquent rhetorician the suspect motives of deceit, fraud, and counterfeit. We can discern a dissimulation within all persuasion. We can detect in metaphor the ruse of consent. Here is Cheyfitz: "The skilled translator, or rhetorician, like the skilled overseer with a slave, must use force in transporting a word from its proper, or 'natural,' place, but conceals that force, or tries to, under the semblance of the word's willingness to give up its property in itself" (*Poetics of Imperialism,* 37).

Taney's rhetorical skill evokes the skill of the translator, which skill's secret is to dissemble force into an occasion of willfulness, to simulate dis-possession as a reminiscence of self-possession: a "turning" or "wresting" of constitutional syntax toward another signification "of some affinitie . . . with it," and "so convenientlie, as that it seeme rather willinglie ledd, than driven by force." When translation looks more like transparency, coercion and dispossession like fugitiveness and disobedience, the lexicon of race "seeme rather willinglie ledd" toward property, and declensions of person-hood appear to provide a frame for the racialization of property. In the po-etics of property, circa 1857, the work of the skilled translator on the word is hardly discernible from that of the skilled master on the slave. Consider Sanford's plea before the Court: not guilty "of the said supposed trespass" on the grounds that "he gently laid his hands upon [Dred Scott], and only restrained him of such liberty as he had a right to do" (*Dred Scott,* 693). Diminution of force ("gently"). Amplification of will ("only restrained . . . of such liberty" as Sanford had a right to claim). Consider, too, the terms of Taney's defense of Sanford: the constitutional Preamble "speaks in general terms of the people of the United States . . . does not define what descrip-tion of persons are intended to be included under these terms . . . [and] uses them as terms so well understood that no further description or definition was necessary" (*Dred Scott,* 703). The force of translation dissembles be-neath the ruse of intent in a disavowal of dispossession that is itself both the-ater of legal positivism and revel in the metamorphosis of persons into property. Recall, finally, the guiding assumption in *Dred Scott:* "There are two clauses in the Constitution that point directly and specifically to the ne-gro race as a separate class of persons, and show clearly that they were not regarded as a portion of the people or citizens of the government then formed."

Taney assumes a principle justifying obedience to the Constitution that, in effect, makes the "letter of the law" "seeme" like the "spirit of the law" (*mens legum, ratio legis*), 1787 like 1857.[134] Judicial fidelity to the letter is tantamount, in this instance, not to a jurist's obeisance to the framers' intent but, rather, to a principle of textual transparency ("not only the same in words, but the same in meaning") that, finally, executes with a force unseen the immediate purposes of the judicial translator: "The Constitution rec-ognizes the right of property of the master in a slave, and makes no distinc-tion between that description of property and other property owned by a citizen . . . an ordinary article of merchandise and property." As Taney's rhetoric manipulates force and purposiveness into the whimsy of willful dispossession, his interpretive acts of translation (interests of "feeling," "reflex," and "passions") evaporate into the ether, leaving only the pure transparency of original and authentic "intent."

Taney's interpretive victory is to find an efficacious racial calculus within a document that steers clear of any mention of either "blacks," "whites," "the negro race," or "Caucasians" (hopelessly imprecise slang from the perspective of the law), a document so coyly evasive of the popular vocabulary of "masters," "slavery," and a "right of property" that, when it turns to the question of slavery, treats slaves merely as fractional, migratory, and indebted "persons" and treats the possession of property as a vicissitude of personhood. Racial inscription authenticates lines of legal precedent. In language that does not mean what it says (a position we would have to assume as Taney's given his substitutions), the Constitution draws a "line of division" between "the citizen race" and "the African race (707), a line sharpened once "merchandise and property" are substituted for "person"; "slavery" and "traffic guaranteed" for "the migration and importation of . . . persons"; "the slave escape[d]" for persons whose "labor may be due"; "the dominant race" for "citizens"; and "the negro race" for "free persons" as well as "other persons." In *Dred Scott,* complex legal declensions of personhood acquire a lay lucidity in grammars of race. One simple circumstance, writes a concurring jurist, Dred Scott's indisputable status as "a negro of African descent, whose ancestors were of pure African blood," dictates that he cannot "by correct legal induction . . . be clothed with the character and capacities of a citizen" (730), that he remain, by law, a "subject of individual power and ownership," "governed at [the citizens'] own pleasure" (730). The plaintiff's "sojourning" into free territory "made no difference" to his status as slave on account of the a priori matter of his race, a difference that made all the difference in the legal calculation of his personhood. Dred Scott's circumstance, the mark of race, preserves the law of slavery and the tentacles of possession. Divested of the legal accouterments of the "citizen," the southern slave on free soil is henceforth clothed only in the distressed habiliments of race: sign of an alchemy in which the person dispossessed at law of him- or herself appears, also, in the law, as distinctly self-possessed ("debt"); ornament of a social rank so inferior as to leave its bearer hovering precipitously on the market's border between merchants and merchandise (for "migration" redeems "importation" with the ease of a numismatic equivalent); adjunct to a calculus so exact as to serve adequate to signify the latter's differential estimates of value, wealth, and representation (oblique measures of property in "other persons"). In the deepest of ironies, the law absolves itself of guilt over the theft of another's personhood by personifying property—making slaves culpable in their exchange, merchants at market who bear the gift of their persons, and agents who, willing to give up their property in themselves, are guilty finally of the most egregious perfidy.

"If anything in relation to the construction of the Constitution can be regarded as settled," Taney abjures, as he reads from a manuscript held in tremulous hands, on March 6, 1857, eleven years after this case of property-taken-flight began, "it is that which we now give to the word 'citizen' and the word 'people'"(*Dred Scott,* 709)—two words that, clearly, on his interpretive holding, and by his skillful translation, fail to overlap in the orbit of racial proscriptions and rights of possession they respectively assign their chosen subjects.

The law knows the fugitive as a nondescript. The fugitive threatens it with illegibility. "Aporia," "crisis," and "novelty" are the terms I have used to indicate this threat—that dilemma when a "right to an unchanging world" or a "right to a reasonable return on investment" is met by the illegibility of property that has taken flight. However, by oscillating between sundry doctrines of property and an unfolding poetics of property, my readings have tried to signal something more. In the final assessment, the fugitive is not simply an aporia in the law but is, rather, the occasion for the law to figure its own authority. Jurists have available doctrines of property whose filigreed relations are uneven and discontinuous. The fugitive incites this noncorrespondence whether defenders of the bar are faced with wayward slaves (recall that, because of the principles governing conflict of law doctrine, competing lines of precedent in the Dred Scott matter could protect principles of "attachment," "reversion," or a proverbial "once-free-forever-free" liberty) or inescapably erosive and ephemeral, transient and fugacious sounds (where, in the case of *White-Smith,* sounds are property when fixed in a visible writing, while in "The Right to Privacy" they achieve such protections only as a kind of "secret-writing," in those invisible scribbles of the private self). Something quite different occurs at the level of a "poetics" of property. There, discontinuity of doctrine appears to be offset by the coherent exposition of a form—the "person."

In the opening pages to this chapter I observed that, when faced with the heightened abstraction and intangibility of the turn-of-the-century market's emergent properties, American jurisprudence tended to deploy two distinct interpretive strategies. On the one hand, through what might be called the "incarnation" of the word, the law steels the market against the uncertainties fostered by a conception of property that then appeared so broad as to be able to embrace every valuable interest known to the law. An important example of this faith in the "letter" appears in Oliver Wendell Holmes's correction of the commonsense perception of contract as a "meeting of minds": "The making of a contract depends not on the agreement of two minds in one intention, but on the agreement of two sets of external signs . . . [and] as the signs may be addressed to one sense or another—to sight or to hearing—on the nature of the sign will depend the moment when the contract is made." On the other hand, faced with novel forms of wealth and ownership, the law mobilizes a work of analogy. It "fits" the world to its representations through a "series of successive approximations" (again, Holmes's phrase). The coherence of legal precedent (stare decisis) is, as I argued, the formalized result of a set of informal associations, subterranean affiliations connected and made "the law" by repeated association. Another way to state the matter would be to say that the law achieves its ends by positing forms, by engendering forms out of the archives of culture. The "person" is one such form, one effect of the traffic between incarnation and figuration; an effect registered in the subordination of property to the contract relation, which subordination results in the perception of property as a relation between people, and not, as had earlier been thought, between people and things. With regards to this last observation, you should recall my early and provisional conclusion that, as an evolved function of the contract relation, property rose to the status of pathetic fallacy; a personification of individual "interests" through the legal figuration of specific "outcomes"; a formalization of a way of thinking about future actions; a means of substantializing acts as a form of property. Property law is in this reading simply a code of fantasized intentions.

In my reading of *Dred Scott v. Sandford* against *Leviathan* I have tried to track this double movement of legal culture and have tried to excavate the poetic and methodological precursors to a turn-of-the-century interpretive practice of the law. Incarnation and figuration together make up the paradox of positivism. When Taney makes an appeal to precedent—when he invokes "the intent of the founding fathers" and "the plain meaning of the words" and when he speaks of meanings that are "distinctly and expressly affirmed"—his ostensible task is to define the limit of the practical power of the legal system to preserve itself. Yet when he combines an appeal to "plain words" (which gives form to a foundational collective "will," to a regime of consent) with a figured persona held to that founding moment's standard of "consent" (the fugitive slave), he essentially enforces on both framers and slaves a single vision of "original intent"—the former of which limits the text's meaning while the latter limits property's flight. The shadowy "Negro" of Taney's interpretation—a translation of the Constitution's fractional, migratory, and indebted "person"—offers a figuration of legal authority. In short, the "force of law" is figured in the fugitive's will, duty, and broken promise.[135]

The whole purpose of this series of readings has been twofold. An important objective has certainly been to demonstrate the complicated reasoning that had to go into legal improvisation around questions of race and property, the point of which has been to give back to race its proper historical specificity. Yet through these readings, I have also wanted to draw into the orbit of literary studies a number of concerns regarding the structure and workings of American "legal culture." I have wanted to make apprehensible the intersecting lines of flight from the law to culture and from culture to the law. The movement from the law to culture is largely predictable, a matter of intended consequences. This movement has been registered in the preceding pages through methods that make clear how the law posits form, how it engenders a form, how it gives life to the figure of the person (within positivist jurisprudence). The movement from culture to the law is considerably more difficult to register—largely unpredictable and a matter of unintended consequences. One way to make this movement apprehensible is to read our received methods of exposition against the grain. Arguably, the destiny of the concept of the person back into the arena of culture changes the culture from which it was taken or, better, changes our perception of that culture. Thus, having figured out the specific form of property that the law engenders—the "Negro," a racial form of the "person" that figures the law's authority, its power to screen the commodification of personhood beneath the specter of promise, to offer theft in the Pandora's box of the gift—we can track anew the efficacy of that form in multiple spheres of culture. This chapter shall achieve its close, then, by offering a series of readings of specific texts—concerning the origins of blackface minstrelsy, the theft of voice—readings informed by the above archaeology of legal form.

IMPERSONATION

It was Karl Marx who warned of the difficulty of drawing the line between a generous inheritance and a selfish usurpation, gift from theft, when he proposed that, at best, Louis Napoleon Bonaparte III could expect to be characterized by history as a "grotesque mediocrity" and "caricature" of his uncle, Napoleon the First.[136] For certain, the heir can expect the power of a name, but, with a "swindler's" deceit, this particular scion to the Napoleonic legacy—an "adventurer blown in from abroad" (607)—clumsily assumes his place in the Napoleonic line when he "hides his trivially repulsive features under the death mask of Napoleon [I]" (596). *"C'est le premier vol de l'aigle,"* Marx states, citing the imprecise source of a certain "Countess L.," the mistress of M. de Morny, whose witticism, he adds, "is applicable to every flight of the *eagle,* which is more like a *raven*" (616). When, like revolutionaries past, Louis Bonaparte rises to prominence on the "time-honoured disguise and . . . borrowed language" (595) of revolutions past, specifically the eighteenth Brumaire of Napoleon I's coup d'état (November 9, 1799), a recalcitrant and adverse war of position gives way to the wan commensurability of universal suffrage. In the adventurer nephew, France's conservative peasantry finds its universal equivalent ("the most simple-minded man in France acquired the most multifarious significance. Just because he was nothing he could signify everything save himself").[137] Detached from each other and from any "intercourse with society [i.e., the bourgeoisie and other classes]," and of dubious origin (*von zweideutiger Herkunft*) at best, the peasantry or "lumpen proletariat" are unproductive of any meaningful forms of value: "Their mode of production isolates them from one another, instead of bringing them into mutual intercourse" (608). A pseudoclass, the lumpen "cannot represent themselves," are not capable to produce themselves as a class, and thus "must be represented" (608). It is here that Napoleon III steps into the breech and "represents" a nonrepresentative class, an act that frees the state from "its putative grounds in production" but that, by exacerbating the disjunct between representations and what they represent, bears the added cost of further fomenting the crisis of representation in French society.[138] Bonaparte was the proverbial shadow without the substance.

"C'est le premier vol de l'aigle": the fugitive has become emperor, and flight theft. Napoleon III emerges as the mirror of the contradiction at the heart of the June Days, a revolution that generates not only "confusions of cause and effect" but "passions without truths, truths without passions; heroes without heroic deeds, history without events," which contradiction is also, for Marx, constitutive of all commodity form and exemplified by money [*Geldform*] itself, the "absurd form" [*Verrückten Form*] or "fantastic form" in which the commodity gold is hit on as the standard for all

exchange. In *Capital*'s formula, when distressed money changes hands it takes on the "fantastic form" of its obscene (L., *obscēnas,* adverse) standard. In the *Eighteenth Brumaire*'s elaboration, what is true for specie is true also for personality—for the more the imposter traffics in the mask of Napoleon the First, the more the raven comes to resemble an eagle. In the nephew, Marx proposes, the French have "not only a caricature of the old Napoleon, they have the old Napoleon himself, caricatured as he would inevitably appear in the middle of the nineteenth century" (597). The French have in Louis Bonaparte a counterfeit that satisfies as an equivalent. And Hegel warns as much when he remarks, as Marx maintains in his famous paraphrase, that "all great world-historical facts and personages occur, as it were, twice . . . the first time as tragedy, the second as farce" (594). As Marx goes on to warn, the tradition of generations past "weighs like a nightmare on the brain of the living"— or, in line with his consistently theatrical rhetoric, the social republic of the first French Revolution "haunts the subsequent acts of the drama like a ghost" (*Eighteenth Brumaire,* 603). Human agency, in the *Eighteenth Brumaire* formulation, is much like the acquisition of a language, where "the beginner who has learnt a new language always translates it back into his mother tongue, [and where it can also be said that] he has assimilated the spirit of the new language and can produce freely in it only when he moves in it without remembering the old and forgets in it his ancestral tongue" (*Eighteenth Brumaire,* 595). Foreign language echoes eccentric literary form. Farce, we learn in the *Eighteenth Brumaire,* that degraded and imitative literary form, which in 1851 comes in the guise of an insurgent's theft of another's persona, is the practice that captures (in its usurpatious yet munificent, fugitive yet cyclical motions) the ambivalence and absurdity of all commodity exchange. At midcentury, tragedy descends into farce, eagles into ravens, and politics becomes a drama of "death mask[s]" and "borrowed language," "caricature" and "disguise." All of which is to say that, from Marx's perspective, the problems of French society spring from an imperialism of the literary, from the migration of literary tropes and theatrical conventions beyond their proper domains and into the sphere of civil society.

The class struggle in France is certainly not the subject of this chapter, which should calm any worries that I have either unjustifiably flipped the script or raised the stakes beyond what previous claims will bear. I introduce the *Eighteenth Brumaire* at this juncture because, in its effort to tease out the conflicting temporalities of gift and theft, to give force to a conception of human agency as an act of translation (and not origination), the text clearly assigns to impersonation a distinct work of occultation: a "work" brought to our attention by a lexicon of form and fugacity, parody and production, representation and caricature. Marx's principle insight in the *Eighteenth Brumaire,* as previously noted by other scholars, is that human beings make their own history, although not under conditions of their own choosing.[139] That this act of making or *poesis* comes in the form of an act— an ungrounded caricature, a nimbus of theatrics, an *autopoesis*—flies in the face of that category valorized above all others in Marx's hermeneutics, the category of production. Marx depends on the category of production as the ultimate source of value and is for this reason averse to Bonaparte's particular form of parody, an aversion expressed in Marx's antitheatircal postures. Bonaparte's theatrics parody his uncle's works, sharing a degree of superfluity with other perpetrators of "unproductive" work: "Alongside decayed *roués* with dubious means of subsistence and of dubious origin . . . were vagabonds, discharged soldiers, discharged jailbirds, escaped galley slaves, swindlers, mountebanks, *lazzaroni,* pickpockets, tricksters, gamblers, *maquereaux,* brothel keepers, porters, *literati* hacks, organ-grinders, ragpickers, knife grinders, tinkers, beggars—in short, the whole indefinite disintegrated mass, thrown hither and thither, which the French term *la bohème.*"[140] Like the "frivolous professions. . . [of] men of letters . . . players, buffoons, musicians, [and] opera-singers" rebuffed in Adam Smith's *Wealth of Nations,* the work of the members of this mass "perishes in the very instant of its production."[141] Fleeting exertions, these laborer's efforts are all parodies of production, representations of labor (such as might be given by an actor) that are not to be mistaken for the real thing ("Unthinking Sex," 33). But parody does not so much overwhelm production as occult it. Parody is a literary form that imitates theatrical convention; but it is also, by its very definition as a form, inherently reproducible and can thus make little claim to first instances and originary grounds. I follow Edward Said's insights here: "Originality, in one primal sense . . . has to be loss, or else it would be repetition; or we can say that, insofar as it is apprehended as such, originality is the difference between primordial vacancy and temporal, sustained repetition. . . . The best way to consider originality is to look not for first instances of a phenomenon, but rather to see duplication, parallelism, symmetry, parody, repetition, echoes of it."[142] Parody makes a display of the occultation of origins, of the supersession of value's putative grounds in production. Bonaparte's impersonation makes a spectacle of the fecundity of imitation.

In a fortuitous and distinctively American play on Marx's *Eighteenth Brumaire,* a play no less salient for its lack of intent, James Weldon Johnson, in *Black Manhattan* (1930), finds origins to the institution of "Negro minstrelsy" in inexorable repetitions, in impersonations that, measure for measure, vacillate between gift and theft. Early and professional "Negro theatrical talent," Johnson writes, could be found in an array of venues both high and low; but it was on the minstrel stage, he clarifies, that the "real beginnings of the Negro in the American theatre were made."[143] Yet, no sooner does Johnson offer this apparently empirical and falsifiable historical claim, he adds, a sentence later, this measurably more commonsensical assertion: "Negro minstrelsy, [as] everyone ought to know, had its origin among the slaves of the old South" (87). And by the latter account, "every plantation" guarded its own "troupe of black minstrels," a "talented band" of performers who could "crack Negro jokes, and sing and dance to the accompaniment of the banjo and the bones . . . [whenever] the wealthy plantation owner wished to entertain and amuse his guests" (87). But again, no sooner does Johnson fix on one origin over another than a third appears. The "full entry of the Negro" on the professional minstrel stage takes place after the Civil War, Johnson claims, "towards the end of the sixties" when, ironically, all-black troupes such as Lew Johnson's Plantation Minstrel Company stole back from white blackface minstrels cultural forms of alleged plantation origin: "These troupes . . . accepted wholly the performance pattern as it had been worked out and laid down by the white minstrels . . . even to blacking their faces, an expedient which, of course, never entered the minds of the original plantation artists" (89).

Repetition and racial impersonation—this tit for tat of gift and theft—appears to mark the triumph of an ideal that, elsewhere, falls under the sign of "contractualism." That is, Johnson's account presents us with a vision of exchange between equals, of a consensual production by the plantation's "troupe of black minstrels" for "the wealthy plantation owner." Nowhere is this "formal equality" more poignantly displayed than in accounts of the interlocking histories of black culture and blackface minstrelsy, specifically in the "authoritative" account of the alleged origins of the latter—from which Johnson quotes extensively and to which I want now to turn. This account, written by Robert P. Nevin for the November 1867 number of the *Atlantic Monthly,* begins with an anonymous "actor" described, by turns, as "a superficial man," "deficient in the more profound qualities," and "destitute of all the distinguishing, though shallower, virtues of character.[144] Our actor, whose dealings seem always, from Nevin's vantage, "marked by tact and shrewdness," roamed the streets of his native Cincinnati with his "wits upon the alert" for any opportunity that "might be turned to professional and profitable use." A character "deficient" of "profound qualities" and a desire for profit combine in proportions adequate to produce the following (apparently chance) encounter:

> As he sauntered along one of the main thoroughfares of Cincinnati . . . his attention was suddenly arrested by a voice ringing clear and full above the noises of the street, and giving utterance, in an unmistakable dialect, to the refrain of a song to this effect:—"Turn about an' wheel about an' do jis so, An' ebery' time I turn about I jump Jim Crow." Struck by the peculiarities of the performance, so unique in style, matter, and "character" of delivery, the player listened on. Were not these elements—was the suggestion of the instant—which might admit of higher than mere street or stable-yard development? As a national or "race" illustration, behind the footlights, might not "Jim Crow" and a black face tickle the fancy of pit and circle, as well as the "Sprig of Shillalah" and a red nose? Out of the suggestion leaped the determination; and so it chanced that the casual hearing of a song trolled by a negro stage-driver, lolling lazily on the box of his vehicle, gave origin to a school of music destined to excel in popularity all others. (608–9)

On chance encounter with a voice indelibly and "unmistakeabl[y]" marked by "character," this "obscure actor"(609) loses his anonymity to become the famous "T. D. Rice." [145]

Accident gives way to enterprise when Rice quits Cincinnati for Pittsburgh, where, scheduled to serve duty at the "Old Drury," he prepares in addition "to take advantage of his opportunity" (609)—much as he had done initially on his native Ohio soil. At Griffith's Hotel, Wood Street, Pittsburgh, Rice encounters "a negro" named Cuff—who, as "an exquisite specimen of his sort" (609) was, unlike the "destitute" Rice, utterly gorged with the lucre of character. Cuff won a "precarious existence" making the most out of the desolate economic terrain between minstrelsy and industry, by, on the one hand, "letting his open mouth as a mark for boys to pitch pennies into" (609) and, on the other, "carrying the trunks of passengers from the steamboats to the hotels" (609). Rice manages with only "slight persuasion" to "induc[e]" Cuff to accompany him to the theater, where the stevedore finds himself "ordered" to disrobe and permit Rice "to invest" of the cast-off apparel. Rice, the account alleges, quickly and expediently satisfies his illicit duties in the previously mentioned play—a play mounted under the distinctly antitheatrical ban "of the Scotch-Irish Calvinists" (609)—and reemerges, a legitimate performer, in the colorfully distressed habiliments of Cuff: "an old coat forlornly dilapidated," "a pair of shoes composed equally of patches and places for patches on [the] feet," and "a coarse straw hat in a melancholy condition of rent and collapse" (609). To make the "apparition" (609) complete, Rice adds "a dense black wig of matted moss" (609) and "shade[s] his own countenance to the 'contraband' hue" (609).

Rice's impersonation creates an instantaneous effect, reducing the noise of gallery, box, and pit, declivitously, from the resounding "crash of peanuts" to a mere "murmur and . . . bustle of liveliest expectation" (609). The din of pit and circle has nearly completely given way to silence when Rice fills the theater with his purloined refrain: "O, Jim Crow's come to town, as you all must know, / An' he wheel about, he turn about, he do jis so, / An' ebery time he wheel about he jump Jim Crow" (609). The effect is "electric"—with demonstrations of "deafening" proportions following quickly on "each succeeding couplet and refrain" (609). Pittsburgh's "Old Drury" echoes with a call and response of a none-too-orthodox sort.

As performer and audience engage in raucous repartee, Cuff, crouched "in dishabille" "quietly ensconced" out of sight, learns of the "near approach of a steamer" (609) to which he for competitive reasons must devote his attentions *tout de suite*. Cuff, it seems, had jockeyed with a formidable competitor, another black man by the name of Ginger, for supremacy in the baggage-carrying business. Subsistence through industry or the continued mortgage of his person are the options, Nevin portends, Cuff tosses about in his mind. "Liberally as he might lend himself to a friend," the journalist writes, "it could not be done at [the] sacrifice" of granting Ginger "the advantage of an undisputed descent upon the luggage of the approaching vessel" (609). The price of any lapse in business acumen is both pecuniary and public. To cede competitive advantage to Ginger, Cuff would not only "forfeit all 'considerations' from the passengers," but would also prove himself "a laggard in his calling . . . [and] cast a damaging blemish upon his *reputation*" (609, emphasis mine).

Choosing industry over minstrelsy, Cuff, from the restless interstice of his own "liberal" patience—"a minute or two of fidgety waiting" (609)—hazards a plea in a "hurried whisper" (609–10): "Massa Rice, Massa Rice, must have my clo'se! Massa Griffif wants me,—steamboat's comin'!" (610). Cuff's plea falls on deaf ears, for it comes in the immediate wake of a jab, by Rice, at a Pittsburgh politician, which "set the audience in a roar in which all other sounds were lost" (610). The *Atlantic*'s correspondent provides an account of Rice's theft that reveals more than perhaps a purely journalistic "accounting" would normally permit:

Waiting some moments longer, the restless Cuff, thrusting his visage from under cover into full three-quarter view this time, again charged on the singer in the same words, but with more emphatic voice: "Massa Rice, Massa Rice, must have my clo'se! Massa Griffif wants me,—steamboat's comin'!"

A still more successful couplet brought a still more tempestuous response, and the invocation of the baggage-carrier was unheard and unheeded. Driven to desperation, and forgetful in the emergence of every sense of propriety, Cuff, in ludicrous undress as he was, started from his place, rushed on the stage, and, laying his hand on the performer's shoulder, called out excitedly: "Massa Rice, Massa Rice, gi' me nigga's hat,—nigga's coat,—nigga's shoes,-gi' me nigga's t'ings! Massa Griffif wants 'im,—STEAMBOAT'S COMIN'!!"

The incident was the touch, in the mirthful experience of that night, that passed endurance. Pit and circle were one scene of such convulsive merriment that it was impossible to proceed in the performance; and the extinguishment of the footlights, the fall of the curtain, and the throwing wide of the doors for exit, indicated that the entertainment was ended.

Such were the circumstances—authentic in every particular—under which the first work of the distinct art of Negro Minstrelsy was presented.

Next day found the song of Jim Crow, in one style of delivery or another, on everybody's tongue. Clerks hummed it serving customers at counters, artisans thundered it at their toils to the time-beat of sledge and of tilt-hammer, boys whistled it on the streets, ladies warbled it in parlors, and house-maids repeated it to the clink of crockery in kitchens. Rice made up his mind to profit further by its popularity: he determined to publish it. Mr. W. C. Peters, afterwards of Cincinnati, and well known as a composer and publisher, was at that time a music-dealer on Market Street in Pittsburgh. Rice, ignorant himself of the simplest elements of musical science, waited on Mr. Peters, and solicited his co-operation in the preparation of his song for the press. Some difficulty was experienced before Rice could be induced to the correction of certain trifling informalities, rhythmical mainly, in his melody; but, yielding finally, the air as it now stands, with piano forte accompaniment by Mr. Peters, was put on paper. (610)

Rice's "Jim Crow" was, in Constance Rourke's words, words that echo Nevin's "touch that passed endurance," "the Negro . . . pictured in firm, enduring outlines." This most famous account of the origins of blackface minstrelsy is largely a product of Nevin's fancy, and more apocryphal than "authentic" with each enumeration it receives. And so dense is the account with financial motive and economic verbiage that it seems impossible to account for Rice's impersonation, with whatever variations one does or does not intend, without also adding considerably — and usuriously — to Rice's speculative investment in black forms as "stock in trade." So inevitable is fiscal metaphor in accounts of minstrelsy that recent scholarship has seen it as an institution of capital and commerce.

For Eric Lott, the minstrel show partook of a "commodified logic," evident, as just one example, in the *Atlantic Monthly*'s talk of "opportunity and investment, lending and ownership, subsistence and competition." [146] The paradigm of origins governing Nevin's account is that of an original act of exchange, in which mixing between white performer and black understudy takes place through a transfer of ownership — often by means of theft but occasionally through payment. Rice's vestment is Cuff's divestment, and the theft that embarrasses Cuff "nevertheless entails both his bodily presence in the show and the titillating threat he may return to demand his stolen capital" (19). The play of presence and absence in the Nevin account — Cuff replaces Rice as the account's center of attention, to strip Cuff is to make him all the more necessarily visible — suggests a certain uneasiness and anxiety about the very primitive accumulation this account of minstrelsy's origins celebrates (19). Nevin's narrative, which reads, Lott notes, "like a master text of the racial economy encoded in blackface performance" (19), realizes "that the minstrel show flaunted as much as it hid the fact of expropriation and its subtex[t of] enslavement" (62). When spectacle, minstrelsy's plunder can be seen as a narrative substitute for slavery, "a comfortable alternative to the idea of black labor" (59). When denial, the general intention of an illusory and far from consensual "transfer of ownership" is revealed to be an actual "forgetting of the unremunerated labor of slavery, a denial often difficult to sustain as repressed economic facts return" (59). By the terms of this assessment of the minstrel show, financial metaphor and economic prattle intensify the link between culture and capital, literalize white interest in and profit from capital possessed by blacks (in themselves in the form of labor, or in each other in the form of "authentic" black cultural practices), capital necessary to the market's workings — necessary, to be precise, to an impersonator's working of the cultural marketplace.

To others, the minstrel show participates in a nineteenth-century capitalist "romanticism," a relaxation in the profit motive in which blackness comes to symbolize all the pleasures that the accumulating capitalist had given up but still longed for. From the representation of blacks by a unionized immigrant class as indolent though threatening hirelings to their literary representation as dulcet accessories, profit-minded Englishmen and Americans, argues David Roediger (following George Rawick), "cast Blacks as their former selves."[147] The freshly minted capitalist and his white laborer underling—representatives of a Northern Jacksonian urban working class, an antebellum artisanate—met the West African, in Rawick's words, "as a reformed sinner meets a comrade of his previous debaucheries."[148]

But another form of property comes into view when this apocryphal tale of theft is read through the lens of later meditations on property, personhood, and "the right to one's personality." The Negro stage driver's "character" inheres, importantly, in his voice; for, from an anonymous source Rice hears "a voice ringing clear and full above the noises of the street." Rice's impersonation—his theft of the stage driver's voice and "character" and his theft, moreover, of the valet's vestments—intrudes on both their free labors, trespasses on their property in themselves, dispossesses them of themselves as property. However, when Cuff's mute appeals go "unheard and unheeded" and are met by Rice's "happy hit," "successful couplet," and "convulsive merriment" (when, in Rice's mouth, the stage driver's pilfered song fills in for Cuff's silence, *causes* that silence) the extent to which Rice's theft signals more substantive transformations in the conception of property comes to light. The stage driver's voice is made exchangeable—turned into investment—when accompanied by the vestments of Cuff. Voice ripens into property when theft becomes gift (when "slight persuasion induced" Cuff to permit the masker "to invest himself in the cast-off apparel"), and impersonation looks a great deal like translation as defined by Puttenham and lent a certain jurisprudential heft by Taney: "a kind of wresting of a single word from his owne right signification, to another not so naturall, but yet of some affinitie or convenience with it" (a force concealed beneath the semblance of the word's willingness to give up its property in itself). As is true in the case of *Dred Scott v. Sandford,* in this postbellum allegory of antebellum conceptions of market exchange and race, inalienable personhood turns into fungible good when the bearer of that personhood promises it to the market. In the nineteenth-century poetics of property, black personae are presumptively expropriated through the generous designs of the gift—presumptively translations; presumptively repetitions; presumptively mechanical reproductions.

Pro Bono Publico

The angel of the Lord said to her, "Return to your mistress, and submit to her."
The angel of the Lord also said to her, "I will so greatly multiply your descen-
dants that they cannot be numbered for multitude." And the angel of the Lord
said to her, "Behold, you are with child, and shall bear a son; you shall call his
name Ishmael; because the Lord has given heed to your affliction.

GENESIS 16 : 9 – 11

CHAPTER TWO

The Fugitive's Properties

UNCLE TOM'S INCALCULABLE DIVIDEND

By the publication of Mrs. Stowe's book, the creations of the genius and imagination of the author have become as much public property as those of Homer or Cervantes. Uncle Tom and Topsy are as much *publici juris* as Don Quixote and Sancho Panza. All her conceptions and inventions may be used and abused by imitators, play-rights [*sic*] and poetasters. They are no longer her own—those who have purchased her book, may clothe them in English doggerel, in German or Chinese prose. Her absolute dominion and property in the creations of her genius and imagination have been voluntarily relinquished. All that now remains is the copyright of her book.

STOWE V. THOMAS (1853)

I travel'd round de country an' felt dat I was free,
    For I was cold and starvin' from de elbow to de knee,
But Massa has forgib me, an' I know dat all am right
    Tho' if it gives you pleasure, I'll run off eb'r night.

UNCLE TOM ("WAIT FOR THE WAGON," IN *SOUTHERN* "*UNCLE TOM'S CABIN*" [DAN RICE, 1854])

Plagiary, fr. L. *plagiārius,* one who abducts the child or slave of another, a kidnapper; a seducer.

FICTIONS OF FINANCE: PUTTIN' ON OLD MASSA

"It has been thought," recalls Oliver Wendell Holmes, Jr., in his master-work *The Common Law* (1881), "that to shoot at a block of wood thinking it to be a man is not an attempt to murder, and that to put a hand in an empty pocket, intending to pick it, is not an attempt to commit larceny."[1] Holmes offers this analogy evidently certain as to the legal (as opposed to merely rhetorical) import of metaphor. And yet, while certainly curious, the twinned image of a personified block and an empty pocket should come as little surprise, since murder and larceny ascribe the limits of the very law— criminal and civil, public and private, respectively—that Holmes takes as the subject of his inquiry into the fundaments of liability. The first crime deals with harm to persons and the second with harm to property. Despite the perceived antinomy between persons and property, the limits to law are in fact quite intimate; for, as Holmes himself observes, the "early forms of liability" given effect in ancient Greek and Roman law tend frequently to render insensate things legally culpable, scored throughout as that law had become by a "metaphysical confusion" and "personifying language" whose principal consequence remained the "personification of inanimate matter" (33, 11). And what is more, as we move across those posthumous yet now classic textual elaborations of property—John Locke's *Second Treatise of Government* (1690), David Hume's *A Treatise of Human Nature* (1740), Adam Smith's *An Inquiry into the Nature and Causes of the Wealth of Nations* (1776), G. W. F. Hegel's *Philosophy of Right* (1817–18)—this intimacy appears even further confirmed by liberal explanations of persons that turn inexorably on the legal, political, and philosophical movements of property. Ultimately, Holmes's analogy tests those limits but finds equipoise in an underlying reasoning quite intricate in its folds; a reasoning pertinent, in the main, to the establishment within nineteenth-century American jurisprudence of thresholds of liability. I offer it here to exploit its density as metaphor, to explore the curious belatedness of its metaphysical power; for an "empty pocket" exempt from theft underscores the most basic ontological conceits in the common law conception of property, conceits inimical to the very putative and conjectural financial pursuits of late-nineteenth-century market capitalism—which gets me to the second and more pertinent reason I begin with Holmes's common law conceit.

Whereas Holmes's metaphor preserves an ontology as old as the Roman legal concept of *dominium* (or *proprietas*, "the right of possession"), concurrent with his thinking a miraculously fertile speculative marketplace comes increasingly to require forms of security more comfortably allied with the consensual promises and ungainly reciprocities of a credit economy's constituent creditors and debtors. Holmes, of course, wants above all to adumbrate the limits and fundaments of a "common law" and, thus, imagines a subject who exceeds its grasp, who stumbles carelessly across its commonsense boundaries, who violates unwittingly its perfectly coherent values. This offender of the common law thinks he has shot a man, but he has not; he thinks he has lit on a pocket full of portable goods, but he has not. He finds only valuelessness where he had expected there to be value, which misrecognition of man's (or the pocket's) value seems finally to affirm both the necessity and the accuracy of the common law's discriminations.

What is more, for Holmes these misrecognitions do much to confirm the final impropriety of the subjective in the law — of an "intention" improper for reasons of its potential for error and its perceptual dubiousness, improper due to its curious capacity to see things as both themselves and not themselves. The common law, as Holmes would have it, shares much with its tort law descendant, each designating a space within the law indifferent to intention — indifferent because the former takes intention not as the motivation behind the criminal's acts but, rather, wishes to read intention back into history as the foundation of judges' discrete decisions; indifferent, too, because the latter, a product of the nineteenth-century invention of "negligence," seeks to uncover consequences without intentions. In both, intention simply does not matter. Yet, the tendency for error from which Holmes seems to want to flee, the tendency to shuttle between what a thing is and what it is not, to see one thing in another — the propensity for "fancy"—is the very dynamic reciprocity that characterizes the emerging market economy of late-nineteenth-century America, the very incoherence that makes finance capitalism work.[2] This era's burgeoning speculative marketplace is marked by nothing so much as its embrace of the principles and tenets of contract law, which, unlike its tort affiliate, gives rather generous scope to intention as one of the many sources of value. A more literary way of phrasing the matter would be to say that error holds the place of narrative uncertainty in a rational economics conceptually at odds with (but necessarily fueled by) both — a necessity and an error glimpsed, arguably, in the breadth between "substance" and "shadow" that critics of speculative exchange often invoked, in those credit exchanges where the "substance" of an agreed on exchange value accrues added market value only with the help of the "shadow" of interest. It is to correlate figures of error that I want ultimately to direct my attention: for example, fugacity, translation, punning. Yet, as a preliminary, a simple way of marking the shift that interests me here is to say that credit finds itself uneasily pertinent to those conceptions of property and liability of long and esteemed provenance, those conceptions predicated on absolute (i.e., coherent and error-free) conceptions of value. There should be little surprise, then, both that Holmes fails to see the lineaments connecting his own figuration of error to the instruments of an emerging finance capital and that he offers one final grudging demurral: "The absolute protection of property, however natural to a primitive community more occupied in production than exchange, is hardly consistent with the requirements of modern business."[3]

A common retreat (another tale of the "fall" from production to consumption), and one that I suspect proved clarifying to Holmes as he grappled with the period's critical market upheavals — specifically with a speculative market more interested in values without goods, in wealth without substance, than in the arguably more tangible pursuits of farming and industrial manufacture.[4] In this chapter, I will take these upheavals as indicative of a transitional moment in American finance and commercial law and will propose that skepticism regarding the ontological certainty of speculative value occasioned the resurgence of a debate (dating as far back as England's transition in the sixteenth century to a commercial society) over the abstract representation of value as both an economic necessity and a moral and epistemological threat. At the crux of this debate one finds the representation of speculation itself as a moral activity — a representation that, in the majority of cases, falls along a continuum between two extremes. To some, because speculation was based on an always-deferred system of credit (L., *crēditus, crēdēre*, to trust, believe), its ensuing wealth was nothing short of a patent falsehood. The members of the speculative class — bankers, brokers, financiers — were mere pretenders to commerce, devious manipulators who took advantage of the market by trading on the abstract value of goods rather than introducing materiality into the economy. The world of credit was, for the skeptic, one of smoke and mirrors, for it rested on the perceptually dubious foundation of faith and expanded and contracted through means of largely subjective stores of affect. In a word, this world was more likely to run on rumor than resources. To others, the speculator's labor affirmed the abstraction implicit in property; for both the economy and the government depended for their solvency and stability on abstract market machinations. Relatedly, money lent on grounds of reputation and honesty was not anathema to social well-being; rather, it was the core of sociality itself. Credit made value out of the very intangible and impermanent bonds among people and nations. It was the most literal expression of interest — something, in Hannah Arendt's description, "which *inter-est,* which lies between people and therefore can relate and bind them together."[5] Its elusiveness was taken as a communal, public good — *pro bono publico.*

In general, we find one or another (or, more often, some combination) of these postures in the nineteenth-century discourse of speculation—in everything from the Congressional debate over the Fugitive Slave Law of 1850 to Harriet Beecher Stowe's response in *Uncle Tom's Cabin* (1852), from legal opinions on the problem of translation as an infringement of another's property right to others on the right to prices as property, and from economic treatises claiming Adam Smith's *The Wealth of Nations* as intellectual precursor to those anticipating John Maynard Keynes's *The General Theory of Employment, Interest, and Money*. I offer a literary reading of this transitional era in American finance and law, ranging across economic primer and legal opinion, literary text and cinematic adaptation to uncover what I would term a "social text of fugitivity"—interweavings of legal and literary discourses in which figurations of the fugitive (as errant and inconstant) shape economic transactions and the representation of speculative value. What interests me in this regard are, on the one hand, legal cases that function as aesthetic instruments, engendering a type of social character who is the embodiment of ambivalence about capitalism's mechanisms of valuation and profit and, on the other, literary texts that play a role in the fashioning of a new concept of the self, one that answers to the problems of affect in valuation, incertitude in the market, and deferral in the world of credit. I will get to these crossings between law and literature shortly, but first I want to range over some key terms and arguments in the discourse of speculation and to offer some brief considerations of historical context that suggest why the fugitive remains pertinent to these deliberations.

I said earlier that many of the terms in the nineteenth-century debate over speculation dated back to early-modern England, and it would seem important to explore the implications of this genealogy at this juncture. Beginning in the late sixteenth century, various institutions in English society (i.e., the legislature, courts of equity) worked to curtail usurious forms of lending; profits taken, in the language of Jeremy Bentham, "[at] a greater interest than the law allows . . . [or] a greater interest than it is usual for men to give and take."[6] *Usura* describes a prearranged profit on loans beyond a certain statutory rate of interest and, for many at the time carried hints of a social infraction, of profits drawn beyond one's personal *interesse* (med. L., a relation of concern in respect of advantage as well as disadvantage [in the French juridical sense of *dommages et intérêts*]).[7] As Guyora Binder and Robert Weisberg observe, the line separating *usura* from *interesse* had for long been difficult to draw, due in part to the seemingly irreconcilable differences between two strands in Continental theology and law (both of which had begun to affect English thought). The first position was "objectivist" and held that any lending with a guaranteed return more than the value of the loan was not only illegal but also immoral. The second position—the "subjectivist" or "nominalist" one—held that "there was no reliable external measure of the morality of a loan."[8] A balance began to be struck between these positions with the passage of various laws against usurious lending in 1571 and 1624—laws limiting annual rates of interest to eight pounds (for most members of the lending class) and five pounds (for brokers and solicitors) for every hundred pounds on loan (Fr. *pour cent*). Older law described certain loans at interest as prima facie usurious, and English society, in turn, took violations of a statutory rate of interest as a technical yet complementary expression of the moneylenders' violations of the natural boundaries of class and status ("they were social climbers trying to fashion themselves into higher-status figures" [*Literary Criticisms of the Law*, 519]). The laws against usury were aimed at suppressing, in this regard, "an emerging Renaissance humanist definition of selfhood, a self free to fashion itself into a new social identity" (*Literary Criticisms of the Law*, 519).

The distinction between *usura* and *interesse* became easier to draw in part because the Renaissance-era developments in the law of usury were accompanied "by the emergence of a new social imagery appropriate to the new character type of the legitimate money merchant," one who was honest in his dealings, charitable with his acquired wealth, and morally selective in his lending. By 1700, the moneylender had ceased to be perceived as an "absconding charlatan" and had taken on the character of "the sympathy-invoking hero of the economy, the passive figure who suffered the accidents of the natural and economic world in order to enhance the movement of capital" (*Literary Criticisms of the Law*, 523). Technical developments within commercial law were thus entwined with the creation of a type of social character whose empathic extensions of credit, reputation for upright dealing, and suffering beneath the vicissitudes of the market reflected the social opprobrium against usury. Lending became morally neutral with transformations in the law. It was the lender himself who captured the moral norms and tensions of a society paranoid about early capitalist economics: "The new legislation focused on creating a model character of the properly interested moneylender, rather than drawing a line between specific good and bad actions. No one loan on its face could be determined to be usurious or not; the context—the character of the lender—was decisive" (*Literary Criticisms of the Law*, 519). Emergent techniques of wealth generation in English law depended on this dramaturgic model of the self.

The merchant, the banker, the broker—as expressions of financial "character" they proved not only economic stereotypes within the unfolding narratives of wealth generation but also the very aesthetic conduits by means of which individuals, even groups, could "try to redeem their sense of social identity from its material origins" (*Literary Criticisms of the Law*, 507).

Taking my cue from this Renaissance historicism, I argue in this chapter for the necessary reciprocity between dramaturgic act and legal form within the competing narratives of nineteenth-century finance capital.[9] Admittedly, the terms of the debate had shifted considerably by the nineteenth century, and, while rhetorics of the "objective" and the "subjective" still seemed relevant, the debate over value in American jurisprudence and economics had acquired its own distinct methods and logics. On the one side was the "marginal revolution," whose adherents used the new methods of statistics and calculus to account for "consumer desire."[10] The marginalists advocated using mathematics to determine value that, given the conditions of the market, frequently fluctuated. To their minds, the market, despite these fluctuations, reflected the workings of various objective economic laws. The key to unlocking these laws was the "will theory of contract," which, though it took the desires of contracting parties into account, led not to a subjective theory of value but an intersubjective one. While the marginalists acknowledged that value was not intrinsic to an object, they still maintained that subjective desires taken together set an objective (if always changing) value for an item, a value determined by the market. These arguments laid the intellectual groundwork for the professional soothsayers of finance capitalism—the technicians and "chartists" who track movements in stock prices. When the latter spot a sequence of price changes in the same direction over a period of time, they tend to read this persistent pattern as a gauge of future performance and the probability of a specific yield.

On the other side of the debate were those skeptical both that the marginalists could ever be completely successful in establishing an objective value for an item through the use of calculus or statistics and that the chartists' persistent patterns were anything other than random. The argument of progressive legal thinkers and (later) monetarists went as follows. Sometimes one gets rising prices for several days in a row; but, by the same token, sometimes when one flips a coin you also get a long string of "heads" in a row. The persistence in prices occurs no more frequently than a random sequence of heads or tails in a row. That is, the stock market's "persistent patterns" occur no more often than a gambler's runs of luck. Mathematicians and economists would term this behavior "the random walk of value," meaning by that term conditions in which "future steps or directions cannot be predicted on the basis of past actions." As Burton Malkiel puts the matter, "No matter what wiggle or wobble the prices have made in the past, tomorrow starts out fifty-fifty. The next price change is no more predictable than the flip of a coin."[11] Past outcomes may influence the soothsayers' predictions, but they bear no impress on the probability of a specific outcome. To believers in the "random walk of value," the chartists' momentum is a mere statistical illusion.

As this summary of the debate suggests, these problems of errantry, inconstancy, and improbability in the market often bore a negotiated relationship to the problem of affect in valuation (equated in the minds of many with the gambler's instincts)—and for economists no less than for financiers. As one of the period's reformed financiers notes, those traders who traffic in the economy's emerging financial instruments fall prey to "suspicion, overconfidence, timidity and vacillation."[12] The speculator is, in another investor's words, the "opium-eater of finance," and the speculative profession "a master passion, which like Aaron's serpent, swallows up and strengthens itself with other passions."[13] In the final decades of the century, the problem of property appears as the dilemma of an economy that, having forsaken production of goods for the prophesies of speculative exchange, finds itself riding (as Keynes would later put it) "waves of optimistic and pessimistic sentiment," with the end result that the economy's greatest certainty appears paradoxically to be the degree to which it would henceforth be shadowed by the specters of inconstancy and hypersensitivity, volatility and flux.

The competing narratives of the "objective" and the "random" that I have sketched here define the limits of the debate over speculation, and the pragmatic conclusions arrived at in everyday legal affairs often fell somewhere in between. These compromises were usually expressed in the law's particular figurations of character in a speculative marketplace, many of which were of the same order as the properly interested moneylender of Renaissance literature and commercial law (and one might reflect here on the quiet assist provided by literary characters such as Dreiser's Cowperwood or Howells's Lapham). I want to draw attention to a distinct but related order of compromise and would offer a reconsideration of the above responses to the market as one way of detecting the dramaturgic acts that channeled the individual's participation in political and economic life. On the one hand, the marginalists, while assuming that individual nodes of exchange were subjective, nonetheless grounded the values they discerned in an intersubjective web based in their view on objective economic laws. Consumer desire was, thus, rationalized as a sort of natural and ontological force in the economy (e.g., *homo economicus*). On the other hand, the marginalists' critics, who saw exchange as structured but nevertheless colored with narrative uncertainty, personified the errantry and improbability of the market in the random walk of value. What these responses share is a gesture I pointed to in the previous chapter—the personification of the market—but, as I have also wanted to stress, cultural forms play a role in the composition of the social world, specifically in the crafting of forms of social character that wed the extremes in the market assessment of value (a compromise for the deep moral ambivalence about emergent forms of capital). I have spoken of "character in a speculative marketplace" in this regard, and the figure I have had in mind is the fugitive.

One of the fears sparked by the passage of the Fugitive Slave Law in 1850 was that of an expanded speculation in slaves—a fear not only that the market would now extend from the New Orleans auction block to all parts north but that it would also absorb both escaped slaves and blacks incapable of defending their freedom. But, as I have already suggested, the problem of the speculative market was acutely that of a particular way of being "in" the market, and not just for the speculator but for all market actors as well—an issue of the management of the market's affective dimensions, of value's incertitude, and of credit's deferral. To my mind, it is at this quotidian level that the figuration of the fugitive as errant and wayward—as a flaneur of sorts—correlates with the representation of value's inconstancy and the speculator's languorousness. This correlation is one I track, in what follows, across a range of texts invested in the representation and codification of economic routine: from a translation case that uses the fugitive's flight as a figure for textual circulation (*Stowe v. Thomas* [1853]) to a speculation case that cites it as precedent (*Chicago v. Christie* [1905]); from the representation of profligacy and wantonness in *The Wealth of Nations* (1776) to the representation of credit fraud through the mockery and minstrel accents of the cakewalk (traditionally, the slaves' satire of their masters' manners) in *The Marrow of Tradition* (1901).[14] In all, I will want to trace the tendrils linking the fugitive of midcentury jurisprudence to the dandy of literary and minstrel culture.

The path I will have to follow is a complicated and tricky one—straying beyond the comforts of the literary text to engage both economic treatise and legal opinion. It may help matters to state in as simple a manner as possible the correlation out of which the following reading arises: in the nine-teenth-century drama of economy, the slaves' "puttin' on old massa," basis for minstrelsy's cakewalk, is the cultural "compromise" that weds the ex-tremes of the marginalists' intersubjectivity and the mathematicians' ran-dom walk of value. On the one hand, the cakewalk's mockery signifies like a mirroring and, in that respect, captures the intersubjective dimensions of marginalist economics. On the other hand, its mockery signifies more like class aspiration (remaking oneself as one's master) and, thus, captures the sense of a "random walk" that, by definition, takes the future to be radically cut off from the past. A cultural practice of the legally commodified satisfies the conceptual demands of an emergent commodification. That is, the plantation ceremonial of the cakewalk is entwined with the creation of a type of social character—the aspiring, improvident, devil-may-care dandy whose chief labor involves "puttin' on airs." Slave "character" migrates from the plantation to the minstrel stage and, in that movement, comes to be imbricated in emergent forms of economic subjectivity (and this migra-tion from culture to law suggests, in yet another way, how blacks as a sub-ordinate class got a head start on modernity, floating free of constraints of tradition and property long ago codified in the common law). By following economic transactions and the cakewalk through their various textual iter-ations, I hope to provide a narrative in which it becomes clear that legal forms and legal procedures play a compositional role in modern culture, and, reciprocally, literary and cultural texts assist in the fashioning of new social identities. The interpretive task of the pages to follow is to read liter-ary texts, economic transactions, and legal forms "for the tropes and fictions that enable the formation and perpetuation of a commercial society and culture" (*Literary Criticisms of the Law*, 510).

It shall become clear before long that Stowe's sentimental novel *Uncle Tom's Cabin* stands as more readily pertinent to the coupling of law and literature, imaginative labor and speculative valuation, than many scholars of that text have for much of its history presupposed. As the gospel of nine-teenth-century sentimental ideology (of the obligation to feel when "in" the market), as well as a text critical of the speculative mania that promptly flourishes on the passage of the Fugitive Slave Law, Stowe's venture in mar-ket critique flirts with a late-nineteenth-century drama of credit economy, a drama that primarily consists in the deontologization of value, or the spec-ulative turn away from substantive justifications of value that critics of the period's economy descried as the law's embrace of "counterfeit" goods and "pretended" exchange, as the narrowing of all wealth generation to subjective and passionate play. *Uncle Tom's Cabin,* in intimate proximity to late-nineteenth-century speculative economy, risks absorption into the era's aura and logic of credit (its aura of passion and logic of contract). This risk is made manifest in the minstrel accents, the scents of revel, the whiffs of delight foregrounded in antebellum as well as postbellum, sentimental as well as blackface, and literary as well as theatrical and cinematic *Uncle Tom*s.

Stowe's fondness for a lexicon of affect should be of vague acquaintance to very few, the argot of empathy putting an insistent (and memorable) pressure on the tongues of slaveholder and abolitionist alike ("Showing the Feelings of Living Property on Changing Owners"; "while blood marked every step . . . she saw nothing, felt nothing"; "you allow yourself to feel too much"; "There is one thing that every individual can do,— they can see to it that *they feel right*").[15] Yet, of comparable relevance, Stowe's supplement to the novel, *A Key to Uncle Tom's Cabin,* displays an equally obdurate indebtedness to the principles of sentimental economy. Nowhere is this debt more unabashedly displayed than in its author's meditations on the African's personality and "peculiarities of nervous constitution":

> The vision attributed to Uncle Tom introduces quite a curious chapter of psychology with regard to the Negro race, and indicates a peculiarity that goes far to show how very different they are from the white race. They are possessed of a nervous organization peculiarly susceptible and impressible. Their sensations and impressions are very vivid, and their fancy and imagination lively. In this respect the race has an oriental character, and betrays its *tropical origin.* Like the Hebrews of Old and the oriental nations of the present, they give vent to their emotions with the utmost vivacity of expression, and their whole bodily system sympathizes with the movements of their minds. When in distress, they actually lift up their voices to weep, and "cry with an exceeding bitter cry." When alarmed, they are often paralyzed, and rendered entirely helpless. Their religious exercises are all colored by this sensitive and exceedingly vivacious temperament. Like oriental nations, they incline much to outward expressions, violent gesticulations, and agitating movements of the body. Sometimes, in their religious meetings, they will spring from the floor many times in succession, with a violence and rapidity that is perfectly astonishing. They will laugh, weep, embrace each other convulsively, and sometimes become entirely paralyzed and cataleptic.[16]

This psychology proves the inspiration for a rather perverse writing practice, for an infectious writing practice. The African's "nervous" disposition suffuses all corners of slavery's postlapsarian garden, even (it should come as no surprise) the "Moorish" vistas of Augustine St. Clare's Lake Pontchartrain estate. And one wonders, in this regard—when the latter is described as surrounded by "arabesque ornaments [that] carried the mind back, as in a dream, to the reign of oriental romance in Spain" and the former, as we have just seen, as not only of "tropical origin" but "oriental [in] character" and, in his or her bodily kinetics, "like oriental nations"— one wonders, given this descriptive vocabulary, how Stowe will see fit to wrest the slave's personhood from the pervasive reach of slavery's property rights, how she will achieve, finally, the denouement promised by the tense of her original subtitle, "the man that *was* a thing."

It will take the sensitive critical eye of Hortense Spillers to notice that the slave's oriental sensuousness does not stand alone (nor, as Stowe implies, simplistically so) as that "peculiarity which goes far to show how very different [Africans] are from the white race," but that, resting in fatal opposition with the child Eva's "lush sensuality," it is the twinned figuration of slave and charge as fonts of desire that enacts the very renunciation of want mandated by Stowe's era of her women readers. We have in hand, in the case of *Uncle Tom's Cabin,* a novel written "by, for, and about, women" (in Jane Tompkins's memorable phrase), this last nominative of which, when deployed in the above phrase, presupposes in its exclusion, Spillers contends, the Chloes and the Topsies and the Dinahs whose desires, while often and loudly and declaratively expressed, seem persistently to fall on deaf ears. The captive woman's desire-lost provides a "fictional cypher" for the satiety and fulfillment of woman fully self-possessed (i.e., Stowe's optically white and prototypically bourgeois readers). "Woman" in sentimentality's imaginary equates with "nondesiring woman"; or, in the formulation attributable to Gillian Brown, "women's plenitude obviates desire." Thus "immun[e] from desire," women signify "the imagined state of possession, that is . . . the goal of the pursuit of happiness . . . the embodiment of perfect ownership" (*Sensational Designs,* 29-30). Theological terror, as James Baldwin put the matter some time ago, provides this ur-text in the protest genre with its constitutive energy, with a halting "terror of damnation" for "being caught in traffic with the devil" ("Everybody's Protest Novel," 17-18). Desire absolutely renounced (or, what comes to essentially the same thing, desires fully achieved) thus comes as a consequence of a specifically theological requirement of sacrifice. This renunciation, Spillers adds, occurs "under the sign of an indirection . . . subtle in its appearance" ("Changing the Letter," 43)—Eva's unassuming yet decisive claim, whispered in her father's ear, "I want him" (236). In this reading, the child is dispatched to do a woman's job, and character more thoroughly than usual serves as an expression of authorial will: "The female child figure—in her daring and impermissible *desire*—stands in here for the symptoms of a disturbed female sexuality that American women of Stowe's era could neither articulate nor cancel, only loudly proclaim in the ornamental language . . . of disguise and substitution" (44). In short, Eva frees "woman" of all earthly desire. Such a reading, fueled by a lexicon of "desire," seems compelling; appropriate, even, given how quickly and efficiently the novel's reflections on "the Negro's" "nervous constitution" correlate with matters of want. I am one reader willing decidedly to accede to the force of this argument, but some further and compelling elisions in Stowe's *Key* seem to me worthy of note.

"Mother love" (or, again, what amounts to essentially the same thing, a sense of shared sentience, empathic identification, and intimacy between right-thinking citizens and the enslaved) is enmeshed in *Uncle Tom's Cabin* (novel as well as "key") in a version of the "polymorphous perverse." On the face of it, when Stowe ruminates on "the negro race['s] . . . nervous organization" she appears unperturbed to paddle about in musings whose provenance stretches as far back as (if certainly much farther than) Thomas Jefferson's exculpatory *Notes on the State of Virginia* (1787). To the abolitionist, slaves' emotions are "susceptible and impressible" and their "sensations and impressions are very vivid"—little different from the ambassador's assertion, in the "Laws" installment of his *Notes,* that, in the case of American slaves, "their existence appears to participate more of sensation than reflection."[17] Yet by midcentury, there appears an added wrinkle to these reflections on the slave's "curious . . . psychology": "They give vent to their emotions with the utmost vivacity of expression"; "they incline much to outward expressions, violent gesticulations, and agitating movements of the body"; "their whole bodily system sympathizes with the movements of their minds." I see in these reflections a tendency to wed excessive emotionality to gestural excess. In Stowe's sentimental imagination, affective resonance elides with kinesics, and passions ostensibly spiritual in origin make cozy company with a received choreography of the slave body. Sympathy encodes a larger work—"their whole bodily system sympathizes with the movements of their minds"—the work of translation. Stowe professes interest in the emotional and the internal, but, clearly, on the evidence, she is to a comparable extent fascinated by the gestural, more taken, specifically, with the transit (or traffic) from a grammar of emotions to a repertory of gesture, from passion to pantomime.

A slight twist of the hand. Those "comic evolutions of . . . hands, feet, and whole body" (*Uncle Tom's Cabin*, 44) that, performed by Little Harry before master and trader, incite trade and enhance speculative value. A frenzied Topsy "turning a summerset or two" (*Uncle Tom's Cabin*, 352). The minstrel Tom's sundry *par me la*. All prove syntactic elements in a sentimental grammar of the body, a vocabulary whose referent appears to be the subjective affect and elusive sensation Stowe strives so single-mindedly to represent. *Uncle Tom's Cabin*'s repertory of gesture amplifies and effervesces into the text's myriad "minstrel accents" as it proliferates across various media; and that kinesics of which we get a glimpse in the *Key* proves, finally, the "key" to unlocking the text's economic import.

Stowe's *Uncle Tom's Cabin* provides a palimpsest for a Reconstruction and post-Reconstruction drama of economy. A drama of impetuousness, economic languorousness, and wanton gain lies hidden in a nimbus surrounding the profligate Toms, Adolphs, Topsies, and sundry cakewalking vassals of those blackface productions of *Uncle Tom* that quickly follow the publication of Stowe's novel. Suffused with the themes of wanton excess and irrational expenditure, the blackface *Uncle Tom*s of the latter half of the century wed unpredictable and volatile figures of sentiment to the movements of property and the fluctuations of profit. This ethos of prodigality (of the speculative fall into errantry and deferral) is captured in the whimsical and festal adjuncts to Stowe's sentimental *Uncle Tom*. This theme—this *fort/da* between fugacity and minstrelsy—is given poetic enactment, early on, in the refrain of Dan Rice's blackface Uncle Tom (cited in epigraph):

> I travel'd round de country an' felt dat I was free,
>> For I was cold and starvin' from de elbow to de knee,
> But Massa has forgib me, an' I know dat all am right
>> Tho' if it gives you pleasure, I'll run off eb'ry night.

It is perhaps on suspicion of these nascent connections between speculation and minstrelsy that Charles Mackay would see fit, in his *Memoirs of Extraordinary Popular Delusions and the Madness of Crowds* (1841), to begin that history with speculative disasters of worldly renown (beginning with the *tulpenwoerde* of seventeenth-century Holland) and to end it with an account of the "vile" and "senseless" ditties, "grotesque" and "uncouth" antics of Thomas Danforth Rice's "Jim Crow."[18] What I will want to show over the length of this chapter is the specific capacity of *Uncle Tom's Cabin*'s governing tropes to figure speculation's traffic in abstract values (versus goods) and, thus, to transform the conditions of exchange in the contexts of law and everyday life. *Uncle Tom's Cabin* provides pretext, subtext, and context in the nineteenth century's emerging drama of speculative economy.[19]

PRO BONO PUBLICO

My queries spring, as in the last chapter, from a labyrinth of property concerns. In this section, I want to tease apart a web of contested claims surrounding the speculative contract—as, variously, the very core of the speculator's intangible property and anathema to real property given that contract, based on a promise, is thus conceptually intimate with notions of will and affect, credit and belief. There is an etheric trigger at the heart of contract (i.e., the parties' intentions) and the task of much commercial law is to afford it appropriate legal weight—to make the virtual material. The meaning the speculator assigns to the terms of his contracts is the understanding of speculation's phantomal goods that lends them substance as legal property. I argue, in what follows, that a step in this process is to be found in the poetics and procedures of intellectual property law. This last resolves a particular quirk in the concept of literary property (one that is legally relevant to the speculator's property right in intangible goods), specifically that of the janiform vision of literary characters and literary property as partly the objects of private appropriation and authorial monopoly and, in competing measure, sites of a redundant ownership that preserves the public's interest (nurtures the "public domain," to be exact).[20] This peculiar form of ownership allows literature to be "possessed" inexhaustibly. In terms of the relations between literature and economics, I have in mind here the "pyramiding" characteristic of abstract money in a credit economy (i.e., money in credit economies, like a compressed metaleptic chain, can be in multiple places at once, which principle of excess founds the financier's profit and productivity). Of the latter, "good will" provides a most illustrative example.[21] In the next few pages, I seek to limn this interest in property and aesthetics to the evolving interests of capital, to forms of credit and finance that parrot this characteristic of the literary. I will do so by paying particular attention to the role of *Uncle Tom's Cabin* in the resolutions of commercial and intellectual property law.

A key moment in these literary economies can be found in the eccentric (though far from sui generis) holding in *Stowe v. Thomas* (1853), referred to in the epigraph to this chapter. In that case, the court ruled that Harriet Beecher Stowe had no power to protect her "conceptions and inventions" against unauthorized translation and theft. Lawyers for Harriet Beecher Stowe argued that no property right "stands on better ground and is more deeply rooted" than the right to copyright. The right to one's literary work, they maintained, is "original . . . founded on nature, [and] acknowledged . . . at common law."[22] The defendant in the case, Stowe's lawyers charged, had translated her *Uncle Tom's Cabin* into German in the columns of the Pennsylvania daily *Die Freie Presse* and had done so without her permission, which permission she had already granted "at much expense" to the "competent German scholar" Hugo Rudolph Hutton (201). The translation in dispute, "a mere or bare translation," called "for no creation on the part of the translator" (202). His effort could be measured "at best . . . a voluntary and wrongful mixture of his labour with that which belongs to another" (203). Language constituted one of nature's finite resources, Stowe's counsel proposed (with faintly Lockean conceits), and a "particular language—words of one tongue as distinguished from words of another—are but the signs of [an author's] ideas" (202). It is therefore the case that, in violation of the common law principle of absolute dominion, a "perfect translation will present the identical creation and mental production, in a way that the sign is never thought of" (202).[23] In sum, redundancy amounts to theft. Thomas had merely adorned Stowe's literary composition in "the new dress of another language," a "change of dress" that should not, on its own, "annihilat[e] the most important subject of his [*sic*] right to property" (205). The court ought properly to conclude that an unauthorized translation was an infringement, her lawyers abjured, otherwise "both the original work and the translation must be regarded, with respect to further translation, as *publici juris*" (203)—translated, as the "common property" of all.[24]

It is incorrect, Thomas and his lawyers rebutted, to measure how much they had taken, "for we have taken all," and to measure how much they had added, "for we have added nothing" (205). "We concede and we boast that we have taken every sylable [*sic*], comma and i-dot of the original"; consequently, the question was only "how have we taken, and what have we done with it" (205). It would not do to charge Thomas a copyist "so far as he appropriates," and an author "so far as he contributes his own exertion"; in fact, it would be prudent and in the interest of all involved, they argued, to eschew the very notions of appropriation and labor within their copyright deliberations, as they muddled more than they clarify. The law had already recognized, defense abjured, that "every copyist, every reprinter contributes his own exertion, and every author appropriates thoughts from others" (205–6). The court gave the nod to the arguments of the defendant's counsel and restrained Stowe in her attempts to keep *Uncle Tom's Cabin* "locked up in a learned tongue"—it did so, notably, in full faith that the protection of "public property" served a "public good."

Justice Robert C. Grier, writing for the majority, held that an author's monopoly is in "reproducing the material, mechanical engine of the communication, the body of the book," a monopoly granted in the interest of the "general diffusion of the communication" (206). The author's property "in the creation of his mind," cannot be vested in the author "as abstractions [*sic*]." Property extended solely to the "concrete form" he gave them and "the language in which he had clothed them" (206). Copyright was "the exclusive right to multiply the copies of that particular combination of characters that exhibits to the eyes of another the ideas intended to be conveyed" (206–7). The identity of a book "does not consist merely in the ideas, knowledge or information communicated, but in the same conceptions clothed in the same words"—the same conceptions "clothed in another language" might not be considered the same composition (207). The *Stowe* court carefully maintained the *fort/da* between private property in "the body of the book" and public property in "information," the preclusion of theft and the encouragement of exchange, in the extraordinarily rich passage with which this chapter began:

> By the publication of Mrs. Stowe's book, the creations of the genius and imagination of the author have become as much public property as those of Homer or Cervantes. Uncle Tom and Topsy are as much *publici juris* as Don Quixote and Sancho Panza. All her conceptions and inventions may be used and abused by imitators, play-rights [*sic*] and poetasters. They are no longer her own—those who have purchased her book, may clothe them in English doggerel, in German or Chinese prose. Her absolute dominion and property in the creations of her genius and imagination have been voluntarily relinquished. All that now remains is the copyright of her book; the exclusive right to print, reprint and vend it, and those only can be called infringers of her rights, or pirates of her property, who are guilty of printing, publishing, importing or vending without her license, "copies of her book." A translation may, in loose phraseology, be called a transcript or copy of her thoughts or conceptions, but in no correct sense can it be called a copy of her book. (208)

The case was quixotic in more ways than one, with Stowe's lawyers eager to defend an "absolute dominion" curiously outmoded and misplaced in an era already quite comfortable with textual reproduction. The court's contradictory aim was to affirm the immateriality of public property in texts, while acknowledging and protecting the necessary materiality of the subject of copyright.[25] Specifically, the *Stowe* court faced a difficulty common to much midcentury American copyright law: to trace the residues of rights "voluntarily relinquished," that is, to maintain a material ground for the author's property in the face of her decision to abdicate her inalienable but unprofitable common law right to her manuscript for "a qualified right to a printed text that remained elusive in its generality and unreclaimable from the public realm."[26] On the scales of all copyright exercises in justice were balanced the interests of private accumulation and profit against protections of the public domain, or those portions of copyrighted works that were "owned by no one" and were "available for any member of the public to use."[27] The Pennsylvania court reasoned, like other courts of its time, that since statutory copyright granted specific rights to the author of a literary (or other) work, copyright carried with it a dedication to the public of aspects of that same work: "Since Congress had expressed statutory copyright in terms of specific rights, any other literary rights, whether or not they had once been protected at common law, must pass into the public domain upon the vesting of statutory copyright" ("Public Domain," 978). *Stowe v. Thomas* affirmed the doctrine that copyright law afforded no protection for characters and figures possessed of a certain obviousness, conventionality, or stereotypicality—the position that copyright offered no right of property to patterns and codes, conventions and formulas, the clichés that were "bound to recur" in the act of textual production.[28]

In the thinking of Paul de Man, this unfettering of the cliché constitutes translation's most treasured sacrilege, to bring into focus "certain disjunctions, certain disruptions, certain accommodations, certain weaknesses, certain cheatings, certain conventions, certain characteristics that don't correspond to the claim of the original, so that the original loses its sacred character—of being the original in any sense [—] because a translation brings out all that is idiomatical [*sic*], all that is customary, all that is quotidian, all that is nonsacred, all that is prosaic in the original."[29] Alleged to lack the characteristics of "creative genius," these characters were "common property" and "should be available to all as the tools of discourse" ("Beyond Metaphor," 767n. 182, 769). Significantly, these same wayward characters (surrendered to the public and perversely owned by all) proved to be fictions integral to the period's financial revolution, to its reconceptualization of ownership, profit, and the logic of production.

The terms of the *Stowe* opinion—"absolute dominion" versus "general diffusion," an "exclusive right" in the material "body of the book" versus immaterial conceptions "*publici juris*"—anticipated the concerns of a turn-of-the-century property law newly focused on the abstraction implicit in property:

> Property is everything which has exchangeable value.[30]
>
> "Property" has ceased to describe any *res*.[31]
>
> The term "property" "means only the rights of the owner in relation to [land]." "It denotes a right . . . over a determinate thing." "Property is the right of any person to possess, use, enjoy, and dispose of a thing."[32]
>
> Not merely physical things are objects of property, but the expected earning power of those things is property; and property is taken from the owner, not merely under the power of eminent domain which takes title and possession, but also under the police power which takes its exchange-value.[33]
>
> A patent right, a copyright, a right of action, an easement, an incorporeal hereditament, may be property as valuable as a granite quarry; and the owner of such property may be practically deprived of it,—such property may be practically taken from its owner,—although it is not corporeal. So those proprietary rights, which are the only valuable attributes or ingredients of a landowner's property, may be taken from him, without an asportation or adverse personal occupation of that portion of the earth which is his. . . . Property is taken when any one of those proprietary rights is taken, of which property consists.[34]

The reconception of property as every species of valuable right and interest threatened, in the view of some, you recall, to engulf all legal relations; and this expansion in the scope of property (this unfettering of prior restraints on the reach of wealth interests) demanded the attention of jurist and philosopher alike to tame the rambunctious excesses of the market. The *Stowe* court's conception of this vexed abstraction as the tension between the principles governing private interest and public gain, private property and the public commons, suggested, at once, that the fear of abstraction was nothing short of a fear of overexpropriation (a fear resolved, momentarily, in the legal recognition of the modesty of authorial right and the magnanimity of public interest). Yet the court's language of beneficence and virtue suggested, more important, that its deliberations were haunted by a specter at least as old as *The Wealth of Nations* (1776), Adam Smith's famous treatise on political economy and the morality of commercial enterprise (on the rationality that leads from individual productivity to that most important public good, national prosperity, from subject to structure).[35] I will digress here for just a moment, then, to reflect more specifically on some of that text's meditations on property (and personality), a digression that seems important not only because *Wealth* was extremely popular among American jurists, legal thinkers, and neoclassical economists during the final decades of the nineteenth century (second only, perhaps, to Smith's own *The Theory of Moral Sentiments* in that regard) but also because its figuration of the tension between scarcity and abstraction by way of a symbolic economy of the parsimonious and the prodigal retains an uneasy pertinence, providing a clarifying backdrop to our thinking on the relationship between fiction and finance.

In *Wealth,* Smith screens an overzealous accumulation of capital behind the "invisible hand" of public interest ("capitals are increased by parsimony, and diminished by prodigality"; "every prodigal appears to be a public enemy, and every frugal man a public benefactor"; "every individual necessarily labours to render the annual revenue of the society as great as he can.... He is in this, as in many other cases, led by an invisible hand to promote an end which was no part of his intention" [259–62]). *Wealth*'s fabulation of human nature is famous for managing profitably to distinguish the frugal man's investment from the prodigal's perversion. As the story goes, the frugal man accumulates "valuable commodities," "endeavors as much as he can . . . to employ his capital in the support of domestic industry," "maintains productive rather than unproductive hands," and manages, as an unintended consequence, yet through means unknown to him, to establish "a perpetual fund for the maintenance of an equal number in all times to come."[36] The prodigal, on the contrary, whose spending responds to a "passion for present enjoyment," "perverts" this fund from "its proper destination" in conduct whose unintended consequence (still unknown but now logically inferable) is to "feed the idle with the bread of industriousness." The prodigal's is a "trifling" and "selfish" disposition and leads him "not only to beggar himself, but to impoverish his country" (261, 263). *Wealth* so quietly intimates spiritual with fiduciary belief, so skillfully purges human nature of wastefulness, as to make the love of monetary gain a building block of civil society:

> With regard to profusion, the principle that prompts to expense, is the passion for present enjoyment; which, though sometimes violent and very difficult to be restrained, is in general only momentary and occasional. But

the principle that prompts to save, is the desire of bettering our condition, a desire that, though generally calm and dispassionate, comes with us from the womb, and never leaves us till we go into the grave. In the whole interval that separates those two moments, there is scarce, perhaps, a single instance in which any man is so perfectly and completely satisfied with his situation as to be without any wish of alteration or improvement of any kind. (263)

The interdependent web of assertions articulated in the above passage—between a rational and normative interest in accumulation, on the one hand, and an irrational and wanton expenditure, on the other—depends on a string of theoretical positions that Smith (in what is essentially an equation of theoretical speculation with objective description) takes as the "laws" governing human nature. In all, frugality reads as "rational," for it is concerned, minimally yet primarily, with the maximization of profit and satisfaction, efficiency and (if it might be quantified) justice. The profligate fails to "confin[e] his expense within his income" and, thus, "encroaches upon his capital," which, from the vantage of the "accumulation of capital," can only be glossed as "irrational." On the evidence of the frugal man's discipline, classical political economy assumes a dynamic of emulation in which all men strive privately, yet analogously and uniformly ("the private interests and passions of men naturally lead them to divide and distribute the stock of every society . . . in the proportion which is *most agreeable* to the interest of the *whole* society").[37] *Wealth* underscores belief in the deep morality of production, offering a sanguine proposal for "bettering our condition" that counterpoises the temporality of the "calm and dispassionate" (that desire that "comes with us from the womb, and never leaves us till we go into the grave") against the volatility and inconstancy of the prodigal's "passion for present enjoyment."

Classical political economy's outcomes appear unrelentingly merry and beneficient.[38] The logic of private property encourages owners to put their time, labor, and care into the development of their investments, enables them, in theory, to exclude others from capturing the value of their individual investments on the assumption that property is a finite and bounded resource, that is, on the assumption of a "naive" conception of property (an assumption hinted at in Smith's reference to "the stock of every society").[39] Exclusive control enables owners to identify other owners and for all to exchange their objects of investment until such goods arrive in the hands of those who value them most highly. In this world, it is widely held that private property works in the public's interest, for it provides a medium in which goods are exchanged to the great cumulative advantage of all.[40] But in this very sanguine proposal of liberal governmentality, the drama of private property has all the makings of a tragedy. Tragedy is certain to result when the rational pursuit of gain conflicts with the constraints of finite resources—"economics" in its most acute modern form or what gets emplotted, more familiarly, as "the tragedy of the commons."[41] Notably, it is in the interest of assuaging this threat, Albert O. Hirschman has observed, that Smith offers the "invisible hand" in the first place. His innately moral and providential "hand" figures efficient distribution, constant equilibrium, and self-correcting valuation and, thus, answers to the problem of scarcity and risk ("tragedy"). All men, in Smith's view, are actuated by a "desire of bettering [their] condition," which desire (or "self-interest") remains beneficent and innocent to the extent that it remains fueled by rational deliberation, advanced toward the end of efficiency, and inspired by the possibility of mutual gain. Smith makes a powerful economic case for the unfettered pursuit of private gain, final assist to the modern transformation of the "deadly passions" of avarice, greed, and covetousness into the "innocent interest" in accumulation.[42] His *Wealth* offers a prudent and passionless "interest" as the logic that protects the common good within a culture of scarcity. In Smith's political economy, innocence forestalls tragedy when faced with property's naïveté.

One need not scratch too deeply the surface of Smith's personifications to see a temporality of investment hidden beneath the ur-capitalist's diligence and the prodigal's reckless expenditures, nor need one look with too keen a set of lenses to see a morality of commerce in the penumbra that shades these personalities. "Interest" forestalls capitalism's melancholia, holding in abeyance private property's implicit tragedy.

Curiously, the conception of the "public" and the "private," of the "passions" and the "interests," in classical political economy and real property law is without parallel in the sphere of intellectual property, as *Stowe* makes readily apparent. For, where in real property the public commons is viewed as a finite domain, in intellectual property the public domain lacks only limit; where in real property expropriation for purposes of private accumulation wields hardship and tragedy for all, intellectual property doctrine encourages such expropriation from the commons; and where classical political economy forestalls tragedy through principles of rational action and beneficent exchange (i.e., self-interest, the profit motive, the "invisible hand"), the burdens, hardships, and duties of copyright fall heavily on the shoulders of the regime's presumed beneficiary, the author. Jeremy Waldron, the scholar of copyright, has put the matter this way: when the author is viewed as the bearer of a right to profit through private accumulation, the copier assumes the form of a thief, one who has failed to perform his or her requisite duties; yet when the author appears the beneficiary of a statutory and limited monopoly, the copier becomes the very embodiment of free enterprise values, a personification of the useful enjoyment of riches found at the public weal.[43] Neither author nor translator, artist nor copyist, seems the inevitable bearer of specific duties in a limitless commons, an open-endedness within legal signification captured with greatest eloquence in defense counsel's claim, in *Stowe,* that "every copyist, every reprinter contributes his own exertion, and every author appropriates thoughts from others" (205–6).

In this light, it is worthy of note that the *Stowe* court resolved copyright's impossible contradiction between the author's monopoly and accumulation, on the one hand, and laissez-faire exchange and dissemination, on the other, through the "translation" of Tom and Topsy's circulation into the ungovernable and unpredictable movements of the fugitive. Textual dissemination is figured as a kind of textual wandering that mimics, in many respects, the errantry of the very fugitive slaves on which Stowe modeled her critique of property. Of equal importance, the court's representation of the public domain (of the public's property in Stowe's text) as wayward slaves bodies "[to] be used and abused" by the nearest entrepreneur calls to mind the coevalness of the fugitive slave—as contractual person and pilfered property, a subject capable of sentiment and an article of property (or, to recall the words of William Goodel, hybrids "moveable by their nature" yet "immoveable by the operation of law"). The doubleness of the fugitive stands in for the public's interest in the ostensibly private text, for a collective and nonrivalrous possession of the object of private accumulation. The specter of bodies naked, freely circulating, and vulnerable to the interests of the nearest free-marketeer figures the fungibility of the literary as commodity, embodies the limitless profitability of the book both as private object of appropriation and public capital asset—that redundant and public "ownership" necessary to the production of literary property as market commodity.[44] In all, the *Stowe* court conjures forth a disinterested *agent of transfer* in its efforts to resolve the problem of textual translation, much like those barterers on the cusp of a money economy who (as Marx explains in the *Grundrisse*) give in to the assumption by a particular commodity of the power to measure and to purchase—that is, to translate—all others, which is simply a version of the assumption that (as the "universal commodity") money speaks the language (*Warensprache*) of all commodities.[45] But this implication of a relation between linguistic translation and monetary transaction figured in the fugitive is more than a scholar's fancied critical inference; and, importantly, the *Stowe* case possesses even greater bearing on this connection than I have been able here to suggest, as the intimacy of the aesthetic with the economic that that case thematizes had an already quite thoroughly established and lengthy history.

The term "translation" (as a great many scholars of literature and economics have noted), in the Latin form *translatio,* means not only "figurative term" (Gr., *metaphorein,* "transfer of meaning") but also "a transfer of property" ("All Contract is mutual translation, or change of Right" [Hobbes, *Leviathan* (1651)]); and, further, this union of the poetic and the economic redounds in the German word for translation, *Übersetzung,* which applies both to the linguistic transfer of meaning and to the economic transfer of property occasioned by contract.[46] Marx sustains that this interlinguistic translation (*Entfremdung,* translation from the mother tongue) provides monetary alienation (*Entäußerung*) with principles both immanent and irrepressible: "Language does not transform ideas, so that the peculiarity of ideas is dissolved and their social character runs alongside them as a separate entity, like prices alongside commodities. Ideas do not exist separately from language. Ideas that have first to be translated out of their mother tongue into a foreign [*fremde; ausländisch*] language in order to circulate, in order to become exchangeable, offer a somewhat better analogy; but the analogy lies not in language, but in the foreignness of language" (*Grundrisse,* 162–63). Emphasizing foreignness, Marx stresses in turn language's implicit figurality, this last of which, according to Paul de Man, translations faithfully execute in the form of the ontologically groundless interchange between one language and another: translations "put the original in motion . . . giving it a movement which is a movement of disintegration, of fragmentation. This movement of the original is a wandering, an errance, a kind of permanent exile if you wish, but it is not really an exile, for there is no homeland, nothing from which one has been exiled" ("Conclusions,"92). A translation establishes a relation of language to language (and not, as in the case of the original poetic or literary creation, of language to a meaning, "to a statement that is not purely within the realm of language" [81]). To this degree, to the degree to which de Man's claims for translation give the lie to the ideological assumption of a matter ontologically prior to thought (or, echoing Marx, "ideas" independent of "language"), his "exilewhich-is-not-an-exile" captures with an uncanny precision the implications of an errant Uncle Tom and, by turns, the economic consequences of the translation case. The *Stowe* case's emphasis on interlinguistic translation (*Entfremdung*)—its repudiation of the plaintiff's metaphoric affirmation of "real estate," or the claim to "absolute dominion" that carries with it the presupposition of an ontological "thing"—provides a literary correlate to the logic of speculative economy, to the perfection of capital achieved, for example, in gambling, where "money need relate only to itself (M-M′) rather than suffering the indignity of trade (M-C-M′)."[47]

The potential implicit in a vision of literary trope and aesthetic formula as financial "asset" is not lost on the free-marketeers of finance capitalism. The *Stowe v. Thomas* translation dispute and other more orthodox holdings in intellectual property law (*Millar v. Taylor,* 1769; *Donaldson v. Beckett,* England 1774; *Wheaton v. Peters,* 1834; *Jefferys v. Boosey,* England 1854; *Bleistein v. Donaldson,* 1903) acquire broadened economic consequence when cited as precedent in arguments for and against the right to prices as property—a pivotal concern in the speculative finance economy of the turn of the century. Commercial law acquires a sense of infinite profits when it appropriates the principles governing the circulation of fictions (or, better, the translation between economic and literary media) as capitalism's principle of operation and transvaluation.

In the case of *Board of Trade of the City of Chicago v. Christie Grain and Stock Co.* (1905), representatives of the Chicago Board of Trade sued to restrain the proprietors of competing (and illegal) "bucket shops," brokerage offices that appeared to be actual grain exchanges and in which customers "could trade on simple price differences but could neither buy nor sell real bushels of wheat, bales of cotton, lots of pork bellies, or actual shares of stock."[48] The bucket shops, plaintiff's counsel accused, obtained the price quotations on sales of grain and provisions for future delivery "through a known breach of the confidential terms" on which the board had agreed to communicate said quotes to Western Union. Such vice was further compounded, they added, by the fact that the shops traded in prices alone, counterfeiting the board's legitimate exchange in goods alongside prices.[49] In sum, the shops screened their theft behind a spectral, counterfeit ruse. The bucket shops' counsel countered that the board boasted of a trade that at best ranked of mere pretense, as traders in the pit of the exchange made no intention of either delivery or receipt of goods "in ninety five per cent of the transactions" and as they tended cynically to fulfill these contracts by dumping fake products on the market just when farmers arrived with the real (242). The defense trotted out volumes of intellectual property law in an effort to reduce the board's price quotations to mere information. This move, if successful, would have made prices ineligible for protection as property, at least on the evidence of received copyright statute. As nothing that lacked "corporeal substance" could be the object of property, they argued, the disputed quotations "are not property and cannot be impressed with a right of property" (and here lawyers cited as precedent both *Stowe v. Thomas* and *Wheaton v. Peters* [*Chicago*, 241]).[50] Similarly, nothing could be the object of property "which is [neither] capable of sole and exclusive enjoyment" (*Millar v. Taylor*) nor "of distinguishable proprietary marks" (*Jefferys v. Boosey*); and, when absent those marks, publication for one necessitates that one "publish for all."[51] On this established authority, lawyers for the bucket shops located the right to property in mental or literary effort "fundamentally upon the creative faculty," which belonged, if to anyone, to the members who transacted in the pits of the exchange and not to the Board of Trade, a mere scrivener whose responsibility was to record and gather up others' labors (241). Sanctuary for a traffic in the "idea" of wheat (phantom goods concocted out of units of time and bits of information), the board was nothing short of, in the defendant's words, "the greatest of bucket shops" (246); and, thus, in the case then before the court, differences in degree had unfortunately been presented as differences in kind.

Regardless, a jurisprudence evidently disposed to load the dice for enterprise found support for the claims of the "legitimate" financial sector. If there was authority to be drawn for capitalization and finance in the extraordinary and peculiar protections of literary property, then the nod was in the direction of the plaintiff, according to Oliver Wendell Holmes, author of the opinion of the Court. The production of prices "stand[s] like a trade secret" as it reflects the board's particular "expertise," and, when considered to consist of a kind of literary "work" based "fundamentally upon the creative faculty," said prices seem undoubtedly "entitled to the protections of the law" (241, 250). The fact that "others might do similar work, if they might"—like plagiarists, copyists, or, as in the case cited, *Bleistein v. Donaldson*, lithographers—"does not authorize them to steal the plaintiff's."[52] The making of contracts to buy and sell nonexistent commodities was not a "pretended" trade that smacked of gambling but an honest "endeavor to forecast the future and to make agreements according to . . . prophesy" (247). The dissemination of this "market news" was "highly beneficial to legitimate commerce" and "clothed with a public use" (237, 249): "In a modern market contracts are not confined to sales for immediate delivery. People will endeavor to forecast the future and to make agreements according to their prophecy. Speculation of this kind by competent men is the self-adjustment of society to the probable. Its value is well known as a means of avoiding or mitigating catastrophes, equalizing prices and providing for periods of want" (247).[53] Holmes reasons: "It is true that the success of the strong induces imitation by the weak, and that incompetent persons bring themselves to ruin by undertaking to speculate in their turn. But legislatures and courts have recognized that the natural evolutions of a complex society are to be touched only with a very cautious hand, and that such coarse attempts at a remedy for *the waste incident to every social function* as a simple prohibition and laws to stop its being are harmful and vain" (*Chicago*, 247–48, emphasis mine). He continues:

> No more does the fact that the contracts thus disposed of call for many times the total receipts of grain in Chicago. The fact that they can be and are set-off sufficiently explains the possibility, which is no more wonderful than the enormous disproportion between the currency of the country and contracts for the payment of money, many of which in like manner are set off in clearing houses without any one dreaming that they are not paid, and for the rest of which the same money suffices in succession, the less being needed the more rapid the circulation is. (*Chicago*, 250)

Waste was no index of social ill, no measure of illegality, no cause for remedy. The board's abundance and excess of contracts was the very warp and weft of wealth in modern economies.[54] The "proportion" of "pretended buying and selling" (to cite defense counsel)— of contracts balanced against other contracts, rather than against commodities exchanged—threw no light, in Holmes's assessment, on the question of the proportion "of serious dealings for legitimate business purposes" measured against "those which fairly can be classed as wagers or pretended contracts" (or, in a word, gambles).

The U.S. Supreme Court's recognition of the consubstantiality of aesthetics and economics tamed, for a spell, the fear of inflated values and intangible properties—the fear, in short, of those ascendant strains of finance capitalism that, gathered beneath the sign of "credit," solicited belief.[55] The Court redeemed the buying and selling of things that did not exist by broadening the definition of "common interest" to include "an interest in the production of markets and prices" (*Card Sharps*, 172)—a conception of aesthetic production (prices as prophetic figuration) that served to suborn copyright precedent's identification of "general diffusion" with publicness and the absence of property protections. What the Court allowed moral sanction is the board's claim that, as its members were linked to the larger economic community by a basic principle of risk—that is, as its commodity speculators had incurred the "rights" as well as the correlate "liabilities" of a holder of property—speculation as a practice served the "public good." What the Court allowed further substantive constitutional protection was the argument that the definition of "production" ought properly to include the production of prices and markets, as well as professional knowledge and expertise (a version of what the defendants had described as the "creative faculty"). This argument, on the Court's final ruling, "altered the metaphysical structures that governed a logic of production" and "transferred the moral power of production to intangible things" (*Card Sharps*, 172, 196). In essence, by legitimizing the selling of property that one did not own, the Court confirmed the fiction that all property was one's own to begin with—that it is, at its core, the mere effect of one's abstract, subjective, and aesthetic imaginings (even though those subjective desires would often seem recondite from the vantage of the law). In *Chicago*, fiction served ancillary to finance as an immanent principle of capitalism's operation and valuation.

Lawyers for both parties placed before the Court a diverse array of speculation's mechanisms, from the ludic inconstancy and prophetic cast of its valuations to the abstraction and fictionality of its products. The judges, however, remained largely agnostic on these matters, preferring to steer clear of the moral juggernaut that awaited them. Of course, Holmes's remarks on the tendencies of "the strong," "the weak," and "the incompetent" seem an exception, but even he notes that, for long, "legislatures and courts have recognized that the natural evolutions of a complex society are to be *touched only with a very cautious hand*" (and the reach of that "cautious hand" extends, we are to assume, to the present). Rather than take up these larger questions of the morality of commerce, the judges ruled on the much narrower (though no less critical) question of whether prices warrant status as property. This last pivoted on their construal of contract, and, in this respect, the terms of their ruling foregrounded speculation's place within what both legal historians and constitutional scholars consider the "golden age" of laissez-faire philosophy in constitutional law: the period in turn-of-the-century American jurisprudence during which courts elevated the notion of "freedom of contract" to a constitutional right and in which the correlate doctrine of "formal equality" achieved its apotheosis. Before returning to *Chicago*'s link between prophetic forecast and literary work (and the place of copyright precedent in the forging of that link), I want to consider some of the wider ramifications of this pivotal moment in constitutional law.

The rise to prominence of laissez-faire philosophy was a result, in large measure, of the continued reassessment throughout the course of the century of the "will theory of contract." By the terms of the will theory, the basis for enforcing a contract was a "meeting of minds" or convergence of the wills of the contracting parties. This premise led most courts in the direction of one of two conundrums in the majority of everyday contract disputes: on the one hand, how to enforce a contract (how to respect it as a "meeting of minds") without acquiescing to the unusual or idiosyncratic understanding of one of the parties; and, on the other, how to determine when the state could either enforce or refuse to enforce a contractual agreement between parties (distinctions that, it is worthy of note, roughly correlate with the subjectivist and objectivist strands in early-modern thought, respectively). To solve the first puzzle was essentially to move away from the second and to further the law's transformation of its standard of value from an earlier "doctrine of consideration" to the fluctuating and fluid measures of the "will theory."

Where eighteenth-century jurisprudence's doctrine of consideration had subjected contract and other forms of valuation to substantive and static measures of "intrinsic value" or "just price," the will theories of nineteenth-century jurisprudence reduced all contract to the voluntary agreement of the interested parties as the standard of fairness—the *nuda voluntas* traditional law had rejected as too subjective and, hence, too perceptually dubious. The former position reflected the longstanding belief that the justification of contractual obligation derived from the inherent justice or fairness of the exchange (a determination that there existed no exorbitance of price). Advocates of "just price" asserted that value ultimately was intrinsic and morally justified. Their position was that values and prices, though subject to fluctuation, oscillated around a "natural" quantity—the quantity of labor required to produce the object. "Values and prices were thus generally, or on the average, or in the long run determined by labor, which in moral theory entitled the owner to both the object and its value."[56] In the financial revolution of late-nineteenth-century America, justifications of value rooted in the inherent fairness of the exchange (all principles of substantive justice) appeared arbitrary and perceptually uncertain, intrinsically ambiguous if not utterly groundless. Legally, as all goods came to be thought of as infinitely fungible, value itself appeared to be a category so purely subjective that the only legitimate basis on which to make its assignation was the concurrence of necessarily psychological individual desires. This position on value marked the triumph of a critique of intrinsic value that had for long striven to void mere "exorbitancy of price" as legitimate ground on which to seek legal remedy for a contract: "It is the consent of parties alone, that fixes the just price of any thing, without reference to the nature of things themselves, or to their intrinsic value; and . . . therefore, a man is obliged in conscience to perform a contract that he has entered into, although it be a hard one."[57] In the thesis of Morton Horwitz, speculative markets for future delivery are difficult to explain within a theory of exchange based on giving and receiving equivalents in value: "Futures contracts for fungible commodities could only be understood in terms of a fluctuating conception of expected value radically different from the static notion that lay behind contracts for specific goods; a regime of markets and speculation was simply incompatible with a socially imposed standard of value."[58] This transformation in the conception of value assumes that all parties to a contract are equal, since, where things have no "intrinsic value," there can be no substantive measure of exploitation. Thus, as "modern contract law [is] . . . born staunchly proclaiming that all men are equal because all measures of inequality are illusory," laissez-faire economic philosophy encounters its penultimate expression in yet another of liberalism's talismanic phrases ("all men are created equal")—a coincidence between economic theory and legal rhetoric that is largely to the benefit of both.[59]

The midwife here is *Lochner v. New York*—also known as the Sugar Baker's case—a case passed in the year 1905 (the same year, incidentally, as *Chicago v. Christie*).[60] In *Lochner,* a majority of the U.S. Supreme Court, over strong dissent, voided state attempts to limit bakers' hours to ten per day on the argument that such legislation violated the "due process" clause of the Fourteenth Amendment. The central legal issue concerned whether employees should be permitted unlimited "freedom of contract" or whether the number of hours they could work should be limited under the "police powers" of the state. The latter, in the assessment of the majority, was merely that "delusive name" that held the place of "the supreme sovereignty of the State," an obfuscating screen for its "meddlesome interferences with the rights of the individual" (56, 61). This position, if it were rephrased in the period's language of value, might well have read as follows: Should the value of labor be determined by the contractual exchanges between employer and employee or by some external judgment as to its "intrinsic value?" As the case's numerous dissenters took pains to point out, citing as authority precedents that were of this very tribunal's own authorship, the liberty secured by the Constitution did not extend to each citizen "an absolute right . . . to be, at all times and in all circumstances, wholly freed from restraint."[61] The recognized constitutionality of certain forms of state power was so obvious, added Justice Holmes, in his own ringing dissent, that the majority's central claim could be seen as a rather naked assertion of the financial class's will-to-power: the claim that "the liberty of the citizen to do as he likes so long as he does not interfere with the liberty of others to do the same" was the principle that governed an array of "fundamental" rights (e.g., the right of private property, the right of free contract). The majority's embrace of this principle insinuated into the sacred precincts of constitutional doctrine "an economic theory which a large part of the country does not entertain," transforming laissez-faire doctrine into "the right of a majority to embody their opinions in law" (75). Their embrace of "the word liberty in the Fourteenth Amendment," he pointedly charged, reeked of sacred principles "perverted," a turning of "liberty" against the very "rational and fair man" who would see the statute in question as "a first installment of a general regulation of the hours of work" or, dare he have altruism in mind, as "a proper measure on the score of health" (76).

Scholars often speak of "pre-*Lochner*" and "post-*Lochner*" eras because the case in many ways ushered in the paradigm shift that proved a key defense of the will theories of nineteenth-century jurisprudence—that transformation in thought, which I referred to at this chapter's start, known as "the marginal revolution."[62] For the followers of this intellectual movement, the problem of value in contract—of a freewheeling "liberty" versus substantive and utilitarian state interests—was no problem at all. Just because the parties to a contract might hold an eccentric understanding of the meaning of its terms, legal thinkers warned, one should not conclude that courts could not arrive at "general theories that would provide uniformity, certainty, and predictability of legal arrangements"; and just because value appears to be subjective, the marginalists claim, it is not necessarily the case that the market does not obey objective laws. The *Lochner*-era (1897–1937) rulings on labor emancipated law and economic thought from the labor theory of value, opening value up to the possibilities of the subjective.[63] But *Lochner* itself enshrined the principle that market value was, more specifically, "intersubjective" (the proverbial "meeting of minds"); therefore, it did not follow, the marginalists and their legal supporters claimed, that value failed to be objective. As I said earlier, the law could (and did) turn to the new methods of statistics and calculus to transform the various "subjective" desires of contracting parties into a set objective (if always changing) value for an item. In theory, the voluntariness of contract (its basis in mutual promise) was not an imputation of the courts but, rather, the market's impartial and self-executing norm. The market was therefore not only objective; it was also, importantly, neutral. These were the case's express legal conceits, at least from the vantage of its defenders; but for its critics, these principles held their own submerged contradictions.

Leading the way in the Progressive assault on freedom of contract, Holmes pointed out in his *Lochner* dissent and in earlier writings that there were limits to the statistical. For sure, he concedes, in "Law in Science and Science in Law," the use of statistics in law promises "an increase in the knowledge of measure" that may counter the "inflated and unreal explanations," "unreal formulas," and "inadequate generalizations" on which the law is so often based.[64] Yet statistics were of limited use in the calculation of value, especially the high-stakes game of the legal calculation of value. Jurists and their marginalist comperes could never be entirely successful in establishing an objective value for an item through the use of calculus and statistics. And this was true, Holmes felt, because statistical models offered probabilities, not certainties. The legal basis for assigning value was often "a judgement or intuition more subtle than any articulate major [economic] premise," which was one reason why Holmes further warned that "general propositions do not decide concrete cases" (*Lochner,* 76). Holmes implicitly faulted the *Lochner* majority for relying too much on a belief that the market was governed by a set of objective, fixed laws when in a famous line he declared that "the Fourteenth Amendment does not enact Mr. Herbert Spencer's *Social Statistic*" (*Lochner,* 75).

What frustrated marginalist method, from the vantage of Progressive critique, were the expansive possibilities of what we might term the "literary" (or the imaginative potential of the "aesthetic"). I describe this problem of prediction as "literary" because the marginalists could only ever confront the limit to the statistical by personifying the market—by invoking either the "reasonable man" of common law jurisprudence or the rational actor (*homo economicus*) of neoclassical economics—but it is possible to define this limit more precisely. In credit economies the sum is greater than the parts, and the excess or variable that makes value incalculable (or never accurately calculable) by the measures of statistics is the subjective itself—the individual subtleties that add up to what Holmes called "unreal expectations," which Keynes later termed the "optimistic and pessimistic sentiment" of crowd behavior and which more recently, in an effort to explain the overvalued stock market of the Internet economy, Alan Greenspan termed (following Robert Shiller) "irrational exuberance." I would call this incalculable variable "character"—an individualized suffering, subverting, and exploiting of economic conditions that yields the necessary (and productive) narrative uncertainties of the speculative marketplace.

In the post-*Lochner* critique of laissez-faire constitutionalism, economic theory and legal praxis do not always mix. Turn-of-the-century commercial law struggled to heal the breech between speculative value and contractual form. In *Chicago,* the Court tried to resolve the tension between speculation's infinite possibilities (its potential to commodify all spheres of life, even the most sacred) and the speculator's narrow property interest, but that resolution left unresolved a number of important concerns: how to keep from succumbing to the peculiar meanings and understandings of the parties to a speculative contract when the only goods were counterfeit and imaginary ones with no correlates in the real; whether, given the fictive nature of speculative goods, it was ever appropriate for courts to override the individual autonomy of parties and impose their own ideas of justice and the appropriate measure of value; whether utilitarian efforts to govern the speculative market were justified given that the traffic in question occurred, by definition, in the uncertain contexts of the future; and, finally, whether the very recognition of a property interest in *Chicago* was anathema to the laissez-faire conception of the neutrality of the market. Ruling as it did, the *Chicago* Court expressed its indifference to these larger concerns, but in this regard it was not at all out of sync with the wider legal culture. As Brook Thomas has pointed out, one of the great failures of turn-of-the-century political culture "was the way in which the legal system made future generations so vulnerable to the unpredictability of an economic chance world. It did so in part by using contract to limit the liability of the powerful rather than . . . using the faculty of promising to create a future of limited reliability."[65] *Chicago* and *Lochner* attenuated future liability and simultaneously reaffirmed the principles behind "freedom of contract," throwing into sharp relief the problematic desire to manage uncertainty, to fill in that future space of emptiness that is, in the assessment of Hannah Arendt, common to all cultures of contract.

In *The Human Condition* (in a section titled "Unpredictability and the Power of Promise"), Arendt argues that making and keeping mutual promises (and covenants) provides a remedy for "the chaotic uncertainty of the future" (237). Unpredictable futures arise, she notes, out of a "two-fold darkness of human affairs." On the one hand, the future remains uncertain because of a "darkness of the human heart," a "basic unreliability of men who never can guarantee today who they will be tomorrow"—man (and I use the masculine pronoun advisedly) is unable "to rely upon himself or to have complete faith in himself (which is the same thing)" (244). On the other hand, the future's uncertainty simultaneously arises out of "the impossibility of foretelling the consequences of an act within a community of equals where everybody has the same capacity to act" (244). The body politic that relies on mutual promises leaves the unreliability of men and the unpredictability of human affairs as they are, "using them merely as the medium, as it were, into which certain islands of predictability are thrown and in which certain guideposts of reliability are erected" (244). Contracts provide just such "islands of predictability," as Arendt conceives the matter, but, as such, they also threaten the freedom of the body politic based on covenants and promises. She continues: "The moment promises lose their character as isolated islands of certainty in an ocean of uncertainty, that is, when this faculty is misused to cover the whole ground of the future and to map out a path secured in all directions, they lose their binding power and the whole enterprise becomes self-defeating" (244). This "misuse" is equivalent to "sovereignty," or "a mastery which relies on domination of one's self and rule over others," one that preserves a capacity "to dispose of the future as though it were the present" (245).

Sovereignty in this sense is always a failed project (about which I will say more presently)—a consequence, for Arendt, of our utter inability either to predict the consequences of any deed or even to plumb its motives. "The reason why we are never able to foretell with certainty the outcome and end of any action is simply that action has no end" (233). The consequence of any deed is wildly open-ended, which "could be a matter of pride if men were able to bear its burden"; but, as Arendt goes one to observe, men have always known that "he who acts never quite knows what he is doing, that he always becomes 'guilty' of consequences he never intended or even foresaw, that no matter how disastrous and unexpected the consequences of his deed he can never undo it, that the process he starts is never consummated unequivocally in one single deed or event, and that its very meaning never discloses itself to the actor but only to the backward glance of the historian who himself does not act" (233). And, what is more, action has no end for reasons of the "web of human relationships" into which all action is thrust (184). There is the world of objective reality and then there is the world of "words and deeds" exchanged between men (a web of action that, though subjective and intangible, is "no less real than the world of things" held in common): "It is because of this already existing web of human relationships, with its innumerable, conflicting wills and intentions, that action almost never achieves its purpose; but it is also because of this medium, in which action alone is real, that it *'produces' stories with or without intention* as naturally as fabrication produces tangible things" (184, emphasis mine).

I said earlier that the turn-of-the-century history of contract consists largely of a confrontation between contractual form and speculative value. From the vantage of Arendt's theory of action, this history looks a great deal like those optical illusions of gestalt psychology that, depending on context, resemble either a vase in black or two faces in profile. In this case, one perceives either growing "islands of security" or a vast "ocean of uncertainty," either a mastery of one's self and others or an "action [that] almost never achieves its purpose." Defenders of "freedom of contract" painted all interference with this "liberty" as an expression of "the supreme sovereignty of the state," but ironically their search for objective market values ranked with Arendt's conception of sovereignty — the attempt "to cover the whole ground of the future and to map out a path secured in all directions." For them, the island became a continent; and their critics, if armed with Arendt's theory of action, might well have seen the soothsayers' attempts to base predictions of future performance on past outcomes as an attempt "to dispose of the future as though it were the present." Contrarily, those who argued against a property interest in the speculator's imaginary goods wanted above all to leave the calculation of speculative value to the uncertainties of the "free (that is, unregulated) market." This arena was marked by incertitude — it "'produces' stories with or without intention" and is thus incalculable — in part because it was governed by the darkness (in the sense of gloom as well as opacity) of character itself. In these "oceans of uncertainty," Arendt proffers, "we [are] condemned to wander helplessly and without direction in the darkness of each man's lonely heart, caught in its contradictions and equivocalities" (237).

The strain between the closures of contract and the open-endedness of deed and action, between paths of prediction and "misty wanderings and hidden ways" (to cite DuBois's beautifully resonant phrase), makes Harriet Beecher Stowe's *Uncle Tom's Cabin* and *Stowe v. Thomas* more relevant to late-nineteenth-century questions of speculative economy than has heretofore seemed safe to assume. Arendt's stories without intention describe what I have termed the narrative uncertainties of the market. Within Arendt's political theory, uncertainty is signified by the vagrant course of all action—"we [are] condemned to wander helplessly and without direction"—and I would argue that in *Stowe v. Thomas* the ungovernable movements of the fugitive serves as a legal figure for this uncertainty. This disinterested agent of transfer poised on the cusp between languages preserves imaginative space within the law *for* that uncertainty, for the final incalculability of value. It is in this light that a deeper exploration of *Uncle Tom's Cabin* seems warranted—a text that, penned in response to the passage of the Fugitive Slave Law of 1850, both criticizes that law's valorization of contract and warns of the speculative mania likely to follow the law's ratification. Better, it is in light of speculation's perceived unpredictability and moral uncertainty that an inquiry appears justified into those fin de siècle versions of *Uncle Tom's Cabin* roughly coincident with the late-nineteenth-century market revolution and into a particular array of festal and whimsical figures in the theatrical, cinematic, and minstrel adaptations of Stowe's text. In retrospect, these figures seem not only to have been engendered by Stowe's earlier legal failure but also to personify the very ludic inconstancy and volatility, pretense and counterfeit, passion and subjective affect of the speculative forms of valuation that characterize the period's credit economy.

TOM'S *PAR ME LA*

Famously, Stowe's Uncle Tom and Topsy (her stereotyped "conceptions and inventions") follow an itinerary as wayward and prodigal as Justice Grier's holding seems originally to have promised; and, with comparable renown, Henry James's florid remembrance of *Uncle Tom's Cabin*'s sundry representational occasions provides an account of this text's circulation that clarifies the cultural consequences of judicial opinion with phrases aesthetically luminous:

> There was . . . I think, for that triumphant work no classified condition; it was for no sort of reader as distinct from any other sort. . . . [It] had above all the extraordinary fortune of finding itself, for an immense number of people, much less a book than a state of vision, of feeling and of consciousness, in which they didn't sit and read and appraise and pass the time, but walked and talked and laughed and cried and, in a manner of which Mrs. Stowe was the irresistible cause, generally conducted themselves. . . . Nothing in the guise of a written book, therefore, a book printed, published, sold, bought and "noticed," probably ever reached its mark, the mark of exciting interest,

without having at least groped for that goal *as* a book or by the exposure of some literary side. Letters, here, languished unconscious, and Uncle Tom, instead of making even one of the cheap short cuts through the medium in which books breathe, even as fishes in water, went gaily roundabout it altogether, as if a fish, a wonderful "leaping" fish, had simply flown through the air. This feat accomplished the surprising creature could naturally fly anywhere, and one of the first things it did was thus to flutter down on every stage, literally without exception, in America and Europe. If the amount of life represented in such a work is measurable by the ease with which representation is taken up and carried further, carried even violently furthest, the fate of Mrs. Stowe's picture was conclusive: it simply sat down wherever it lighted and made itself, so to speak, at home; thither multitudes flocked afresh and there, in each case, it rose to its height again and went, with all its vivacity and good faith, through all its motions.[66]

Familiarly, it is James's preference for colorful semantics and complex syntactics that marks off the peculiar volatility and fugacity of both book and principals, the latter of whose moves to outwit their "literary side" highlight, ironically, the infinite fungibility of the literary as commodity: "Our earliest aesthetic seeds. . . . Careless at once and generous the hands by which they were sown, but practically appointed none the less to cause *that peculiarly flurried hare to run*" (95, emphasis mine). While "letters" "languished," in his words, characters "went gaily roundabout" through various media, "violently" and with a "vivacity" that, he adds later, not only served as the occasion for a "free play of mind" but provided as well "the thrill of an aesthetic adventure" to which he and his cohort "intellectually condescended" (94–95). One imaginative possibility available to James and his associates is suggested by Stephen A. Hirsch, who has more recently remarked that "he [i.e., Uncle Tom] became, in his various forms, the most frequently sold slave in American history."[67]

Notably, given that adapters afforded the minstrel emphases of Stowe's text the greatest amount of "free play," James's "aesthetic seeds" more commonly preserved racial burlesque, the ersatz merriment and darky antics of a panoply of shuffling Toms and hysterical Topsies (James's "wonderful 'leaping' fish") who had been joined in their cultural ubiquity by a cast of fugitive Elizas, imitative Adolphs, calculating Legrees, and indolent St. Clares. James was a customer at the more ribald of the popular theatrical offerings, Phinneas T. Barnum's display of H. J. Conway's *Uncle Tom's Cabin*, which, opening on November 7, 1853, at Barnum's American Museum

Theater in New York, charged from the box lengths behind the first theatrical version (C. W. Taylor's run at Purdy's National Theater on Chatham Street, New York, between August 23 and September 10, 1852) and sprinted aggressively against its strongest competitor (George C. Howard and George L. Aiken's Troy Museum Theater piece, which, on July 18, 1853, replaced Taylor's version at Purdy's). The hustle and bustle was certainly worth the effort in the final tally, for these versions stand out against a sea of parodies, revisions, and thefts, achieving immense fame and influence within months of the appearance of Stowe's sentimental novel in serial form—an immediacy that testifies to the violence and vivacity James recollects.[68] Eventually (and importantly given our concerns), the text's original fame on the popular stage was further enhanced by the turn-of-the-century invention of the cinema (conspicuously not noted by James), with several burlesques, rebuttals, and adaptations following quickly on the release of the first film version of Stowe's text: Edwin S. Porter's *Uncle Tom's Cabin; or, Slavery Days* (1903).[69]

As the first cinematic rendering of the most popular novel and most performed theatrical spectacle of the American nineteenth century, Porter's *Slavery Days* secured an unimpeachable seat within film history, on top of which it preserved much in the way of additional historically significant technical achievements (e.g., the longest and most expensive film to that date, the first film to use intertitles—i.e., titles within the main body of a film).[70] Its antecedent theatrical *Uncle Tom*s balanced antislavery sentimentality against the equivocating antics of the blackface minstrel stage; and, as the cinematic adaptation of Aiken's dramatization, *Slavery Days* affected minstrel procedure as well, perhaps nowhere more perspicuously than when revelry accompanied the rituals of the slave marketplace. We are met, for example, in "Rescue of Eva," by a half-dozen captive persons, who, assembled larboard of the riverboat *Robert E. Lee* (just arrived, we presume, to the New Orleans docks), perform a standard English square dance, prodded along by a baker's dozen of spectators who clap in ordered syncopation with the dancers' steps. In the scene's most abandoned moment of improvised festivity, one of their number break out into a wild and dissembling "buck and wing," and all this before plot has any opportunity to commence. But, then, once the plot begins, and, before St. Clair, Aunt Ophelia, and Eva (the misspellings and misappellations are Porter's) manage altogether to disembark, the latter tumbles from the gangplank, with degrees more purpose and intent than Stowe's original plot had implied, into waiting depths that, despite their resemblance to an orchestral pit, here serve duty as "the Mississippi." Uncle Tom plunges in after her, and, when the pair resurfaces, St. Clair purchases Tom as "reward" for his valor (with the effect that, curiously, accident obscures desire ["I want him."] as the inducement to exchange).

An apposite incursion of mourning into merriment occurs in "Auction Sale of St. Clair's Slaves," where, again, festivity serves preludial to plot. The scene opens with another congeries of enslaved subjects, who, as they await narrative's launch, display a rich anthology of subaltern cultural practices, from shooting craps to jigging and "pattin' Juba" (a flat-footed dancing and percussive use of the body meant, in the manner of call and response, to move ancillary cultural practices along).[71] This economic, bodily play comes to a succinct close when, on the arrival of auctioneer and trader, the sale of Tom and Emaline (again, a Porter misspelling) proceeds with dispatch and resolve. At scene's end, Tom and Emaline, each with one hand in the grasp of their new owner, Simon Legree, kneel and raise the other heavenward in desperate entreaty.

The persistence of plantation festivities and darky antics confirms *Slavery Days'* propensity to wed the market to the minstrel, the torturous to the festive — thematic proclivities that, given the original's established array of tropes, we might describe as "genetic." But the prominence of plantation and minstrel pleasures in advance of (in anticipation of and in contrast to) the deeply recessed sufferings of persons exchanged implies an unusual order of priorities. The film appears to offer two contrasting visions of the production of value: on the one hand, a vernacular gymnastics that produces a species of (pace Pierre Bourdieu) "cultural capital," and, on the other, a traffic in slaves whose particular, ritualized incidents of fungibility preserve "capital" in its most narrowly economic form. Yet to the degree to which the shuffling antics of the film's nameless chattel precede matters of plot, and these preludes appear at every turn to anticipate incidents of exchange, the "story" the film seems intent to tell is that slavery stopped profligacy and idleness, that exchange arrested ludic play — or, better, that the market ambitions of the speculative class transformed profligacy into profit, dance into dollars. In short, when arrested idleness gets read as idleness *tout court,* the "peculiar institution's" states of vassalage effect a transubstantiation of a most fecund sort.

As I have emphasized from the start, what interests me is a turn-of-the-century economy increasingly irrational and aesthetic, ungovernable and unpredictable (what the literary critic Bill Brown designates the "somatic economy" dislodged from a rationalized system of production and remu-

Figure 2. Stowe paid her debts to the minstrel stage with a character such as Adolph, who holds the place of the devil-may-care dandy and suffers an "absolute confusion as to *meum tuum* with regard to himself and his master." Edwin S. Porter's filmic adaptation would add cakewalking vassals to St. Clair's Lake Pontchartrain estate—with the effect of painting both master and slave with the brush of economic languorousness. (Photo courtesy Library of Congress, Prints and Photographs Division, 929)

neration), and, in this respect, what strikes me as significant in Porter's take on *Uncle Tom's Cabin* is both his adaptation's suturing of profligacy to profit and his culminating figuration of that hybrid act in one of the most promiscuously (and contradictorily) volatile and disciplined turn-of-the-century minstrel forms—the cakewalk (see fig. 2).[72] Centerpiece in the vignette "Tom and Eva in the Garden," Porter's cakewalk doubles class aspiration with libidinal pleasure in a tableau vivant whose semantic excesses mime the famed polymorphous perversity of the St. Clare Louisiana estate, screening both the scandal of desire that is this scene's literary though largely inscrutable point of narrative departure and the constitutive indolence with which Stowe charges all slave economy.[73] At the opening of the scene, four pair of St. Clair's slaves enter their master's "pleasure grounds" through an arched opening in one of its famed verandahs. The ostensible last word in tailoring—donning standing collars and swallowtail coat, top hats, and umbrellas in lofty altitude—the couples strut in a figure eight, displaying a courtliness of manner evocative of the "high steppers" and "smart coons" of an itinerant minstrelsy. One couple next takes center stage, prancing forward as they kick their feet high and far ahead of their obliquely angled bodies, shuffling across the screen as the female of the pair flirtatiously dangles her hem back and forth across her thigh, stepping gingerly backward along the same axis, and, in their most gymnastic pose, "hoofin'" their way back across the frame, the man on one knee shuffling backward, as his partner hops, her neck craned precipitously in arrears and her foot poised equally precariously on his remaining knee. The emphasis seems always to be on dissonance, with chest and buttocks thrown aggressively in opposite directions, as if to stress the body's ability (as a kind of translating or catalyzing machine) to wed states heretofore antagonized and incommensurate. As a matter of physicality become semiotics, the echo here is of slave economy itself. Needless to say, this couple leads the entourage off screen in a daintily stylized promenade.

Porter's *Slavery Days* is as much a tribute to the "Tom shows" of minstrel theater fame as it is to Stowe's original novel. Porter's cakewalk certainly pays its respects to the novel's extemporized moments of minstrel festivity, and it no doubt taps into the same cultural zeitgeist as American Mutoscope and Biograph's *Cakewalk* and *Comedy Cakewalk* of the same year (1903)—those "society dances" of turn-of-the-century fame made famous by professional white dancers such as Irene and Vernon Castle (such as their appropriately titled "Castles in the Air").[74] However, its greatest debts are to the vaudeville walks of more recent popularity—of which Primrose & West's Big Minstrels (1898; fig. 3) and Richard & Pringle's/ Rusco & Holland's Big Minstrel Festival (1898; fig. 4) prove the more studied precursors—as well as to turn-of-the-century "Tom shows" such as Palmer's *Uncle Tom's Cabin* (1899; fig. 5) and Al W. Martin's "mammoth production" of *Uncle Tom's Cabin* (1898). This last would see fit to hawk its version of Stowe's melodrama as "the most sumptuous occurrence that is likely to happen," all absent Uncle Tom's piousness, Ophelia's spinsterish wisdom, even Topsy's eccentric antics—pieties that have here been replaced with the sly mockery and extravagant jollity of white swells on parade (fig. 6).

The cakewalk achieved immense fame at the turn of the century. Broadway accounts of the dance's putative origins (Will Marion Cook and Paul Laurence Dunbar's *Clorindy, the Origin of the Cakewalk* [1898]) played alongside Times Square revues (Bert Williams and George Walker's *In Dahomey* [1898]). A minor appearance of the cakewalk in the work of "black

Figure 3. By "puttin' on old massa," the cakewalker proved, like many a speculative financial instrument, the mere "shadow without the substance." The cakewalker violated the
boundaries of class and status (and, before the war, property), which had the effect of representing emancipation as a form of social climbing and the emancipated's subjectivity as an
entirely speculative enterprise. (Photo courtesy Library of Congress, Prints and Photographs Division, LC-USZ62-24432)

musical theater"—Harrigan and Hart's *Cordelia's Aspirations* (1883) includes a number titled "Sam Johnson's Cakewalk," and John W. Isham's
The Octoroons (1895) closes with a "Cakewalk Jubilee"— can be balanced
against the pride of place lent within the "big colored shows" of an urban
vaudeville stage (*Black Patti's Troubadours;* Sam T. Jack's *Creole Company;*
and *The South before the War Company*). There was even a national championship held at New York's Madison Square Garden in 1897, which no
doubt lent the dance an aura of sophistication and cultural authority. The
cakewalk's perfume of class aspiration and satire on white manners lured
even the likes of Mr. and Mrs. William K. Vanderbilt, who, in a play to make
themselves once over out of the stuff of which they had originally been
made, perfected the cakewalk with the tutelage of black theater great Tom
Fletcher.[75] Musical modernism seemed also to crave the cakewalk's racial
masquerade, its persistent dialectic of play and discipline, as even Claude
Debussy penned a "Golliwog Cakewalk" before long. Yet for all its popular

Figure 4. Turn-of-the-century walks such as this one wed minstrelsy and plantation cere-monial. A descendant of the chalk-line walk, the cakewalk permitted the slaves' satiric com-mentary on their masters' cotillion. Master and mistress would award the prize cake to the couple who danced the best; and the absence of both in this broadside would seem to im-plicate minstrel festivity (as well as emancipation) in a structure of ingestion as introjection. (Photo courtesy Library of Congress, Prints and Photographs Division, LC-USZ62-26102)

appeal, it was the dance's appearance as literary trope in Charles Chesnutt's *The Marrow of Tradition* (1901) that sounded the themes of sentiment and speculation, affect and economy in greatest harmony with the dance's ap-pearance in turn-of-the-century *Uncle Tom* adaptations.[76]

In Chesnutt's novel, Tom Delamere (young white aristocrat, gambler, and on-again, off-again heir to his grandfather old Mr. Delamere's estate) impersonates Sandy Campbell (the patriarch's bovinely faithful black ser-vant) on two separate occasions—first, in a cakewalk and, second, in a rob-bery of his aunt that results in her death. Tom's imposture proves as cun-ning as those trickster schemes of animal form and African provenance given artful literary and human contour by Chesnutt himself in *The Conjure Woman,* his dialect tales of that same period (1899); for he was not only "unexcelled in cakewalk or 'coon' impersonations, for which he was in large social demand" but he had also long "regarded Sandy . . . as a very comical darkey" whose similarity to the minstrel stage's various personae implicitly left him open to designs of human counterfeit. (One wonders, incidentally, about Tom's "nigger in the woodpile," i.e., about a possible

Figure 5. Investment: "He became, in his various forms, the most frequently sold slave in American history" (Stephen A. Hirsch, "Uncle Tomitudes: The Popular Reaction to *Uncle Tom's Cabin,*" in *Studies in the American Renaissance,* ed. Joel Myerson (Boston: Twayne, 1978), 303-30). (Photo courtesy Library of Congress, Prints and Photographs Division, LC-USZ62-28514)

Figure 6. The Random Walk of Value: Stowe's Aunt Ophelia cursed slavery for its "shift-lessness," for fostering a type of social character who either "did nothing" or "did not take the most direct way to accomplish what they set their hands to do." The dancers' peregri-nations in Martin's adaptation suggest that it was slaves who exemplified the institution's fiscal imprudence, for their "puttin' on airs" figures the errantry, inconstancy, and efferves-cence of value in style. (Photo courtesy Library of Congress, Prints and Photographs Di-vision, LC-USZ6-520)

connection between "cunning" [OE, *cooninng, coonning, counninge*] and the minstrel "coon's" imposture.) In debt and bereft of his family's accrued honor, Tom parodies Sandy in a cakewalk performed for the delight and in-struction of Northern visitors to the southern town of Wellington ("Tom was merely the shadow without the substance, the empty husk without the grain," thought one character, though another would admit that despite all "[he] can get credit"—in this case, that which has accrued to a black ser-vant described, variously, as "honest as any man" and "capable of a certain doglike fidelity" [24, 96, 99]). Redolent of the very themes of credit and credibility, fugacity and order currently of interest, Chesnutt's vision of racial masquerade deserves citation in the fullness of its poetic insight:

> In order to be perfectly fair, and give their visitors an opportunity to see both sides of the question, they accompanied the Northern visitors to a colored church where they might hear a colored preacher, who had won a jocular popularity throughout the whole country by an oft-repeated sermon in-tended to demonstrate that the earth was flat like a pancake. . . . In order to

give the visitors, ere they left Wellington, a pleasing impression of Southern customs, and particularly of the joyous, happy-go-lucky disposition of the Southern darky and his entire contentment with existing conditions, it was decided by the hotel management to treat them, on the last night of their visit, to a little diversion, in the shape of a genuine Negro cakewalk.

On the afternoon of this same day Tom Delamere strolled into the hotel, and soon gravitated to the bar, where he was a frequent visitor. Young men of leisure spent much of their time around the hotel, and no small part of it in the bar. Delamere had been to the club, but had avoided the card-room. Time hanging heavy on his hands, he had sought the hotel in the hope that some form of distraction might present itself.

"Have you heard the latest, Mr. Delamere?" asked the bartender, as he mixed a cocktail for his customer.

"No, Billy; what is it?"

"There's to be a big cakewalk upstairs to-night. The No'the'n gentlemen an' ladies who are down here to see about the new cotton fact'ry want to study the nigger some more, and the boss has got up a cakewalk for 'em, 'mongst the waiters and chambermaids, with a little outside talent."

"Is it to be public?" asked Delamere.

"Oh, no, not generally, but friends of the house won't be barred out. The clerk 'll fix it for you. Ransom, the head waiter, will be floor manager."

Delamere was struck with a brilliant idea. The more he considered it, the brighter it seemed. Another cocktail imparted additional brilliancy to the conception. He had been trying, after a feeble fashion, to keep his promise to Clara, and was really suffering from lack of excitement.

He left his bar-room, found the head waiter, held with him a short conversation, and left in his intelligent and itching palm a piece of money.

The cakewalk was a great success. The most brilliant performance was by a late arrival, who made his appearance just as the performance was about to commence. The newcomer was dressed strikingly, the conspicuous features of his attire being a long blue coat with brass buttons and a pair of plaid trousers. He was older, too, than the other participants, which made his agility the more remarkable. His partner was a new chambermaid, who had just come to town, and whom the headwaiter introduced to the newcomer on his arrival. The cake was awarded to this couple by unanimous vote. The man presented it to his partner with a grandiloquent flourish, and returned thanks in a speech that sent the Northern visitors into spasms of delight at the quaintness of the darky dialect and the darky wit. To cap the climax, the winner danced a buck dance with a skill and agility that brought a shower of complimentary silver, which he gathered up and passed to the headwaiter.

Ellis [a rival to Tom in romantic affairs] was off duty for the evening. Not having ventured to put in an appearance at Carteret's since his last rebuff, he found himself burdened with a superfluity of leisure, from which he essayed to find relief by dropping into the hotel office at about nine o'clock. He was invited up to see the cakewalk, which he rather enjoyed. But the grotesque contortions of one participant had struck him as somewhat overdone, even for the comical type of Negro. He recognized the fellow, after a few minutes' scrutiny, as the body-servant of old Mr. Delamere. The man's present occupation, or choice of diversion, seemed out of keeping with his employment as attendant on an invalid old gentleman, and strangely inconsistent with the gravity and decorum that had been so noticeable when this agile cakewalker had served as butler at Major Carteret's table, on the occasion of the christening dinner. There was a vague suggestion of unreality about this performance, too, which Ellis did not attempt to analyze, but which recurred vividly to his memory on a subsequent occasion. (117–19)

The cakewalk's disciplines can be traced to the antebellum plantation celebration of the "chalk-line walk" (or "water dance"), a straight walk along a path or "chalk line" in which dancers made their way with a pail of water perched atop their heads.[77] A source of competition, the chalk-line walk proffered a prize to the couple adjudged to have walked the line with the most erect posture and having spilled the least amount of water or none at all. Peppered initially with such longstanding prances and ceremonials of black plantation culture as the buck-and-wing, pigeon wing, ring dance, ring shout, jig, and reel, the cakewalk came eventually to occasion satiric commentary on the minuets, quadrilles, and waltzes of Anglo-American cotillion: "Us slaves watch the white folks' parties when the guests danced a minuet and then paraded in a grand march. . . . Then we'd do it too, but we used to mock 'em every step. Sometimes the white folks noticed it but they seemed to like it."[78] Conscious, undoubtedly, that it was they who were being burlesqued, master and mistress often assumed the responsibilities of judgment and mastery, offering the prize cake to the couple most adept at the "cuttin' of figgers": "Sometimes de slave owners come to dese parties 'cause dey enjoyed watchin' de dance, and dey 'cided who danced de best."[79] The cakewalk's mockery of white promenade, while tinged with a note of irreverent wisdom, sounded a note of underlying rebellion as well; for the parodic slave could just as often be found to layer his affectations with pantomimes of the labor he had for this brief instant been lent a reprieve—mimicking, without tool or load, the acts of shucking corn and pitching hay that formed the theoretically inescapable, diurnal rhythms of plantation life. In form, this dance was the dance of dialectic—a dialectic between play and mastery, volatility and discipline, freedom and fidelity, a display strained between the baroquely "exaggerated" and the rigidly "hypercorrect" (or what the folklorist Roger Abrahams describes as the tension between the "heating up" of nether regions and "the coolness of the dancer's head").[80]

Tom's impersonation of Sandy is minstrelsy's cakewalk chapter and verse, with Tom "dressed strikingly" and "conspicuous[ly]"and his gestures ornamented with a "grandiloquent flourish," all of which, in the eyes of one, made the victor appear "overdone" and "grotesque." The atmospherics here suffuses with "a superfluity of leisure" and the entire spectacle of "the joyous, happy-go-lucky disposition of the Southern darky" is put on as a scene of instruction for "No'the'n gentlemen an' ladies" poised to invest in a "new cotton fact'ry." And while Tom's blackface play on the "body-servant" Tom points, variously, to a black vernacular pantomime of labor, on the one hand, and a minstrel darky's antics, on the other—it gestures, however faintheartedly, toward the themes and incidents of speculative economy. Tom and Ellis's "superfluity of leisure" preserves the vacuum in disciplined modes of economy marked off architecturally by "the card-room"—the arena of speculation's economic twin, gambling. Curiously, the narrator notes in addition that this space is one in which those "burdened" with leisure and time might find a reprieve. Here "time hang[s] heavy"—free from the rational protocols of work, production, and investment (and one need only recall, regarding this last, the prudent aphorisms of Benjamin Franklin's Poor Richard: "If time be of all things the most precious, wasting time must be . . . the greatest prodigality [since] lost time is never found again; and what we call time enough always proves little enough").[81]

In this colony of idleness, this province beyond work, the cakewalk emerges as an odd mirror of production. Certainly, Tom's disciplined performance in the cakewalk itself garners him "by unanimous vote" the disputed laurel; but it is his ornamental and superfluous "darky dialect," "darky wit," and "buck dance" that win him additional financial remuneration. The whole scenario is layered in the dress of usury and interest, of infidelity and inflationary returns, of a crisis in credit that breeds hints of incredulity ("there was a vague suggestion of unreality about this performance"; "the grotesque contortions of one participant had struck him as somewhat overdone"). There is in Tom's performance suspicion of representational disparities, not least of these is that mismatch between a performer's "skill and agility" and his audience's affective "spasms of delight," here brought back into alignment through the seemingly unearned and excessive (but nonetheless remunerative) "shower of complimentary silver." Subsequent discovery of a "torn and crumpled bit of paper" that had "plainly formed part of the wrapper of a package of burnt cork" reveals to all that Tom's story had all along been a cynical play for undue credit: "Tom Delamere, to get the money to pay his gambling debts, committed this foul murder, and then tried to fasten it on as honest and faithful a soul as ever trod the earth" (222–23, 225–26). This "damning piece of evidence" reveals, moreover, that that narrative of credit fraud was, despite all fiduciary incentive, only a heartbeat away from acts irredeemably immoral: "It was but a step from fraud to crime." For my purposes, however, it is Tom's more foppish "step"—equal parts freedom and fidelity, imitation and immorality—that proves a significant figuration of the period's reconceptualization of value, for in his prancing Tom not only takes a gambit at another's credibility but he does so with moves that suffice to balance the debts of a speculator accrued under an unchecked gambling "instinct."

There seem to be considerable affinities between the writings of Chesnutt and the legal opinions of Holmes. Chesnutt's *Marrow* reprises Holmes's *Lochner* dissent. The call, in both literary and legal text, is for arrest, for the informal (or formal) containment and regulation of speculative economies. Chesnutt, having elided Tom's blackface impersonation with his literal act of larceny, disparages all interracial cultural performance as a species of credit fraud. Tom, absent any intrinsic value, detached from "the marrow of tradition" (he was "the shadow without the substance, the empty husk without the grain"), finds redemptive currency in the established coin of the realm—Sandy's "character," or, what amounts to the same thing, the mask of blackness. The critique of speculative economy deploys racial burlesque as its temporary ethical framework and fictional cipher. Speaking in two registers, *Marrow* asserts that, if one is not interested to contain the speculative economy (an economy that consists, almost in its entirety, as in the cakewalk, of a vortex of intersubjective exchanges), then one is open to the egregious excesses of its valuations; excesses in which property exists but in which it can only appear beneath the questionable auspices of theft.

To this point, I have followed a route circuitous in its path, tossing roundabout much like James's "wonderful 'leaping' fish" from literary property to commercial law, from intrinsic value to the "marginal revolution," and from the dissemination of literary figures to the mockery and discipline of the cakewalk. There is, however, a method to my madness. My argument, as this chapter's opening salvos can only have faintly indicated, is that, in the case of Stowe's *Uncle Tom's Cabin,* the plot of the text anticipates the circulation of the text (its logic becomes a chronologic, so to speak)—that the adapters of Stowe's sentimental treatise are "reading" that text for its economic meanings (centrally, for its claim to the triumph of affect in the market) with the unintended consequence that Stowe's figures of wantonness and profligacy offer figures for the fugacity of speculative value. Familiarly, a figure such as Adolph mocks and emulates the manners and dress of his master Augustine St. Clare. Stowe figures intersubjective exchanges that both cite the ambitions of Dandy Jim and other such impetuous outcasts of the minstrel stage and anticipate in addition the cakewalks of the "Tom shows." This mockery, as Chesnutt so compellingly figures it, partakes as much of the poetics of speculative economy as of minstrelsy's predictable stage antics.

Uncle Tom's Cabin provides a "grammar book" in the late-nineteenth-century drama of speculative economy, a ready archive for the era's rewriting of the ethics and values of market exchange. In order to understand the significance of this relation between literature and economy I must consider the historical and legal factors that led nineteenth-century property law in the direction of the subjective and its triumphant embrace of the will theories of contract. I must consider, as well, the theoretical problems of credit (of affect versus rationality as mechanisms of valuation and of the relation between the aesthetic and the economic in nineteenth-century American legal and economic thought). In this respect, the metaphorics and metaphysics of substance with which this chapter began (Holmes's comedic hypothetical on breaches of property and person) are still relevant to our concerns. It is a major premise of this chapter that the economic risks of pretense and prophecy—the turn toward the subjective values of the fictive and the probable—to the degree to which they form the warp and weft of a system of credit, coincide with the vicissitudes of "thinking" and "intending" Holmes claims are inimical to common law. A return to *The Common Law* appears warranted, then, if only because a rehearsal of that text's lexicon of liability will provide us with some axioms in our efforts to engage prospective property in a speculative world.

CASTLES IN THE AIR

The assessment that a wrong has been done for which the law must punish is the common law's measure of liability, according to Holmes; and to determine a person liable, to determine him or her culpable once a harm has been done, "attempt" and "intent" must precede the harm. Attempt is an "overt act," a matter of "conduct" (*Common Law*, 65). To intend a harm, however, is to possess "foresight that certain consequences will follow from an act, and to wish those consequences working as a motive which induces the act" (53). To have foresight, moreover, is to be aware of causality, to possess "a picture of a future state of things called up by knowledge of the present state of things" (54). The probability of a future outcome (the "picture") need only be a matter of "common knowledge"—"not what this very criminal foresaw, but what a man of reasonable prudence would have foreseen" (54). *The Common Law* seizes on this "common knowledge," as I suggest in this chapter's opening, asserting unequivocally that a block of wood is not calculably equivalent to a man and that an empty pocket cannot serve as an occasion for theft.

We can determine liability, Holmes urges, if we follow certain protocols of harm, attempt, and intent. In cases of murder and manslaughter, the standard of assessment is extremely high, resting largely on the harm inflicted but referring necessarily to the original intent. Murder may be defined as "unlawful homicide with malice aforethought," but the balance of liability is always tipped toward the harm done.[82] A finding of "malice aforethought" in the case of murder is not a finding of the mens rea, or actual wickedness, of "the defendant's mind" (62); it is, rather, a holding that the wrong-doer has not met "the legal standard of action under the circumstances" (63), whatever maliciousness he actually had "in" mind. Murder is, thus, a rigorous calculus of unlawful harm and malicious intent, a combination so strict as to produce the comedic postulate with which we began: "To shoot a block of wood *thinking* it to be a man is not an attempt to murder." Intent, imagining, thinking count for little in the law's calculus of bodily harm and "malicious mischief" (65). Murderous thoughts, while morally repugnant, are no more actionable than licentious, covetous, or adulterous ones: "The law only deals with conduct" (65). Similar standards apply in the case of larceny, which covers a class of acts minor and harmless in themselves but harmful (i.e., criminal) if "followed by other acts on the part of the wrong-doer" (66–67).[83] The purpose of the civil law's punishments is always to prevent harms "foreseen as likely to follow" specific acts under specific circumstances (67). Jurists are only to measure the harm of loss of property against the ground of expectation and probability, not actual events—ground that appears precarious except when measured against the thief's necessarily volatile and indeterminate mental or moral state of mind. Innocuous acts may remain innocuous acts, but to prevent such acts from becoming culpable ones the law must act on innocence. To light a match is not likely to do harm; to light it in proximity to a haystack is. To put a hand in a pocket is not likely to result in theft; to put it in stranger's is.

Yet as Holmes repeatedly warns, the thief's innocuous sleight of hand ought rarely to encounter the restraining arm of the law under conditions of "malice" as traditionally conceived (a term whose modest scope encompasses, from the perspective of the law, "foresight of consequences" or what the reasonable man, as judged by external standards, could foresee; again, custom or common knowledge and not, "as in common speech," intent to do harm or malevolence). On the basis then of these examples of law at its extreme, Holmes infers the following general rule, proffers the following judicial compass: "Acts should be judged by their tendency under known circumstances, not by the actual *intent* which accompanies them" (66). The common law, whose many forms of liability "spring from the common ground of revenge" (37), ought remain ever careful to hold its vengeance out of range of ill will, choosing "not [to] punish every act which is done with the intent to bring about a crime" (68). "The importance of the intent is not to show that the act was wicked, but to show that it was likely to be followed by hurtful consequences" (68). Thus, while intent offers evidence that a reasonable person might envision a specific harm, intent is neither prima facie criminal nor in essence morally wrong: "There is no law against a man's intending to commit a murder the day after tomorrow" (65), or against "thinking" a block of wood to be a man nor an empty pocket full. There is no law, in other words, against imagining, no agency to negotiate the whimsies of thought.

Writing in the midst of a debate about the moral foundations of private law—a law that for many was ideally apolitical and whose sole function lay in the vindication of the private rights of individual parties—Holmes sought to banish moralism from civil as well as criminal law through the eschewal of personal blame and individual "states of mind." The common law brooks no quarter for blameworthiness, recklessness, or moral wrong and casts on the mens rea a look of profound indifference (a persistent theme of much of Holmes's writing, from "Codes, and the Arrangement of the Law," published just following the end of the Civil War, to "Privilege, Malice, Intent" and "The Path of the Law," which, though written in the 1890s, sacrifice the sedimented lessons of a real world idiom for a putatively transcendent law of negligence): "The law is full of phraseology drawn from morals, and by the mere force of language continually invites us to pass from one domain to the other without perceiving it, as we are sure to do unless we have the boundary constantly before our minds. The law talks about rights, and duties, and malice, and intent, and negligence, and so forth, and nothing is easier, or, I may say, more common in legal reasoning, than to take these words in their moral sense, at some stage of the argument, and so to drop into fallacy."[84] Not even the criminal succumbs to said fallacy, Holmes notes in addition. The "bad man" cares not a wit for either the morality or the logic of the law; his principal concern is for the "prophecy" that, on certain of his actions, the law will make him bear the "disagreeable consequences . . . of imprisonment or compulsory payment of money" (173). Miscreants seek neither praise nor blame, and, from Holmes's perspective, neither should the law.

> The law takes no account of the infinite varieties of temperament, intellect, and education, which make the internal character of a given act so different in different men. It does not attempt to see men as God sees them, for more than one sufficient reason. In the first place, the impossibility of nicely measuring a man's power and limitations is far clearer than that of ascertaining his knowledge of law, which has been thought to account for what is called the presumption that every man knows the law. But a more satisfactory explanation is, that, when men live in society, a certain average of conduct, a sacrifice of individual peculiarities going beyond a certain point, is necessary to the general welfare. If, for instance, a man is born hasty and awkward, is always having accidents and hurting himself or his neighbors, no doubt his congenital defects will be allowed for in the courts of Heaven, but his slips are no less troublesome to his neighbors than if they sprang from guilty neglect. His neighbors accordingly require him, at his proper peril, to come up to their standard and the courts, which they establish, decline to take his personal equation into account. (108)

The objects of moral scrutiny—intent, imagination, motive—prove too personal, too idiosyncratic, too volatile, and, hence, too great a threat to the law's express desire for stability, order, and predictability. Here as elsewhere—in more studied formalizations of contract—Holmes frees the law from those intersubjective constructions of economy implied by moral philosophy (to which I will turn presently). Any embrace of subjectivity, in Holmes's assessment, turns arrogant what is a fundamental humility of the law ("The prophesies of what the courts will do in fact, and nothing more pretentious, are what I mean by the law" ["Path of the Law," 172–73]). Custom preserves the law's modesty, serves adequately as a "legal standard" of prophecy and predictability. Based in experience, customary standards provide neutral constraints on the application of justice, a temper to the extremes of an anarchic individualism, on the one hand, and potentially tyrannical impositions of the state, on the other. A legal "right," as a consequence, neither includes the protection of necessarily individual and particular "states of mind" (provides no measure for a society to defend morals and virtue), nor does it formalize the powers of state sovereignty (the popular sovereignty and legislative supremacy invoked by continental positivists as the legitimate foundations of all lawmaking); it is, rather, from the vantage of the common law, no more than a legal conclusion, a mere practical and logical consequence of experience. "Duties," Holmes puts the matter some years earlier, "precede rights logically and chronologically."[85] The term "humble" describes the nature of the law. Customary standards—a legal regime in which the duties of all are logically antecedent to individual rights—both underscore this fundamental humility and confirm a lived sense that "a large part of the advantages enjoyed by one who has a right are not created by law" (*Common Law,* 220). Custom seconds natural rights that, ordained by powers greater than either state or man, preserve an interest in the quiet enjoyment of property. A simple example (Holmes's simple example) illumines this modest proposal: "The law does not enable me to use or abuse this book which lies before me. That is a physical power which I have without the aid of the law. What the law does is simply to prevent other men to a greater or less extent from interfering with my use or abuse" (*Common Law,* 220).

Reading as the bedrock of property's enjoyment? The book as "legal standard" of expectation and probability—exemplar of an absolute right to property and locus of subjectivity in vacuo? This is an ill-chosen metaphor, to put the matter charitably, especially considering its being offered at century's end, when the properties associated with a burgeoning finance capitalism found their most apt analogy in this most idiosyncratic object of property and when the rights that accrued to ideas and their expression helped to focus a renewed (but at that point economic as well as literary) sense of the abstraction implicit in property. Doubtless, Holmes has objectivity in mind when he strikes custom as the mother lode of legal order and uniformity, economic certainty and predictability. The law of his era struggled to place market society's increasingly abstract, dynamic, and tumultuous economic operations in sync with legal principles, and Holmes is no advocate of restraint on this score: "For the rational study of the law the black-letter man may be the man of the present, but the man of the future is the man of statistics and the master of economics" ("Path of the Law," 186–87). However, a property standard based in a conception of the customary—in a way, the ideal of a kind of impartial Frostian fence making— provides little help in the near-infeasible struggle over silence as property (the central stake in cases involving trade secrets); a certain impatience with morals and motive restrains, at the very least, efforts to determine whether solicitation of old customers rises to the crime of theft or merely presents one of the many vagaries of competition (the distinction at issue in matters of good-will); and dread of anarchic and inscrutable "states of mind" holds in abeyance those objects of legal scrutiny unique for the apparent purity of their abstraction (prices versus goods as property). Custom, in other words, imagination's principal antagonist, inhibits enterprise and the practices of credit—practices themselves predictive of the risks and profits of distant and future changes to value in the market.

Credit's prophecies appear far more the reflection of a state of mind than a prediction cut from the bedrock of custom (they are what Keynes would describe, near the end of Holmes's tenure on the U.S. Supreme Court, as an "expectation" or "forecast" based on "partly existing facts" and "partly future events").[86] The economic actor in a credit economy, Thorstein Veblen offers in *The Theory of Business Enterprise* (1904), resorts to the market "as a vent for accumulated money values and a source of supply of capital," while his or her companion in a money economy resorts to the same "as a vent for products and a source of supply of goods."[87] The agents of credit economy (the financiers, speculators, brokers, and corporate managers of nineteenth-century finance capitalism) manipulate not consumable commodities but "putative" values in "an interminable process of valuation and revaluation"—of futures balanced against futures, "puts" advanced against "calls," bull options "hedged" against bear options—that is, in a "presumptive" reading based on the "recurring valuation" of present assets against "imagined future events."[88] "The trust-maker is in some respects a surrogate for a commercial crisis [or what Henry Crosby Emery would call the market's '*Konjunktur*']" (*Business Enterprise,* 128; *Speculation,* 108). His business is, as Veblen adroitly terms it, "the business of manipulation," for he wields pecuniary gain by cultivating "interstitial adjustments" between the value of commodities, securities, and other forms of property. His interest is to manipulate the "magnitude" of "disturbances of the system" into profit, to make them as "large and frequent" as possible, "since it is in the conjunctures of change that [his] gain emerges" (28). The trust-maker turns liquidity—the buying and selling of assets "as expeditiously

and as advantageously as may be"—from vice to virtue—his "trust" appearing suspiciously implicated with transient interest, temporary ownership, and putative value (157). Profit is a variable of perturbation in the
credit economy of nineteenth-century capitalism and responds little, if at
all, to concerns of industry's "heightened facility" or the public's "widespread hardship" (28).

Forecast and manipulation, disturbance and conjuncture, trust and tran-
sience, speculators and financiers (or, with measurably less legitimacy,
gamblers and policy players): the agents of credit economy operate "economically with the unmeasurable material of dreams" (*Card Sharps,* 149).
And no doubt, to a defender of objective legal standards, it is only a matter
of time before a speculative market sector more interested in liquidity than
longevity, solvency than service dances provocatively beyond the reach of
the law: "The absolute protection of property, however natural to a primitive community more occupied in production than in exchange, is hardly
consistent with the requirements of modern business" (*Common Law,* 100).
As Holmes seems implicitly to concede, then, the speculative fabulations of
a credit economy contradict (and threaten to undermine) accepted notions
of property, custom, and prophecy. Subjectivity spawns chaos. In short,
the credit economy of nineteenth-century America not only poses a challenge to natural rights assumptions about property (and productivity) as
the ultimate source of wealth but also threatens to render obsolete traditional expressions of virtue.[89]

In this regard, neither the institution of credit finance nor suspicion with
regard to its workings appear as novel concerns to turn-of-the-century
American economic analysts and to jurists such as Holmes. The consequences of credit have been sighted elsewhere. In the assessment of J. G. A.
Pocock, Britain's "financial revolution" of the mid-1690s (a revolution that
entailed the founding of the Bank of England, the rise of the stock market,
the development of the national debt, and the creation of a system of public credit) instituted a diversity of measures that permitted English society
"to maintain and expand its government, army and trade by mortgaging its
revenues in the future."[90] This turn toward a secular and historical future
proved an affront to received conceptions of property and virtue. The ancient function of property (in the tradition recorded by Aristotle) was to
preserve personal autonomy, to provide a prerequisite *oikos* to civic engagement within the polis. Property furnished the individual "with power,
leisure and independence" and the opportunity "to be autonomous" as
"autonomy was necessary for him to develop virtue or goodness as an actor

within the political, social and natural realm or order" (103).[91] Property provided personality with both its extension and prerequisite, conferring an independence that embroiled the individual in as few as possible contingent relations with others. Within this characteristically Hellenistic ideal, property preserved virtue as a form of autonomy in action, protected the unity of personality in political action. Virtue was thus an ideal of the uncorrupt and the incorruptible provided through various mechanisms and protections of the undifferentiated personality.[92] However, as early-eighteenth-century social critics frequently came to realize, the mediation implicit to a system of credit—the alienation of the self-defense of property into the hands of a remunerated and professional mercenary class, on the one hand, combined with a correlate renunciation of heritable property for emphasis on the circulation of goods and money, for an interest in accelerated rates of commerce, on the other—risked corruption and led to the construction of new principles of government and a novel image of social personality.[93] With the emergence of the public funds came the realization that fiscal indebtedness provided both a functional and an epistemological paradigm of a society living by speculative beliefs—"by men's expectations of one another's capacity for future action and performance"—that is, in short, a society adrift from the material anchor of landed property (98). These speculative expectations are not simply beliefs in another's capacity to repay what he had borrowed but the "boomtime beliefs" that oblige men "to credit one another with capacity to expand and grow and become *what they were not*" (as a precondition of the augmentation of wealth [98, emphasis mine]). Again Pocock:

> Government stock is a promise to repay at a future date; from the inception and development of the National Debt, it is known that this date will in reality never be reached, but the tokens of repayment are exchangeable at a market price in the present. The price they command is determined by the present state of public confidence in the stability of government, and in its capacity to make repayment in the theoretical future. Government is therefore maintained by the investor's imagination concerning a moment which will never exist in reality. . . . Property—the material foundation of both personality and government—has ceased to be real and has become not merely mobile but imaginary. (112)

In the world of credit finance, faith in government follows the fluctuations of "passion, fantasy and appetite," forces whose amplification tends not only to be narcissistic but also "to be without moral limit" (112). Credit's prophecies find root in imagination rather than experience (since there is no way of experiencing the future), passion rather than reason (since the latter can ill predict the effect of conduct heretofore nonexistent), and fantasy rather than faith (since even the most rigidly apocalyptic Christian prophesy cares little to predict the volatile fluctuations of the market [98]). The very paradigm of government, both its functional prerequisite and its code of intelligibility, is credit. Reducing governmental stability to financial prosperity, public credit transforms the relations of citizenship—both the relations between government and its citizens, and those between citizens themselves—into relations of credit, relations between debtors and creditors. "The increasingly complex and dynamic relationships and processes we call 'economics' began to surpass in importance the political relations among people, swallowing up the ancient *polis* as they swallowed up the *oikos*" (105). The market's Whig advocates as well as its Tory critics fear for a politics humbled at the foot of "a self-generated hysteria" (113). Sensitive to the irrationality of speculative value (in the case of the former) and fearful of the ontological uncertainties of credit wealth (in the case of the latter), both perceive government and personality to kneel obsequiously before "the despotism of speculative fantasy" (112).

The intellect of the early eighteenth century applied itself to the stabilization of this "hysteria"—to a reunification of personality in the face of that anarchic passion that threatened it with corruption from within. As passion seemed ineradicable and irrepressible, David Hume's *Treatise of Human Nature* (1739-40) founded economy on the distribution of sympathy. In that text, Hume argues that social and economic personality—"our reputation, our character, our name"—follow closely on the contagious circulation of feelings.[94] Section 9 ("Of the Love of Fame") of book 2 ("Of the Passions") of Hume's *Treatise* offers the hypothesis that economic personae rest comfortably within sympathetic arrangements—the hypothesis that, in Hume's words, "the pleasure, which we receive from praise, arises from a communication of sentiments" (374). It is the intimacy of the affective with the economic, for one, that leads those men "of good families, but narrow circumstances" to "seek their livelihood . . . among strangers"; for, more acutely sensitive than most to "being contemn'd" by those persons "acquainted with their birth and education," Hume reasons, the prodigal seeks to reduce this contempt through affiliation with strangers. The prodigal's "poverty and meanness . . . sit[s] more easy upon [him]" when he pursues his efforts in the company of strangers (372). And again, it is the intimacy of the affective with the economic that, conversely, leads those who receive undue credit for their efforts to crave the very approbation the prodigal spurns. Plagiaries, Hume notes appositely, "are delighted with praises, which they are conscious they do not deserve; but this is a kind of castle-building, where the imagination amuses itself with its own fictions, and strives to render them firm and stable by a sympathy with the sentiments of others" (374). ("Plagiary," from L., *plagiārius*, one who abducts the child or slave of another, a kidnapper, a seducer.) What the prodigal spurns, the plagiarist husbands: the tendency for the opinions and sentiments of others to fuel our store of pride and amplify our fund of credit or that fund of beliefs in our ability to attain levels of wealth, power, and satisfaction we had heretofore failed to achieve. Confirmed both by the prodigal's flight and the plagiarist's fictions, sympathy founds fortune. In fact, the circulation of affect is no more and no less than the very trope of credit economy (an early and foundational trope, we could argue, for the inflation endemic to speculative financial cycles): "No quality of human nature is more remarkable, both in itself and in its consequences, than that propensity we have to sympathize with others, and to receive by communication their inclinations and sentiments" (367).

Adam Smith's contribution to midcentury thought on affect and the social, *The Theory of Moral Sentiments* (1759), sharpens this kaleidoscope of reflections and representations. In the chapter of that text titled "Of Sympathy," Smith argues that as we have no immediate experience of what other men feel, as our senses are ill equipped to inform us of how or what another man suffers, "it is by the imagination only that we can form any conception of what are his sensations."[95] It is only through imagination that sympathy can take place, so, when confronted (as in Smith's portrait) by "our brother . . . upon the rack," our only choice, if we hope to represent to ourselves the feelings of the person who suffers, is to represent our own feelings to ourselves: "By the imagination, we place ourselves in his situation, we conceive ourselves enduring all the same torments, we enter as it were into his body, and become in some measure the same person with him, and thence form some idea of his sensations, and even feel something which, though weaker in degree, is not altogether unlike them" (1.1.1.2). All sympathy is a function of this theatrical mirroring—so much so that the mirror of sympathy in which the spectator represents to himself the feelings of the sufferer on the rack (and through which he places himself in the position and person of that sufferer) finds itself reflected once over in the experience of the person who knows he is being viewed. The sufferer, similarly incapable of knowing what spectators feel as they face him, consequently "must represent to himself in his imagination what they feel as *they* represent to themselves in *their* imaginations what he feels" (*Figure of Theater*, 172). "As they are constantly considering what they themselves would feel, if they actually were the sufferers, so he is as constantly led to imagine in what manner he would be affected if he was only one of the spectators of his own situation. As their sympathy makes them look at it, in some measure, with his eyes, so his sympathy makes him look at it, in some measure, with theirs, especially when in their presence and acting under their observation" (*Figure of Theater*, 22). When passion proves irrepressible yet nonetheless inscrutable, best to turn it to good use. Again Pocock: "If speculative man was not to be the slave of his passions, he had to moderate these by converting them into opinion, experience and interest [what Montesquieu in the *Esprit de Lois* (bk. 19) described as the conversion of '*crédit*' into '*confiance*'], and into a system of social ties which these things reinforced; and the reification followed by exchange of the objects on which his passions focused was an excellent means of socializing them" (115).

When economic writers of this period in British history attempted to explain even further the dynamics governing this emergent credit economy, they encountered a market that consisted of little feeling yet of an overabundant and apparently loosely interconnected sequence of valuations, of causes and effects, of wage rates and interest rates, of monetary supply and volume of trade.[96] The minutiae of market interaction appeared to them so obedient to the laws of cause and effect (e.g., a high commodity price can be counted on to stimulate an increase in its supply), that causes and effects were held to partake of the status of conditions; and conditions, no doubt, became variables open to manipulation. These writers traced order back to the human bargainers who incited the circulation of goods and the imputation of value—bargainers who, against the potentially anarchic voluntarism of their actions, seem to converge on the same estimation of value. "Behind this convergence analysts discerned the influence of the profit motive. Self-interested individuals determined value in their bargains; the aggregate of those discrete private bargains determined the rates and prices that prevailed over the entire market. Thus observers concluded that the law-like regularity of economic relations came from a consistent force inside each market participant" (*Capitalism and a New Social Order*, 30–31). The market's internal dynamic appears to be located in (and at all points reducible to) an internal drive within each person. This force equates with economic rationality, that human deliberation of fiduciary "interests" based on strict mathematical expectations, correct equations of market with intrinsic value, and the maximization of profit and satisfaction. Uniform estimations of value betray a consistent force within each market participant. Every person is the same, and wants the same thing(s). Every man, in short, is a version of *homo economicus*. What is more, these individuals have initiated market exchanges so as to maximize their interests, which interests can only be justified through appeal to the self-interests of others. Emulation, it follows, the incessant striving after private ends that reflects a fundamental human sameness (a more precise version of the lawlike dynamic intrinsic to the market as a whole), prompts every market actor "to commit her and his resources most advantageously and, when disciplined by competition, [leads] inexorably to the greatest good for society" (*Capitalism and a New Social Order,* 32). Rationalist determinism, the assumption of an eternal and essential sameness, allowed early analysts of the financial revolution to "explain why the dynamics of emulation and differentiation intrinsic to the market system did not lead to anarchic expressions of idiosyncratic desire."[97] In answer to the market's indeterminacy and the risks incident to credit (a promise of spectacular profits wed inextricably and asymmetrically to a threat of cataclysmic loss), these writers offered an architecture of sympathetic mirrors as the imaginary order so necessary to a liberal political economy. In answer, more pragmatically, to the freewheeling speculation and abstraction of early market culture that had recently led to the moral panics of the South Sea Bubble of 1720 (an effervescence of extravagant financial proposals inspired by the astoundingly successful initial subscription to the South Sea Company) and John Law's Mississippi Scheme of 1719–20 (in which Law's Banque Générale issued paper money, prospered, and finally collapsed under its overextended credit), these writers offered a prudent and honest, rational and informed economic deliberation. These last guarantee the twin objectives of civil society: public welfare and personal well-being. In the idealized arenas of a rational market, comprehensive knowledge and precise calculation preserve efficiency and save value from the volatility, inconstancy, and irrationality of whim and sentiment.[98]

All previous embrace of the economic nectar of affect aside, many nineteenth-century political economists, bourgeois reformers, and reformed financiers—especially those faithfully wed to an ideology of the deep morality of production, of making something and exercising a trade—held to the opinion that the credit economy of America's finance sector continued to threaten traditional expressions of virtue. These analysts of the economy saw no need to distinguish their fear that there were those participating in the economy whose only efforts were affective from their fear that there were those participating in the economy whose only products were fictive (what Aristotle termed *chrēmatistikē,* or the activity of "money making," which is "not productive of goods in the full sense").[99] The speculator, in particular, personified America's newly ascendant credit economy and was perceived to bear an irreverent attitude toward property. That attitude proved not only deeply troubling to believers in a kind of yeoman agrarianism ("who saw independence, rooted in ownership of property, as the preserve of the republic") but troubling as well to those who feared all trade "completely demoralized," in the words of one market analyst, "by its subjection to fictitious speculative conditions" (*Speculation,* 98). Speculation, as described in James Fennimore Cooper's *The Chainbearer,* relies on the "dark machinations of a sinister practice of the law."[100] Law provides speculation with diabolical sanctuary. The speculator, who neither produces for a market nor consumes goods for his own or others' use, is held to have reaped without sowing and to have done so unfairly; for, making something out of nothing, one land reformer accuses, he fans the miraculous fertility of finance capitalism into an achieved yet "unearned increment."[101] Henry Ward Beecher warned of the questionable character of those who received unearned credit, those who, in his words, took selfishly "without rendering an equivalent."[102] Fear of credit's magical ability to create wealth and suspicion of the creditor's idleness were multiple sides of the same currency. In the assessment of Lydia Maria Child, the speculative sector made cozy company with an "unwholesome excitement," which could turn even the most "honest, ignorant, [and] peaceful" man into "a raving maniac!"[103] As Emery warned, finally, the "possibility of making quick and large gains from fluctuations in prices" proved so great that a large number of "irresponsible persons" were led to the speculative market, and their trading could at times seem to "partake of the unreasoning nature of all crowd action" (*Speculation,* 188).

The practices of credit extension and financial speculation were perceived by period reformers and economists alike (as some moral philosophers previously had sensed) to be the product of imaginative rather than physical effort, to be fueled by sentiment rather than reason. Consequently, credit and finance offered patent evidence, in their view, of a selfish and atomistic pursuit of gain that posed an antisocial threat to the public good. Those practices of wealth production gave rise to fears of the insubstantiality and ontological uncertainty of vaporish and flighty profits, gains offensive both to a conception of the market as an arena for the circulation of tangible goods and to an ideology that stressed work as the only legitimate origin of wealth. The fear that the credit economy ran on unreasoning (and hence unreal) waves of impulse and sentiment presented a philosophical and psychological version of the fear that *homo ludens* (man at play) eclipsed *homo faber* (man at work) in the theater of finance capitalism. As the discouraging words of Beecher, Child, and others confirmed, accusations were rife that the speculator affected the foundation of economics and, hence, introduced irrationality into a process protected only (and ideally) by the cautious deliberations of the rational. No more than a gambler to some, the speculator encouraged false hopes for quick profits. These false hopes begat wild passions that destabilized an economy based on rational and productive effort, and this implicit fraudulence was itself betrayed by the sham and counterfeit goods on which the speculator made his living (the "phantom hogs" and "wind wheat" undersold farmers accused them of conjuring, and the "pretended contracts" competitors charged them with making).[104] There was a fear of those who neither produced nor consumed participating in the economy, a fear that those who pretended to resources they neither had nor deserved—from speculators, gamblers, striking workers, and fugitive slaves to, curiously, plagiarists, translators, and copiers—nonetheless received a free ride on unearned credit.

It is worthwhile to pause for a moment to consider Holmes's peers in critique: Henry Ward Beecher, William Fowler, and Lydia Maria Child. Odd company for Holmes, this congeries of abolitionists, feminists, and social reformers (offensive company, in a way, to the pragmatic and morally agnostic legal scholar), yet a nexus made all the more interesting in light of Holmes's own early dalliance with abolitionist politics. Holmes's impatience with moralism and blame marked, in large measure, a retreat from youthful indiscretions he shared with his Harvard University mentor, Ralph Waldo Emerson. The student was, in his own words, "a pretty convinced abolitionist," a youth shocked by the insensitivity of "the nigger minstrels" and the "painfully blunt" "morality of Pickwick," and one so "deeply moved by the Abolition cause" that he thought it his duty to serve in "a little band intended to see Wendell Phillips through if there was a row after the meeting of the Anti-Slavery Society."[105] His "abstract conviction" to serve in the Union ranks (though "borne along," he suggests, "on the flood of some passionate enthusiasm") remains unquestioningly certain—rooted in those "examples of chivalry [which] help us bind our rebellious desires to steadfastness in the Christian Crusade of the 19th century."[106] He reminds a skeptical father, Oliver Wendell Holmes, Sr., "I never I believe have shown, as you seemed to hint, any wavering in my belief in the right of our cause . . . [and] am as ready as ever to do my duty"; yet, it remains "maddening to see men put in over us & motions forced by popular clamor."[107] This tyranny of popular sentiment proved the sting of the "passionate enthusiasm" that spurred him to serve in Phillips's guard. And Holmes, like Emerson, who after the Civil War abandoned the individualism and anarchism of his youth, soon abandoned his flirtation with abolitionism, finding distasteful its appeal to sympathy and sentiment, conscience and morality. In retrospect, abolitionists appeared prey to an "emotional state" that "catches postulates like the influenza"—and, like them, he too succumbed to a "frame of mind" equivalent to "the martyr spirit."[108] Abolitionists subordinated abstract convictions to the "fanaticism" of their own moral arrogance: "The abolitionists had a stock phrase that a man was either a knave or a fool who did not act as they (the abolitionists) *knew* to be right."[109] To take Holmes at his word, we might say that he derived from his Civil War and abolitionist experiences the lesson that all passionate appeals to conscience and morality invariably result in the destruction of a fragile social order.[110] His writings everywhere evidence fear of the anarchic and disorderly implications of appeals to individual conscience and morality. My point here is neither that impatience with morals in the common law makes palatable more ethically suspect concerns nor, even, that Holmes chastises the abolitionists merely for the energy of their righteousness. It is, more precisely, that the legal aversion to "states of mind" and the moral antipathy to "unwholesome excitement" answer to the same concern. Each answers to the problem of sentiment in the market, to the problem of affect in valuation. The problem of nineteenth-century economy is the problem of how the value of things will be determined and whether such value shall spring from the wanton passivity of the "opium-eater" financier or, appositely, whether it shall respond to the volatile strivings of the "raving maniac." In either case, what gives legal scholars and moral reformers pause is the threatened return of the "deadly passions" of avarice, greed, and usury; for what the speculator augurs is the incomplete transformation of the passion of covetousness into the interest in accumulation.

In the financial dialogue of the period, the only way to make the art of finance socially salubrious was to distinguish the passions that seemed to fuel speculation's randomness and volatility from the vicissitudes of "the gambling instinct" (Veblen, Keynes); and for defenders of rational economics, the only way to do so was to (in short) burst the critics' bubble. To

the nineteenth-century inheritors of laissez-faire reasoning, it was not speculative values that were unreal but the bubbles and manias speculators were
accused of spawning. The so-called speculative bubble could not exist in
principle since market prices, whether of stocks or tulips, always reflected
their objective value. The market was, in this respect, "efficient." Speculators, in this argument (which was a mere adaptation, notably, of the eighteenth-century "doctrine of consideration"), simply "discovered" values;
and, thus, when their prices moved they did so randomly (even, at times,
volatilely) because they reflected all information relevant to their value.
(That is, in the tautologies of this argument, values moved randomly in response to new information, which, by its nature, was random.)[111] To believers in the immanence of rationality, the "random walk of value" was not
(as it is often assumed) a response to what the economist James Medbery labels, ungenerously, in 1870, "animal spirits," but was rather a consequence
of knowledge.[112] To them, if markets were efficient, and if values moved
randomly, then the activities of speculators were neither irrational in motivation nor destabilizing in effect.

Contrary to this reasoning, John Maynard Keynes offers, in his *General
Theory of Employment, Interest and Money,* that the knowledge in which
the theory of the "rational bubble" trusts suffers from "extreme precariousness" at best and mania of its own sort at worst.[113] He admits to times
when "the market will be subject to waves of optimistic and pessimistic sentiment" and concedes, further, that these waves are clearly "unreasoning";
yet, they are also, in a sense, "legitimate" where "no solid basis exists for a
reasonable calculation" (*General Theory,* 154). Decisions regarding the future, whether personal or economic, cannot depend solely on "strict mathematical expectations," since the basis for making such calculations does
not exist; thus, those who seek to predict values must often fall back "on
whim or sentiment or chance" (*General Theory,* 163). Crowds of investors
tend to build their hopes, as others have put the matter in paraphrase of
Keynes, "into castles in the air"—a figure that resonates with the drone of
"praises [that are] a kind of castle-building" surrounding Hume's plagiaries, "where the imagination amuses itself with its own fictions, and strives
to render them firm and stable by a sympathy with the sentiments of others"
(*Human Nature,* 374). Speculative investments hold a certain value to one
investor because he or she expects to sell to another at a higher price. An investment is able to hold itself up "by its own bootstraps," as it were—which
conceit feeds the Keynesian creed, *Res tantum valet quantum vendi potest*
(A thing is worth only what someone else will pay for it). The speculator's

labor, then, is to determine how the market will value an asset "under the influence of mass psychology," and he garners reward for keen foresight of changes in this valuation arrived at "a short time ahead of the general public" (*General Theory*, 154). In this respect, the contemplations of the speculator and the tricks and ruses of the gambler are surprisingly difficult to discern: "The actual, private object of the most skilled investment to-day is 'to beat the gun' . . . to outwit the crowd, and to pass the bad or depreciating, half-crown to the other fellow. This battle of wits . . . is, so to speak, a game of Snap, of Old Maid, of Musical Chairs—a pastime in which he is victor who says *Snap* neither too soon nor too late, who passes the Old Maid to his neighbour before the game is over, who secures a chair for himself when the music stops. These games can be played with zest and enjoyment, though all the players know that it is the Old Maid that is circulating, or that when the music stops some of the players will find themselves unseated."[114] When the luck turns, the crack play is *sauve qui peut*.[115]

This uncomfortable intimacy of passion with profit, irrationality with increase, wantonness with wealth informs my reading of *Uncle Tom's Cabin* across time and between media. Before returning to that reading, it may be worth pausing to consider the trajectory that stretches from Hume's embrace of sympathy as the *primum mobile* of economic emulation to Keynes's argument for the irrepressibility of affect in speculative valuation. Passion's sweetness turned sour in the mouths of nineteenth-century jurists and reformers. What started as a celebrated truth of moral philosophy turned into a repressed truth of nineteenth-century reform; and this repressed truth came to be figured as the economy's literariness, its volatility and uncertainty, its ludic inconstancy, its randomness and incalculability. By the time Keynes penned his *General Theory,* the specter of inconstancy was made to obey a principle of randomness explained either as an effect of the inherently fortuitous circulation of knowledge or as the "irrational" yet "legitimate" whimsy that attended all speculative valuation. Regardless, credit's volatility was first subject to the rigors of that dynamic of shared belief and credulity that Montesquieu had termed earlier "*confiance,*" or public confidence, and that Hume explored in terms of the narcissistic vortices of "sympathy." Of the eighteenth-century revolution in credit, Pocock admonishes that "we should be aware of the possibility that different modes of property may be seen as generating or encouraging different modes of personality" (103). These gerunds—"generating or encouraging"—should give us pause, for they imply a methodology in which personality is epiphenomenal and, in turn, betray Pocock's vision of the literary and the figurative as mere symbolic projections of a more historically decisive political-economic drama. One's ability to credit another with the capacity to become what he or she is not—one's ability to speculate—seems nothing more nor less than the ability to exchange with others fictions of themselves; hence, Hume's "communication of sentiments" and, in Smith's enlargement, the *dédoublement* that structures all acts of sympathy and, by extension, all economic emulation. On this insight it thus seems a plausible inference that different modes of personality are less generated and encouraged *by* different modes of property and are more acutely the very performative structures, the very tropes of reciprocity, and the very dramaturgic acts from which these "different modes of property" devolve, out of which exchange (especially the affective and abstract exchange of credit) occurs.

It seems a further reasonable postulate that the economic implications of literature are, in large measure, to highlight the aesthetic nature of all economy, to draw into focus the language and logic that poetic and economic systems share and in such a way (as Kurt Heinzelman has persuasively essayed) as to make apprehensible the ways in which economics substantiates the imaginative—that is, philosophical as well as aesthetic—validity of its discursive formulations.[116] In light of the evidence before us it seems reasonable to draw provisional conclusions more common to the practice of Renaissance historicism, in particular that historicism adduced by scholars such as Patricia Parker and Lorna Hutson. As Hutson observes, "What economic implications literature has are bound up with its rhetorical and dialectical undoing and transforming of the media through which relations of service and exchange had hitherto taken place," which transformation includes the literary's effect on the flexibility of legal procedure in the area of property transmission and credit relations (*Usurer's Daughter*, 9). In this light, I consider one of "the fugitive's properties" that figure's waywardness, that very peregrination of form which in *Stowe v. Thomas* promises to transform the dynamics and dimensions of ownership and to aggravate further the incalculability of Stowe's measures of profit, value, and gain. That legal trope's movements of metamorphosis and fugacity parrot the "random walk" of value and, arguably, on the evidence of Al W. Martin's "fashionable cake walk" (and other minstrel adaptations), provide text and subtext to blackface *Uncle Tom*'s white swells on parade. The slave's wantonness (in *Uncle Tom's Cabin*) expresses not an eternal truth about whites' imaginations or blacks' economic capacities but a historically specific transition in socioeconomic relations in which Stowe's rhetoric of sentiment is implicated.[117] I offer, then, one last proposal. Perhaps the fugitive's waywardness and, elsewhere and elsewhen, the slave's wantonness are together expressive of the "incalculable dividend" of all credit valuation—to cite Keynes once again, figurations of the "whim . . . sentiment . . . [and] chance" immanent to all credit economy—aesthetic forms that capture the "extreme precariousness" of all investment.

We turn, then, to the panoply of forms that risk absorption into the drama of credit economy I have laid out here, for it is on their scrutiny that we clarify further why race remains pertinent in this connection. Again, as in the argument of the previous chapter, this argument has its roots in a transformation in the conception—or "poetics"—of property. What I want to draw into focus is a midcentury American jurisprudence keen to subordinate the metaphysics of property to the contract relation, to figures of obligation, duty, and promising—a jurisprudence that, once again, in the face of governmental crisis, appears willing to recast political relations between citizen and state as economic relations between creditors and debtors.

THE SOCIAL COVENANT OF PROPERTY

In the opinion of Daniel Webster, declared during his controversial Seventh of March speech (1850), all law—from the law of territorial expansion to that of fugitive persons—"stands . . . on the ground of a contract, a thing done for a consideration."[118] Acts of legislation are "the act[s] of men" and, thus, carry with them the "obligations," "injunctions," and "duties" typically enjoined on the parties to a contract (528, 533, 540, 544). Sensitive, perhaps, to his peers' uncertainty as to the identity of the parties to which he referred—constitutional framers or members of the Thirty-first Congress, Northern Whigs, Free Soilers, secessionists, "Young America" expansionists, or proslavery Unionists—Webster chose to cover all the proverbial bases. He urged, first, affirmation of the Joint Resolution of March 1, 1845, for the admission of Texas as a state. The resolution admitted "New States, of convenient size, not exceeding four in number, in addition to [the] State of Texas . . . under the provisions of the Federal Constitution," with the added condition that in "such State or States as shall be formed out of . . . territory north of [the] Missouri Compromise line, slavery or involuntary servitude . . . shall be prohibited."[119] Webster, eager to bracket the contentious question of slavery, admonished his peers to concede one simple point: that above and below said "line" (36°30″ of north latitude) "there is no land, not an acre, the character of which is not established by law; a law which cannot be repealed without the violation of [that]" contract" made between the several parties that make up "the great number of Northern votes [and] the entire Southern vote" (530). When members of the "Northern Democracy" consented to the resolution "their eyes were all open to its true character," and their vote (or contract, or promise) was given "under pledges, absolute pledges, to the slave interest" (531). The members of Webster's Congress had no alternative but "to carry into effect all that [their predecessors] have stipulated to do" (537):

> I wish it to be distinctly understood, that, according to my view of the mat-
> ter, this government is solemnly pledged, by law and contract, to create new
> States out of Texas . . . and, so far as such States are formed out of Texan ter-
> ritory lying south of 36°30″, to let them come in as slave States. That is the
> meaning of the contract which our friends, the Northern Democracy, have
> left us to fulfil; and I, for one, mean to fulfil it, because I will not violate the
> faith of the government. What I mean to say is . . . [that] to wit . . . when new
> States formed out of Texas are to be admitted, they have a right, by legal stip-
> ulation and contract, to come in as slave States. (537)

The parties to the Joint Resolution of March 1, 1845, had left the Thirty-first Congress "to take the odium of fulfilling the obligations in favor of slav-ery . . . or else the greater odium of violating those obligations" (533). To choose the latter course, Webster warned, was to replace "the sense of fra-ternal affection, patriotic love, and mutual regard" with mere "excuses, evasions, [and] escapes" (540); it was "careless" to substitute "fanatical idea[s]" and "false impression[s]" for "a fixed and settled character" al-ready assigned "every foot of land in the States or in the Territories" and "by [a] law which cannot be repealed" (541, 539).

Adherence to "the exactness of [the] letter" in no way contradicted a principled stand against slavery, even Webster's, for long before the meet-ing of the Twenty-eighth Congress to discuss Texas's annexation or that of the Thirty-first to discuss Henry Clay's compromise resolutions, delegates to the Constitutional Convention had guaranteed "the exclusive authority of the several States over the subject of slavery as it exists within their re-spective limits."[120] These guarantees left untouched "historical truths" of antislavery sentiment, truths that Webster repeated in the interest of serving present legislative purposes (525). They included the principled objective "to leave slavery in the States as [the Convention delegates] found it"; the further objective, on the assumption that the Congress held the "power . . . to prevent the spread of slavery in the United States," to execute that power "in the most absolute manner"; and the belief, in Webster's reading, that the drafters of the Constitution "thought that slavery could not be continued in the country if the importation of slaves were made to cease" (523, 525). Congressional legislators could remain both bound "in honor [and] in justice" to ensure these guarantees, and, like Webster, staunchly opposed to the expansion of the institution of slavery: "I frankly avow my entire unwillingness to do anything which shall *extend* the slavery of the African race on this continent"; "I shall do nothing . . . to favor or encourage its further *extension*"; "We are to use the first and the last and every occasion which offers to oppose the *extension* of slave power."[121] Webster's supplication approaches divine reverence, as he imagined himself bound by the burden of prior pledges. "I know, Sir, no change in my own sentiments," he proclaimed—an assertion of constancy and credibility in which he appears imprisoned, yet also, ironically, liberated by duty.

Webster counseled his peers to confirm the Clay compromise, for they, like he, were duty bound to honor and respect the terms of Texas's inclusion into the Union, yet bound equally sternly to honor the Constitution's provisions abolishing the slave trade and obligating the states to return fugitive slaves. "There has been found at the North, among individuals and among legislators," he warned, ventriloquizing southern grievance, "a disinclination to perform their constitutional duties in regard to the return of persons bound to service who have escaped into the free States. . . . Every member of every Northern legislature is bound by oath . . . to support the Constitution of the United States; and the article of the Constitution which says to these States that they shall deliver up fugitives from service is as binding in honor and conscience as any other article. No man fulfills his duty in any legislature who sets himself to find excuses, evasions, escapes from this constitutional obligation" (540). Clay's initial provisions assuaged an antislavery northern conscience by allowing for the admission of California into the Union with her free Constitution and by calling in addition for the expedient abolition of the slave trade in the District of Columbia, as well as for just compensation to the owners of slaves in the District and Maryland. Yet the compromise's drafters were just as intent to satisfy calls to adhere to constitutional and legislative duty (to satisfy southern grievance), for the bill calls for Congress additionally to make "more effectual provision . . . for the rendition of fugitive slaves," for the continuation of slavery itself in the state of Maryland (with the option that slavery may there be terminated if the state of Maryland and the people of the District agreed to do so), and declared as well that Congress had no power to interfere with the slave trade between the states.[122] Clay eschewed consistency of principle in the interest of union. Webster, reciprocally, sacrificed logic on the altar of consistency. He reduced slavery to an issue of "territory"—the credibility of his promise "[to] do nothing . . . to favor or encourage its further extension" having, in this debate, squarely been put on the line. This reduction left him room adequate to argue that Congress could strengthen the Fugitive Slave Act of 1793 without committing the morally abhorrent act of extending slavery. Confident in the inviolability of constitutional vision (the utopian faith that to cease "the importation of slaves" was immediately to attenuate the institution's reach, if not ultimately to shepherd it toward its final demise), Webster appeared to call for the attenuation of the slave market while preserving existing property interests. His valorization of the inviolability of contract reduced the Constitution to a single principle, and one captured in the article that, over the remaining half-century, would serve as American capitalism's holiest writ: "No state shall . . . coin money; emit bills of credit; make any thing but gold and silver coin a tender in payment of debts; pass any bills of attainder, ex post facto law, or law *impairing the obligation of contracts*" (art. 1, sec. 10, para. 1). The result of his efforts ("An Act Respecting Fugitives from Justice, and Persons Escaping from the Service of their Masters" [1850]) reads, consequently, like free-labor contract, like lapsed free-labor contract:

> And be it further enacted, That when *a person held to service or labor in any State* or Territory of the United States has heretofore or shall hereafter escape into another State or Territory of the United States, the person or persons to whom such service or labor may be due, or his, her, or their agent or attorney . . . may pursue and reclaim such fugitive person . . . with proof . . . by affidavit . . . of the identity of *the person whose service or labor is claimed to be due as aforesaid,* that the person so arrested does in fact *owe service or labor* to the person or persons claiming him or her, in the State or Territory from which such fugitive may have escaped as aforesaid, and that said person escaped, to make out and deliver to such claimant, his or her agent or attorney, a certificate setting forth the substantial facts as to *the service or labor due from such fugitive* to the claimant, and of his or her escape from the State or Territory *in which such service or labor was due* to the State or Territory in which he or she was arrested, with authority to such claimant . . . to use such reasonable force and restraint as may be necessary under the circumstances of the case, to take and remove such fugitive person back to the State or Territory from whence he or she may have escaped [emphasis mine].

The Compromise of 1850—one part Clay's engineering, another part Webster's marketing—cut a narrow path between two markets whose differences were hardly discernible. On the one hand, the compromise's myopic abolition of the District's slave trade expressed full faith in the constitutional position that actual "trade" in persons was the sole and formal expression of the slave "market," yet, on the other, taken alongside a strengthening of the Fugitive Slave Act of 1793, the compromise's provisions also lent added faith to the perception that the extradition of fugitive persons occurred independently of issues of market "value" and valuation. Extradition here appeared untouched by the brush of economy, and "delivery" free of the forces of supply and demand.

Webster's crazy-quilt logic proved the object of unrelenting political and moral rebuke.[123] His infinite regression into "excuses, evasions, [and] escapes" of his own design triggered everything from Henry David Thoreau's paean against "Webster's Fugitive Slave Bill" and Ralph Waldo Emerson's 1851 and 1854 addresses on "The Fugitive Slave Law," to Theodore Parker's comparison of Webster to yet another infamous "son of New England," Benedict Arnold.[124] Frederick Douglass, in his 1852 oration "What to the Slave Is the Fourth of July?" assailed the compromise's principal sponsor for his efforts to arrogate to himself the authority of the revolutionary fathers and, with "scorching irony" and masterful rhetoric, answered, point-for-point, both Webster's and his predecessors' inexcusable hypocrisy ("a fiery stream of biting ridicule, blasting reproach, withering sarcasm, and stern rebuke," appropriate, in Douglass's estimate, to the moral precariousness of much proslavery defense).[125] Shall the slave trade rest as a purely foreign affair?

> In several states, this trade is a chief source of wealth. It is called (in contradistinction to the foreign slave-trade) *"the internal slave-trade."* It is, probably, called so, too, in order to divert from it the horror with which the foreign slave-trade is contemplated. That trade has long since been denounced by this government, as piracy . . . denounced with burning words . . . as an execrable traffic. . . . It is, however, a notable fact, that, while so much execration is poured out by Americans, on those engaged in the foreign slave-trade, the men engaged in the slave-trade between the states pass without condemnation, and their business is deemed honorable. (*Douglass Reader*, 119)

Shall slavery rest as a purely state institution?

> By an act of the American Congress, not yet two years old, slavery has been nationalized in its most horrible and revolting form. By that act, Mason & Dixon's line has been obliterated; New York has become as Virginia; and the

power to hold, hunt, and sell men, women, and children, as slaves remains no longer a mere state institution, but is now an institution of the whole United States. The power is coextensive with the star-spangled banner, and American Christianity. (*Douglass Reader,* 121)

"What, to the American slave, is your 4th of July?" he queries derisively (and conclusively): "A day that reveals to him, more than all other days in the year, the gross injustice and cruelty to which he is the constant victim. To him, your celebration is a sham; your boasted liberty, and unholy license; your national greatness, swelling vanity; your sounds of rejoicing are empty and heartless; your denunciations of tyrants, brass fronted impudence; your shouts of liberty and equality, hollow mockery" (*Douglass Reader,* 118–19). In Douglass's wake, there was little left of the argument from "admirable law-forms" (Emerson) and established legal precedent. Few, of course, matched Douglass for either clarity of critique or unimpeachable moral posture. Others certainly provided their own brands of critique, however. John Greenleaf Whittier penned a poem that matched Douglass's "scorching irony" with the venom of an epitaph written before the fact but in the end offered up "thanks for the Fugitive Slave law; for it gave occasion for [Harriet Beecher Stowe's] 'Uncle Tom's Cabin,'" a text that would prove the period's deepest and most sustained critique of Clay's and Webster's legislative designs.[126]

Their subsequent differences aside, Stowe and Douglass at this moment crooned in concert. Stowe reveals, in the "Concluding Remarks" to *Uncle Tom's Cabin,* that a particular shift in public debate compelled her, over the course of fifty-two weeks, to make serial installments of the novel in the Liberty Party and Free-Soil organ, the *National Era* (Washington, D.C.). She has heard, she says, "with perfect surprise and consternation," and from the mouths of "Christian and humane people," echoes of Webster's talk of extradition "as a duty binding on good citizens" (*Uncle Tom's Cabin,* 621). These "deliberations and discussions as to what Christian duty could be on this head" (*Uncle Tom's Cabin,* 621–22) risked conformity with Webster's valorization of contract; they assented to his translation of the rights of citizenship into the duties of contract and secured a level of intimacy between civil and religious community and the demands of the marketplace. "Shall the whole guilt or obloquy of slavery fall only on the South," she asks, when there are "multitudes of slaves temporarily owned, and sold again, by merchants in northern cities?" (*Uncle Tom's Cabin,* 624). This "accession of slave territory" and provision requiring the "remanding [of]

escaped fugitives" had opened "so boundless a market" that all those bearing the brand of blackness tempted "the avarice and cupidity of the northern slave-raising states" (*Key to Uncle Tom's Cabin,* 143–44). The Fugitive
Slave Law compelled all citizens to see the slave just as the master saw the
slave, as "only so many stamps on his merchandise" (*Key to Uncle Tom's
Cabin,* 144). The accounting was rather simple, taking inventory of both
body and soul. "The black baby in its mother's arms was a hundred-dollar
bill"; intelligence would "raise his price two hundred dollars"; fidelity
would add "two hundred dollars more"; and piousness, she proposed, "let
that also be put down in the estimate of his market value, and the gift of the
Holy Ghost shall be sold for money" (*Key to Uncle Tom's Cabin,* 144). "The
probability is that hundreds of free men and women and children are all
the time being precipitated into slavery," poised as they were in "slave-
exporting," "slave-raising," or "slave-consuming stat[es]" (*Key to Uncle
Tom's Cabin,* 144, 173). Douglass warned that slavery had been "national-
ized," that under this "hell-black enactment" the "oath of two villains is
sufficient . . . to send the most pious and exemplary black man into the re-
morseless jaws of slavery (*Douglass Reader,* 122). In Stowe's view, the consubstantiality of nation and market that followed on reverence for such vil-
lainous "oaths" certainly warranted condemnation but what would appear
to her even greater cause for alarm—what the equation of market demands
to "fulfi[l] the *obligations* in favor of slavery" with the "*duty* binding on
good citizens" seemed finally to effect—was an opening of the slave market
to the sprawling modern world of infinite abstraction ("so boundless a market," she portended). The compromise "enactment" gave the nod to the invisible, intangible, and miraculous fertility of speculative capitalism, leaving little to distinguish the inviolability of contract from the violations of
slavery. With ownership separate from possession (the condition of speculation), markets were then constrained only by the limits of the imagination,
given pass to a heretofore "inviolable sphere," with market values that were
then mere indices of the slave's "fluctuations of hope, and fear, and desire"
(*Uncle Tom's Cabin,* 556).

Important for our concerns, *Uncle Tom's Cabin* has been taken as a defense of "private feelings" and what Stowe calls "an atmosphere of sympathetic influence" (624) over and against "public interests" and the market
from the moment it appears in Dr. Gamaliel Bailey's *National Era.* Sentimentality's task is to endow the slave with sentience on the evidence of the
reader's identification with scenes of seduction and violation, brutality and
sadistic pleasure; and the methodological prerequisite to this system of af-

fect is the universalizing rhetoric of "nervousness" with which this chapter began.

> Their sensations and impressions are very vivid, and their fancy and imagi-
> nation lively. In this respect the race has an oriental character, and betrays its
> *tropical origin.* Like the Hebrews of Old and the oriental nations of the pres-
> ent, they give vent to their emotions with the utmost vivacity of expression,
> and their whole bodily system sympathizes with the movements of their
> minds. When in distress, they actually lift up their voices to weep, and "cry
> with an exceeding bitter cry." When alarmed, they are often paralyzed, and
> rendered entirely helpless. Their religious exercises are all colored by this
> sensitive and exceedingly vivacious temperament. Like oriental nations,
> they incline much to outward expressions, violent gesticulations, and agitat-
> ing movements of the body. Sometimes, in their religious meetings, they will
> spring from the floor many times in succession, with a violence and rapidity
> that is perfectly astonishing. They will laugh, weep, embrace each other con-
> vulsively, and sometimes become entirely paralyzed and cataleptic.

Stowe embraces *avant la lettre* what Mark Seltzer terms "the feelings of living property"—quite acutely in what is perhaps the text's most memorable
analogy, that exemplary situation in which "the negro, sympathetic assim-
ilative . . . [and of] a refined family" becomes "the bond-slave of the coars-
est and most brutal [master]," much as a chair or table "that once decorated
the superb saloon" finds itself "battered . . . defaced" and reduced "to the
bar-room of some filthy tavern" (480–81). A baroque analogy, for sure, but
one whose extravagance provides that most important distinction between
person and property—"that the table and chair cannot feel, and the *man*
can." Taken alongside slavery's indifference to sentiment, this fatal distinction makes up, ultimately, in Stowe's words, the institution's "bitterest apportionment" (480–81).

Stowe's assertions of sentiment rise to the status of feminist and abolitionist convention in the novel's ambitious attempt "to bind persons to the
nation [and to humanize degraded subjects] through a universalist rhetoric
not of citizenship per se but of the capacity for suffering and trauma at the
citizen's core."[127] Surplus pleasure and surplus pain rectify that soulless-
ness of persons and fetishistic radiance of things characteristic of slave
economy, in particular, but, through it, in Stowe's view, market capitalism
at large. A nation of affect (an "empire of love") supplants a nation of logic
and rationality, obligations and duties.[128] The letter of the law (in this case,
a prescription that approaches theological mandate) is here unforgettable:

"There is one thing that every individual can do,—they can see to it that *they feel right*... the man or woman who *feels* strongly, healthily and justly, on the great interests of humanity, is a constant benefactor to the human race" (624). "Pain alliances" (to use Lauren Berlant's term) safeguard the citizen against those social covenants of property defended by Webster and his ilk: the inviolability of contract; the ideology that political authority derives from "social contracts" among equal and independent men (which ideology serves not only to preserve a laissez-faire, atomistic conception of the individual but also provides adequate grounds for the translation of the rights of citizenship into the duties of contract); and, finally, visions of the republic that reduce its manifold purposes to the twin aims of the guarantee of property and the enforcement of contracts, enabling those of entrepreneurial spirit "to shape the state to the market ambitions of capital."[129] Strong in its advocacy of sentiment, weak in its critique of contract, strong in its defense of heart and home, weak in its conception of market forces— Stowe's *Uncle Tom's Cabin* is often taken to privilege a domestic reprieve over the rigors of economic critique, to valorize that sanctuary or "separate sphere" (again, in Stowe's words, that "atmosphere") distinct from the sphere of the market.[130]

For certain, it is the inviolability of contract that produces, in Stowe's analysis, those inaugural "embarrassments" (53) of Mr. Shelby that sever affective bonds and leave Harry, Eliza, and Tom valuable in the way of trade and speculation. Shelby's "imprudence," his tendency to "speculat[e] largely and quite loosely" and to "involv[e] himself deeply," estranges his charges "from every familiar object" (51, 104), making homelessness (consider: L., *familiaris*, "of or pertaining to a household") the text's very principle and medium of narrative progression. Fiscal indiscretions leave his "notes" in "the hands of Haley," with the effect that the benevolent and paternalist master falls "in this man's debt," and, in turn, "this man" (who, nameless in his initial description, triggers suspicion of the market's anonymity) acquires "power over him" (51, 89). Furthermore, it is the inviolability of contract that has raised "the catching business," in Stowe's estimation, to "the dignity of a lawful and patriotic profession." Thanks in large measure to the Fugitive Slave Law of 1850, Haley—a recent inductee into "our aristocracy," as Stowe puts the matter—satisfies his desires "to elbow his way upward in the world" (41, 132). On the sacredness of promises made in the market, and the patent blindness of the law of contract "to details of subject matter and person," the word of a "low man" such as Haley (who does not seem "to come under the species" of "gentleman") secures rather putative and conjectural strings of "enterprise" (41, 127).[131] It is this word that assures an indebted Shelby that the agreed exchange shall "balance . . . the debt" (43), the acquisitive St. Clare that religion and "calculatin faculties" (235) are currently "up in the market" (236), and partners Loker and Marks that once they capture Eliza and "take the gal to Orleans to speculate on" (128) she will be certain to "bring a clean profit of somewhere about a thousand or sixteen hundred" (129). It is the inviolability of contract, finally, that has made the price of "carelessness and extravagance" (471) on the part of the proprietors of personhood "hopeless misery and toil" for any slave thrown on the vicissitudes of the market. Through "indolence and carelessness of money" and a general "wasteful expenditure of the establishment," Augustine St. Clare's estate accrues immeasurable monetary debt, whose consequence ensures that Tom shall never find a home of any worldly sort again. St. Clare's indolence and passion for "good times" reads as the cruelty of the illusorily immortal. "Have you ever made any provision for your servants, in case of your death?" queries Miss Ophelia. Without such provision, she cautions, "all your indulgence to them may prove a great cruelty" (446). St. Clare's response—"No . . . Well, I mean to make a provision, by and by . . . O, one of these days" (446)—is telling for its glibly halting and elliptical indifference. Shelby's "imprudence," taken alongside similar weakness on the part of St. Clare, leaves the enslaved in danger of being "temporarily owned, and sold again," of being easily and quickly "precipitated into slavery." The master's profligacy leaves the bondservant rife for the nearest trader eager "to elbow his way upward in the world."

Yet curiously, even those personae whose purpose is to rouse the reader's sympathetic feelings are painted in colors of rampant inefficiency, profligacy, and extravagance. The "self-indulgent" Adolph's "absolute confusion as to *meum tuum* with regard to himself and his master" leads him to be, "to the full, as careless and extravagant as his master" (305–6). "As to Adolph," his effete master admits, "the case is this: that he has so long been engaged in imitating my graces and perfections, that he has, at last, really mistaken himself for his master; and I have been obliged to give him a little insight into his mistake" (270). So prone is Adolph to "putting on airs"—to making "appropriations from his master's stock"—that one is likely to find him moving among the colored circles of New Orleans beneath the absconded moniker of *"Mr. St. Clare"* (321). The inefficient Aunt Dinah, meanwhile, has so "perfectly scorned logic and reason" (finding refuge in "intuitive certainty") that her domestic preparations are performed in a "peculiarly meandering and circuitous" manner and "without any sort of calculation" (311). Dinah's impropriety reigns in the perverse economics of slavery ("Dinah had ruled supreme" [310]). Thus, where Ophelia seeks in Dinah's kitchen "a fine damask table-cloth," she instead finds cloths "stained with blood" from misemployment in the estate's smokehouse ("O Lor, Missis, no; the towels was all a missin'—so I jest did it"); where she seeks a grater, she instead finds nutmeg ("Laws, yes, I put 'em there this morning,—I likes to keep my things handy"); and where she seeks pottery, she instead finds pomade ("laws, it's my har *grease,*—I put it thar to have it handy" [313]). Such impropriety offends Stowe's Ophelia ("But the waste,—the expense!"), the personification of a "domestic economy" that holds "shiftlessness" to be the "great sin of sins," a "mode of procedure" lacking in "a direct and inevitable relation to accomplishment of some purpose then definitely had in mind" (247, 309, 317). The profligate, the prodigal, the inefficient—"people who did nothing, or who did not know exactly what they were going to do, or who did not take the most direct way to accomplish what they set their hands to do"—these people "were objects of her entire contempt" (247). In the looking-glass world of slavery most popular at midcentury, transient interest rivals perseverance and economy, and present enjoyment vies with the secure prospects of rational calculation (echoes of Adam Smith's prodigal). Shiftlessness rivals slavery itself as the "great sin of sins."

Debt, speculation, prodigality: Stowe's moral objection to slavery is on its face the protest of an ascetic, a repudiation of idleness, waste, and the temptations of the flesh—the *auri sacra fames*—which, as Max Weber famously has argued, provides a pious anchor to the restraint and rational tempering of American capitalism.[132] Taking her clues from an ascetic Protestantism, Stowe writes cruelty as "indulgence," thoughtlessness as "imprudence," and obduracy as inefficiency and "shiftlessness." All the same, so readily does she paint master and slave with the same brush of economic languorousness, and so quickly is she willing to lend slave owners, slaves, and speculators an indistinguishable and singular economic "character," that one wonders if all has been deferred in her scrutiny of the institution of slavery, which institution's various political and moral postures abolitionist critics had heretofore appeared quick to conflate with its disparate personae. We would be hard pressed, in fact, to distinguish this antebellum (and ostensibly "antislavery") disdain for "shiftlessness"—or corresponding embrace of efficiency, rationality, and systematic regulation—from Reconstruction charges of the Negro's undisciplined wantonness and idleness. For many at midcentury, the very distinction ranks as moot.

The real issue of emancipation, writes George Fitzhugh, in *DeBow's Review,* is how capitalism shall counter the "crying evil that negroes work too little."[133] The task of the postbellum state is, rather simply, Fitzhugh augurs, to induce the freedman to forsake his "idleness and indolence" and to "become a regular, industrious and productive laborer," in short, "to bring negro labor under the dominion of capital" (416).

> Political economy stands perplexed and baffled in presence of the Negro. Capital can get no hold on him. Fashion cannot increase and multiply his wants, and make him again a slave, in the vain effort to supply artificial wants. How will the convention deal with a being that, being liberated, seems resolved to remain, really not merely, nominally free? How make him work ten hours a day, whose every present want can be supplied by laboring three hours a day? . . . To give the negro emulation, ambition, to make him aspiring, provident, covetous of wealth, competitive, and resolved, at any cost of labor, "to keep up with the times and fashions," will be as knotty a subject as the solution of the Riddle of the Sphinx, or the untying of the Gordian Knot. (416–17)

Fitzhugh startles as the heir apparent of antislavery critique, sharing with abolition's spokeswoman-designate a scrutiny of wantonness couched in language that poises indolence against industry, subsistence against profit, and present enjoyment against future increase.[134] As a problem of character—of "Negro" character—wantonness persists as an analytical category within Reconstruction's "political economy." The racial and economic accents of Stowe's novel seem integral on this score, providing a grammar that soon answers Fitzhugh's queries regarding that discipline that shall "give the negro emulation, ambition, [and] make him aspiring, provident, [and] covetous of wealth."

Stowe might be exempted from making such a spurious bequest on the acknowledgment that her critique of indolence and prodigality is no more than a quixotic volley at specters from the minstrel stage. Without a doubt, Stowe's market transactions (economic spark for her sentimental fodder) readily call to mind the entr'acte stunts of the antebellum minstrel stage. Take the sale of Harry in the opening chapter as one example. Her benevolent Mr. Shelby cries out to a newly appraised Harry: "Hulloa, Jim Crow! . . . show this gentleman how you can dance and sing." Harry croons "one of those wild, grotesque songs common among the negroes, in a rich, clear voice," the narrator informs, "accompanying his singing with many comic evolutions of the hands, feet, and whole body, all in perfect time to the music" (44). Despite these efforts, Shelby remains unsure as to whether the debt has been cleared, and chides Harry further, "Now, Jim, walk like old Uncle Cudjoe, when he has the rheumatism." We learn, in what follows, that "instantly the flexible limbs of the child assumed the appearance of deformity and distortion, as . . . he hobbled about the room, his childish face drawn into a doleful pucker, and spitting from right to left, in imitation of an old man" (44). "Fling in the chap," the speculator barks, "and I'll settle the business—I will" (44–45). A midcentury reader would need little in the way of "thick description" to see minstrel repartee as the exchange that incites valuation, the flow of capital, and the closure of contract. This same reader would need little in the way of translation to see here a Shelby who plays "Mr. Interlocutor" to Harry's "end man"—courtly, stilted, and artificial straight man to an archetype of excess and enjoyment, imitation and indolence. Finally, it is worthy of note in this regard that St. Clare's Adolph is taken not only to "puttin' on airs" in imitation of his master's "graces and perfections" but also to "examining Tom through an opera-glass, with an air that would have done credit to any dandy living" (256). It thus goes without saying that Adolph's affectations mime the studied form and strenuousness of the cakewalk.

Many of the same inheritances can be found in the untutored speech of the enslaved, from the wistful anticipation encoded in Aunt Chloe's syllabic redundancy ("Bery nice man, de Gineral! He comes of one of de bery *fustest* families in Old Virginny!" [73]), to the syntactic arrhythmia of Dinah's heavily consonantal speech ("Lor now! If dat ar de way dem northern ladies do, dey an't ladies, nohow"). Such grotesqueries certainly fell soothingly into ears accustomed to the mellifluous cadences of an artisanate's Yankee dialect, particularly that idiom that Stowe had herself perfected in earlier tales written for the *National Era*, as well as into the ears of an urban working class newly attuned to such popular treatises as "Sambo's 'Dress to He' Bred'rin" (1833) and the prophylactic ditties of Daniel Emmett's Virginia Minstrels ("Cross Ober Jordan"), Stephen Foster's *Plantation Melodies* songbook ("Ring de Banjo" [1851], "Old Folks at Home" [1851]), Christy and Wood's Minstrels, Thomas Danforth "Daddy" Rice's "Jump Jim Crow," and numerous other minstrel burlesques.[135] What is more, Stowe's penchant for linguistic substitution, reduction, and ellipsis captures the essential fungibility of language, that signifying fluidity lost on all but the functionally illiterate.

It is, famously, Shelby's Sam's "especial delight" to "edify" the "various brethren of his color" with "ludicrous burlesques and imitations" of the political speeches he would often attend with his master (*Uncle Tom's Cabin*, 136). Sam lays claim to the "vocation" of orator, in which capacity he demonstrates an incomparable "talent" to make "capital out of everything that turned up"—capital "to be invested for his own especial praise and glory" (136).

> Dis yer matter 'bout persistence, feller-niggers . . . dis yer 'sistency 's a thing what an't seed into very clar, by most anybody. Now, yer see, when a feller stands up for a thing one day and night, de contrar de next, folks ses (and nat'rally enough dey ses), why he an't persistent,—hand me dat ar bit o' corncake, Andy. But let's look inter it. I hope the gen'lmen and der fair sex will scuse my usin' an or'nary sort o' 'parison. Here! I'm a trying to get top o'der hay. Wal, I puts up my larder dis yer side; 'tan't no go;—den, cause I don't try dere no more, but puts my larder right de contrar side, an't I persistent? I'm persistent in wantin' to get up which ary side my larder is; don't you see, all on yer? (139)

Sam's oration on moral principles reads as minstrel "stump speech" once removed and echoes the form and accents of midcentury burlesque, following the latter's linguistic practice as it turns toward mocked economic and political prattle. The minstrel persona Julius Caesar Hanibal's scientific treatment of "satire and sentiment," *Black Diamonds* (1855), is, like Stowe's scripting of Sam's oration, quick to wring comedy from the argot of the presumed economically and linguistically unassimilated: "I hab come, as you all know, from 'way down in ole Warginna, whar I studded edicashun and siance all for myself. . . . De letter ob invite I receibed from de komitee from dis unlitened city, was full ob flattery as a gemman ob my great disernment, ediction, definement, and research could wish." [136] Linguistic alchemy also turns the king's shilling into fool's gold in this "Burlesque Political" from Byron Christy's *New Songster and Black Jester . . .* (1863):

> FELLER CITIZENS:—Correspondin' to your unanimous call I shall now hab de pleasure ob ondressin ebery one of you: an I'm gwine to stick to de pints and de confluence where by I am myself annihilated.
>
> When in de course ob human events it becomes necessary fur de colored portion ob dis pop'lation to look into and enquire into dis inexpressible conflict. It is—it is—it is—to return to our subject.
>
> Dis is a day to be lookin' up, like a bob-tailed pullet on a rickety henroost, or—or, any other man! [137]

Revolutionary rhetoric (for Christy's abolitionist contemporaries, the persuasive script of political mnemonic) tosses about aimlessly on the pre-
tender's tongue. A sort of negative "alchemy"—a translation that sounds
more like monstrous transmutation or, contrarily, more like devaluation
than arrival at a recognized equivalent—is minstrelsy's principle of fungibility, as, most emphatically, the Declaration of Independence achieves
minstrel deflation in Christy's gruesome reiteration (his "nonsense" effect-
ing a certain sense given the original text's duplicity on the matter of slavery). This linguistic economy ranks as a comedic version of the rhetoricians' *agnominato* and *paronomasia* (the play on a word's sound and the
play on a word's sense, respectively), which poetics permits "ondressing"
to substitute for "addressing," "inexpressible" for "irrepressible," "annihi-
lated" for "anointed," and "unlitened" for "enlightened." Minstrel sloven-
liness is only the most visible sign of this negative linguistic operation, for
Stowe's clear fascination with minstrelsy's linguistic economies is represented not only by her characters' *antistoecon* ("Master Sam's suavities," in
which he proclaims "when I study 'pon it, I think de straight road de best,
deridedly" [115]) and *barbarismus* (Sam's further warning "boys like you,
Andy, means well, but they can't be spected to *collusitate* the great principles of action" [138, emphasis mine]); nor is this passion for linguistic imprecision entirely satisfied by her characters' repeated use of figures of ellipsis (Dinah's use of "Lor" in place of "Lord," or Aunt Chloe's "curis" in
place of "curious," or, as in Uncle Tom's remonstration, "I'm afeard you
don't know what ye're sayin'. Forever is a *dre'ful* word, chil'en; it's awful to
think on 't. You oughtenter wish that ar to any human crittur").[138] The refusal of "plain speaking"—the propensity for indirection—is perhaps most
frequently (and most brilliantly) displayed in a surfeit of malapropisms and
puns (Chloe's "particular fancy for calling poultry poetry," or "confection-
ers" "perfectioners" [374–75], or Sam's warning to all the assembled, on
discovery that Eliza has "done clared out," and in errant deployment of Renaissance proverb, that "it's an ill wind dat blow nowhar. . . . Yes, it's an ill
wind blows nowhar" [92, 96]).[139]

Prances or prattle, "comic evolutions" or comic declensions: however
such antics strike the eye or ear—whatever provenance one assigns to
Stowe's slaves' "puttin' on old massa" or whatever insight and irony one
perceives in her numerous references to "Jim Crow" (44, 352)—we are cautioned against exempting *Uncle Tom's Cabin* from more cynical critiques of
race, economy, and discipline on the mere grounds that Stowe chases
(however imprudently) after minstrel ghosts, while Fitzhugh aims squarely

at "freedmen and free men." Such a claim proves weak and unsustainable, if only for the reason that Stowe's minstrel imitation and Fitzhugh's market emulation appear finally to be multiple sides of the same currency. Certainly it is the case that Fitzhugh craves a different mimicry than that paraded on the minstrel stage, seeks a mode of economic emulation based in old-fashioned (dare I say "common law" and "naive") views of property, discipline, and frugality. Yet when viewed through the kaleidoscope of mid- to late-nineteenth-century *Uncle Toms*, whose performance history frames the era of emancipation, there seems little doubt that minstrelsy's would-be strivers are the very economic actors conjured, pejoratively, though unintentionally, by Fitzhugh's witty turn of phrase ("To give the negro emulation, ambition, to make him aspiring, provident, covetous of wealth, competitive, and resolved, at any cost of labor, 'to keep up with the times and fashions,' will be as knotty a subject as the solution of the Riddle of the Sphinx, or the untying of the Gordian Knot"). Fitzhugh's command "to keep up with the times and fashions" is a doubly resonant phrase, then, calling to mind both the sartorial (an Adolph who sports his master's "elegant figured satin vest" [*Uncle Tom's Cabin*, 256]) and the economic (the Negro who needs "increase and multiply his wants" ["Freedmen and Free Men," 416]). The difference between an abolitionist drama of imitation and a Reconstruction theory of emulation is startlingly difficult to discern.

Stowe's translations of the affective into the economic suggest that this premiere antebellum sentimentalist's concern with adverse pain and surplus pleasure masks an ancillary interest in the habits of thought, disciplines and pedagogies, duties and obligations given occasion by the passage of the Fugitive Slave Law. Beneath Stowe's critique of Webster's valorization of contract there appears another layer of economic knowledge, a defense of capitalist discipline and rationality—a defense, in essence, of the virtues of prudence, thrift, and efficiency aimed (admittedly obliquely) at the emerging onslaught of a market activity morally threatening in the temporariness of its interest, in the perceptual dubiousness of its valuations, and in its irreverent attitude toward established social covenant, a defense of discipline aimed at the festal market whimsy of speculation. Here, at points, Stowe and Webster speak in unison, the former seeking by means of an aggrieved prudence what the latter resolves through the sanctity of promise. Yet, arguably, at cross-purposes with Stowe's critique of Webster's defense of the inviolability of contract—at odds with her critique of the law's fortification of the subject's *nuda voluntas*, which, as I have tried to show, leads her into the darkened labyrinths of the slave's own "nervous system"—at cross-purposes with this critique are the very ceremonials and so-liloquies that undoubtedly and unimpeachably, if admittedly unintention-ally, lay claim to minstrel provenance. Stowe's text provides an archive of representations of "the Negro" as *homo economicus manqué* that make abo-litionist aspirations for slave emancipation the very subtext of a Recon-struction drama of speculative economy.

When Stowe commanded the nation's citizenry to privilege a dialectic of passion and pain as that structure of affect that would free them from the law's "accursed principle[s of] mathematical accuracy" (*Key to Uncle Tom's Cabin*, 82), her express objective was to make available for public scrutiny not only the classical phenomenology and inextricable entailment of body and soul but also the final inalienability and nonfungibility of the latter, whatever fate the former might encounter in even the most abstract and speculative of markets (Tom to Legree: "No! no! no! my soul an't yours, Mas'r! You haven't bought it,—ye can't buy it! It's been bought and paid for, by one that is able to keep it;—no matter, no matter, you can't harm me!" [508]). Sentimentality's governing conceit was, through the promise of ac-cess to the enslaved's "private feelings," to rouse in turn the sensibilities of those most callously hardened by slavery. *Uncle Tom's Cabin* opened the floodgates to the "Negro's" interiority—and, inexplicably, out streamed a fiduciary impropriety fueled by reservoirs of passion and an unmeaning lin-guistic creativity seemingly unstaunchable in its burgeoning significations.

But what if, in the last instance, in a kind of semantic frugality, the latter is the only available sign for the former, the symptomatic externalization of its subjective effect? What if the inevitable outcome of the sentimentalist project against "shiftlessness"—an admittedly secondary dimension of that project—is an elision of economic languourousness with linguistic slovenli-ness? What if, for reasons that will continue to escape us, Stowe's professed commitment to the sentimentalist project—her attempt, before all, to make her readers achieve a kind of empathic identification, to feel as the bonds-man, she imagined, had heretofore been made forcefully to feel—at least in-termittently led Stowe herself to see, by which I mean led her to expel from her imagination all those ancillary somatic concerns that had driven her to write in the first place, and to wish to make her readers see, by which I mean single-mindedly to fix their attentions on, those things that, before all, nec-essarily lay between herself and her readers, the only things readily available to both her and her readers, the very words on the page.

That is, what if this semantic frugality led both author and reader to see in all its dense materiality the orthographic spectacle displayed in, say,

Sam's "habit *o'bobservation*" (103) or, similarly, to see (and, hence, to hear), in all its deafening phaneric display, the ear dialect of those boisterous slaves strung along Legree's coffle (*"Ho! ho! ho! boys, ho! / High—e—oh! high—e—oh!"* [490])?[140] And what if that paucity of resource meant, finally, that the most poignant and persuasive way Stowe might represent the moral crisis of slave market activity—an "immoral economy" exemplified by the errantry and inconstancy of slave speculation—was through the indifference to verbal exactitude and effervescently profligate significations of the slave's (not the slaveholder's, not the speculator's) corrupt and dadaistic speech, through the vassal's gradual unlimbering of stable semiotic reference, through the *acyrologia* of the slave's pun. "Poetry suthin good," avers Aunt Chloe to her enslaved cohort, referring, in that pun, both to the words on the page and to the estate's free-range tenants—a fecund production of meaning that she herself had earlier theorized when, breathless with exasperation, she complains, "words is so curis, can't never get 'em right" (375).[141]

CUTTIN' OF FIGGERS

Those impresarios who chose to appropriate and revise Stowe's text seemed to see what she herself was willing to show but apparently unwilling to see. C. W. Taylor, in a pattern others would follow, combined his "serious" hour-long, uninterrupted anti-*Tom* adaptation with *Otello*, a burlesque of Shakespeare's play performed by minstrel great "Daddy" Rice. Arguably, Shakespearean burlesque provided a largely superfluous farcical counterpoint since, in the *Tom* melodrama, Rice stood alongside the comic personae of Jerusha Jenkins and Everlasting Peabody (both characters born of Taylor's pen) for interpolated numbers with such odious titles as "Chorus (Nigga in de Cornfield) Kentucky Breakdown Dances."[142] George C. Howard was no less intent to distill the novel down to the ethical extremes of melodrama and minstrelsy (what one viewer described, ambiguously, as "the most ghastly [horrendous or livid?] of the painful story") when he chose to mount his cousin George L. Aiken's version of *Uncle Tom's Cabin* at the Troy Museum Theater in 1852.[143] Curiously, Aiken made the case for his melodrama with a plot completely absent the figure of Uncle Tom, an omission he strove to make up for, under the pressure of the play's popularity, with the production of a second play of the more emphatically melodramatic title *The Death of Uncle Tom; or, The Religion of the Lowly.* He chose eventually to correct for this omission with the release of a "complete" version of *Uncle Tom's Cabin.* This last made pretense to realize Stowe's work in its entirety by remaining attentive to the very phrasings and dialogue of the novel, yet, despite claims of textual fidelity, added the comic personae Phineas Fletcher and Gumption Cute, along with various blackface *chansons:* "Uncle Tom's Religion"; "I'se so Wicked!" a number Howard wrote for the character Topsy; and "Old Folks at Home," a Stephen Foster ditty popularized at about that time by the Christy Minstrels and (in the Howard-Aiken production) crooned by a shuffling Uncle Tom:

> Way down upon the Swanee ribber,
> Far, far away
> Dere's wha my hear is turning ebber,
> Dere's wha de old folks stay.
> All up and down de whole creation,
> Sadly I roam,
> Still longing for de old plantation,
> And for de old folks at home.
> All de world am sad and dreary,
> Ebry where I roam,
> Oh! darkeys how my hear grows weary,
> Far from de old folks at home.[144]

Foster's lyric resolved dissonances between the mournful and the burlesque by means, familiarly, of minstrelsy's most common metonymy: a longing for "de old folks" hardly distinguishable from a longing for "de old plantation." The melancholia of traumatic partings so perfectly affected proslavery romance as to produce a text whose janus-faced demeanor guaranteed appeal to full well all partisans in the slavery debate.

Phinneas T. Barnum purchased H. J. Conway's *Uncle Tom's Cabin* with just such purpose in mind: to mount Conway's politically ambivalent production at his American Museum Theater in New York in direct challenge to Howard's Troy Museum piece. Barnum promised to represent "SLAVERY AS IT IS" (in mockery of many a slave narrative's title page) and to steer clear of any representation that might "foolishly and unjustly elevate the negro above the white man in intellect or morals." He guaranteed, that is, to offer for public consumption a "true picture of negro life in the South" that appealed "to reason instead of the passions," embracing it in "all its abhorrent deformities," "cruelties," and "barbarities."[145] Barnum's realist conceits took the form of a Shakespearean pledge to "nothing extenuate / Nor set down aught in malice" (*Othello,* 4.2) yet seemed challenged outright by Conway's selective and embellished citation. An auction scene—one of the institution's "barbaries," it was implied—was punctuated by a "Plantation Jig . . . Mr. Gray/Banjo Accompaniment . . . Mr. Brown"; and Conway took great thematic license when Topsy, already a legendary shuffler and prancer, was made to dance in "The Quadroon Lady's Maid's Burlesque *Pas de Trois*" (*Goodbye to Uncle Tom,* 271). H. E. Stevens confirmed the wisdom of Barnum's revision when, two months into the Barnum-Howard feud (in January 1854), he opened his own version of *Uncle Tom's Cabin* at the Bowery Theater in New York starring Thomas "Daddy" Rice and substituting other actors for Rice only when two other well-known burnt-corkers, Frank Brower and John Mulligan, were able to assume the leads of Uncle Tom and Topsy, respectively.

It is in Aiken's *Uncle Tom's Cabin,* finally, that prophetic speculations and minstrelsy's profligate significations commingle to greatest narrative effect; especially in the exchanges between trader Haley and Gumption Cute, a self-described "gentleman in distress" and a "done-up speculator" who serves as minstrel counterpart to Stowe's acquisitive broker.[146] Cute tries his hand at numerous speculations, from a form of antebellum "school-marming" ("keeping school" in an academy for instruction "in the various branches of orthography, geography, and other graphies"), to evangelical proselytizing (or, as he put it, the "Spiritual Rappings"), to contracting as overseer on a cotton plantation (657–58). In all his efforts (efforts, in toto, in his words, "to get bank-notes—specie-rags, as they say"), Cute speculates only to chalk up losses on account of withheld payment, religious skepticism, and accrued debt, respectively. Keen, however, to capitalize on Cute's predilection (absent expertise) for conjectural markets, Marks, the lawyer retained to capture Eliza and Harry, proposes yet another capital venture. A remedial lesson in markets and management follows:

> *Marks:* How should you like to enter into a nice, profitable business—one that pays well?
> *Cute:* That's just about my measure—it would suit me to a hair. What is it?
> *Marks:* Nigger catching.
> *Cute:* Catching niggers! What on airth do you mean?
> *Marks:* Why, when there's a large reward offered for a runaway darkey, we goes after him, catches him, and gets the reward.
> *Cute:* Yes, that's all right so far—but s'pose there ain't no reward offered?

Marks: Why, then we catches the darkey on our own account, sell him, and
   pockets the proceeds.
Cute: By chowder, that ain't a bad speculation!
(658–59)

This lesson in pelf and usufruct is not lost on Cute, nor are the lineaments
connecting fiscal planning and blackface profits ("we catches the darkey on
our own account"), for the minstrel rumblings straining beneath its surface
are given free reign when he sights Topsy, a "juvenile specimen" (in Cute's
view) of the putative blackface minstrel troupe "Day & Martin." Cute be-
guiles Barnumite designs in the following exchange with his new find,
"Stove Polish" (fig. 7):

Cute: By chowder, I've got a great idee. Say, you Day & Martin, how should
   you like to enter into a speculation?
Topsy: Golly! I doesn't know what a spec-spec-cu-what-do-you-call-'um am.
Cute: Well, now, I calculate I've hit upon about the right thing. . . . Topsy, you
   can make my fortune, and your own, too. I've an idee in my head that is
   worth a million dollars.
Topsy: Golly! is your head worth dat? Guess you wouldn't bring dat out South
   for de whole of you.
Cute: Don't you be too sever, now, Charcoal; I'm a man of genius. Did you
   ever hear of Barnum?
Topsy: Barnum! Barnum! Does he live out South?
Cute: No, he lives in New York. Do you know how he made his fortin?
Topsy: What is him fortin, hey? Is it somethin he wears?
Cute: Chowder, how green you are!
Topsy: Sar, I had you to know I's not green; I's brack.
Cute: To be sure you are, Day & Martin. I calculate, when a person says an-
   other has a fortune, he means he's got plenty of money, Charcoal.
Topsy: And did he make the money?
Cute: Sartin sure, and no mistake.
Topsy: Golly! Now I thought money always growed.
Cute: Oh, git out! You are too cute—you are cuter than I am; and I'm Cute by
   name and cute by nature. Well, as I was saying, Barnum made his money
   by exhibiting a *woolly* horse; now wouldn't it be an all-fired speculation to
   show you as the wooly gal?
Topsy: You want to make a sight of me?
Cute: I'll give you half the receipts, by chowder!
Topsy: Should I have to leave Miss Feely?

Figure 7. "I spect I grow'd." A *persona mixta* who violates the natural ontology of being and substance, Topsy permits, like the monetary *diabolus,* the generation of something out of nothing. (Photo courtesy Library of Congress, Prints and Photographs Division, LC-USZ62-2564)

Cute: To be sure you would.

Topsy: Den you hab to get a woolly gal somewhere else, Mas'r Cute.

Cute: There's another speculation gone to smash, by chowder!

(672–73)

Topsy's thoughts on money are an implicit echo of her infamous thoughts on her own personhood in Stowe's original text:

"Who was your mother?"

"Never had none!" said the child, with another grin.

"Never had any mother? What do you mean? Where were you born?"

"Never was born!" persisted Topsy, with another grin, that looked so goblin-
   like, that, if Miss Ophelia had been at all nervous, she might have fancied
   that she had got hold of some sooty gnome from the land of Diablerie. . . .

"Tell me where you were born, and who your father and mother were."

"Never was born," reiterated the creature, more emphatically; "never had no
   father nor mother, nor nothin'. I was raised by a speculator, with lots of
   others. Old Aunt Sue used to take car on us."

The child was evidently sincere, and Jane, breaking into a short laugh, said,

"Laws, Missis, there's heaps of 'em. Speculators buys 'em up cheap, when
   they's little, and gets 'em raised for market. . . .

"Have you ever hear anything about God, Topsy?"

The child looked bewildered, but grinned as usual.

"Do you know who made you?"

"Nobody, as I knows on," said the child, with a short laugh.

The idea appeared to amuse her considerably; for her eyes twinkled, and she
   added,

"I spect I grow'd. Don't think nobody never made me." (356)

Stowe leaves a thin film of pathos dusting the scene, allowing minstrel drollery to shine through her professed interest in mother love and the domestic. It is by means of frequently missed apprehensions, in fact, that Topsy rises to the status of the novel's principal force *for* literalization, a central tool in the condemnation and deflation of speculative economy. The unlettered slave's incomprehension, while it serves as instrument of a deafening dehumanization—Topsy's self-annihilating spin on what it means to be "born and raised"—serves, too, as an occasion for the muted mockery of capitalism's infinite abstractions and limitless fecundity. Aiken, of course, makes capital humor out of Topsy's renowned poverty of intel-lect (Cute: "I've an idee in my head that is worth a million dollars"; Topsy:

"Golly! is your head worth dat?"; Cute: "Do you know how [Barnum] made his fortin?"; Topsy: "What is him fortin, hey? Is it somethin he wears?"). The whimsical slide from Cute's imagined "fortune," to Barnum's "fortin," to Cute's "green," to, finally, Topsy's "brack" makes light of the distinctions between capital investment and comedic spectacle, southern planters and northern vaudevillians, emphasizing instead as its epigrammatic close those irreconcilable tensions between protocols of production and speculation ("Did he make the money? . . . I thought money always growed"). What is given to readers of the novel as "I spect I grow'd" comes back to theater patrons, scarcely processed, as "I thought money always growed," and, largely lost in translation, antislavery critique comes to play a far second to an unmeaning linguistic creativity and struggle with conceptions of money economy. Topsy's ignorance of abstraction (money-as-produce) secures nascent links between slaves and specie, being and substance, persons and property, what Stowe termed, you recall, slavery's "bitterest apportionment."[147]

Yet, it is not for no reason that Ophelia appears shadowed by fears that she might have taken possession of a little devil—"if Miss Ophelia had been at all nervous, she might have fancied that she had got hold of some sooty gnome from the land of Diablerie"—one whose perversion of the natural ontology of things permits, like the monetary *diabolus,* the generation of something out of nothing.[148] To Ophelia's question ("who made you?")—a question whose emphasis on things and persons "made" seems not only to exemplify the era's valorization of production but, ironically, coming from the mouth of the novel's most complacent critic of slavery, to effect the institution's own displacement of the biological onto the economic—to this question, Topsy's response of "nobody" seems the encapsulation of speculation *tout court,* a diabolical generation (making something out of nothing) confirmed in the syntax of the double negative ("nobody never made me"). Though Topsy's punctuation of this famous colloquy ("I spect I grow'd") offers the novel's most memorable mockery of speculation's miraculous generation, the errant significations and diabolical supplements of linguistic economy more often form the very warp and weft of Topsy and Miss Ophelia's figurative repartee.

> "Our first parents, being left to the freedom of their own will, fell from the state wherein they were created."
>
> Topsy's eyes twinkled, and she looked inquiringly.
>
> "What is it, Topsy?" said Miss Ophelia.

"Please, Misses, was dat ar state Kintuck?"

"What state, Topsy?"

"Dat state dey fell out of. I used to hear Mas'r tell how we came down from
    Kintuck."

St. Clare laughed.

"You'll have to give her a meaning, or she'll make one," said he. "There seems
    to be a theory of emigration suggested there." (368)

Or, again, in Aiken:

Ophelia: Not till to-day have I received any authority to call you my property.

Topsy: I's your property, am I? Well, if you say so, I 'spects I am.

Ophelia: Topsy, I can give you your liberty.

Topsy: My liberty?

Ophelia: Yes, Topsy.

Topsy: Has you got 'um with you?

Ophelia: I have, Topsy.

Topsy: Is it clothes or wittles?

Ophelia: How shiftless! Don't you know what your liberty is, Topsy?

Topsy: How should I know when I never seed 'um?

(655)

With regards to the slave's accidental pun, her corruption of the letter, St.
Clare's thrill is the b'hoys' thrill: "I do like to hear the droll little image
stumble over those big words" (*Uncle Tom's Cabin*, 369). The pleasure
here, no doubt, is that Topsy, both a force for literalization ("My liberty? . . .
Has you got 'um with you?") and a force for usurious generation ("was dat
ar state Kintuck? . . . Dat state dey fell out of"), speaks a version of Bakhtin-
ian *heteroglossia*.[149] Her wordplay yields a tension or competition between
two fundamentally different modes of speaking: one that remains a force for
literalization and another that, with equal persistence, in the movement of
the interrogative, remains emphatically outside the literal, emphatically
usurious.[150] Standing at the crossroads between the speculator's and the
promoter's designs, Topsy brings speculation's wanton ambitions and minstrelsy's linguistic and cultural profligacy into an imagined and uneasy
alignment. Unaware of the workings of the economy's financial instruments, Topsy becomes a fecund mechanism of generation herself. She personifies the very principles of finance capitalism—a miraculous fertility
that appears capable of making something out of nothing ("I spect I
grow'd."); an infinite fungibility and asset liquidity ("fortune" becomes

"fortin" becomes "green" becomes "brack"); and, finally, when considered in light of her infamous scene of theft, a rampant profligacy and irreverence toward the established social covenants of property, a diabolical disdain for the natural ontology of being and substance ("I 's so wicked").

Credit economy and punning phrases, Marc Shell informs us, share a disdain for the real. Credit money, those *chiffres* bearing the imprimatur of a creditor's (government or person) promise, those IOUs that hold in an insignium or signature the creditor's "character" (e.g., Shelby's "notes"), disaggregate the name from what it is supposed to (what it *used* to) represent, gold itself: "In the institution of paper money, sign and substance — paper and gold — are clearly disassociated, much as word is disassociated from meaning in punning" (*Money, Language, and Thought,* 19). Credit money — the extreme form of paper money and quintessence of symbolic economy — thus augurs, as Marx held in *Das Kapital,* an idealist transcendence, or conceptual annihilation, of commodities; and, similarly, that untutored speech that spurns referential precision, in the form of either Topsy's punning phrases or her slave compatriots' pidgin locutions, allows for the suppression, if not the complete obliteration, of "original" meanings. Puns break the neck of meaning. They negate it, as Emerson warned, speaking specifically of the idiom of his age, through ciphers (Arab., *çifr,* "zero" or "naught") in which "old words are perverted to stand for things *which are not*" just as "a paper currency is employed, when there is no bullion in the vaults."[151] A pun is a test of literacy, a solicitation to assent to the speaker's multiple and unorthodox loci of meaning. Punning, it follows, like paper money, achieves accidental connections (or, better, drawing on the example of the latter, protean and fugitive connections) between signs and referents, either through the play on a word's sound (through the *paranomasia* of Topsy's query: "Was dat ar state Kintuck? . . . Dat state dey fell out of"), through the mule-headed persistence of the slave's malapropism (taking "liberty" for consumable "wittles"), or through the *acyrologia* (from Gr., "incorrect in phraseology") of that eye dialect that spews forth from the mouth of the aspiring charge ("I think de straight road de best, *deridedly*"; "boys like you . . . can't be spected to *collusitate* the great principles of action"). Such "signifyin'" functions, as Henry Louis Gates notes, as an extended linguistic sign in which meaning is not proffered and fixed but is, rather, "deferred" because the relationship between intent and meaning "is skewed by the figures of rhetoric or signification" of which the texts in the tradition of signifyin(g) consist.[152] These intentional deviations from the ordinary form or syntactical relation of words, he continues, introduce "a

measure of undecidability" into the discourse, "such that it must be interpreted or decoded ['de-ciphered'] by careful attention to its play of differences" (53). The "play" here is of a prototypically deconstructive sort: that
"movement of *supplementarity*" within all structure that remains contingently open and vertiginously ludic on the persistent absence of a totalizing
"point of presence [or] fixed origin," given the absence of a neutralizing
and reductive "center."[153] The force of the pun, in short, is that of deferral.

Expanding on this now classic formulation (the famed "linguistic turn"),
both Georges Bataille and Jacques Derrida after him discover in
signification's "play" an occasion for the reassessment and reconceptualization of economy as it has been traditionally understood. The origin of economics, notes Bataille, ought to be located in the desire for loss, not gain.[154]
Economy begins with surplus or, in his words, "unproductive expenditure" ("life starts only with the deficit of these systems," with the excesses
signified by classical economy's correlate aesthetic and cultural phenomena—"luxury, mourning, war, cults, the construction of sumptuary monu-
ments, games, spectacles, arts" [118, 128]). Attention to the principal
sources of modern economic profit—usury and debt, fiscal crisis and
credit, loss and obligatory surplus—reveals the extent to which passional
gain ought properly to replace the reciprocities of barter in the history of the
origins of economic exchange. Even "the most lucid man," Bataille muses,
when given to the "permissible debauchery" of making wagers at risk of
"the loss of insane sums of money," preserves something of the "states of
excitation" and the unquantifiable "agonistic" excess of this libidinal economy. The strenuously rational investor lacks, at such moments, "a *utilitarian* justification for his actions" (117). Bataille adds: "It does not occur to
him that a human society can have, just as he does, an *interest* in considerable losses, in catastrophes that, while conforming to well-defined needs,
provoke tumultuous depressions, crises of dread, and, in the final analysis,
a certain orgiastic state" (117). This last adjective perhaps overstates the
matter, but it warrants assertion that Bataille constructs this vision of waste
as a challenge to capitalism's myth of its own origins in barter for gain (the
"so-called myth of primitive accumulation" [*Das Kapital*]); for he finds in
the "reasonable conceptions" (128) of both utilitarianism and Marxism undue reliance on restitution and dialectics, respectively, as the *primum mobile* of economic activity. The principle of classical utility, for one, protects
a notion of self-interest that is only valid when made to obey the "necessities of production and conservation," when limited to "acquisition . . . and
to the conservation of goods" (116, 117). In the "closed system" of economic

activity exemplified by Adam Smith's "invisible hand"—which preserves "public interest" through altruistic sketches of "private gain"—economic activity follows, on order, the rationality of balanced accounts, of "expenditure regularly compensated for by acquisition" (118). Similarly, the notion of private accumulation, Marxism's alternative to the fictions of classical political economy, obeys the dialectic of goods subject to value, of use value counterpoised with exchange value. Presumptive of exchange, Derrida responds, formulations such as these take closure to be their necessary (and utopian) moment in large measure because the figure of the circle stands "at the center of any problematic of *oikonomia*" (e.g., "circular exchange, circulation of goods, products, monetary signs or merchandise, amortization of expenditures, revenues, substitution of use values and exchange values").[155] It is this governing motif of circulation that leads to the commonplace that all economic narrative follows an "*odyssean* structure" of "return to the point of departure, to the origin . . . to the home" (6–7). Fatefully, he continues, any law of repatriation is anathema to the felt contingencies of fiduciary "interest" (and we are reminded here of that unfamiliarity, i.e., of that "homelessness" that is the chattel's fate, an impossibility of return that proves *Uncle Tom's Cabin*'s very mechanism of narrative progression).

Both Bataille and Derrida, inspired by Marcel Mauss's study of potlatch civilizations (in whose ceremonials considerable gifts of riches are offered openly and with the goal of humiliating, defying, and obligating a rival), settle on the "gift" as that form that interrupts restrictive and reciprocal economy.[156] Gifts, Derrida observes, refuse the closures of economy, "ope[n] the circle so as to defy reciprocity or symmetry" (7)—gifts presuppose, we might say, following Pierre Bourdieu, "an improvisation," introduce "a constant uncertainty," a certain "charm."[157] Borrowing chiefly from Mauss's assertion that the "ideal" within this economy "would be to give a *potlatch* and not have it returned," Derrida makes the further proposition that, for gift to exist at all, "there must be no reciprocity, return, exchange, countergift, or debt"; gift is annulled "each time there is restitution or countergift" (12). For the gift to maintain its foreignness to the circle, it must impose an eccentric element into the circuits of exchange; this imposition takes the form, in Mauss's phrase, of "an obligatory time limit or term" (Mauss quoted in *Given Time*, 38–39). Thus, the difference between a gift and every other operation of exchange, as Derrida puts the matter, in his characteristically tautological prose, is that "the gift only gives to the extent it *gives time*" (41); this last of which preserves in the gift an excess, an exaggeration, a delay, a (not at all surprisingly) "certain *deferral/differing*" (38).

There is in the gift something more than itself—the sense of being *"excessive in advance, a priori exaggerated"* that accompanies the demand to "return-more-later"—which excess or temporizing difference "sets the circle of economic exchange going" (42). Time, in this formulation, appears "as that which undoes [the] distinction between taking and giving . . . between receiving and giving"; and, thus, because time itself cannot be exchanged, because it remains eccentric to the closures of economy, time works best as a metonymy, as "less time itself than the things with which one fills it," what one does "in the meantime," or "the things one has at one's disposal during this time" (3). This metonymy of time, this sense of the gift as "a priori exaggerated," is the very operating principle of Bataille's notion of expenditure, for the latter preserves debt in glory's humiliations, finds usurious interest in honor's obligatory surplus. Value is more than the ledger's express assets: "Wealth is multiplied in *potlatch* civilizations in a way that recalls the inflation of credit in banking civilizations: in other words, it would be impossible to realize at once all the wealth possessed by the total number of donors resulting from the obligations contracted by the total number of donees" (122). With gift and glory much the same obtains as with credit and capital.

Stowe, like Derrida and Bataille, preserves against her better judgment the very "shell and kernel" of speculative economy, locating in the grotesque phonics of her faithful retainers and "fashionable dilettanti" (137) a measure of credit economy's unproductive expenditure, of its "libidinal" economy. Of course, to see Bataille in Stowe requires that we assume a great many poststructuralist principles. It requires that we accept that the principle effect of a traffic in gifts (what distinguishes gift exchange from the simple exchange of goods) is the circulation of time, and that, on the obligations that accrue to the gift, time serves as a metonymy, as that form that holds the giver's glory and the recipient's humiliation. It requires that we accept the analogy implied in the paragraphs above, between an archaic mode of exchange and modern credit economy, which analogy precedes recognition of an identity between the gratuitous "'interest' in considerable losses" and that gratuity that fuels credit economy, keeping the latter endlessly fecund and its closure endlessly delayed. And, on acceptance of these two rather complex formulations, it then makes sense to return gift to the logic of credit, for reasons that the process of circulating gifts contains a specificity (term, time, "interest"), which remains pertinent to cold economic rationality. And, finally, these premises can reasonably be held in alignment with the insight of Marc Shell that punning dialect serves adequate as the literary form that most forcefully foregrounds the deferral of meaning, the noncommittal relation to a referent, and that this semiosis is shared by literature and economy alike.

If we accept these propositions, then my earlier suspicion that the syllabic idiocies of Stowe's wayward vassals are the symptomatic externalization of the speculative economy's subjective effect appears warranted. Nonsense, we come to see, serves not only as the indicia of a meaning deferred; uttered within the confines of the various texts of *Uncle Tom's Cabin,* the nonsensical is both the sign and the very substance of irrationality itself. Syntactic arrhythmia, nonsense phrasings, grotesque utterances are a metonymy for "intuitive certainty" and for the errantry, expiation, and excitation of a bevy of indolent laborers. Subjects of sentiment and objects of empathy, the idle vassals of Stowe's *Uncle Tom's Cabin* offer aesthetic figures for credit economy. Their speech's "shiftlessness" thickens the speculator's profiteering and the fiscal "imprudence," "carelessness and extravagance," and "wasteful expenditure" of the novel's various plantation topoi. Linguistic imprecision is the sign for that "indirection" of motives Ophelia most feared—sign for obeisance to passion, for the will's "desire" to "steal away" from the dominion of reason. In essence, punning's fugacity is a sign for the peculiar fecundity of the slave's market circulation. We are reminded here of Ralph Ellison's remarks regarding the "'darky' entertainer" who embraces the blackface mask in catharsis and with "relish": "Motives of race, status, economics and guilt are always clustered here."[158]

We are at last in a position to start bringing this chapter to a close, and so it now seems appropriate to reconsider the text that originally led me to suspect that Stowe's *Uncle Tom's Cabin* provided a medium through which, over the latter decades of the nineteenth century, a plethora of speculative instruments and mechanisms acquired a certain historical density and dramaturgic intensity, a particular way of working through textuality, and a peculiar means of personifying (i.e., performing) that form of textuality that was its subjective and passionate "property": Edwin S. Porter's *Uncle Tom's Cabin; or, Slavery Days.* Unfortunately, on the matter of Porter's adaptation, there is a problem. Where we find word play in Stowe's original novel, Porter's *Slavery Days* greets us with not a word of speech. Porter and Edison, *silent* filmmakers, have not a single pun with which to work; thus, it would seem that, in order to tap the residual energies of blackface minstrelsy, they would have had to mine (and "mime") them otherwise. If we reconsider some of what I have said to this point on the matter of economy, this embedded strategy should, with little additional effort, begin to reveal itself to us.

I have just suggested that, in *Uncle Tom's Cabin,* slaves stand alongside slaveholders and speculators as figures of fiscal and linguistic "imprudence"; and, in my discussion of the economic "character" that circulates among them, I have called specific attention to the slaves' linguistic imprecision and to what I saw as an analogy between punning and usury. In this last connection, linguistic "nonsense" serves as the most oft-encountered sign of fiduciary impropriety; the slaves' linguistic imprecision provides, as I put it, the symptomatic externalization of the economy's subjective effects. And if we think back to my discussion of the crisis of speculation, we see how this analogy (which is, finally, a relation of poetics to property) had ramifications in the culture at large. The turn-of-the-century crisis of speculation was one in which some, faced with the fragility of subjectivity as a basis for valuation, took recourse in rationalist determinism (in the claim, rooted in the classical political economy of Adam Smith, to an eternal and essential sameness), while others, conceding a certain place to rationality and deliberation in the market, conceded, moreover, to legitimate and necessary, though analytically dubious, "waves of optimistic and pessimistic sentiment." The case of *Chicago v. Christie* provides us with one instance of this dubious economic effect. Taking recourse in the fugacity of speculative value, the majority in *Chicago* protected the production of phantom goods out of units of time and bits of information as "the self-adjustment of society to the probable" and did so by assigning to speculation the character of a "creative faculty" akin to the production of literary ideas. In *Stowe v. Thomas* (cited, ironically, for the plaintiff in *Chicago*), the majority, through an errant "Uncle Tom and Topsy," conjured forth a disinterested agent of transfer and figured the errantry of value in the ungovernable and unpredictable movements of the fugitive—and in *Chicago*'s extension of this logic to the defendant, textual circulation tamed fears of credit, of principles of exchange that solicit passion and belief.

I have said, too, that the cakewalk was marked, more often than not, by a certain semantic excess; and, if we think back to that discussion, it appears that the cakewalk's particular translation of rhetoric into gesture, motion into kinesics would read as follows. The cakewalker's burlesques are gestural and performative adjuncts to the rhetorical trope of *antanaclasis* (Gr., "reflection, bending back"), a homonymic pun in which one word is used in two contrasting, usually comic, senses (as, e.g., when a men's clothing store advertises "Law suits our specialty"). The cakewalker offers a satiric performance whose linguistic breadth between literal labor and poetic flourish—the slave's application of *dire* and *vouloir dire*—represents a "version" of emancipation commonly referred to, in other quarters, as "signifyin(g)."[159] That said, it is in and through the minstrel stage antics of Zip Coon, Sambo, and Dandy Jim, personifications of the Negro's putative self-promoting and gaudily imitative nature, that from mid- to late-century the cakewalk would serve more popularly as a significant point of white commentary on black affectation of the former's manners and customs. The play here, arguably, is classically rhetorical (the master's *recipricatio*), an effort to "trope-a-trope" (if we might signify on Henry Louis Gates, Jr.), to make a final bid for appropriation through mastery of the "slave's trope." The cakewalk's dynamic of "playing *at*" (of emulation with a slight note of mockery, of imitation with an element of usurious interest) is what has always interested me, finally; and, importantly, the consequence of the dissemination of this cultural form is something like the deontologization of its putatively "authentic" and "originary" value, the evaporation of its gestures into a nimbus of interracial reflections and imitations.

Putting these insights together—the first concerning economy, the second kinesics—with my analysis of the structure of the film, and, in particular, its structure of improvised abandon and mournful plot (of abandon as logically prior and an inducement to plot, to slavery's plots of exchange), leads me to the following conclusion. On the assumption that, in the turn-of-the-century discourse of credit economy, a narrative of rational bourgeois acquisitiveness (*homo economicus*) was wed precariously to belief in the irrepressibility of affect in valuation, that is, on the assumption that credit is marked by a structure of internal difference, the effluvia of blackness serve as the sign of this difference, as the marker of speculative "interest." What is more, the structure of *Uncle Tom's Cabin; or, Slavery Days* displays this peculiar imbrication of whimsy in rationality. In *Slavery Days,* the received drama of Uncle Tom attains to the status of diegesis, defined as the posited events and characters of a narrative taken, as it were, "in themselves," without reference to their discursive mediation, that is, "the story as it is received and felt by the spectator."[160] Diegesis, or an emphasis on preexisting knowledge of Uncle Tom and his ilk, is confirmed by intertitles that, preceding each scene, do not so much "tell" the story as coax it from the sanctuaries of memory ("Eliza Pleads with Tom to Run Away"; "Phineas Outwits the Slave Traders"; "The Escape of Eliza"; "The Welcome Home of St. Clair, Eva, Aunt Ophelia and Uncle Tom"; "Tom and Eva in the Garden"; "Death of Eva"; "St. Clair Defends Uncle Tom"; "Auction Sale of St. Clair's Slaves"; "Tom Refuses to Flog Emaline"; "Marks Avenges Death's [*sic*] of St. Clair and Uncle Tom"; "Tableau. Death of Tom"). To the contrary, then, the film's cautiously delineated darky antics, positioned as they are in anticipation of plot, take on a more primary narrational function. The film's improvised moments of festivity operate, it seems reasonable to conclude, from this end of the twentieth century, much like the "song and dance" numbers in the genre of the musical—"fun and frolic," that is, rise to the status of the "extradiegetic" ("the primary agency responsible for relating events, it is always exterior and logically prior to the fictional world itself, which it encloses").[161]

I said earlier that to cut the border between narrative and play in this way (to cut it here, at the convergence of mourning and merriment) enforces a certain economic plot onto *Uncle Tom's Cabin:* that plot in which it appears that a speculative slavery transformed profligacy into profit, dance into dollars. However, if we consider the film's particular layering of the cakewalk's antics onto sentimental narrative, another possibility awaits. To move from received, disciplining story into the whimsy and pleasures of extradiegetic abandon is tantamount, in this instance, to stepping out of plot and into economy, out of a tale of discipline and bourgeois acquisitiveness (i.e., *homo economicus,* primitive accumulation, the "invisible hand") and into the festivity and merriment, the inconstancy and volatility of credit economy. Recall, a society living by speculative beliefs was one in which men thrived on the expectation of one another's capacity for future action and performance, one that lived by faith in men "to credit one another with the capacity to expand and grow and become *what they were not*" (*Virtue, Commerce, and History,* 98, emphasis mine). The cakewalk's vortex of imitations, its governing principle of "playing at" (*recipricatio, antanaclasis*), and all with a necessary gratuity, captures the essence of this inflationary economy. For whites to play at being blacks playing at being white (or, vice versa, if one might still at this point believe in an origin to this revel's nimbus of reflections, to its mirror of production); this is what it means for an economy to be grounded in a "meeting of minds"; this is what it means to "credit" others with the capacity to become "what they were not"; this is what it means for blackness to serve as a sign of internal difference, of difference from oneself.

Sine Qua Non

All this, with what preceded, and what followed, occurred with such involutions of rapidity, that past, present, and future seemed one.

HERMAN MELVILLE, *BENITO CERENO* (1856)

CHAPTER THREE

Counterfactuals, Causation, and the Tenses of "Separate but Equal"

> We are beggars in these respects. . . . Our only national melody, Yankee Doodle,
> is shrewdly suspected to be a scion from British art. All symptoms of invention
> are confined to the African race, who, like the German literati, are relieved by
> their position from the cares of government. "Jump Jim Crow," is a dance native
> to this country, and one which we plead guilty to seeing with pleasure, not on
> the stage, where we have not seen it, but as danced by children of an ebon hue
> in the street. Such of the African melodies as we have heard are beautiful. But
> the Caucasian race have yet their rail-roads to make.
>
> MARGARET FULLER, "ENTERTAINMENTS OF THE PAST WINTER"
> (1842)

IN PLAIN BLACK AND WHITE

It is a better-than-even bet that Margaret Fuller had pass within her hearing,
on some occasion during "the past winter," budding qualification of railway coaches beneath the adjectival marker "Jim Crow." Adept on "woman
in the nineteenth century" and denizen of many a Cambridge salon, Fuller
no doubt possessed an astute sensitivity to transformations in social code;
and, thus, we can presume she knew that, in Massachusetts, in the year just
prior to her publication of "Entertainments," ministers of that industry
found fit to wrest Thomas Danforth Rice's infamous "Jim Crow" appella-
tion from its minstrel deployments and apply the same to the railroad's segregated travel compartments.[1] On the face of it, Fuller's reflections on
American culture—on cultural privation matched by a guilt borne of surreptitious witness—fall just short of that tidy figuration of "'Jim Crow' segregation" by which, in the rhetorical nonchalance of century's end, Americans would come to associate their experiences in the public sphere. Yet so

closely does she come to such an alignment, her words deserve some attention for the contradictions and incommensurable differences that they do manage to draw into an imagined (if uneasy) alliance. What I have to suggest is that, oddly enough, reflections on seasons past affect the work of a profoundly dark augury. Fuller's assertion that "the African race" had been "relieved by their position from the cares of government" certainly lends a benign cast to slavery's dispossessions, proving an article of bad faith; but her claim also finds resonance later in the century in the various disfranchisement maneuvers that, following Reconstruction, served assuredly to divest the recently emancipated of any significant role in (though not any passionate care for) government. And, though Fuller's elision of vernacular American culture with the counterfeit of blackface minstrelsy betrays an occult formation familiar to most (then and now), interesting to consider, in addition, are the ways in which she marks Africans and Africanness with the stamp of invention. Interesting, too, is her added concession that "the Caucasian race have yet their rail-roads to make."

The peculiarity of this last should not go unremarked, as it proffers a vision of the future that correlates with Fuller's allusion to the African's immunity from the *vita civile*. With a single stroke of the pen, Fuller achieves a multitude of ends: on the one hand, she assimilates "the African race" to "symptoms of invention," while, on the other, she exempts Anglo America and the railroad from any similar inventive purpose. In retrospect, not only can we say that the railroad has captured for the better part of America's history the country's passion for mobility, but also we can claim that it has satisfied an equally fervent passion for invention. Certainly, few nineteenth-century technologies rival the railroad for the satisfying manner with which it combined desires for mobility and inventiveness, desires that would become "national" before long.[2] Still, it seems odd how easily Fuller distinguishes culture from technology or, drawing on the language of the first chapter (recall Blind Tom), the aesthetic from the mechanical since, from the perspective offered by subsequent practice of racial segregation, and, given our current vogue for the concept of "machine culture," the two seem so intimately and eternally conjoined.[3]

Some of what motivates Fuller's discriminations can be found in contemporaneous deployments of the symbolically weighty image of the train as history. Here is Charles Dickens's use of that venerable metaphor in *Dombey and Son* (1846–48):

> The first shock of a great earthquake had, just at that period, rent the whole neighbourhood to its center. Traces of its course were visible on every side.

Houses were knocked down; streets broken through and stopped; deep pits and trenches dug in the ground; enormous heaps of earth and clay thrown up; buildings that were undermined and shaking, propped by great beams of wood. Here, a chaos of carts, overthrown and jumbled together, lay topsy-turvy at the bottom of a steep unnatural hill; there, confused treasures of iron soaked and rusted in something that had accidentally become a pond. Everywhere were bridges that led nowhere; thoroughfares that were wholly impassable; Babel towers of chimneys, wanting half their height; temporary wooden houses and enclosures, in the most unlikely situations; carcasses of ragged tenements, and fragments of unfinished walls and arches, and piles of scaffolding, and wildernesses of bricks, and giant forms of cranes, and tripods straddling above nothing. There were a hundred thousand shapes and substances of incompleteness, wildly mingled out of their places, upside down, burrowing in the earth, aspiring in the air, mouldering in the water and unintelligible as any dream. Hot springs and fiery eruptions, the usual attendants upon earthquakes, lent their contributions of confusion to the scene. Boiling water hissed and heaved within dilapidated walls; whence also, the glare and roar of flames came issuing forth; and mounds of ashes blocked up rights of way, and wholly changed the law and custom of the neighbourhood.

In short, the yet unfinished and unopened Railroad was in progress; and from the very core of all this dire disorder, trailed smoothly away, upon its mighty course of civilization and improvement.[4]

Much can be (and has been) said about this passage, but I would draw your attention to the hiatus between metaphoric form and the dramatic survey that proves the occasion of its unfolding: "The yet unfinished and unopened Railroad was in progress; and from the very core of all this dire disorder, trailed smoothly away, upon its mighty course of civilization and improvement."[5] This last clause describes history itself or, better, a particular vision of history as culture-become-nature, architectures of human will apprehended as a direct and natural disturbance. And, in the form of Dickens's "great earthquake," this act of history, deterministic in its force, overrides all other human habits and purposes, making the latter appear both modest and ultimately submissive ("blocked up rights of way"). Yet in Dickens's dramatization of upheaval, he preserves something of history's stochasticity, some place for an apparent randomness within deterministic system. "Dire disorder" is the phrase chosen to describe this railroad, "traces of [whose] course," though "unfinished," were visible, yet finally as perceptually "unintelligible as any dream." A railroad "in progress" whose evident skeleton appears chaotic preserves a belief, regarding history, that the end is unknown at the beginning, that chaotic event of an indeterminate order might still intervene, that the future preserves some measure of contingency.

Something of the order of this contingency motivates a vision of "railroads" that "the Caucasian race *have yet* . . . to make"—an odd choice of tense, as private interests had been engaged in an industrial revolution of transport since the charter of the first American railway, the Baltimore and Ohio, in 1827.[6] Fuller seems, thus, like Dickens some seasons after her, engaged in a historiography of cultural forms, in the work of temporizing elements of lived (as in "living") culture, of culture in situ. "We are beggars in these respects. . . . Our only national melody, Yankee Doodle, is shrewdly suspected to be a scion from British art. . . . Such of the African melodies . . . we have heard are beautiful." Again, as I have already suggested, the compliment here is an article of bad faith, implied confession that the slaves built a national culture—the nation's only culture—in essence, that the slaves built "America." National culture equates with slave culture in this assessment. Even so, Fuller's reveries might be translated as follows: We cannot lay claim to an Anglo-American vernacular culture, have yet to carve out our own path in that regard, have heretofore lacked title to a proper place within the culture; therefore, it stands to reason that, of all that is left to do, the "Caucasian race have yet their rail-roads to make." "Jim Crow" provides an indicia of seasons past because, following Fuller's logic, "African melodies" and other putative forms of black culture are just that, forms received, inheritances, objects of primogeniture, a past preserved in amber. Contrarily, the time of Anglo America is a future perfect, a time yet arrived, whose contingency and idealism remain the privileges granted to those on the road of history—or, holding to our original metaphor, aboard the proverbial train.

The determinist and the stochastic, past and future, necessity and contingency, Jim Crow and the railroad: these are the oppositions and governing logics sketched above. In America, at the height of the debate on racial segregation in public accommodations, the issues at hand, though admittedly couched in a more pedestrian vocabulary, partook of the very oppositions and governing logics that I sketch in these opening paragraphs. Writing in the immediate wake of the *Civil Rights Cases* of 1883, in which the U.S. Supreme Court upheld racial segregation in public venues, both George Washington Cable and his principal journalistic antagonist, "New South" ideologue Henry Grady, confirmed as much when they conceded one simple fact: the constellation of issues central to the debate over, as the latter phrased it, "the social intermingling of the races" (i.e., denial of access, equal accommodations, "public safety") often adhered in the aggregate to a particular phenomenology of time; this kaleidoscope, we might add, on the evidence of their writings, distills politics into a set of perceptions of a piece with the antinomies adumbrated in the above reflections on Fuller and Dickens. Racial discrimination in the public sphere protected that social and quasi-legal penumbra at the threshold of "formal equality," at the limit of the rights guarded by the Reconstruction Amendments— those cautiously phrased legislative maneuvers, familiar to all partisans in the debate, that draw to a close all institutions and practices of "slavery and involuntary servitude," those protections of a right to the franchise independent "of race, color, or previous condition of servitude," and, most complexly, and perhaps most pertinently, those strictures restraining all state interference with the "privileges and immunities" of federal citizenship, as well as those protections of "life, liberty, or property" against deprivation "without due process of law," which last guarantee, further, "the equal protection of the laws."[7] Racial segregation bore a negotiated relationship to each of the Reconstruction Amendments, Yet for all that, "equal accommodations" as a matter of law stemmed most directly from the "equal protection" clause of the Fourteenth Amendment; and, as I have already stated, this particular relationship was often imagined to be a temporal one.

In Cable's assessment, those making "the freedman's case in equity" struggled, undoubtedly, against a certain petrifaction of the freedman's concerns. It is for this reason, arguably, that his essay of the same title takes the form of a fable of arrested development. The "black man's liberty," he proposed, had in the North "withered away" as a matter of politics, while in the South it remained "petrified," stuck in a perpetual frost: "Now this painful and wearisome question, sown in the African slave trade, reaped in our Civil War, and garnered in the national adoption of millions of an inferior race, is drawing near a second seedtime. For this is what the impatient proposal to make it a dead and buried issue really means. It means to recommit it to the silence and concealment of the covered furrow."[8] What form had this interrupted itinerary taken? On the one hand, the laws protecting the "Freedman's liberties" had met "that reluctant or simulated acceptance of their narrowest letter . . . a virtual suffocation of those principles of human equity which the unwelcome decrees do little more than shadow forth" (59). On the other, having proffered a certain security of life and property, these same emancipatory decrees then made it possible for whites to "hol[d] the respect of the community, that dearest of earthly boons, beyond [the freedman's] attainment" (67). The adherents of "the old regime," Cable descried, stand at the entrance of every public privilege and place—"steamer landing, railway platform, theater, concert hall, art display, public library, public school, courthouse, church, everything"—and flourished before the freedman's gaze "the hot branding iron of ignominious distinctions" (69). The threat—the social *Stoff* of segregation—found support in the efforts of bench and bar to "evad[e] the law" (68). Yet neither judicial gymnastics, nor political maneuvers, nor settled social aversions, Cable continued, can account for the persistence of a state of affairs that properly belonged to regimes long past. The fault rested, chillingly enough, on the shoulders of the freedmen: "Nothing but the habit, generations old, of enduring ['the habit of oppression'] could make it endurable by men not in actual slavery" (68). A thought experiment, Cable proposed, would help to clarify this point: "Were we whites of the South to remain every way as we are, and our six million blacks to give place to any sort of whites exactly their equals, man for man, in mind, morals, and wealth, provided only that they had tasted two years of American freedom, and were this same system of tyrannies attempted upon them, there would be as bloody an uprising as this continent has ever seen. We can say this quietly" (68). Or, better:

> Suppose, for a moment, the tables turned. Suppose the courts of our Southern states, while changing no laws requiring the impaneling of jurymen without distinction as to race, etc., should suddenly begin to draw their thousands of jurymen all black, and well-nigh every one of them counting, not only himself, but all his race, better than any white man. Assuming that their average of intelligence and morals should be not below that of jurymen as now drawn, would a white man, for all that, choose to be tried in one of those courts? Would he suspect nothing? Could one persuade him that his chances of even justice were all they should be, or all they would be were the court not evading the law in order to sustain an outrageous distinction against him because of the accidents of his birth? Yet only read white man for black man, and black man for white man, and that—I speak as an eyewitness—has been the practice for years, and is still so today, an actual emasculation, in the case of six million people both as plaintiff and defendant, of the right of trial by jury. (68–69)

As I said earlier, Henry Grady also admitted to a stalled emancipatory project, to a vision of the present as the winter of the freedman's discontent ("the revolution faltered"; "the line halted"; "there was hesitation, division,

uncertainty"; "forces of the revolution . . . held in arrest").[9] In his response
to Cable, an essay entitled "In Plain Black and White," Grady rebutted the
call for a "just assortment" of the races according to standards of "decency"—denied, that is, Cable's preference for affinities of class above race.
Assuming a uniquely Southern state of affairs, in which a certain "instinct . . . keeps the two races separate," yet between which no "kindlier
feeling, closer sympathy or less friction" existed, Grady reasoned, "the
South must be allowed to settle the social relations of the races according to
her own views of what is right and best."[10] The Southerner, black as well
as white, had wisely recognized "what was essential," had refused to seek
"to change what was unchangeable" (916). The races in the South had
achieved accord on this matter, contrary to a compelling yet erroneous
northern public opinion. Equal accommodations, not at all surprisingly,
and in poignant anticipation of the stratagems of state suzerain George Wallace, functioned as a variable of state sovereignty, the latter of which presented an abstract expression of liberal self-possession. Defenders of the
South's unique culture requested leave for "the right of character, intelligence, and property to rule. . . . [—] qualities . . . lodged with the white race
of the South" (917). Again, as was proposed in the plea of Grady's interlocutor, only an intellectual exercise of a certain imaginative strenuousness
could provide adequate proof of "the clear and unmistakable domination of
the white race of the South" (917). Matching his adversary's "habit, generations old, of enduring" with an aristocrat's habit of "domination," Grady
proffered the following: "If the blacks of the South wore white skins, and
were leagued together in the same ignorance and irresponsibility under any
other distinctive mark than their color, they would progress not one step
farther toward the control of affairs. Or if they were transported as they are
to Ohio, and there placed in numerical majority of two to one, they would
find the white minority there asserting and maintaining control, with less
patience, perhaps, than many a Southern state has shown" (917). Needless
to say, Grady's hypothetical history (of blacks disappeared beneath clanish
"white skins"), his gradual unlimbering of a lived present from the sedi-
ments of the past, contributed to those "various wishful schemes that
would banish [blacks] from the nation's bloodstream . . . from its conscience and historical consciousness," contributed to those fantasies of
"benign amputation" that Ralph Ellison assailed so trenchantly in "What
America Would Be Like without Blacks."[11] And what is more, the very title
of Grady's essay—"In Plain Black and White"—performed this work of
forgetting. His pun on "black and white" reduced racial blackness to the

signifier; and this reduction of social substance to the writing on the page, of the contingencies of race and history to the purified contours of an abstraction, expressed the intellectual labor operative within the pages of the essay itself—a labor whose governing forms and attendant logics I want now to explore.

In this preliminary foray into the law of racial segregation, I have chosen to scrutinize journalistic palaver as a prelude to my discussion of established legal doctrine and, thus, admit to treading lightly over cautiously delineated and historically significant lines of argument. I do so with a specific purpose in mind. I would draw your attention to the rhetorical form and vocabulary common to these arguments both for and against "equal accommodations." One wonders, certainly, about the vocabulary of causation (ponders how a valorization of what is deemed "essential" and "unchangeable" matches against "chances of even justice" and "accidents of birth") and ponders, further, the import of that shared metaphor of an itinerary interrupted ("this painful and wearisome question" remains "petrified"; "the revolution faltered," "the line halted"). But what seems most startling here is less the vocabulary of causation and more the form in which that vocabulary appears, that form captured in Cable's and Grady's flexible gymnastics of the mind ("were we whites of the South to remain every way as we are, and our six million blacks to give place to any sort of whites exactly their equals"; "suppose, for a moment, the tables turned"; "if the blacks of the South wore white skins"; "if they were transported . . . to Ohio, and there placed in numerical majority of two to one"). At a pivotal moment in the arguments both for and against segregation, at that moment when the alibi explaining the persistence of the past reveals it to be a matter of "habit," the claim to historical precedent acquires a conditional or subjunctive mood—"what if?"—expresses itself through the form of a counterfactual. It is through the counterfactual form—which, mirror-like, transposes the actual world into its imaginary and inverted equivalent—that partisans in the debate over racial segregation sustain a multiplicity of "case[s] in equity," of equality under the law, of "equal protection." What is more, the counterfactual form preserves that dialectic of necessity and contingency that characterized our inaugural metaphor, the train as history, and nowhere more resplendently than when "unchangeable" modes of affiliation meet "accidents of birth." The doctrine of separate-but-equal accommodations in the public sphere arguably encounters its correlate legal and logical form in the counterfactual.[12]

Counterfactuals are defined as those if-then statements or contrary-to-fact speculations that constitute both a necessary feature of all literary and legal hermeneutics and a common component of historical and philosophical inquiry. Counterfactual statements are taken as "pertaining to, or expressing, what has not in fact happened, but might, could, or would, in different conditions" (*Oxford English Dictionary,* 2d ed.); and they thus often assume the form of a conditional assertion, which consists "of two categorical clauses, the former of which, expressing a condition introduced by *if* or equivalent word, is called the *antecedent* (in Grammar *protasis*), the latter, stating the conclusion, is called the *consequent* (*apodosis*)." [13] A counterfactual supposition allows one, in literary analysis, to imagine what a text from the past would mean if it were being reauthored in the present; it is the very conditional that permits a text to be transported to other worlds, "yielding further local meanings not only to contemporaries but also for those in other historical spheres" (e.g., "Would Chaucer intend that sort of meaning in the present world?"). [14] In legal analysis, similarly, counterfactuals allow one to make inferences regarding causation, to infer not merely what happened or will happen, but, in addition, "what *would* have been the case if some actual event, which in fact happened, had not happened." [15] Accordingly, H. L. A. Hart and A. M. Honoré propose that the legal counterfactual can in most instances be reduced to two simple formulaic questions— "Would Y have occurred if X had not occurred?" And, "Is there any principle which precludes the treatment of Y as the consequence of X for legal purposes?" The first is a question of fact, the second of legal policy, and as Hart and Honoré note further, the only element in causation that is "factual"— or independent of shifting protocols of policy—is the relation of sine qua non, the "without which, not" condition. Therefore, when the response to the first question is a negative answer, "X is referred to not merely as a 'necessary condition' or *sine qua non* of Y but as its 'cause in fact' or 'material cause'" (*Causation in the Law,* 104). A law that reasons in this conjectural mood is able to adjudicate injury and harm, able to distinguish an event's "necessary conditions" from its cause sine qua non—that is, to discern those conditions that are "necessary" in the sense that they form a set of circumstances jointly sufficient to produce a particular consequence, from an event's express cause, which, to be a sine qua non, must be "necessary on the particular occasion for the occurrence of the event" (*Causation in the Law,* 106–7). So, for example, a lighted cigarette thrown into a wastepaper basket can be treated both by common sense and the law as the cause sine qua non of a fire, whereas the oxygen that fueled it would rise only to the status of a "necessary condition." And employing the language of literary analysis, we can add that a counterfactual keeps the former from eroding into the latter; that is, it keeps a relation of causation from the always-present threat of its deconstruction into a metonymy, into a "chain" of relations so extended as to lack any causal significance.[16]

Certainly, a law that reasons in this subjunctive vein does more than simply establish "that on some particular occasion some particular occurrence was the effect or consequence of some other particular occurrence" (*Causation in the Law,* 9–10). It enacts the very presumptions that assign "eventfulness" to any two discrete phenomena. The law's insights are in these instances largely Enlightenment in origin, for it is David Hume who offers that the necessity in causation does not "lie in objects" but "belongs entirely to the soul, which considers the union of two or more objects in all past instances."[17] All assertions of cause linking two discrete phenomena, he proposes further, sustain a covertly general set of propositions, exemplify an abstract claim that kinds or classes of events (such as those considered in the particular case) are invariably connected.[18] Again, Hart and Honoré: "The doctrine that, whenever we make a singular causal statement asserting that two particular events are causally connected, we are logically committed to one or more general propositions asserting a universal connection between kinds of events, is not one that is ever stressed in legal writings on causation" (15). It is to Hume, therefore, that legal doctrine may turn for the authority justifying counterfactual inferences; yet it is through him that, covertly, the counterfactual's subjunctive mood obtains the status of abstract law, that necessity ripens into causal logic. To tauten these lines linking law to philosophy, I would like to say a few more words on the counterfactual's lineage.

Counterfactuals are linguistic expressions common to literary and legal argument—rhetorical forms consistent with liberal conceptions of justice within the classical philosophical tradition. They represent a species of Kantian rationality (specifically, the "categorical imperative"), an example of what John Rawls has termed the "original position."[19] Rawls offers a description of the original position in his seminal work *A Theory of Justice;* there he describes it as a principle that free and rational persons would accept as defining the fundamental terms of their association were they to reason from an initial position of equality (10). The original position is neither an actual historical state nor a primitive condition of culture; it is, rather, the "appropriate initial status quo," which Rawls understands as a "purely hypothetical situation characterized so as to lead to a certain conception of justice" (11). Important for our concerns, this hypothetical position of equality can only be achieved when one willfully puts on a "veil of ignorance," when one nullifies "the effects of specific contingencies that put men at odds and tempt them to exploit social and natural circumstances to their own advantage" (118). Persons meet this condition when they have been deprived of the kinds of information that would allow them to rank their own prejudices above justice; of their unique place in society, their gender, race, class, sexual orientation, and religious affiliation; of their personal fortune, intelligence, or strength; and of their individual rational plan of life. The veil of ignorance is predicated on further exclusions of knowledge — on exclusions regarding the content of persons' determinate conceptions of the good, the particular circumstances of their own society, even the generation to which they belong (118). I will say more by way of conclusion regarding counterfactual form, the pursuit of equality as a principle, and the veil of ignorance (along with other like conditions). What I want to emphasize at this juncture is what appears to my eyes as a tacit limit to the form, one reached when the counterfactual is returned to the philosophical tradition leading to Rawls's original position, and one that renders the form largely ineffectual for those who seek to understand not hypothetical states of origin but actual ones, not fictional events but real ones.

There is an irreducible tension within any counterfactual speculation between the principle of equality and the history of rights (and their violation), between the pursuit of justice and the search for truth — and this tension is certainly operative when the framework for the form's use is a legal one. On the one hand, the counterfactual can be taken as a safeguard of rights, as an instrument that allows one to weigh the historical pressures on rights and to ascertain whether, under a different set of circumstances, the right in question (say, the Constitutional grant of equal protection to all) would be preserved. It is the very instrument for producing counterhistorical accounts of an event that can then be weighed against each other — all in the hopes that the right shall remain constant. Yet from another vantage (and this is the one preserved in the tradition extending through Kant and Rawls), the counterfactual valorizes the principle of equality over a history of rights, takes the former to stand logically and ontologically prior to the latter; and, what is heuristically troubling, what pushes the counterfactual to the limit, this principle can only exist in a vacuum (it requires the evacuation of historical consciousness). Rawls's tool for the latter, the veil of ignorance, presumes that restrictions on all knowledge of particulars is fundamental in the working out of a theory of justice, for, once deliberations of the latter sort are opened up to a knowledge of circumstance, the outcome is biased by arbitrary contingencies. Again Rawls: "If the original position is to yield agreements that are just, the parties must be fairly situated and treated equally as moral persons. The arbitrariness of the world must be corrected for by adjusting the circumstances of the initial contractual situation" (122). It thus seems that the counterfactual remains an irrepressibly dialectical form, one caught between the Scylla and Charybdis of principle and history; it might be used to protect the principle of equality, but, by the same token, it might also be used to clarify the historically saturated situation from which the principle emerged in the first place.[20] Whether jurist or journalists, then, one embraces this form at one's own peril—certainly if one's objective is to produce a compelling account of injury.

Thus, where legal and philosophical analysis displays a manifest affinity for counterfactual speculation, the discipline of history finds it difficult to embrace counterfactualism's arbitrary relation to fact. When the counterfactual takes the form of a thought experiment that starts from a fictional supposition (as in both legal analysis and speculative history it often does), its effect is to construct an alternative social imaginary that performs a negative operation on the certitude of historicist conceit: for example, "suppose the American economy had developed without the railroad"; "suppose the Confederacy had won the Civil War"[21] This exercise in counterhistory cleaves the present into parallel and simultaneous presents —"What would the present economy look like without the contribution of slave labor?"—a move that lacks plausibility, in the view of some scholars, because it subordinates a self-identical and experientially grounded "now" to the vicissitudes of an alternative "history of events which have not happened."[22] This conjectural historicism is thus, at its most benign, anachronistic.[23] Less benign is its relation to causation, and in this regard, historians typically look with suspicion on the very terms that make counterfactualism a necessary instrument in legal causation. Their cause for complaint is threefold.

First, there is the matter of a jurisprudence evidently predisposed to deploy the counterfactual's "what if" in its efforts to assign causation, to distinguish disparate necessary conditions from the singular cause sine qua non and to do so by means of a grammatical conditional. Historians charge that "if" with the responsibility of dividing the single course of history "into necessary facts and accidental facts."[24] Under the sign of this "if," Benedetto Croce warns, in "'Necessity' in History," "one fact in a narrative is graded as necessary and another one as accidental, and the second is mentally eliminated in order to espy how the first would have developed along its own lines if it had not been disturbed by the second" (557). A past event subject to the contingency of an "if" holds the potential to spin off alternative chronologies, which leads to the further possibility of alternative presents. The present is, in this view, "contingent," and counterfactualism consequently "anti-historical" (557). A second difficulty lies in the emphasis on causation. The argument that historical necessity arises out of relations of causation—the claim that "there is necessity in history because the preceding facts in the series entail the succeeding facts in a chain of cause and effect"—warrants dismissal, Croce adds, because the concept of cause was born in the realm of natural science and not history (558).[25] Third, and finally, from the vantage of historical inquiry, necessity and determinism prove multiple sides of the same currency, as Hume had himself observed; and, therefore, Croce concludes, the historian's use of the "conditional" erroneously imports "foreknowledge of the future" into the study of the past (559).[26] When the historian, thinking counterfactually, enlists causality to do the work of history, he or she brings a determinism or a logic to bear on the past's plausible chronologies. The former yields a "forlorn and pessimistic style," while the latter hides a "master-pattern" that rules "the beginning, the development and the end of history" (559). Regarding this "foreknowledge of the future," Croce warns of what we might call (but what he did not) "the burden of history": "[History] instead of appearing as the work of man, requiring to be carried forward and renewed in action, seems to descend upon him like a shower of dislodged stones tumbling from a mountain peak into a valley and crushing him as they fall" (559). Accident, causality, determinism.

There is another way to phrase these difficulties, one that translates them into a language that highlights their pertinence to literary analysis (and a language to which I will return before long). Counterfactuals prove anathema because they betray a structure of internal difference at the heart of all historical narrative. From the counterfactual's suppositional vantage, history is not an accumulation of events. It is, rather, an effect of the frisson between the necessary and the accidental, between the material and the contingent. Historical narrative possesses the characteristic of always appearing intrinsically different from itself, unstably grounded in a fundamental discrepancy between the actual and the suppositional. Yet for all these difficulties, Croce stops short of dismissing the counterfactual on grounds of its impertinence to historical inquiry. The grammatical conditional—for example, What if Daniel Webster and Henry Clay had not colluded to pass the Compromise of 1850?—this sort of "if," Croce notes, "is sometimes useful for underlining the importance of certain decisive acts, and stimulating a sense of responsibility" (557).[27]

Combining these legal and historical insights into counterfactual method, we may safely conclude that legal recourse to counterfactual supposition preserves the link between historical "necessity" and legal responsibility. When a jurist reasons counterfactually, his or her attribution of cause presumes the assignment of responsibility. Where an event is established as a sine qua non, as a necessary precursor to the particular event (i.e., injury) in question, responsibility flows from the assignment of causal origins. Contrarily, once an event is established as accident, as historically contingent, the law can abdicate responsibility for making any alteration or remedy in the present. When courts assent to the counterfactual's logic of historical necessity, they do so for reasons that are *pro tanto* rigorously individualistic.

This much said we can perhaps return to Cable and Grady, those sparring journalists, and to the essence of their exchange, the costs of "social intermingling," with an altered sense of the stakes at issue in the nineteenth-century debate over racial segregation. We see, in the editorially permissive pages of the *Century,* a journalism that plays fast and loose with the rigors of legal deliberation. Cable and Grady, drawing abstractions from the counterfactual's conjectural syntax, abandoned individual responsibility for a universal model of duty and a collective sense of blame.[28] An "instinct [that] keeps the two races separate"; "the habit of enduring"; "the habit of oppression": immutable and timeless, this lexicon of instinct promises the obstinacy of historical "necessity" (for Grady, you recall, the habits of Southerners were "what was unchangeable"). Yet despite all, in the narrative form these standards of behavior assume, they fail additionally to achieve the status of event, cause, sine qua non. At best, habit rises to the status of "condition," of necessity absent responsibility. There is nothing the law can do here, as racial "instincts" fall beyond its reach (according to this journalistic — and preliminary — meditation on racial segregation).

Importantly, these discrete conjectural speculations as to how the social might operate if "the tables turned" and "the blacks of the South wore white skins" anticipated the arguments for and against the legal provision mandating separate-but-equal accommodations in the public sphere, arguments that would achieve their apotheosis in the U.S. Supreme Court case *Plessy v. Ferguson* (1896). In that case, Homer A. Plessy challenged as unconstitutional Louisiana's Separate Car Law, which mandated racial segregation in railway transport. *Plessy v. Ferguson* established as matters of federal law the juridical doctrines protecting separate-but-equal racial accommodations in the public sphere. On the evidence of the opinion of the Court, penned by Justice Henry Billings Brown, credit for the terms and underlying logics of the Court's ruling might well go to Cable and Grady. The greatest weakness in Plessy's argument, according to Brown, consisted in the assumption that any enforced separation of the two races "stamps the colored race with a badge of inferiority."[29] Inferiority was no instrument of the social and was certainly beyond the purview of the act in question. It was associated with the law in question "solely because the colored race chooses to put that construction upon it"—due largely, that is, to the fecundity of the freedman's imagination. "Inferiority" was a private and psychological affair and, thus, not entitled to federal constitutional remedy: "The argument necessarily assumes that if, as has been more than once the case, and is not unlikely to be so again, the colored race should become the dominant power in the state legislature, and should enact a law in precisely similar terms, it would thereby relegate the white race to an inferior position. We imagine that the white race, at least, would not acquiesce in this assumption" (*Plessy*, 551).[30] That jurisprudence that attended to the doctrine of "equal protection" would seem to partake not so much of a logic as of a rhetoric. Once more, a circumstantial historicism provided that heuristic that put the law of "equal accommodations" to the test of constitutional "equal protection." And, again, in echo of that distinction of civic equality from social inequality, venerated by both Cable and Grady, Brown abjured: "The object of the [Fourteenth] amendment was undoubtedly to enforce the absolute equality of the two races before the law, but in the nature of things it could not have been intended to abolish distinctions based upon color, or to enforce social, as distinguished from political equality, or a commingling of the two races upon terms unsatisfactory to either" (*Plessy*, 544). "Legislation is powerless to eradicate racial instincts," he concluded, "or to abolish distinctions based upon physical differences" (*Plessy*, 551).

Plessy marked a memorial end to all the promises of the post–Civil War era, from the Reconstruction amendments to more informal assurances of black participation in New South industrialization and civic life. Moreover, borne on the crest of a growing wave of legally suspect maneuvers by whites against blacks and blatantly illegal aggressions, *Plessy* served also as a monumental juridical culmination of the post-Reconstruction "reign of terror." Among the events and phenomena that gave rise to *Plessy*, one of the most important was the compromise reached between candidates Rutherford Hayes and Samuel Tilden during the 1876 presidential election, in which

Hayes promised federal subsidies for the uncompleted Southern railroad as well as the withdrawal of federal troops from Louisiana and South Carolina. A coveted southern "home rule" was thus secured if and when Southern Democrats supported him as a candidate. Concomitant with Hayes's promises was the growth of white protective societies and patrols with names such as the Regulators, the Jayhawkers, and the Black Horse Cavalry, which in their impress on the cultural landscape were together outmatched by the resurgence, of course, of the Invisible Empire of the Knights of the Ku Klux Klan. The Compromise moment was also marked by the passing of the antislavery political generation of Thaddeus Stevens, Charles Sumner, and Benjamin Butler, among others—an exit from the political stage that, combined with the disfranchisement of blacks through systems of gerrymandering, poll taxes, elaborate and confusing election schemes, complicated balloting, literacy tests, convict disqualifications, and dubious "grandfather" clauses, all served to reestablish an almost exclusively white and hostile electorate.[31]

I shall have a great deal more to say about this history, about *Plessy* and separate-but-equal accommodations, counterfactualism, and the doctrine of "equal protection" before all is done. I note here that what shall remain of interest as I make my way across textual forms and legal opinions are the logical, temporal, and cognitive constraints of "formal equality." As has been the case in previous chapters, what concerns me in the pages to follow are the lineaments connecting legal logic and aesthetic form, particularly that moment of migration from the former to the latter when a certain form of pleading persists as a poetics of form. By "form of pleading" I mean to designate the counterfactual schemes common to a turn-of-the-century equal protection law, those interrupted itineraries (between cause and effect, past and present) that spawn scenarios characterized by alternative chronologies, historical contingency, and fictive suppositions; and in referring to that moment when the civil procedures coincident with equal protection persist as a "poetics of form," I mean to highlight the rather compelling resemblances between this conjectural jurisprudence and a tendency toward an aesthetics of rupture, plots of identity exchange, and themes of repetition and temporal return that recur in the American literature and film of this period.

As in previous chapters, this one is premised on a moment of convergence, of synchronicity—on a perception of resemblance between the ostensibly disjunct discourses of law and cinema; and, as has also been true throughout this book, and consistent in terms of its method, noting a rela-

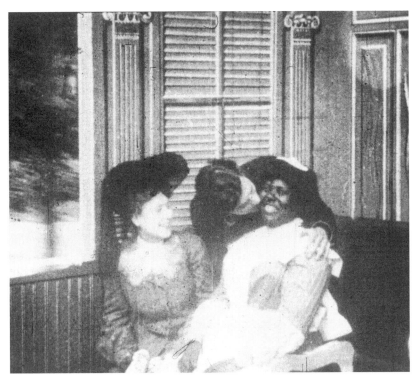

Figure 8. In plain black and white: a film such as *What Happened in the Tunnel* plays out the counterfactual fantasy common to equal protection law—"Suppose, for a moment, the tables turned"—with the effect of reducing blackness and whiteness to fungible units of exchange and thus shrouding an injurious history of race in a veil of ignorance. (Photo courtesy Library of Congress, Prints and Photographs Division, FLA 3680)

tion between these two discrete systems serves as the first step to excavating their historical entailments. I focus in this chapter on two texts — *What Happened in the Tunnel* (fig. 8), an early silent film produced by Thomas Edison's film company in 1903, and the Supreme Court's *Plessy v. Ferguson* (1896) decision. The film consists of a narrative that barely registers as such (about which more in a moment), but which nevertheless pivots on the act of a white woman and her black maid trading places; relatedly, the core constitutional issue in *Plessy* is whether black and white railway cars are themselves essentially interchangeable or, in the language of the time, "separate but equal."

Given my concern with these plots and logics of exchange, I might just as well have focused on a number of other legal, cinematic, even literary texts. For certain, within the last decade of the nineteenth century alone, a number of writers published novels concerned with the fiction of race (we often term them novels of "passing"); and, though not of explicit concern in the pages to follow, these works provide an important context for thinking about the persistence of the counterfactual's counterhistorical imaginary, for thinking complexly about the constraints as well as possibilities of "formal equality." I have in mind here Albion W. Tourgée's *Pactolus Prime* (1890), William Dean Howells's *An Imperative Duty* (1892), Frances E. W. Harper's *Iola Leroy* (1892), Mark Twain's *Pudd'nhead Wilson* (1894), and Charles Chesnutt's *House behind the Cedars* (1900). In each, one or more characters renounce (or are forced to renounce, or choose not to renounce) their black racial identity for a white one. Take Tourgée's novel as the first (if neither the most aesthetically rich nor the best known) example. Pactolus Prime faces the possibility of renunciation twice over, first as a deliberative matter, second out of force. Prime, who was born black and for many years lived life as a slave, was light enough to pass as white and at a certain point in his life (curiously, when he escapes slavery and joins "the Federal lines" during the Civil War) he chooses to do so. Prime graduates from "slave-boy" to lieutenant "P. P. Smith," a man exclusively in possession of "the secret of [his] first life."[32] Later, while recovering from gunshot wounds inflicted by his old master (who had absconded with his former slave sweetheart), Prime undergoes a second transformation of his racial identity; his doctor provides a remedy of "nitrate of silver" for his injuries but does so "in such stiff, old-fashioned doses" as to produce a case of argyria, or a transformation of the pigment in Prime's skin that makes him appear to be "of pure African blood" and leaves him with a most "unnatural mask" (251, 319). The deliberative choice to pass as white is no longer Prime's, though he devotes his life to keeping his racial identity a secret from his "blue-eyed, fair-haired daughter" and argues strenuously with his son Benny about the virtues of passing: "I shudder at the thought that a man should beget souls, whom he knows must transmit the curse of inferiority,—the ever-present thought of injustice and debasement,—to unnumbered generations, transforming the bequest of love into an inheritance of reproach and hate" (320). Important for our concerns, Prime figures the relation between absent genealogy and historical amnesia, passing plots and counterfactual exchanges in his reflections on a life "vainly devoted to obliterating the curse that rested on it": "I have helped some of [my siblings'] children—to become white. I hope their children will be able to forget their origin. The one fortunate thing about slavery was that it left no family tree to blight with the shade of its dead branches the new shoots" (303, 321).

Like Tourgée, Howells, Harper, Twain, and Chesnutt play out the literary fantasy of what would happen if the circumstances of one's life were reversed (at least, that is, if we consider the novels' at the level of plot and consider plot as the purest expression of a text's "deep structure"). The passing novel is, in fact, something like the literary correlate of counterfactual legal form. The very imbalance between a lived white experience and a suppressed (though not entirely forgotten) black one expresses at the level of narrative consciousness a sense of those alternative and parallel chronologies triggered by the counterfactual's "what if?" And the renunciation of one's racial identity (the "oblitera[tion of] the curse"), it stands to reason, ranks as that contingent event that triggers these alternative possibilities in the first place. Significantly, these literary plots anticipate (and in some cases inspire) a range of classical Hollywood films from midcentury: for example, *Adam's Rib* (1949), a film about attempted murder and gender equality (the first as plot, the second as politics) in which, during the climactic courtroom scene, the male and female parties to the crime are made to switch places in the jurors' imaginations and before the viewer's eyes (a visual trick achieved through the combined magic of the filmic dissolve and sartorial drag); *Gentleman's Agreement* (1947), in which the journalist Philip Schuyler Green (played by Gregory Peck) passes as a Jew in order to collect information on anti-Semitism; and (it would seem a mistake not to include within this impromptu canon these three) the famous passing films *Pinky* (1949), *Lost Boundaries* (1949), and *Imitation of Life* (1959). I have laid out these literary and cinematic plots in such detail as a way of providing a context for what follows but also to make clear the specificity of my claims and to provide a sense of the critical possibilities that might spiral out from these claims. What I am most interested in tracing are a set of connections that are (chronologically, at least) more tightly interwoven than the traditions I trace above: connections between turn-of-the-century silent film and a contemporaneous equal protection jurisprudence. Of the former, I am curious about the cinema's shift from visual tricks to narrative and plot, about the ways in which emergent narrative techniques produce mysteries of causation. What draws me to these mysteries are their echoes with a specific legal logic, one that, intent to peel away numerous obfuscating veils of historical consciousness (and to arrive at purified principles of equality), only produces more besides. I have settled on silent film and equal protection law as my objects of aesthetic inquiry because, as should soon become apparent, when filmic form and legal logic turn to consider blackness in the era of segregation they share as well a concern with repetition, recondite causation, and nonlinear temporalities.

This assertion of continuity between an emerging visual poetics and a legal propensity toward conjectural historicism at the juncture where blackness meets principles of equal protection—between, in short, the figurative and the law—proves anathema to a number of hypotheses of recent mint. I have in mind here the theses (advanced by Richard A. Posner, James Boyd White, and, arguably, Wai Chee Dimock) that law and literature, the juridical and the aesthetic, maintain a relation of historical and conceptual obliquity. Posner and White, as I outline in an earlier chapter, see the law as so value neutral in its judgments and so practical in its objectives as to be free of that worry about textual indeterminacy that plagues as well as fuels literature and literary interpretation alike.[33] Dimock describes this relation as the "uneven development" between literature and the law—as the "noncoincidence of boundaries" between the nineteenth-century American novel and Anglo-American analytical jurisprudence, to be exact—the latter of which captures a mode of legal rationality that, stretching from Immanuel Kant through Jeremy Bentham and on to Oliver Wendell Holmes, Jr., becomes over the course of the nineteenth century more "frugal" in its semantics.[34] Construed as a limited arena—free of morals and narrowly economic (or, as in the case of Bentham's utilitarian "moral arithmetic," moral only to the extent conceived as economic)—the language and procedures of the law experience a "contraction in semantics" (*Residues of Justice*, 23). Legal rationality's figurative ascesis is the matter at hand whether one contemplates a Kantian retribution ("an adequate Retaliation after the principle of 'Like with Like' "), a Benthamite utilitarianism (the celebrated axiom that "it is the greatest happiness of the greatest number that is the measure of right and wrong"), or a Holmesian topography of justice (a "path" of "well understood limits, a body of dogma enclosed within definite limits").[35] That law, which subordinates justice to a principle of exchange (and for which the act of barter proves axiomatic), undergoes an attenuation of purpose, this last of which coincides with its becoming "frugal in its semantics" (*Residues of Justice*, 33). And, while the law achieves a diminution of import, Dimock continues, "the luxury of signification became more and more a residual privilege of the novel" (*Residues of Justice*, 33). Literature, that is, came to be possessed of an enviable "semantic latitude."[36]

Conceding at once that literature and law are disciplinarily oblique, with the added proviso that their unevenness is more precisely a matter not of form but of form's absorption into insoluble regimes of knowledge, I want to focus all the same not so much on the absence of kinship between aesthetic forms and jurisprudential practices as on the imbrication of the fictive within the legal, of the imaginary within the pragmatic. I want to scrutinize in the pages to follow the instrumentality of the fictive within legal adjudication. What I have in mind here are what can be thought of generally as "legal fictions" but what might also be called, with greater specificity, following Bentham himself, "logical fictions." I take the latter from *A Fragment on Ontology,* where Bentham explains that words like "right" and "duty" and "obligation" name things that are said to exist but that fall short of existence "in truth and reality." They are, as he describes, "fictions in the logical sense."[37] Though words like "right" and "obligation" lack claim to the ontological certainty taken to be characteristic of material things and sensory impressions, there is a relation between the names of fictions and reality that affords them meaningfulness and even truth — the meaningfulness or truth we would extend, H. L. A. Hart adds, to a statement such as "I have an obligation to report for military service," where the fiction binds the speaker to a certain course of action.[38] I want to see in the conjectural historicism of equal protection law something like the logical fiction's hermeneutic modesty, to see in the turn toward counterfactual speculation some desire (if not need) to lay claim to a lightened semantic burden. These burdens are, importantly, like Bentham's "logical fictions," no less obligatory or binding for being fictions.

A single example from the era of equal protection is worth consideration in this regard. When Albion W. Tourgée, former Union officer and carpetbagger jurist in North Carolina, author of *Pactolus Prime* as well as the Reconstruction laments *A Fool's Errand: By One of the Fools* (1879) and *Bricks without Straw* (1880), and counsel for the plaintiff in error in the case of *Plessy v. Ferguson,* sought to demonstrate how the doctrine of equal protection correlated with and enhanced the Declaration of Independence's assertion that "all men are created equal," he posed a counterfactual query to the members of the federal judiciary. At that moment, he claimed for the law the lush signification others would designate the distinct privilege of the literary (through a "what if . . . " scenario that leaned so heavily in the direction of the literary's lush semiotic landscapes that Tourgée-the-advocate appeared momentarily to give way to Tourgée-the-author). Here is the query as it reads in Tourgée's "Brief for the Plaintiff in Error" (a document to which I shall return presently): "Suppose a member of this court, nay, suppose every member of it, by some mysterious dispensation of providence should wake tomorrow with a black skin and curly hair — the two obvious and controlling indications of race — and in traveling through that portion of the country where the 'Jim Crow Car' abounds, should be

ordered into it by the conductor. It is easy to imagine what would be the result, the indignation, the protests, the assertion of pure Caucasian ancestry."[39] On the face of it, Tourgée's plea is rather simple. He asks the members of the supreme judiciary—all of whom were "white"—to put
themselves in the place of blacks by imagining themselves "with a black skin
and curly hair." This counterfactual flight of imagination replicates the
deepest structures of metaphor, and through it the stakes in equal protection law approached those of fictive persuasion. Law flirted with literariness. I would enlist another literary critic's succinct summary of metaphor
to demonstrate this connection. Metaphor, Harry Berger reminds, in "Metaphor and Metonymy and the End of the Middle Ages," posits a false identity, "A is B," coupled with its implied contradictory, "A is *not* B."[40] In metaphor, we realize that a false identity is being used and feel a "resistance" to
it; this resistance is like going into a higher gear, because the machinery of
interpretation must be brought into play. Once we feel the pressure of the
resistance, of the negation "A is *not* B," we also, Berger adds, "view the
identity assertion as conspicuously imaginary or counterfactual."[41] Metaphor "asserts its fictiveness by indicating the radically different contexts in
which its terms are normally embedded, and then bringing them together
in an imaginary complex," joining them momentarily "in a counterfactual
synthesis" (7). Tourgée's "Brief" asserted the false identity that the judges
at the Supreme Court bench were blacks relegated to the "Jim Crow Car,"
but that identity bore an internal pressure, produced its own resistance—
the frisson born of the knowledge that, to that point, Supreme Court judges
had never been black.

Yet once phantasmatics are allowed entry into pragmatic adjudications,
there is no stopping the counterfactual's accelerated figurality. Tourgée's
plea solicited a work of sympathy. Through it he appealed to his interlocu-
tors to insinuate themselves into another's circumstance, which act of imagining, as Adam Smith explains in *The Theory of Moral Sentiments* (1759),
can be achieved largely through the lightened semantic burdens and speculative exchanges of the aesthetic. Suppositional forms of pleading stimulate sentimental appeal, the latter of which holds the place of (and clears a
space for) a more structurally complex form of imagining—a fantasy scenario that allows one to feel the other's pain and injury. As Smith explains,
"When I sympathize with your sorrow . . . my emotion . . . arises from
bringing your case home to myself, from putting myself in your situation,
and thence conceiving what I should feel in the like circumstances."[42] Sentiment involves an "imaginary change" of situation, he adds, in which "I

not only change circumstances with you, but I change persons and characters" (VII.iii.1.4). The ability to put oneself into another's "case" involves
not simply that one experience what another person feels but that one, in
addition, project oneself into another in order better to understand his or
her circumstance—in short, it involves the ability to feel "as if" one were in
another's situation.[43] The paradox of sentimentality is that, while it clears a
space for one's own affect, it leaves little room for the sentience of those with
whom one is being asked to identify. The trouble, in short, is that sentiment
follows less the model of sympathy, or "the state of being affected by the
condition of another with a feeling similar or corresponding to that of the
other," and more the model of empathy, or the "power of projecting one's
personality into (and so fully comprehending) the object of contemplation"
(*Oxford English Dictionary*, 2d ed.). The dictionary's slippage from subject
to object is telling in this regard, and glimpses of this displacement and effacement of the other come into view in Tourgée's plea when a state of black
injury "easy to imagine" by whites produces nothing more certain and objective than "the indignation, the protests, the assertion of pure Caucasian
ancestry." Counterfactualism in the law, like "sympathy" in moral philosophy, subordinates the afflictions of the aggrieved in its effort to rouse the
sensibilities of those taken to be imperturbably objective; and while both
law and moral philosophy respond to the vicissitudes of form, it is in counterfactualism that the fragile temporal material of feeling gives way to the
forms of equivalence and exchange made possible by the very exercise in
subjunctive rhetoric ("Suppose, for a moment, the tables turned").

There is an added wrinkle, then, to suppositional pleading and sympathetic imagining. The system of sympathy that enables one to feel "as if"
one were in another's situation not only occasions an imaginary transference ("I not only change circumstances . . . but . . . persons and characters
[with you]"); it also obeys the very principles of exchange characteristic of
traffic in the commodity form (the *als ob* of commodity fetishism). Permit
me to give an account of those principles.

In the standard literary account of commodification, exchange is based
on resemblance and similitude—on metaphor—the appearance or self-
announcement of something as something else. Exchange is thus a substitution in which one thing stands in for another and on the basis of
something similar or equal. This "something similar" can only make an appearance with the assist of a synecdochic reduction of all the diverse
"thingly" properties of the commodity, a prior operation in which one part
is made to stand in for the whole. But there is nothing immanent in the thing

that can play this part, that can make exchange happen; for no common part can be reduced from the radical heterogeneity of the thing's possible uses, from its multiple sensible attributes. Therefore, a metamorphosis within things proves necessary—necessary to provide an axis of resemblance around which disparate things may be exchanged. This transformation is called abstraction, an effacement of materiality: "All of its sensible attributes [*sinnlich Beschaffenheit*] are extinguished [*ausgelöscht*]," Marx explains.[44] And, finally, as there is nothing at once particular and common for which an abstraction can substitute, it in essence takes the place of nothing. This positing of exchange value is thus akin to catachresis, the substitution of an improper name for something that has no name of its own: "But if for lack of naturall and proper terme or worde we take another, neither naturall nor proper and do untruly applie it to the thing which we would seeme to expresse, and without any just inconvenience, it is . . . then spoken . . . by plain abuse [or catachresis, the figure of abuse]."[45] Catachresis is a violent figure, more like a rupture in the tropological system than an exchange enabled by the mutual reciprocities of metaphoric substitution, and the very figure that through the force of abstraction can turn a sensuous thing into a supersensible thing [*ein sinnlich übersinnliches Ding*]: "Dissolved or validated by the reductive force of abstraction-in-exchange, use values become exchangeable only as ghosts. . . . The force of abstraction [*Abstraktionskraft*] both de- *and* reanimates commodities; we could say it 'ghosts' them, giving them whatever life [*überleben*] or animation (suspended) they have, without presuming that they had any prior to the abstraction. The same *coup de force* institutes and destitutes them at once."[46]

The terms of this literary narrative of the market are pertinent, surprisingly, to the Supreme Court's deliberations in *Plessy v. Ferguson*. When Tourgée turned to the nine "member[s] of this court" and asked them to imagine themselves "with a black skin and curly hair—the two obvious and controlling indications of race—" the latter took the place of what they were not. With whiteness notably *sur rature*, the supreme judiciary came to look like its blackface mockery, and the counterfactual not only succumbed to tropological form (catachresis) but replicated the structures of market exchange. Blackness was a name in the place of nothing—an abstraction that came to take on the meaning of exchange value *tout court*. Tourgée's "suppose" opened a Pandora's box, with the quaintness of metaphor quickly eclipsed beneath the impositions of catachresis, and sympathy's "fellow-feeling" just as quickly renounced in favor of the *coup de force* of empathic projection. The counterfactual, like the abstraction implicit in commodity exchange, to paraphrase, both "reanimates" and "de-animates," "institutes and destitutes." Tourgée's counterfactual exchange drew on the iconicity of blackness and presumed, in the process, the persistent fungibility of the formerly enslaved, which turn toward abstraction risked effacing the very thing it was meant to make apprehensible: a black experience of segregation as injury. And, what is more, thanks to this counterfactual flight of fancy, the doctrine that "all men are created equal" embraced, as a pragmatic turn-of-the-century legal dispute, the principles governing traffic in the commodity form.

It was this "going into [an ever] higher gear" that made the counterfactual a curious chronotope within equal protection law—this moment when the legal text achieved a momentary ontological humility, leaving a more superficial semantic imprint but one that required in turn a more strenuously literary machinery of interpretation as compensation, a mechanism unceasing in its assent through increasingly abstract tropological registers. At the moment when Cable or Grady, Brown or Tourgée, took on the counterfactual's conditional rhetoric, they essentially flaunted the fictiveness of the law's constructs, and these assertions of fictiveness replaced a more forcefully analytical and pragmatic strategy with a speculative one, abdicating the law's reality principle (the pragmatic adjudication of injury) for an imaginary one to which all parties—and, constitutionally, all citizens—had finally to assent.

Of principal concern in this inquiry into "formal equality" shall be the pertinence of the counterfactual's mirror-like imaginary to the doctrine of equal protection, specifically, the utility of the counterfactual's subjunctive mood to musings on race, causation, and historical responsibility in the turn-of-the-century experience of segregation. Counterfactuals clustered in an unprecedented way in late-nineteenth-century equal protection law. A certain density of counterfactual speculations intruded on constitutional law in response to the Fourteenth Amendment's mandate of "equality." Counterfactualism provided the doctrine of equal protection with its logical correlate, with that "fuzzy logic" that enabled the courts to imagine a separate-but-equal (alternative and parallel) universe.[47] Generally, the claim of those opposed to racial segregation was that acts protecting the practice willfully and purposely made historically necessary (a matter of "instinct") what was historically contingent and accidental—that a law such as Louisiana's, according to Justice Brown, in paraphrase of Plessy's lawyers' brief, "*imports* a badge of servitude" and "*stamps* the colored race with a badge of inferiority." In the pages to follow, I argue that it is by means of counterfactual reasoning that the majority in *Plessy* and related cases circumvented this claim, that they made an end run around history. It was by means of the counterfactual, that is, that jurists manipulated historical causes, arriving inevitably, and fatedly, at the constitutionally valid separate-but-equal present. Testing the plaintiff's social imaginary, his vision of an alternative present — and finding it wanting — the *Plessy* court confirmed why the current present is the *only* present possible. It is on the grounds (if we might call it that) of the counterfactual's ontological modesty that courts required to guarantee equal protection of the laws found an alibi for historical responsibility, that the law improvised a detour around historical causes, around the "event" of emancipation.[48]

I have said that the persistence of this form of pleading as a poetics of form betrays the broader relevance of a singular social imaginary. Detour (as I have described it here) is the imaginary I have in mind. It therefore seems fitting that I turn my attention to various instances of this poetics; scenes that share with Fuller's "Entertainments" a concern with the social efficacy of the railroads, and through which, it will become clear before long, law and cinema come to share the same tracks, as it were.

PARALLEL TRACKS

Track One

We have already noted that Margaret Fuller's antebellum reflections on Jim Crow's migration from pit to politics fall short of that intimacy of popular ditty with the railroads for which, by century's end, the two would become comfortably associated. However, we might expect, given those subterranean affiliations of social intimacy with miscegenation that characterized the segregation of Reconstruction's aftermath ("if intermingled they would fuse" [912], Grady warns), that the congruence of minstrelsy and the social would partake of a seduction and that, in addition, the romances in question would take place on board a moving train. Something like this orgy of forms and personae occurs in *What Happened in the Tunnel.* In accord with theatrical mise-en-scène shared by many concurrent "compartment dramas," *What Happened*'s seduction plot transpires in a railway coach on a railway train that, on the evidence of the blurred landscape glimpsed through the coach's window, has already embarked on its journey. The film's rudimentary narrative consists entirely of the interactions between the three characters seated within the coach: a white woman who, corseted and donning an impressively swollen coiffure, appears the quintessence of the era's cult of true womanhood; her black maid, whose simpler attire (no doubt helped by her race) indicates her subordinate social position; and a smartly dressed man, whose class affiliations with his white counterpart appear indisputable. The film satirizes the theme of women's risk of danger when traveling alone in public. Engaged in the reading of a book, the white woman accidentally drops her kerchief, which, returned by the man seated aft of her and with a gratuitous entreaty, serves as the occasion for the pair to engage in flirtatious repartee. The black retainer casts complicitous, sidelong glances at the pair, until, extempore, the screen goes black. When the scene returns—when the train, that is, emerges from the tunnel through which it has temporarily passed—we see that the maid and her mistress have traded places and that the mistress's paramour kisses the cheek not of his beloved but of her black maid. The women laugh uproariously at the reversal they have managed to stage, while the spurned admirer returns to his seat insulted and repulsed, dejected and embarrassed.

It is the fade to black and the switch enabled by its presumed cavital darkness that interests me in this film, though it ought to be said preliminarily that the humor here is not solely occasioned by the emerging mimetic codes of the cinema (an incident, *tout court*, of modernist visuality). The film plays on a preposterous lark as old as Chaucer's *Canterbury Tales*, specifically the more ribald offerings of "The Miller's Tale" and "The Reeve's Tale," in both of which sexuality gives way to a playing "in the dark" (and in response to which Chaucer's cook intones, "If ever . . . / Herde I a millere bettre y-set a-werk: / He hadde a jape of malice in the derk").[49] This is not to say that the film fails to share a semiotic with the more popular cinematic genres of its time. Its setting within a railway environment certainly links it to actualities such as the Lumière brothers' *Arrivée d'un train en gare de La Ciotat* (1895), though, with the simple inclusion of a splice or "cut" (a device to which we will return), the American short expediently moves film form from the one-shot "attractions," for which the Lumières were known, to a two-shot structure sufficiently complex to intimate "narration" (again, a distinction that we will ponder shortly). What is more, as in Edwin S. Porter's *The Great Train Robbery* (1903) and D. W. Griffith's early Biograph melodramas, *The Lonedale Operator* (1911), *A Girl and Her Trust* (1912), and *An Unseen Enemy* (1912), Edison's film deploys the train as a setting designed specifically to determine narrative action, to organize narrative telos. On the one hand, *What Happened*'s rudimentary narrativity appears to distill the narrative strategies of *The Great Train Robbery*, this last of which provides a complex elab-

oration of the railway's emphases on times and sites of departure and destination, provides, that is, for their elaboration into a set of narrative funda-
mentals. On the other, its ostensible break from (and jocose return to) plot
anticipates the structure of Griffith's melodramatic and signature "last
minute rescue," where temporality assumes dramatic significance for its
own sake.[50] The incursion of the train's setting into film form also echoes an
earlier train film, *Love in a Railroad* (Siegmund Lubin, 1902), which de-
picts a male traveler who repeatedly attempts to sneak a kiss from a woman
passenger only to discover, once the train emerges from a tunnel, that he is
kissing her baby's bottom. Additionally, its emphasis on visual gags can be
found elsewhere in the early genre, most resplendently in a "trick film"
such as Georges Méliès's *Voyage dans la lune* (1902), which uses stop-action
editing and superimposition to substitute one thing or figure for another,
yielding an effect akin to the magician's *nigromantīa*. However, perhaps
more pertinently than these many ancillary generic affiliations, *What Happened in the Tunnel*'s dependence on a "bait-and-switch" narrative calls to
mind the many racial explorations of this plot device that precede and follow this particular Edison offering: *Soap v. Blacking* (Edison, 1903), which
shows a man who, duped into picking up a bar of shoe blacking another
character has substituted for soap, "washes" with the shoe polish, blacken-
ing himself up as in a blackface minstrel; *The Mis-Directed Kiss* (AMBCO,
1904), in which an elderly, near-sighted white gentleman caller accidentally
kisses the hand of his beloved's black maid; and *Nellie, the Beautiful Housemaid* (Vitagraph, 1908), in which three old men answer an ad for the house-
keeping services of a "Nellie White," only to discover, on her arrival, that,
much to their astonishment, Nellie White is actually "black."

Owing to the labors of scholars from Tom Gunning to Lynne Kirby (and
they, in turn, to the work of Wolfgang Schivelbusch), we possess a rather
precise set of knowledges regarding the intersection of the railroad with
early cinema, particularly as that intersection receives a kind of fetal plot in
What Happened in the Tunnel. As Gunning explains, in his sustained meditations on "the cinema of attractions," early cinema was less dominated by
a narrative impulse than was earlier thought—was conceived less as a way
of plotting character, of organizing time as a sequence of events, as a measure of motion with respect to before and after, than it was organized "as a
way of presenting a series of views to an audience," views that fascinated
due in large measure to their "illusory power . . . and exoticism."[51] The
words of Méliès, as cited by Gunning, betray this emphasis: "As for the scenario, the 'fable,' or 'tale,' I only consider it at the end. I can state that the

scenario constructed in this manner has *no importance,* since I use it merely as a pretext for the 'stage effects,' the 'tricks,' or for a nicely arranged tableau."[52] *Curiositas,* or "the lust of the eyes," is the term Saint Augustine lends to this habit—that "disease of curiosity" that craves unbeautiful (in the words of Lacan, "unlust") things and, Augustine adds, on account of which "monsters and anything out of the ordinary are put on show in our theatres."[53] Cinema viewers were, on the evidence, attracted to the apparatus itself, lured by the technology's "aesthetics of astonishment": attracted to and lured by the spectacle of traveling westward through vast expanses of landscape, where, in the case of the illustrated lectures called Hale's Tours, spectators assumed the vicarious role of passengers, seated as they were in theaters outfitted with train clatter audio effects and the appropriate swaying; attracted to and lured by the pure exhibitionism of a close-up used not as an "enlargement for narrative punctuation, but as an attraction in its own right," as in the case of Edwin S. Porter's *The Gay Shoe Clerk* (1903), where a heretofore demur lady lifts her skirt, exposing her ankle for all to see; or, finally, attracted to and lured by the display of objects magically materialized or characters vanished in a puff of smoke, which attractions, in the genre of the trick film, demonstrate the unique illusory properties of cinema.[54] The aesthetic of astonishment would seem to satisfy the Freudian maxim, offered in *Beyond the Pleasure Principle,* that "novelty is always the condition of enjoyment."[55] However, far from being completely indifferent to that suspension of disbelief characteristic of narrative cinema, the cinema of attractions "acts out the contradictory stages of involvement with the image, unfolding, like other nineteenth-century visual entertainments, a vacillation between belief and incredulity."[56]

What *Happened*'s pivotal blackout partakes, according to the terms established here, of a solicitation. By means of its momentary yet complete suspension of all temporal and spatial markers, of all setting and character, and its jocose return to another scene, the film explores the suspicion that cinema, like photography and painting earlier, plays tricks on the human eye. What *Happened*'s "astonishment" effect—its elision of blackness with darkness, of the occlusion of light with the suspension of vision—promotes the principally painterly notion that the eye could be fooled, mobilizes yet again the resurgent fear of trompe l'oeil ("trick the eye").[57] I want to take a moment to summarize this painterly tradition and to explore its relevance to turn-of-the-century film.

Long before the advent of either photography or cinema, the trompe l'oeil painting provides a representation whose chief (and ironic) goal is "to conceal itself as representation" (*Gold Standard*, 161). Trompe l'oeil works are designed to convince the beholder that what he or she sees is not a work of art representing objects but the objects themselves. Thus, trompe l'oeil, from the ancient Greek frescoes to turn-of-the-century American monetary illusionism, participates in an aesthetics whose choice of subject matter (usually flat) and claims on perspectival depth (usually nil) wields devices "for reproducing in the perception of representations the physiology of perceiving the objects they represent" (*Gold Standard*, 162). The naked human eye and its powers of perception, given pride of place *by* this aesthetic deception, prove the ultimate measure and guarantee of epistemological certainty — or, at least, such was the case prior to the advent of photography. Photography poses the greatest challenge to the eye's supremacy because it mechanizes and displaces the latter's perceptive powers — with the principal effect, as one scholar notes, that "vision, which had formerly quite clearly 'belonged' to the individual subject, is expropriated by the machine."[58] Photography and cinema collectively prove an affront to seeing, each promoting "a crisis of confidence in the organ of vision which till then had reigned over all representation as its official standard scientifically."[59] Cinematic trompe l'oeil is thus photography's fraudulence once removed.

A slight corrective: the fade to black provided a solicitation in the form of a deception. The problem faced by the cultural form at large was how to persuade reticent masses that the motion pictures provided "an effective pictorial composition of everyday life in motion," an adequate verisimilitude that was at the same time removed enough from the sphere of their everyday lives ("novel" enough) to warrant their investment in a new entertainment industry.[60] Cinema's dilemma, like the earlier tasks of photography, was to appear both real and unreal: banal, corporeal, and undeniably recognizable, on the one hand, and ideal, desirable, and satisfyingly unfamiliar, on the other. The objective was not simply to ameliorate this dilemma but to transform it into something of a heuristic, to make it an integral part of the cinema's then-emergent grammar of spectatorship. Cinema would thus capture the necessary audience once it converted its founding dilemma of believability into a wellspring of aesthetically conditioned pleasure, once it transformed the "astonishment" at unexpected narrative turns into the willful suspension of disbelief. In *What Happened in the Tunnel*, blackness flickers on and off the screen to remind the viewer of cinema's adequate yet never completely believable realism and mimesis; and, what is more, the film further confirms the limits of cinema's representational power by synchronizing it with the archisemiotics of the railroad. The darkness of the tunnel and the framed panorama of the landscape work in sync with the cinema technology and the fade to black and mise-en-scène to suggest that similar principles of construction and operation are at work.

Lynne Kirby, in her recent study *Parallel Tracks,* reads *What Happened in the Tunnel* as part of the "free-floating visuality" associated with the railroad and the silent cinema, part of the "now you see it, now you don't" perception on which these machines of nineteenth-century visual culture are premised.[61] She argues that in early train films, like early trick films, the "in-between space" (Schivelbusch's term) of the tunnel, its darkness — or, relatedly, the exhibitionist, nonnarrative "attractions" in which, according to Gunning, early cinema seems persistently to wallow — is closely identified with what she terms the "joke space" of substitution. "Joke space" defines a space of displacement, in which a repressed meaning takes the place of an acceptable one, or, as Freud details in his analysis of the obscene joke, that "shame or embarrassment" at an erotic situation that gets displaced into smut, admits by its very nature to the sexual excitement of that original situation ("If a man in a company of men enjoys telling or listening to smut, the original situation, which owing to social inhibitions cannot be realized, is at the same time imagined").[62] In *What Happened,* Kirby observes, following this Freudian model, the substitution is one of black woman for white in which the tunnel plays a pivotal role in the reversal. The prohibitions of turn-of-the-century culture make it such that the substitution provides the occasion for a reversal of opposites: "It is not acceptable to desire respectable white women . . . but it is tacitly acceptable to desire unrespectable (black) women . . . only not in public" (98–99). The black maid, consequently, is invested with a sexuality denied her white counterpart, and her blackness converged with that of the tunnel "in a reversal of opposites whose relationship is normally repressed, i.e., kept invisible" (99). Certainly, social code and narrative expectation are the stuff of all genres; yet in *What Happened,* in its pivotal switch, it is their tenuousness that appears to be relevant. Again Kirby: "The repetition and sameness of train space, in which all spaces are interchangeable and only temporarily occupied by different people is in these early films an excuse to upset expectations and the moral codes on which they are based" (92). In many silent railway films, she adds, "trains functioned as containers, stages for action. . . . The sense in which the railway journey provides a contained space and time, a special 'nowhere' outside the sphere of normal rules and codes of conduct, has been seized on by directors from the beginning of film history" (242).[63]

I have gone to great lengths to catalog a set of *idées reçu* because, without some account either of an astonishment effect that would find pleasure in the extemporized suspension of narrative or, contrarily, of the social density of a phobic plot's substitutions, the multiple valences of *What Happened*'s fade to black might very well do just that, fade from our view. By the terms deployed in the substitution thesis, the fade-out provides the element that pushes this film in the direction of narrative (providing a founding investment in the art of montage), while, by the terms preserved in the astonishment account, this very element proves the device through which ludic participation in an aesthetic of attractions seems finally to be maintained. Yet it is precisely for reasons of this filigreed set of attachments, which seem too easily bundled and resolved by an interest either in narrative or in its hiatus, that the theses displayed seem too canny by half, too handily invested in ways of reading the fade to black that reflect the classical (and, hence, more recently arrived at) techniques of cinema. To propose that attractions take place in narrative's "in-between" spaces, or to say more explicitly that formal gimmick rises to the status of a syntactical unit within an unfolding sexual narrative, is in either case to assume a posthumous knowledge of cinematic convention. I would like to offer an alternative to the Gunning and Kirby theses.

From this end of cinema history, we know that the slip into blackness indicates one of two things. More commonly, in both silent cinema and its sonorous issue, the fade-out indicates narrative's diversion. It is the moment when a film says to all literate readers, we are going to another part of the narrative, or, in the case of the suspense film, here we engage this story's necessary simultaneity (*"Maintenant, à l'autre part . . ."*). Less often, though, in the absence of this first option, almost as assuredly, the fade-out indicates that narrative has ended, that the screen time devoted to the fiction has ceased, that the time of the latter's unfolding has been suspended.[64] Neither "code" applies with any comfortable fit to *What Happened*'s fade to black, for in the wake of the blackout, at the moment of the joke's unveiling, the film reveals that it has been by means of this blackout that narrative has been hidden, occulted—neither diverted nor suspended. A turn-of-the-century spectator would most likely have read the screen's blank darkness after the fact as a masking of the diegesis, as a deliberate concealment. That said, it warrants assertion that in order for the film's joke to work, its implied spectator cannot know that narrative is in the midst of its own occultation. In the instance in question, the blackout promises simultaneity or denouement only riotously to undercut expectations of either an errant or a conclusive sort. It seems fitting, then, to ask a number of questions. What if, sustaining that trompe l'oeil emphasis on perception about which I had earlier remarked and assuming that a classical encoding of form had yet to be fully ensconced, it were possible to read into the authorial "intention" behind the intervening matte a presumption of illegibility and illiteracy? What interpretation might be sustained by an understanding of this film's ideal reader as an ignorant one, one who might "read" the film's blank darkness as a sign of either technological breakdown, narrative unfulfillment, or temporal suspension—as a sign of either accident or chance? What meaning is obscured by a gimmick that throws narrative agency into a "black box"? And, what if, furthermore, given a presumption of ignorance, the whole point of the joke were heuristic, to provide a scene of instruction adequate to display and render intelligible cinema's emerging relevance to both aesthetic form (the blackness of film) and social code (the blackness of the retainer), both diegesis and extradiegesis, that is, given those pertinent historical factors of an emerging visual semiotics and railway segregation (a de facto racial semiotics), both film form and legal logic? What peculiar hermeneutic might be served by coincidences such as these? It is a hermeneutic gesture, finally, one provisionally psychoanalytic (as the foregoing paragraphs demonstrate) yet also classically phenomenological, that will help us to answer these questions, help us to apprehend the naive psychic life of machines, help us to lend accident some worthy significance.

A setting from which our gaze has been diverted but to which it is forced finally to return, and as if instinctually, might be described as a "repetition"—an echo, a return, a coming-back—a thwarting of readerly *Erwartungshorizont* [horizon of expectations], and one, clearly, in the instance under scrutiny, possessed of a signal difference.[65] In the classical phenomenology attributed to Aristotle, where time is said to have elapsed on a perception of motion (where time exists as a measure of motion between "before" and "after"), repetition represents motion arrested, a movement thwarted, an interrupted itinerary, a detour.[66] Further, where in the same phenomenology reason represents the persistence of time's motion ("reason is of what is always or for the most part" [197a20]), it follows that, in accord with repetition's antipathy to linear time, its sign is often that of luck or chance, of the astonishingly unwilled. Aristotle explains: "It is right to say that luck is contrary to reason; for reason is of what is always or for the most part, while luck is present in events that are outside of these. So, since such causes are indefinite, luck too is indefinite" (197a20–22). Chance, it is added, "exists when something occurs in vain," that is, "when that for the sake of which something is done does not result" (197b22–24, 197b30–33). By Aristotle's account, an act sustained "in vain" (an event subject to chance intervention) is bracketed off from the filiations that limn action to consequence. Similarly, a repetition represents a "slice of time" bracketed off from a beginning and an end (what Foucault would more recently designate "heterochronia," or "when men arrive at a sort of absolute break with their traditional time").[67] Outside of time (extempore), repetitions may be said to indicate suspensions of linearity, to insinuate a metaphysics of rupture—a break in the causal chain, an unraveling in the web of causation. Lacan would designate this rupture *tuché* in his translation of Aristotle's τύχη ("chance"): "What is repeated, in fact, is always something that occurs—the expression tells us quite a lot about its relation to the *tuché—as if by chance.*"[68] It is difficult to extricate repetition from chance when, as in a jazz performer's improvised riffs, the former is understood as a suspension of linearity, as a moment of break and return, as a break in the chain of causation.

Recall how Freud explained the compulsion to repeat [*Wiederholungszwang*].[69] When the patient fails to remember the whole of what is repressed in him, when he loses access to the past, he is often obliged to repeat "some portion of his forgotten life" and to do so as "a contemporary experience" (18–19, 35). He ritually acts out the repressed element of his past, as if drawn by some recondite force back to the original scene of drama, experiencing it as if under "some 'daemonic' force" "instead of . . . *remembering* it as something belonging to the past" (18). Thus, when "the pressure of external disturbing forces" wanes, when cultural repressions cease to hold sway, when the subject veers "beyond the pleasure principle," what appears to be an unwilled staging of history replaces the latter's usual expressions—dialogue, memory, reflection (36). As repetitions are always repetitions *of*, within this schema the eruption of seemingly unwilled and idiosyncratic repetitions in the present plays out a journey into the past.

A more complex assessment of the joke's repetition and reversal is now within reach. The blackout—the ability for the blackness of the screen and the darkness of the tunnel to stand in place of one another, and for them both to coincide with the maid's unsettling blackness—participates in a peculiarly social modality of Freud's repetition compulsion. Without assenting entirely to the psychoanalytic blueprint, I would argue that the fade to black's concealment approximates an incident of repression, one whose main consequence is to place "some portion of . . . forgotten life" beyond reach. The fade is a curtain, one whose blackness throws just beyond the

veil of apprehension acts obscene (from L., *sceaena*, ~*ae*, background)—
that is, the blackness of race, an exchange within libidinal economy, an in-
stinctual gesture.[70] Might, then, the reversal augur a particular repressed
history, an ersatz staging of a history beyond reach? Is the film's switch essentially a facetious construction of an alternative history, an instance of the
counterfactual? Are we warranted in the speculation that *What Happened*'s
reversal evidences the persistence of the counterfactual's subjunctive mood,
of the social pressure of its counterhistorical imagination? Could not the
joke be summed up as follows: What if, through some dispensation of providence, blacks were to become white, and whites black, what effect would
that have on the social, on relations of intimacy? Or, similarly, if there were
no railway segregation, if blacks and whites could sit side by side (more precisely, if seats were so standardized as to make their occupants interchangeable), what purchase might one race have on the other's erotic networks of intimacy, and what "necessary condition" would that history, or
that violation of exchange, represent?

Something more than a simple bait and switch lies hidden in the film's
proverbial "black box," more than is revealed in the denouement—but to
see how formal gimmick correlates with counterfactualism's subjunctive
mood I need to provide *What Happened in the Tunnel* with a relevant historical supplement. The supplement comes in the form of that doctrine that
makes blacks and whites, from the vantage of the law, interchangeable, fungible: the doctrine of equal protection enshrined in the Fourteenth Amendment to the Constitution. So, bracketing issues of film form for just a moment, I want now to return to the legal logics, arguments, and jousts
coincident with the first chapters in the era of equal protection.

Track Two

On July 10, 1890, midway through its session, the Louisiana legislature
ratified the Separate Car Act, a statute that provided that "all railway companies carrying passengers in their coaches in this State, shall provide equal
but separate accommodations for the white, and colored races" (*Plessy*,
540). The Separate Car Act was curious for a host of reasons, not least of
which was the manner in which it enabled racial designation, what
amounted to the empowered force of a judicial attribution, without providing any statutory definition (or scientific calculation) of race. The law left
the particular disciplinary procedure of classifying persons to the various
pertinent "officers, directors, conductors and employés of railway companies" and added that, "should any passenger refuse to occupy the coach or

compartment to which he or she is assigned by the officer of such railway, said officer shall have the power to refuse to carry such passenger on his train, and for such refusal neither he nor the railway company that he represents shall be liable for damages in any of the courts in this State" (*Plessy*, 541). In a final proviso, which matched this exemption from liability's pliable responsiveness to tort with a comparably irrepressible awareness of class, the legislature averred that "nothing in this act shall be construed as applying to nurses attending children of the other race" (*Plessy*, 541).

Resistance to the law was organized and swift; with the formation, before gavel's fall, by blacks from New Orleans' Creole community, of the American Citizens' Equal Rights Association, and by autumn of the following year, the organization of a "Citizens' Committee to Test the Constitutionality of the Separate Car Law."[71] The proposed test case was organized by attorneys Louis A. Martinet, an original signatory to the Equal Rights Association manifesto, and Albion W. Tourgée. Martinet and Tourgée floated a range of legal conjectures and corresponding scenarios, all with the intent to challenge both railway practices (de facto segregation) and the existing legal doctrines that protected them (their de jure correlates).

Should the test take as its object of scrutiny the legislature's decision to endow railway officials with the power and authority of a judicial attribution? Would such a challenge, if it proved the arbitrariness of the law's racial classification, demonstrate that the attribution of race permitted by law violated the Fourteenth Amendment's equal protection clause? While conceding that to have a mulatto who was nearly white attempt to board a "white" car would offer an appropriate mise-en-scène in which to stage such a challenge, counsel agreed that a black person who was indiscernibly black might not be refused entrance to a white car. A second strategy, Martinet and Tourgée reasoned, would have to be entertained. Should the committee test the Louisiana law on the grounds that it violated the interstate commerce clause of the U.S. Constitution (Article 1, Section 9)? This test might require a black passenger to book a seat from out of state and be forced into a Jim Crow car on entry into the state of Louisiana; but, as the lawyers once again jointly conceded, given that adjacent states had passed similar legislation, the likelihood was that said passenger would be assigned to a car set aside for the black race from the beginning of his journey. Given these loopholes in the law, the case, it seemed, would have to revolve around the nature of the initial legal action, around a specific performance either enabled or prohibited by the Louisiana statute. Should the client purposely violate the conductor's express assignment, thereby forcing the latter to play that hand that, legally dealt him by the legislature, empowered him to refuse to carry passengers who failed to go to their assigned cars? A challenge of this order promised a means of tarrying with nearly every provision of the Reconstruction Amendments (specifically, the Thirteenth's regard for involuntary servitude and the Fourteenth's guarantees of due process and equal protection). But then, there was by century's end the bitter memory of a recent line of cases in which the federal Supreme Court so constricted the boundaries surrounding that jurisprudence associated with Thirteenth- and Fourteenth-Amendment pleading that even refusal of accommodation on account of race seemed a tight fit.

The first blow was dealt in the *Slaughter-House Cases* of 1873—the first federal judicial examination of the Reconstruction Amendments and a response to several lower-court cases. The original state challenges were initiated by a group of Louisiana butchers who, excluded from an abattoir that proved a near-monopoly on their commerce, the Crescent City Live-Stock Landing and Slaughter-House Company, sued to enjoin enforcement of the company charter. In *Slaughter-House,* the Court ruled against the plaintiffs. The arguments of the plaintiffs' counsel inspired their supporters on the bench to claim that the butchers, having been denied the right to pursue a common calling, suffered a "servitude" comparable to that of ancien régime France, whose revolutionary insurgents tended to associate the term with all restrictions on employment and occupation. In the opinion of the majority, whatever the etymology of the term "involuntary servitude," the requisite provision of the Thirteenth Amendment was aimed clearly and expressly at those practices of bondage coincident with the institution of chattel slavery.[72] Similarly, in *United States v. Cruikshank* (1876), *United States v. Harris* (1883), and the *Civil Rights Cases* (1883) and in further extension of the spirit of compromise, the federal Supreme Court ruled that, contrary to the Fourteenth Amendment's express prohibitions against state actions that violated fundamental constitutional rights, most incidents of mob violence, lynching, and racial discrimination in public accommodations, respectively, rose only to the status of individual acts or private wrongs—breaches of duty, or torts, that were certainly open to civil remedy but were far beyond the purview of constitutional law: "An individual cannot deprive a man of his right to vote, to hold property, to buy and sell, to sue in the courts, or to be a witness or a juror; . . . [for] unless protected in these wrongful acts by some shield of State law or State authority he cannot destroy or injure the right; he will only render himself amenable to satisfaction or punishment."[73] Conscious perhaps of the court's determination to undermine federal jurisdiction in cases involving everything from denials of accommodation to southern mob violence, Martinet and Tourgée decided against staging an expulsion from a segregated railway car, for it would likely serve only to force a conductor to exercise his power to refuse service. They did so in the belief that such an exercise of the law might not result in an arrest and a criminal proceeding—might permit, that is, of a suit for civil damages as the sole legitimate means to test the Louisiana accommodations law. It was settled, finally, that their client must attempt entry into a "white" car with such force and such resolve as to produce his own arrest. The test of the separate car law would thus shift to a habeas corpus proceeding in federal court, "formally to obtain the release of the arrestee, but actually to have the separate car law declared unconstitutional" (*The Plessy Case*, 32).

Lawyers for the Citizens' Committee took as their client Daniel F. Desdunes and arranged with authorities from the Louisville and Nashville (L & N) Railroad to have a conductor of the railway swear out a complaint under the law's criminal provision on Desdunes's refusal to seat himself in the Jim Crow car (for reasons of expense, few railways found the mandate to uphold segregation appealing, and so conspired with black plaintiffs to challenge the law). Desdunes, an "octoroon" and son of one of the founders of the American Citizens' Equal Rights Association, purchased a first-class ticket for the trip from New Orleans to Mobile, Alabama, and, as planned, in accord with all stage directions, suffered arrest for taking a seat in a white car on the L & N. For all his lawyers' legal preparations, Desdunes's case soon took second seat on the judicial docket to another, *Abbott v. Hicks* (1892), in which the Louisiana Supreme Court decided that separate car laws were not intended to apply to interstate passengers and that, when so applied, were an unconstitutional violation of the federal interstate commerce clause. *Abbott* held, in echo of an earlier federal Supreme Court ruling, *Louisville, New Orleans and Texas Railway Company v. Mississippi* (1890), not that separate car laws, if applied solely to intrastate traffic, were categorically valid "but that they were not invalid on interstate commerce grounds" (*The Plessy Case*, 39–40). The commerce clause violation established, the court disposed of *State v. Desdunes* (1892). Having already adjudicated the essential subject matter within this suit, the court had no reason to revisit the relevant issues of law, and certainly no reason to do so in the same judicial season.[74]

Though *Abbott* ushered in the swift dismantling of segregation on interstate lines, having left open the issue of segregated travel within the state (having failed to confront, that is, the pertinence of constitutional protections against "slavery [and] involuntary servitude" and guarantees of "equal protection of the laws" and "due process of law"), the case enabled Tourgée and Martinet to initiate a second legal proceeding. This time, the lawyers chose Homer A. Plessy as their client, a Louisiana "octoroon," like the previous plaintiff, who described himself in legal records as "of mixed Caucasian and African blood, in the proportion of one-eighth African and seven-eighths Caucasian," the "African admixture not being perceptible" ("Brief," 30). Plessy purchased a ticket on the East Louisiana Railway for a journey within the state and, after insisting on boarding a coach reserved for whites, was arrested for violating the separate car law. The case made its way through two layers of state courts (the criminal district proceedings of *State v. Plessy* and, later, the state supreme court's deliberations in *Ex parte Plessy*).[75] Plessy's lawyers, in anticipation it seemed of a federal Supreme Court challenge, argued in these proceedings that even a law governing separate accommodations within the state violated federal constitutional protections of the rights of citizenship. The statute in question established an "insidious distinction" between citizens "based on race"; and, furthermore, "obnoxious to the fundamental principles of national citizenship," Louisiana's racial discrimination in public carriage "perpetuates involuntary servitude" (in violation of the Thirteenth Amendment) and "abridges the privileges and immunities" of all citizens of the United States (in violation of the Fourteenth Amendment).[76] The Louisiana Supreme Court ruled, in denial of Plessy's appeal, that in the opinion of nearly every court that had taken up the matter, statutes that mandated separate accommodations, so long at least as those accommodations are "substantially equal," had been taken "not [to have] abridge[d] any privilege or immunity of Citizens or otherwise contravene[d] the XIV Amendment" (*Thin Disguise*, 72). These cases concurred, writes Justice Fenner, in the principle that "equality, and not identity or community, of accommodations, is the extreme test of conformity to the requirements of the fourteenth amendment"—though, to little surprise, he provides no workable differentiation of "equality" from "identity" (*Thin Disguise*, 72). Not the least bit curious to subsequent judicial reviewers of *Ex parte Plessy*'s scrutiny of the Fourteenth Amendment was the majority's citation practice, its appeal to precedent in *Roberts v. City of Boston* (1849) and *West Chester and Philadelphia Railroad Company v. Miles* (1867), cases involving segregation in schools and railways, respectively, which were rendered prior to the adoption of the Fourteenth Amendment or, in the case of the former, prior to the Civil

War itself.[77] Their rehearing refused, counsel for Plessy were presented with no further barriers to a federal constitutional test.

Nineteenth-century rules of pleading required that those seeking a higher court's review of a case's record detail all procedural inconsistencies and faults in ruling evident in a lower court's decision. Following said rules, Plessy's counsel sued for a "writ of error," filing an "assignment of errors" against *Ex parte Plessy* in the U.S. Supreme Court.[78] Plessy and his lawyers maintained in the assignment that the Louisiana court erred against both Thirteenth and Fourteenth Amendment principles. With regards to the former, the statute upheld on appeal "import[ed] a badge of servitude" by perpetuating "the distinction of race and caste among citizens of the United States"; and, similarly, it promoted "observances of a servile character co-incident with the institution of slavery."[79] What was more, by authorizing railway officers to refuse to carry passengers who contest their coach as-signments and by exempting these same authorities from liability for in-jury—that is, by denying a class of persons that access to remedy (i.e., dam-age suits) available to all other citizens—the law failed to extend "to all citizens alike the equal protection of the laws."

Tourgée elaborated his client's complaint in the "Brief for the Plaintiff in Error" that he filed along with the federal writ. The Louisiana law's assort-ment of "the white and colored races in the enjoyment of chartered privi-leges," he maintained, violated the Fourteenth Amendment to an even greater extent than the writ's emphasis on equal protection admits; for, de-priving the plaintiff of the privileges of traveling as a white man, it dispos-sessed him "without due process of law" of a property right in his reputa-tion. Plaintiffs' counsel reasoned that "in any mixed community" the reputation of belonging to the white race is property "in the same sense that a right of action or of inheritance is *property*" ("Brief," 8). These arguments echoed those Tourgée made in *Pactolus Prime,* where the title character ex-horts his light-skinned assistant Benny (who is secretly his son), "You can't help the rest of the colored race by remaining a nigger, and you can do a good thing for yourself and save your children from an inheritance of woe by making yourself white" (41). This last phrase implies both legacies of in-jury and the social capital that accrues to whiteness, but the rhetoric in Tourgée's "Brief " is more tightly interwoven with that of jurists Samuel Warren and Louis Brandeis's recently published "The Right to Privacy" (1890).

In that article, you recall, Warren and Brandeis argued that in a man's right to his "reputation, the standing among his fellow-men"—the right not

to be defamed, cast publicly in a false light, or intruded on unsolicitously—
"there inheres the quality of being owned or possessed," which quality,
they added, suggests that "there may be some propriety in speaking of
those rights as property."[80] Reasoning in similar manner, Tourgée asserted
that any law that endowed another with "the power to deprive one of the
reputation of being a white man, or at least to impair that reputation" put at
risk something "which has an actual pecuniary value" ("Brief," 8). Tourgée
calculated:

> How much would it be *worth* to a young man entering upon a practice of law,
> to be regarded as a *white* man rather than a colored one? Six-sevenths of the
> population are white. Nineteen-twentieths of the property of the country is
> owned by white people. Ninety-nine hundredths of the business opportuni-
> ties are in the control of white people. These propositions are rendered even
> more startling by the intensity of feeling which excludes the colored man
> from the friendship and companionship of the white man. Probably most
> white persons if given a choice, would prefer death to life in the United States
> *as colored persons.* Under these conditions, is it possible to conclude that the
> *reputation of being white* is not property? Indeed, is it not the most valuable
> sort of property, being the master key that unlocks the golden door of op-
> portunity? ("Brief," 9)

Strong echoes of Warren and Brandeis, certainly; still, Tourgée sounded a
note heard first in the more distant reflections of Jeremy Bentham, for
whom property served as "nothing but the basis of expectation." It was
through the sting of a libelous misrepresentation, then, and one that denied
the plaintiff of all the privileges he might expect as a white man, that the separate car law dispossessed Homer Plessy of his property in himself "without due process of law."

The second, more nuanced violation of Plessy's constitutional rights
concerned the manner in which the state arrogated to itself rights that were
the proper province of federal law. As Tourgée elaborated further, the separate car law, while ostensibly passed with the "peace and comfort" of all
passengers in mind, could only make the most specious claims to serve the
"interest of public order." Rather, the Louisiana law proved a most nefari-
ous preserve of the rights and reasons pertinent to "state sovereignty":
"The history of the times shows that exclusive state control over the persons and rights of the citizens of the state was not only the Gibralter of slavery, but was the chief ingredient of that 'paramount allegiance to the State,'
which was the twin of the doctrine of secession" ("Brief," 21–22). Those

claims to absolute rights that subtended secessionist passions were the very disease in governmentality for which the Fourteenth Amendment was offered as a cure, for when the Amendment brought the "rights, privileges and immunities" of state citizenship within "the scope of national jurisdiction" it essentially made "state citizenship . . . [an] incident of *national* citizenship" ("Brief," 6).[81] Nothing expressed with greater clarity the qualified (and subordinate) nature of state sovereignty than the very inconsistencies that riddled the cases the lower court drew on for authority. Tourgée settled on *United States v. Cruikshank,* a case that arose after a white mob attacked a meeting of blacks in Louisiana, killing upward of a hundred people, and one in which the federal Supreme Court ruled that the censures of the Fourteenth (protecting "life, liberty, and property") applied to state and not private activity (the latter of which the violence under scrutiny was an incident). The court then proceeded, Tourgée noted, "to affirm that 'sovereignty' for this purpose (that is for the protection of the natural rights of the individual) 'rests alone with the State'" ("Brief," 22). *Cruikshank* reads: "[It is the] duty of the States to protect all persons within their boundaries in the enjoyment of those inalienable rights with which they were endowed by their creator" (*United States v. Cruikshank* 553). Laws not emanating from any manmade entity, the *Cruikshank* court reasoned, were rightly protected by federalism's lesser progeny, the state. It was only the protection of a most curious sovereignty, *Plessy* counsel warned, that was served by this particular scripting of "the natural rights of the individual," only the surreptitious defense of a paternalism of the most familiar sort that read the Constitution's protections as particular rather than universal. On the matters of "slavery" and "involuntary servitude" a "universal" affirmation of the rights coincident with being "citizens of the United States" was the express objective, Tourgée asserted, of the Thirteenth, Fourteenth, and Fifteenth Amendments. In much corrective legislation, of which the Reconstruction Amendments are certainly exemplary, a "wrong done to specific individuals or classes is prohibited, not as to those classes alone, but as to *all;* or a specific offense calls attention to possible kindred offenses, and the whole class is prohibited instead of the particular evil" ("Brief," 20). "All" can never be made to mean "some," he cautioned, nor "every person" be properly construed to apply solely to one class or race, "until the laws of English speech are overthrown" ("Brief," 20). "Justice is pictured blind and her daughter, the Law, ought at least to be color-blind"; or, in what amounts to the same thing, counsel averred, the "true construction" of the Fourteenth Amendment's equal protection is not as "a compar-

ative equality"—not merely equal as between one race of persons and another, not merely the parity achieved by means of some principle of equivalence whereby whole classes of persons might be said to have been *made*
equal—but, in a more atomistic (individualistic and liberal-humanist) manner, a "just and universal equality whereby the rights of life, liberty, and
property are secured to all—the rights that belong to a citizen in every free
country and every republican government" ("Brief," 19, 23).

Against the lower court's erroneous genealogies, Tourgée turned the attention of the appeals tribunal to another line of legal precedents. He found
the legal authority for Homer Plessy's claims for a property right in his
whiteness and to the privileges of his federal citizenship in the case of
Strauder v. West Virginia, a case challenging jury disqualification on the
grounds of race (and—for reasons that should now be clear to us—I cite in
full the relevant passage from *Strauder,* the passage Tourgée cited in the
"Brief"): "If in those states where the colored people constitute a majority
of the entire population a law should be enacted excluding all white men,
from jury or service, thus denying to them the privilege of participating
equally with the blacks in the administration of justice, we apprehend no
one would be heard to claim that it would not be a denial to white men of
the equal protection of the laws. Nor, if a law should be passed excluding all
naturalized Celtic Irishmen, would there be any doubt of its inconsistency
with the spirit of the amendment."[82] *Strauder* recognized breadth of principle where *Cruikshank* granted to the emancipatory decrees, as Cable had
so eloquently noted, only the most "reluctant or simulated acceptance of
their narrowest letter . . . a virtual suffocation of those principles of human
equity which the unwelcome decrees do little more than shadow forth."
Cruikshank attended with such zeal to the Fourteenth Amendment's restrictive provisions, as Tourgée read the case, that it neglected completely
those affirmative clauses that procured and protected the rights of federal,
national citizenship; those clauses that define "all persons born or naturalized in the United States" as "citizens of the United States and of the state
wherein they reside." *Cruikshank* wrested the provision's abstract language
(of "any person," "no State," and "any law") from its "plain meaning"—
Tourgée's phrase—with one final, fatal result, "to exclude all other force
and consequence" ("Brief," 19–20). So narrowly did *Cruikshank* read the
Fourteenth Amendment's first section that it failed to see that that contribution of the amendment was "in strict accord" with the Declaration of Independence—a document, Tourgée reminded, "which is not a fable as
some of our modern theorists would have us believe."[83] So determined was

the *Cruikshank* court to preserve a blinkered view of the amendment's provisions, to see them as directed solely and exclusively toward "the protection of the colored citizens," that any court that took that opinion as authority and law would similarly fail to see that the doctrine of equal protection correlated with and enhanced the Declaration's assertion that "all men are created equal"—would fail to see, finally, that the amendment ranks universality above particularity. I cite once again Tourgée's query to the court:

> Suppose a member of this court, nay, suppose every member of it, by some mysterious dispensation of providence should wake tomorrow with a black skin and curly hair—the two obvious and controlling indications of race—and in traveling through that portion of the country where the "Jim Crow Car" abounds, should be ordered into it by the conductor. It is easy to imagine what would be the result, the indignation, the protests, the assertion of pure Caucasian ancestry. But the conductor, the autocrat of Caste, armed with the power of the State conferred by this statute, will listen neither to denial or protest. "In you go or out you go," is his ultimatum. ("Brief," 35–36)

Tourgée called for a work of empathy, implicitly, but the warning could neither be misunderstood nor phrased more sharply: were the court's nine justices sufficiently to engage this imaginative counterfactual work, they would then "feel and know" that an "assortment of the citizens on the line of race" ranked as "a discrimination intended to humiliate and degrade the former subject and dependent class" ("Brief," 36).

It is important to come to some understanding of why Tourgée (and, before him, the *Strauder* court) called for a work of empathy, for a balanced measure of how "people like us" might experience a law against how others might respond to the same law, or, contrarily, why in the case of Grady (and, before him, the *Cruikshank* and *Slaughter-House* courts) the response called for was a more entrenched inclemency. Perhaps most important, we should wonder why both Tourgée and Grady deployed counterfactuals to achieve such disparate ends. Of *Cruikshank,* moreover, it seems appropriate to ask the following: Why risk the assertion that the protection of "inalienable rights" was the "duty of the States" when that phrase and those rights (in the form of those "unalienable rights" asserted in the Declaration of Independence) were so foundationally lodged in an arena beyond and before the law, and, as most at the time would have agreed, the states and their powers mere outgrowths of these same "unalienable rights"?[84] From *Slaughter-House* similar doubts followed: Under what constitutional doc-

trine was it possible to maintain, as the Court did, that "involuntary servitude" was aimed exclusively at chattel slavery, and the Thirteenth Amendment's meaning thus fixed at the moment of its ratification (circa 1865), and
the amendment itself unique, where constitutional provisions go, in its irrelevance to subsequent concerns? We might want at the same time to ask
why Plessy's lawyers made the admittedly extraordinary claim to a constitutionally guaranteed property right in his reputation as white—all with
appropriate accounting—so soon after Warren and Brandeis would extract
a "right to one's personality" from the bedrock of copyright and long before
any court would conclude that one's public persona had any "pecuniary
value."[85] Relevant to our concerns with "formal equality," we could ask too
why these same lawyers charged that racial classifications violated the Thirteenth Amendment's restraints against "involuntary servitude" when
classifications of any sort, whether they benefited or harmed individual
members of a group, would by definition appear to violate the Fourteenth's
provision that no state should "deny to any *person* within its jurisdiction the
equal protection of the laws."

Claim to a property barely cognizable by law? Superfluous assertion of
the residues of slavery's inequities? Appeals that partook more of empathy
than of the established legal practices of the day, in the latter of which the
more customary "appeal" to precedent ensured reproduction of the law's
authority? Empathic claims more responsive to the vicissitudes of psychic
identification than rooted in textual reference and the "letter of the law"?

It would not place too great a burden onto either the letter of the law or
the act of legislative authorship to suggest that the fault here lies in the
meaning of "equality" as that term is enshrined in Section 1 of the Fourteenth Amendment. How precisely courts were to determine the equality
signified in the Constitution's equal protection clause had been, since the
convening of the Thirty-ninth Congress in 1866, a matter of no small dispute. It has in fact been proposed, by everyone from Eric Foner to Ronald
Dworkin, that the authors of the Fourteenth Amendment deliberately opted
for vague standards when it came to the constitutional need to restrain government from any denial of due process of law and to guarantee the equal
protection of the laws and that it was their decision to use language lacking
in any precision that caused much of the consequent legal and political controversy.[86] Dworkin observes, in his consideration of the moral foundation
of rights, *Taking Rights Seriously,* that unlike those constitutional guarantees and restraints that take the form of fairly precise rules—such as the
Fifth Amendment's guarantee to each citizen of the right to be free from

compulsion "to be a witness against himself" or, similarly, the Sixth Amendment rule securing to the accused in a federal criminal proceeding the right to "an impartial jury"—unlike these rights, the Fourteenth Amendment's equal protection clause "makes the concept of equality a test of legislation, but it does not stipulate any particular conception of that concept" (226).[87] There can be little doubt that the clause's authors intended to outlaw whatever policies would violate equality, specifically those pertaining to the recently emancipated, but, beyond that, they "left it to others to decide, from time to time, what [equality] means" (226). At the very least, the clause's guarantee of the individual right to equality can mean two things, can refer, that is, to two distinct rights: the right to equal treatment and the right to treatment as an equal.

In Dworkin's elaboration, the right to equal treatment entitles one "to an equal distribution of some opportunity or resource or burden" (227)—the distribution signaled, for example, by the doctrine of "one person, one vote"—and, relatedly, the right to treatment as an equal embraces, and with detectably sharper moral objective, the right "not to receive the same distribution of some burden or benefit, but to be treated with the same respect and concern as anyone else" (227). Where the moral appeal in the right to treatment as an equal lends it the appearance of a foundation, relative to that standard the right to equal treatment appears derivative, a variable of the *lex scripta,* a secondary effect of the former right's moral fundament.[88] The equal protection provision could remain vague and lacking in any precise elaboration of the particular instances the clause's drafters had in mind, for these legislators "assumed that these restraints could be justified by appeal to moral rights . . . which the constitutional provisions . . . might be said to recognize and protect" (133)—rights signaled by standards of equality, cruelty, fairness, and legality. Another way of phrasing the matter, again following Dworkin, would be to designate the right to treatment as an equal the Constitution's concept of equality and the right to equal treatment its specific conception of equality. When the clause's framers appeal to the concept of equality they mean to instruct subsequent legislators and jurists to extend true parity of effort and insight to all parties concerned, an appeal reflective of the belief that legal deliberations may suffer from the moral defect of inequality, which, of its many consequences, might result in an erroneous distribution of benefits and burdens. Those to whom the framers appeal have the added responsibility of "developing and applying" their own conception of equality as controversial cases arise (135). The legislators who voted initially on the right to equal protection may each have had their own particular conceptions of how this moral appeal could be applied, but each held his conceptions only "as his own theory of how the standard he set must be met" (135). Where the theory might change, the standard could not. Dworkin elaborates: "When I appeal to [equality] I pose a moral issue; when I lay down my conception of [equality] I try to answer it" (135). The difference between the right to treatment as an equal and the right to equal treatment is thus that of a standard that occasionally calls forth its nonetheless necessary test.

The legal hermeneutic Dworkin describes, stimulated by a vague standard of equality, opens the law up to a limitless array of "conceptions" as to what a just distribution might look like, opens it up, in fact, to the possibility that one person's unjust and erroneous conception might by another be judged just, as "even responsible men of good will differ when they try to elaborate . . . the moral rights that . . . the equal protection clause brings into the law" (*Taking Rights Seriously*, 133).[89] The elasticity of those foundational moral rights—that porosity to conflicting intention that Bentham caricatured as "nonsense upon stilts"—is arguably what gives rise to the open-endedness of the equal protection clause's application, and, as should come as a surprise to few, these oblique and filigreed relations between law and morals prove the quicksand on which most adjudicators of equal protection disputes stand. These relations had certainly given others cause for concern.[90]

We know from previous discussion that morality proved a veritable minefield in late-nineteenth-century Anglo-American jurisprudence, leading John Austin, Charles Sanders Pierce, Nicholas St. John Green, as well as Oliver Wendell Holmes, Jr., to critique the fallacy of the law's moral foundations.[91] The migration from law to morals (and back) was, as Holmes put it, a function of "the mere force of language," as the lexicon of "rights," "duties," "intent," "negligence," and "liability" was primarily formal in its legal efficacy and, secondarily (i.e., rarely or, better, arbitrarily), able to embrace the meanings of these words understood in their "moral sense." This earlier critique, extended to the question of equal protection, could be expected to take note of the fact that, faced with a Constitution marked occasionally by vague standards (a text of open semiotic texture), courts and legal thinkers would try futilely to answer the question of "which values, among adequately neutral and general ones, qualify as sufficiently important or fundamental or whathaveyou to be vindicated by the Court against other values affirmed by legislative acts?"[92] When Holmes said of the words "rights," "duties," etc., as he did in "The Path of the Law," that "to take these words in their moral sense, at some stage of the argument, [is] to drop into fallacy," he improvised an answer to this question: any "fundamental value" settled on in this manner was "arbitrary from a moral point of view."[93] What this means, finally, the legal scholar Alexander Bickel has been courageous enough to conclude: "No answer is what the wrong question begets."[94]

Dworkin may of course be correct about moral rights — correct in his assessment that less restrictive provisions like the equal protection clause call out for some search for fundamental values — but, by the same token, so may Holmes and the pragmatists. The history of twentieth-century jurisprudence supports even this contradictory claim, for the sustained attempts to fill in the content of the equal protection clause confirm the dangerous "criterionlessness" of the equality implied in that phrase. I noted in the previous chapter that during the "*Lochner* era" constitutional law found reason to embrace a generous miscellany of the tenets and procedures of laissez-faire capitalism, invalidating in a series of cases various sorts of worker protections on the grounds that as "class" entitlements these laws together proved a "meddlesome interferenc[e] with the rights of the individual." Almost coincident with the end of the *Lochner* era — which came to a close in the case of *West Coast Hotel v. Parrish* (1937) — the Court began to elaborate a set of standards by which to judge the content of the equal protection clause, by which to answer "the question of what inequalities are tolerable under what circumstances" (the question, if we extend the *Lochner* reasoning, of when a class or classification might be recognized by law).[95] These standards would come to be known as the "rationality" test and the "strict scrutiny" test, and both would be elaborated, with varying degrees of specificity, and only in a de facto manner, in the case of *United States v. Carolene Products Co.* (1938).[96]

The *Carolene* dispute had nothing to do with either race or racial classifications; it had to do, instead, with a federal statute prohibiting the interstate shipment of processed milk, which the Court upheld on the grounds that all the statute had to be was "rational," and it certainly was that. But in a famous footnote to that case, Justice Harlan Stone, in an effort both to clarify what he meant by "rational" and to suggest the conditions under which he thought that standard would not suffice, laid the groundwork for a stronger standard that the Court might use to determine the constitutionality of racial classifications in the law. When a court saw fit to measure a law or a classification by a standard of "rationality," it held implicitly that the law was constitutional so long as a reasonable person could see a sufficient correlation between the evil or activity targeted and the trait used as the basis of the classification. But, as Stone observes in his footnote, those "statutes directed at particular religious . . . or national . . . or racial minorities," those statutes that may have sprung from "prejudice against discrete and insular minorities," must in addition, he cautioned, "call for a correspondingly *more searching judicial inquiry*" (*Carolene*, 152–53n. 4, emphasis mine).[97] On such occasions, the Supreme Court may have had reason to want to flush out unconstitutional motivations in the case of those classifications aimed at groups known to be the object of widespread vilification, may have had reason to make an analysis of the goals legislators had in mind when passing a law in the case of those classifications commonly understood to be born of "prejudice." From the vantage of late-twentieth-century jurisprudence, the *Carolene* footnote gave birth to rationality's stronger sibling, the "strict scrutiny" test, when it pointed to this "more searching judicial inquiry."[98]

The upshot of all this was that the Fourteenth Amendment's equal protection provision had need of, since its ratification, at least two standards—the "rationality" standard and the "strict scrutiny" standard—yet neither standard took considerable hold on the practice of American jurisprudence until well into the twentieth century. Thus, knowing of the general legal and intellectual antipathy at the turn of the century to conceptions of the law as morally grounded; knowing, too, that the content (that is, the meaning or "conception") of equality was nowhere to be found either in the text of the Fourteenth Amendment or in the known intent of the framers; and knowing, finally, of the absence in the late nineteenth century of the rigid equal protection standards that would take hold during the twentieth, we can assert with considerable assurance that the best the *Plessy* court could strive for with regards to the standard of equality was the mirror-like imaginary of a counterfactual historicism. A second and more discerning look at *Plessy* will reveal this inevitability.

I said earlier that, in one of the principal arguments advanced in *Plessy*, plaintiff's counsel argued that the separate car law dispossessed their client of his proprietary right to his reputation, that it arrogated to the state "the power to deprive one of the reputation of being a white man" ("Brief," 9). A reputation of this sort was, in their view, property endowed with an "actual pecuniary value," which value Tourgée took pains to audit: "Six-sevenths of the population are white. Nineteen-twentieths of the property of the country is owned by white people. Ninety-nine hundredths of the business opportunities are in the control of white people." What I did not make note of earlier was the form of the Court's rebuttal of this property claim. Justice Brown conceded the principle that reputation was property, that it shared the characteristics of property as understood in the common law; but, baffled by Plessy's claims to injury, Brown added that he was "unable to see how this statute deprives him of, or in any way affects his right to, such property" (*Plessy*, 549). The measure of equal protection was rather simple: "If he be a white man and assigned to a colored coach, he may have his action for damages against the company for being deprived of his so called property. On the other hand, if he be a colored man and be so assigned, he has been deprived of no property, since he is not lawfully entitled to the reputation of being a white man" (*Plessy*, 549). Brown's response startles for the ease with which it short-circuited the fundamental questions in all equal protection disputes and for the way in which its syntax allowed him to make a detour around the counterfactual's typical historical concerns: What inequalities are tolerable under what circumstances? Are any of the inequalities in dispute here unjust? If so, what now ought to be done to rectify the injustice? What obligation does the state have to those whose position is worse than it would have been had the injustice not been done? In Brown's rebuttal, there is no history of injury to be found, no inequality exaggerated by the passage of time. Tourgée's audit gave off hints not only of an explanation but also of an accusation, glimpses of a "depriv[ation]" and expropriation whose roots went much deeper than the question of segregation at hand. As we follow the drift of his fractional amplification, from population to property to profit, we get a sense of the exquisiteness of the value in question ("the most valued sort of property . . . the master-key that unlocks the golden door of opportunity"). We get a sense, too, of a ballooning historic deficit as value was absconded from the hands of blacks and spirited into protected coffers to which whites had the only key ("six-sevenths" becomes "nineteen-twentieths" becomes "ninety-nine hundredths"). Brown's response—presentist and antihistorical—interrupted Tourgée's sketch of historical cause and effect, reimagining the inequity in such a way that both the debt and the injury were "forgiven" ("if he *be* a white man . . . if he *be* a colored man. . ."). Through his doubling of the counterfactual's conditional clause (protasis), Brown nullified historical injury, refinancing the state's debt to blacks with a display of presentist conceit.[99] This is the "tense" of separate-but-equal doctrine to which this chapter's title refers; and, though a conceivably minor rhetorical move, we should have no doubts as to the stakes involved in Brown's dismissive stroke of the pen.

Eccentric it may seem, but Brown's ruling has behind it principles recognized by scholars of constitutional law. Robert Nozick, for one, notes that inequalities are certainly matters of justice, even constitutional justice, but cautions that to determine whether an infraction of constitutional principles obtains in the case of an inequality one must do more than take a mere glance at "who ends up with what."[100] As he explains in *Anarchy, State, and Utopia,* there are three topics (or principles) in justice: (1) the original appropriation of a good or entitlement, what he calls "the principle of justice in acquisition," (2) the transfer of holdings from one person to another, and (3) the rectification of injustice in holdings. Most distributions are considered just so long as the original appropriation and any subsequent exchanges are achieved by legitimate means. "Justice in holdings is historical," in this regard, "it depends upon what actually has happened" (151–52). Yet whereas justice may be deemed historical, the history of acquisitions has often fallen far short of a standard of justice—"some people steal from others, or defraud them, or enslave them, seizing their product or preventing them from living as they choose"—in which case, on the perception that a past injustice has shaped the current distribution of goods or entitlements, rectification becomes the principal burden of the law. A court might at this moment administer one of two competing principles of justice. A court may choose to follow an "end-result" principle, which holds that the justice of a distribution depends on "how things are distributed (who has what) as judged by some structural principle(s) of just distribution" (153). An end-result test cares only for "who ends up with what"—as, for example, in the case of welfare economics—and perceives distributions that are structurally identical to be equally just.[101] Contrary to this reading of end states, the alternative principle available to remedy an inequality is a "historical" principle of justice. When a court applies historical principles it considers not only the distribution that a situation embodies but also "how that distribution came about"; it reflects the belief that "past circumstances or actions of people can create differential entitlements or differential deserts to things" (154–55). Jurists who give place to historical principles of justice seek to determine whether a past injustice has shaped present holdings in various ways, and, regardless of whether those causes are entirely identifiable, ask the following: What would have come to pass if the injustice had not taken place? A historical principle of justice thus forces on the law the use of "subjunctive information" (152). It mandates that the arbiters of justice fashion "hypothetical histories," in Nozick's phrase, counterfactual histories to be measured against the actual history that gave rise to the present. "If an existing society was led to by an actual history that is just, then so is that society. If the actual history of an existing society is unjust, and *no* hypothetical just history could lead to the structure of that society, then that structure is unjust" (293). However, Nozick ventures, if the actual distribution of rights and entitlements turns out not to be one of those described in the hypothetical, "then one of the descriptions yielded must be realized" (153).[102]

As the counterfactual form proved one of the principal repositories for "subjunctive information" in equal protection law, it seems both reasonable and of a piece with this chapter's governing themes to locate in the form's circumstantial historicism the kernel of what Nozick designates a historical principle of justice. Both the form and the principle share an affinity for "hypothetical histories"—the former of which achieves these objectives through syntactical structures that tease a singular present into multiple presents. The counterfactual imputes to narratives of historical causation a structure of internal difference, the final purpose of which is most often to give the lie to fictions of radical presentness, to assertions that the actual present is the only present possible. In short, the goal of counterfactualism is to demonstrate the contingency of all historical events; and, both implicitly and explicitly, my argument to this point has been that it is the counterfactual's hermeneutic modesty that occasions the embrace of subjunctive information by constitutional jurisprudence. Yet despite this argument, an alternative and antithetical use of the counterfactual is revealed in segregationist and antisegregationist uses of the form: deployments by both plaintiffs and defendants that suggested, if anything, the necessity of the counterfactual to legal reasoning. The counterfactual's utility to partisans on both sides of the segregation debate makes its import appear largely formal, not ideological—matters of principle, not substance, abstraction, not history. What is more, the counterfactual's ubiquity incites suspicion that the malleability of historical event in response to either legal or authorial intent is so apparently limitless, its contingency so extreme, that the form might finally be able to embrace radically presentist and antihistorical calculations of equality and justice (what Nozick termed "end-states"). Arguably, this interest in "who has what" and indifference to "how that distribution came about" motivated Justice Brown's interpolation of counterfactual form: "If he be a white man and assigned to a colored coach, he may have his action for damages against the company for being deprived of his so called property. On the other hand, if he be a colored man and be so assigned, he has been deprived of no property, since he is not lawfully entitled to the reputation of being a white man."

When Brown invoked counterfactual form he inspirited its embedded promise—the promise of historical contingency, the promise of internal difference, the promise of justice. On the assumption that the counterfactual teases out the present into a synchrony of presents—that, in laying bare a structure of internal difference at the core of all narratives of historical causality, it demonstrates further the impossibility of radical presentness, of the self-identity of the present—Justice Brown's performance of separate-but-equal doctrine (his argument that whites and blacks are due their separate-but-equal universes) reproduced the counterfactual's structure of internal difference, appearing in the process to deliver on the form's promise of historical contingency. However, in *Plessy*, contingency was only mirage, a simulation of form. Brown did not advance the counterfactual's conditional clause ("what if") toward its traditional end of making "white" and "black" interchangeable, which emphasis on the fungibility of race, in echo of most uses of the counterfactual in equal protection law, would have served to demonstrate the contingency of history. It is possible, in fact, to assert that Brown shared with his Supreme Court predecessor Justice Roger B. Taney, author of the opinion of the Court in *Dred Scott v. Sandford,* respect for the distinction between the "letter of the law" and the "spirit of the law," invoking the former without necessarily taking heed of the latter. Brown's invocation of the counterfactual's conditional clause gave expression to its subjunctive mood; Yet so effectively did he tweak the form, he had no need finally to deliver on its consequent (apodosis), to contemplate the consequences for either constitutional principles or jurisprudential methods if "the tables [actually] turned" and "the blacks of the South wore white skins," or "[if] by some mysterious dispensation of providence [he and the other members of the Court] should wake tomorrow with a black skin and curly hair." Another way to state the matter would be to say that Brown's presentist conceit—his vision of the separate-but-equal present as the only present possible—occulted the counterfactual's structure of internal difference, its revelation of the suppositional nature of all historical narrative, its sense that in any "event" in which the law might locate cause and responsibility there may be something else going on—that the event is "contingent" because it possesses importance for a contingent of individuals, because it touches many (from L., *contingentem,* touching together or on all sides, lying near, contiguous, coming into contact or connection).

It appears, from the evidence of what I have said in the foregoing pages, that my principal concerns are quite distinct, if not incommensurate, that what interests me are, in the case of aesthetic form, particular configurations of time, and, in the case of legal logic, the insinuation of fictive premises into pragmatic adjudications. I said earlier that when, in the era of racial segregation, filmic form and legal logic took blackness as their object of scrutiny they shared as well a concern with repetition, recondite causation, and nonlinear temporality. I have been adumbrating this correlation through a focus on analogy, on that moment when (as I put it) "a certain form of pleading persists as a poetics of form." To understand how an argumentative structure that oscillates between the aesthetic and the legal might in this instance be most appropriate, and to see that blackness emerges with great force at this moment as much before the populus as it does before the bar, it is necessary to return to the topic of film form. I do this at the risk, of course, of repetition. But specifically here I hope for a productive circling back, a "cut" to the sphere of the popular that adds coherence.

WHAT HAPPENED IN THE TUNNEL

Where it should be readily apparent that the *Plessy* court made every effort to close the book on the question of segregation in public accommodations, my account of the belatedness of the rise of more rigorous and legally efficacious standards of equality suggests that, with regards to counterfactual thought, the opposite may in fact be the case: that the granting of conjectural foundations to the events of American racial history and institutional forms of injury has a life of its own. In my effort to bring before our attention this "afterlife" of the counterfactual I have emphasized cinematic tropes of repetition and reversal and have limited my remarks to *What Happened in the Tunnel;* however, this early silent is not alone either in its thematic structure or in its play on blackness. In the decade or so following the passage of *Plessy,* the Edison Manufacturing Company and the American Mutoscope and Biograph Company (AMBCO), the major pre-Griffith film production and distribution companies, released approximately seventy early screen novelties (short, one-loop films) with black themes. As can be expected, many of these films—films with titles such as *The Chicken Thief* (AMBCO, 1904), *Watermelon Contest* (Edison, 1900), and *Dancing Darkey Boy* (Edison, 1897; fig. 9)—represent blacks in predictably stereotypical roles. In others, stereotype, while irrepressible, comes to viewers filtered through the lens of those menial and public roles with which blacks were most readily associated in the popular imaginary—roles ostensibly based on day-to-day, face-to-face interactions. I have in mind here films such as *Nellie, The Beautiful Housemaid* (Vitagraph, 1908), *Native Woman Wash-*

Figure 9. The earliest cinematic representations of blacks look the same whether played forward or backward, thus keeping them moving but to no narrativized destination. (Photo courtesy Library of Congress, Prints and Photographs Division, FLA 3021)

ing a Negro Baby in Nassau, B.I. (Edison, 1903), *A Hard Wash* (AMBCO, 1903), and *Jack Johnson vs. Jim Flynn for the Heavyweight Championship of the World, Las Vegas, N.M., July 4, 1912* (Jack Curley, 1912). In terms of formal innovations and subject matter these films are unremarkable when compared to the feature-length works that follow them. On their surface they are stock, generic exploitations of racist stereotypes deeply reminiscent of the long-standing tradition of blackface minstrelsy. Consider these examples.

In *Dancing Darkey Boy*, for example, we are presented with a black boy dressed in khaki shorts, jacket, and hat and shiny leather boots. He dances atop a soapbox for an enraptured audience of older white men. The men clap and shout with energy and abandon, providing their charge with that rhythm clearly necessary to keep him "shufflin' along." The mise-en-scène of black performer and white spectators recalls the dynamics of the antebellum minstrel show. More pointedly, the boy's motions call to mind the breakdowns, shuffles, and acrobatics of the legendary black minstrel performer Juba (William Henry Lane), one of the few black performers to appear in white minstrel theaters.[103] Minstrelsy's involutions of play also

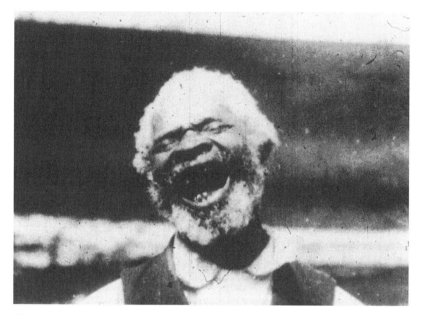

Figure 10. The black subjects of early film were stuck in a temporal whirlpool, in a narcissistic vortex of motion, one that rendered them immediate and stamped them with a quality of "historylessness." (Photo courtesy Library of Congress, Prints and Photographs Division, FLA 3194)

structure the dynamics and objectives in *Watermelon Contest,* where we see four black men, each holding half a watermelon, chew, pit, spit, and swallow with voracious intensity. Minstrelsy's narcissistic vortices of play appear again, and surreptitiously, in *Laughing Ben* (AMBCO, 1902; fig. 10), where a white-haired and toothless old black man, shot in close-up, laughs intensely for the duration of the short film (and none of these films last for more than thirty seconds). As in the minstrel tradition, *Watermelon Contest* and *Laughing Ben* emphasize fat lips, conspicuous teeth, gaping mouths, meaty wagging tongues, and an appetitive insatiability. It is true of midcentury minstrel performance that the attention accorded strategic bodily zones both calls forth a child's-eye view of sexuality and, to cite Roland Barthes, solicits pleasurable engagement with the "'grain' of the voice," with the physical materiality of song; for the wagging tongues and grotesquely enhanced lips of the minstrel show are accompanied by "a vexing and unmeaning linguistic creativity, a proliferation of huge, ungainly, and onomatopoeic words," a lexicography whose ungainliness is matched only by its liminal humanity.[104] Consider Zip Coon's crazy-quilt ditty, a burlesque love sonnet interwoven with snatches of animal fable:

O ole Zip Coon he is a larned skoler,
Sings possum up a gum tree an' coony in a holler,
Possum up a gum tree, coony on a stump,
Possum up a gum tree, coony on a stump,
Possum up a gum tree, coony on a stump,
Den over dubble trubble, Zip Coon will jump.
O Zip a duden duden duden, zip a duden day.
O Zip a duden duden duden, duden duden day.
O Zip a duden duden duden, duden duden day.
Zip a duden duden duden, zip a duden day.
O it's old Suky blue-skin, she is in lub wid me,
I went do udder arternoon to take a cup ob tea;
What do you tink now, Suky hab for supper,
Why chicken foot an' possum heel, widout any butter.
O Zip a duden duden, duden, zip a duden day. . . .
Did you ever see the wild goose, sailing on de ocean,
O de wild goose motion is a bery pretty notion;
Ebry time de wild goose beckons to de swaller,
You hear him google google google google goller.
O Zip a duden duden duden, zip a duden day. . . .[105]

This linguistic profligacy served best to highlight the complementarity of incomprehensibility and animality. Yet unlike in the minstrel stage tradition, the early cinema in question could make no purchase on the "'grain' of the voice" given the considerable constraint of the technology's silence. Scholars of the silent cinema have noted that, lacking in speech, this cinema communicated in part through "stylized gestures," "heavy pantomime," and various "contortions of the face."[106] In this way, the "absent voice . . . is spread over the body of the actor" ("Voice in Cinema," 33). An occluded speech—that element of the theater that would have to wait to emerge on screen—assigns "to the gestural continuum the burden of the conveyance of meaning."[107] On closer examination we can begin to acquire a literacy in this compensatory kinesics.

A second look at *Watermelon Contest,* one that pays closer attention to its temporal organization, might detect in the syncopated bobbing up and down of black heads across a white screen an impulse to document the rhythmic qualities attending the contest. A similar impulse could also be perceived in *A Hard Wash,* in which a black woman vigorously scrubs a baby's bottom in an effort to "cleanse" it of its blackness. Then again, if one were to view these films backward (which I had the accidental opportunity to do in the course of my research) their governing representational code would become even clearer.[108] One would notice that a substantial number of these films look virtually identical whether played forward or backward.

In *Dancing Darkey Boy*, for example, the central, most meaningful action in the film is of the boy shuffling from side to side. There is no object of interest in this brief, half-minute-long film outside of the boy's motion in space. The motion is completely without narrative direction. It lacks even the most rudimentary sense of teleology (the boy aims to move neither from one side of the screen to the other nor from the background to the foreground). Played backward, the film looks essentially the same. Similarly, in *Laughing Ben,* the sole physical action is of the old man's mouth yawning between various degrees of voluminosity and of his head rocking back and forth with fluctuating degrees of intensity. Again, the movement lacks any direction. It aims for nothing. It seems to represent, in fact, a state that is best described as a contented, reflexive interest in itself as motion—as motion turned in on itself. Other shorts that take a minstrel blackness as their ludic point of reference—*Comedy Cakewalk* (AMBCO, 1903), *Cakewalk* (AMBCO, 1903), *Pickaninnies* (Edison, 1894), *Three Men Dance* (AMBCO, 1894), *Negro Dancers* (AMBCO, 1895), and *Dancing Darkies* (AMBCO, 1897)—represent this sense of motion turned in on itself, non-teleological motion, narcissistic motion.

Regarding the mass cultural function of these films as strict amusement and entertainment, Charles Musser places them in the tradition of other cinema novelty genres such as chase films, comedies, facial expression films, fairy tale films, tramp films, and kiss films. He observes that these genres were the most successful ones of this the first era of the cinema because they "isolated a specific characteristic or representational technique to achieve a novel effect: the close view of a kiss, the forward-moving wave assaulting the spectator, even scenes of busy street life 'vitascopicly' presented inside a theater."[109] However, the novelty films of white subjects from this same period, especially those representing white men, suggest a certain dissonance within the cinema's emerging representational economy.

By 1894, these white subjects tend far more often to be nascently teleological, feebly contemplative of an object or objective and crudely narrativized. Certainly nearly all of Edison's kinetoscopes from the earliest period in cinema's development strive toward a rudimentary narrativity, especially the more canonical works such as *Amateur Gymnast* (1894), *The May Irwin Kiss* (1896), *The Leonard-Cushing Fight* (1895), and *The Corbett-Courtney Fight* (1895) (the latter two representing six-round prize fights). The company's first historical subjects, such as *Rescue of Capt. John Smith by Pocahontas* (1895), *Joan of Arc* (1895), and *The Execution of Mary, Queen of Scots* (1895), have clearly articulated beginnings and endings. Most important, works that appear after 1900, such as *Life of an American Farmer* (Edison, 1903), *The Great Train Robbery* (Edison, 1903), *Uncle Tom's Cabin* (Edison, 1903), and *Parsifal* (Edison, 1904) smuggle in an un-reconstructed narrativity from the domains of literature, history, and the theater. The latter category of films, which are often referred to as "story films," are arguably the direct precursors to the feature-length motion pictures that come decades later to prevail in the classical Hollywood cinema. Of the story films, the one work to represent blacks in a narrative situation, Edwin S. Porter's film adaptation of the theatrical version of Harriet Beecher Stowe's *Uncle Tom's Cabin*, stands out in stark contrast against a sea of representations of a temporally arrested blackness. All the same, as late as 1903 the near-entire corpus of black films steer clear of any reference to narrative. Here blacks seem arrested in an earlier cinematic time and place, where the prevailing interest is in motion and its documentation.[110]

From this vantage, it seems almost impossible to avoid the claim that blackness plays a unique and definitive role in the constitution of silent cinema's emergent visual grammar, its visual poetics; for to focus on and emphasize black rhythmic, nonnarrative, cyclical qualities at the very moment when, elsewhere, the cinema gropes eagerly and desperately toward a rudimentary narrativity (toward a sense that the figures on screen are not there as themselves) is to betray a metaphysical use of blackness that is all too familiar. Backward or forward, early silent cinema keeps black subjects moving nowhere or, at least, to no narrativized destination. We might even go so far as to say that, *grace à* cinema's ghostly invocation of minstrelsy's putative black vernacular, one of the signal achievements of this cinema is its ability to inspirit and direct a rhythm and repetition affiliated with blacks and blackness toward a decidedly visual end. A more sustained consideration of repetition may help us to see this connection.

In Western epistemologies of progress, James Snead tells us, repetition signifies as a "natural [and] material cyclicality," a putative stasis that is the antithesis of the modern and mass cultural desire for an "inexhaustible novelty."[111] From the dawn of Francis Bacon's scientific progressivism, through René Descartes's Enlightenment humanism, on into G. F. W. Hegel's historicism, the encounter with repetition in the West can be interpreted as a "willed grafting onto culture of an essentially philosophical insight about the shape of time and history" ("Repetition," 59–60). This insight into repetition, when shot through the prism of race, proves the theoretical assumption that gives rise to "black culture" in much Western thought. Hegel betrays as much when he observes that in Africa "there can really be no history. There is a succession of accidents and surprises."[112] His concluding observation is merely the final nail in the coffin of black repetition: "In general, it must be said that [African] consciousness has *not yet* reached the contemplation of a fixed objective, an objectivity . . . called God, the Eternal, Justice, Nature. . . . Thus we find nothing other than man in his immediacy: that is man in Africa . . . . The Negro represents the Natural Man in all his wildness and indocility: if we wish to grasp him, then we must drop all European conceptions" (*Philosophy of History*, 217). Hegel's epistemology implies that the repetition in black cultural forms bears witness to black people's eternally cyclical, nonprogressive nature. For him, blacks are stuck in a temporal whirlpool, in a closed time loop: "There is no goal, no State there that one can follow, no subjectivity, but only a series of subjects who destroy each other" (*Philosophy of History*, 217). They move neither forward nor backward. Repetition captures their "immediacy," their heightened "thereness." Black cultural repetition represents a privileging of stasis and equilibrium.[113] Snead elaborates: "[The African in Hegel's writing of history] is 'immediate' and intimately tied to nature with all its cyclical, nonprogressive data. Having no self-consciousness, he is 'immediate'—i.e. *always there*—in any given moment" (63–64).

Conversely, repetition in European cultural spheres signifies both as circulation, on the one hand, and accumulation and growth, on the other. Faced with the inevitability that repetition will insinuate itself into the dimension of culture (just as it makes its way into "language and signification because of a finite supply of elementary units and the need for recognizability" ["Repetition," 60]), transformation is Western culture's response to its own apprehension of repetition. So, for example, in the ebb and flow of global financial cycles, the specters of repetition (e.g., the closed tautologies of financial accounting) are spirited away in an emphasis on difference, on progress and growth, on credit and interest. Again Snead: "In European culture, the 'goal' is always clear: that which always is being worked towards. The goal is thus that which is reached only when culture 'plays out' its history. Such a culture is never 'immediate,' but 'mediated' and separated from the present tense by its own future-orientation" (67). We are reminded here of that government debt that gives rise to public credit in eighteenth-century Britain, "a promise to repay at a future date . . . which will never exist in reality."[114]

Certainly, musicologists recognize that repetition has proven a focal constituent of musical forms; and, following their lead, we might tentatively graft an array of musical forms onto Hegel's negative (black) and positive (white) valuations of repetition. Repetition structures a plurality of black aesthetic forms, finding expression in the riffs and shouts of gospel melody, the call-and-response structures of jazz improvisation, and the antiphonies of blues lament. As black musical forms tend toward the repetition of shorter monadic units, toward their cyclical recovery, toward a marking of time, they strain against any development or evolution into that yet unrealized, utopian "state" valorized in Hegel's phenomenology—hewing more closely, in this music's prerequisite slave culture, to the rhythms of natural time, with the "rounds" of the dance (of the ring shout or the circle dance) expressing in musical form the diurnal "roundings" of plantation life. Frederick Douglass, of course, provides us with our most memorable expression of this sort of repetition in the first few lines of his 1845 *Narrative:* "I have no accurate knowledge of my age, never having seen any authentic record containing it. . . . I do not remember to have ever met a slave who could tell of his birthday. They seldom come nearer to it than planting-time, harvest-time, cherry-time, spring-time, or fall-time."[115] We can even witness this repetition's sense of recovery in the anaphora of the black folk sermon.[116]

> God is studying your tongue
> God is studying your aspirations
> God ain't studying your manipulations
> God ain't studying your demonstrations
> God ain't studying your words and your wisdom
> God don't want your delay
> God wants your life.[117]

If this mode of repetition assumes an ideal form, that form would be the "cut." The "cut" is, familiarly, that unmotivated, unwilled moment of break and return in African-American music where the beat returns or "cuts" back to the start, back to a moment already experienced and, hence, more easily re-membered. Snead reads the cut's import in this manner: "If there is a goal (*Zweck*) in [black] culture, it is always deferred; it continually 'cuts' back to the start, in the musical meaning of 'cut' as an abrupt, seemingly unmotivated break (an accidental *da capo*) with a series already in progress and a willed return to a prior series."[118] The cut is an embrace of accident and rupture: the accommodation black culture makes to intrusion.

Contrary to this figuration of return, in Anglo-American and Continental aesthetics repetitions tends to occur at the level of the phrase (defined as those units of musical expression "roughly equivalent to a verbal clause or short sentence").[119] I have in mind here those European musical forms that predate African-American influence: the classic Tin Pan Alley ballad form (a thirty-two-bar *aaba* structure), the harmonic progressions of the symphonic, and the blossoming melodies of German *leider*. Richard Middleton ascribes to these forms the character of "discursive" repetition, by which he means that the recognizable phrase—for example, the melody—gets worked into "hierarchical" structures ("out-and-back, away-home patterns complete with a sense of 'narrative closure'"), and into harmonic progressions ("which, as the chord changes pull the listener along, . . . contribute to 'narrativity'").[120] Repetition's "discursivity" makes us aware "of rise and fall, a discursive hierarchy, and thus refers us to *irreversible experiences*" (165, emphasis mine). To choose just one of many possible examples, the discursive can be said to have achieved much of its "goal (*Zweck*)" when the absorption of a volcanic crescendo permits a listener to forget that what he or she is actually experiencing is Wagner's *Ring* "cycle." Snead's summary of Hegel's view of black culture thus seems right on the mark: "Ever-developing European culture is the prototype for the fulfillment of culture in the future; black culture is the antitype, ever on the threshold" (63).

If I were to pull back slightly from these meditations on music and the phenomenology of history and to draw back into focus the films that initially spawned these reflections, a number of consequences would come into focus with respect to the cinematic use of black rhythm, specifically as rhythm relates to the articulation of narrative progression and the felt necessity to represent some semblance of mimesis or realism. First, the very future-orientedness of the signs of inventive Anglo-American culture make it necessary for "the present" or the real to be "worked up" and "worked through." That is, the cinema's own emphasis on invention at the turn of the century, on an inexhaustible novelty and future-orientedness, must stand in opposition to a signifier or signifiers of "the present." To accomplish this, black and white cultural forms are made to inhabit distinctly opposed temporalities, the latter frequently belated with respect to the former: "The African is . . . *always already there,* or perhaps *always there before,* whereas the European is *headed there* or, better yet, *not yet there.*"[121] Second, the particular meanings associated with the repetitive qualities of black cultural expression mean that the forms of blackness can themselves come to do the labor of working up this "present" (or this "real"). The

dancing darkey boy's jig and laughing Ben's jocularity reference this phenomenological association of black rhythm with circularity and immediacy,
with "thereness," with "historylessness" (Hegel's phrase, finally, a translation of *Geschichtslosigkeit*). The boy's inaudible "tap-tap-tap" and the old
man's muted "ha-ha-ha" express these figures' very metaphysical stasis.
Their rhythmic temporality signifies that they are more "there," refusing
narrative and thus not there as characters but as themselves. Embodiments
of rhythm, they appear more immediately accessible than the very mechanism of their representation, a cinema whose inventiveness and novelty
suggests that it occupies a temporality that is almost but not quite here yet.
Blackness is the defining, nonteleological, nonpurposive antithesis to early
cinema's narrative progression. That inventive progression, in turn, is
synecdochic for the purposive activity of American inventive entrepreneurial pursuit. Black rhythm — the production of blackness as the always
already there — is the terminus a quo of cinematic narrative.

In the archipelago of texts I have mapped here—films that appear motivated in equal measure by an interest in race and time—the effort to document motion yields an explicit renunciation of narrative time, a suspension
of the most rudimentary narrative interest in beginnings, middles, and endings (in the nonidentity of past, present, and future). In these films, motion
is often recursive and repetitive, without telos and narrative direction, a
"narcissistic" motion that refers only to itself and to little of extradiegetic
significance, as it appears hermetically detached from (and profoundly unaware of) a social environ to which narrative would emphatically draw its
attention. Beginnings are barely distinguishable from endings, and, paradoxically, the "movement" documented in these films, quite absent narrative direction, achieves something approaching stasis, looping endlessly
with no objective in sight. These films lack beginnings and endings, exhibiting only the feeblest contemplation of past and future, and holding before the eye with a kind of insistence an endlessly cycling and self-identical
present.

In advance of my consideration of circumstantial historicism and *Plessy
v. Ferguson,* the doctrine of separate but equal, and the principle of equal
protection, I promised that a poetics of form would come into focus when
described in a language appropriate to counterfactual "forms of pleading"
and promised, further, that this poetics would become apprehensible once
I managed to exfoliate from the surface of a set of visual representations
forms easily reconciled with a lexicon and logic of time—repetition, self-
identity, internal difference. In the visual poetics I have rescued from the

islanded ephemera of early cinema history, blackness bears the burden of self-identity, as it signifies an immediacy that holds narrative in abeyance, which refuses time's protean dimensionality. *What Happened in the Tunnel* reproduces the structure of self-identity I associate with this textual archipelago and nowhere more vividly than in that trompe l'oeil deception where the darkness of the tunnel and the blackness of the maid coincide with the blackness of the screen. The specter of self-identity in the railway drama is of a piece with the narcissistic and static blackness characteristic of those visual commonplaces I assembled in the foregoing paragraphs. In *What Happened in the Tunnel,* there is an ideal spectator at the threshold of the diegesis. In order for that spectator to perceive the representation (for him or her to understand that what is being perceived is the darkness of the tunnel) the film must partake of an irony, the irony that representation should cease altogether. This arrest is the very ideal of trompe l'oeil, which seeks to have the perception of the representation of the object differ not at all from the perception of the object itself (in this case, blank darkness). There is a second spectator, of course, within the diegesis, who sees no representation either, experiencing something like its opposite: the blindness of a cavernous darkness. In both instances, the hole in the text, its cavernous darkness, is filled in by a blackness that is almost the same but not quite—the frisson of black skin. Yet I still hold to my earlier claim that there is in fact no aporia in this representation, that what appears as narrative unfulfilled is simply narrative occulted—the jettisoning of the causal logic internal to that narrative into a "black box." Within this poetic, blackness bears the burden of internal difference, the burden of accounting for that fundamental discrepancy between those necessary facts and accidental facts, necessary conditions and causes sine qua non that fuel the movement of history. As the narrative moves into the black box and, emerging from it, encounters the frisson of "black skin," it appears that otherness (or internal difference) is the thing that happened in—the "what happened" of—*What Happened in the Tunnel.* The film certainly echoes the structure of *Plessy* in this regard, for in both aesthetic form and legal case, presentist conceit (or the possibility of identity without difference) occults historical contingency and forms of conjecture.

Assuming a homology between *Plessy*'s structure of occultation and the one evident in *What Happened in the Tunnel,* I wish to rephrase the above and to suggest that the latter consists of two films in one—a declarative film that tells us "what *happened* in the tunnel" and an interrogative one that asks us, "*What* happened in the tunnel?" In the declarative film, the joke is a racist joke, and the narrative an erotic one. The joke concerns a kiss, and its humorous insight is achieved at the expense of a black person. The structure is certainly counterfactual here, but what provokes laughter is the specter that race is unassimilable; what incites collective mirth is the absurdity of the fiction that "black" and "white" might be equivalent, interchangeable, fungible. In the interrogative film, the narrative concerns causation, the status of event, history: What caused the switch to happen? Who is behind it? Would the kiss, the offense, the injury have occurred if the switch had not occurred? When the film throws narrative agency into a black box it makes the question of cause appear much less amenable to explanation—less obstinate, certain, knowable. One effect of this occultation is to make the events of history appear all the more inaccessible, all the more suppositional, all the more fictive. In this film, the joke is not a racist joke: the joke is on a racist culture. The joke is on a culture that cannot return to race its proper contingency, that cannot see race finally as an accident of history.

The Rules of the Game

SIN AND RISK

From the vantage of legal history, the nexus of equality, counterfactuals, and *Plessy v. Ferguson* may seem an odd place to end a book that began as a meditation on legal positivism, fugitive property, and *Dred Scott v. Sandford*—not least because the story the book thus tells appears to disregard the formidable upheaval of emancipation itself. Slavery versus segregation, the Fugitive Slave Law versus the Reconstruction Amendments, the rights of the propertied versus the rights of the emancipated: it seems that there is much more that divides these cases one from the other than connects them, any continuity in political sympathies aside. Yet from another vantage (that of a hermeneutic conception of the law) *Plessy* appears to be one of the most appropriate places to end this story. For certain, there are myriad reasons (as much unconscious as not) why I have framed *The Fugitive's Properties* in this historically unorthodox way, yet I would describe my core motivation as follows: *Dred Scott* and *Plessy* offer perhaps the most eloquent expressions of the fundamental split within nineteenth-century jurisprudence between law and morality, a split that would serve to define the limits of legal method for much of the next century. I would go even further and say that these cases deal a fatal blow to the "higher law" tradition (whose believers, such as Ralph Waldo Emerson and Frederick Douglass, appealed to conscience and invoked moral universalism), effectively eschewing the moral language of sin for an ostensibly value-neutral economic language of risk—a privileging of narrowed structures of negligence, causation, and liability that Oliver Wendell Holmes, Jr., celebrated (and defended) as the essential (though occluded) spirit of the law.[1] One effect of this turn toward value-neutral notions of the law is that both *Dred Scott* and *Plessy* can be measured "good" constitutional law based almost entirely on their adherence to form. I thus began this book in an attempt to understand the historical force of the law's respect for form—for forms of argument, rhetorical forms, forms of procedure. I have focused on a "poetics of property" out of a desire to understand legal form as a necessary component in the experience of blacks in America. My argument has been that the issues of personhood and property that slavery elaborates and the issues emanating from the emerging law on intellectual property are part of a fundamental historical continuity in the life of the United States in which the idea of personhood is increasingly subject to the domain of property. Slavery is not simply an antebellum institution that the United States has surpassed but a particular historical form of an ongoing crisis involving the subjection of personhood to property. My strongest affinity has been for rhetorical forms that figure the fugitive's flight—for figures of thought (e.g., personification, analogy, metaphor, catachresis) in which the errantry and inconstancy of evanescent property and speculative value come to be figured in the errantry and inconstancy of the fugitive slave and for figures of speech in which those same issues of property and value achieve a linguistic correlate in a surfeit of malapropisms and puns. By tracking these forms across disciplinary boundaries, I have wanted to make clear that the law innovates in part through borrowing, speciously, from other domains, by "translating" in ways that not only leave the original precedent behind but also disfigure it for the purposes of appropriation. I have extended this poetics of form to include *Plessy* and other tests of equal protection in part to demonstrate a certain continuity between the structures of equivalence in property law and the counterfactual exchanges that underlay the doctrine of "formal equality."[2] I have done so, too, in an effort to sound this poetics within longstanding forms of pleading (e.g., stare decisis, originalism, judicial review).

Throughout, my purpose has been to exploit the potential in an observation the historian Eric Foner has recently made regarding the *Dred Scott* case, to track this potential across constitutional law, case law, and legal theory, as well as other legal constructions. In an essay entitled "Blacks and the U.S. Constitution, 1789–1989," Foner put the matter this way: "To the historian, Taney's interpretation of the founders' intentions regarding blacks is certainly plausible. *Dred Scott* may have been morally reprehensible, but it was good constitutional law, at least if good constitutional law means continually re-enacting the principles and prejudices of the founding fathers."[3] While *Dred Scott* is adjudged by the moral standards of history as "bad politics," by the exacting standards of jurisprudence it is adjudged "good law"—that is, an example of a quite defensible application of method, of a

quite rigorous adherence to procedure, of, in Foner's assessment, the ineluctable movement of "principles."[4]

What this split between law and morals means for *Plessy* is where I would
like to turn by way of conclusion; for *Plessy*, it seems to me, has something
more to teach us about the turn away from morality and toward form as the
prevailing standard of justice, something to teach us about the transformation of the vast continent of American law into what we might call a "procedural republic," one in which procedure itself reigns as the ultimate standard of justice, in which, as Louis Menand has phrased it, "we know an
outcome is right not because it was derived from immutable principles, but
because it was reached by following the correct procedures."[5]

What this split means for the conclusion of *The Fugitive's Properties* is a
slightly different matter, a matter of both scope and possibility where the arguments that flow from this book are concerned; for, in insisting that the
critique of formalism can extend beyond the question of property, that
Dred Scott's interpretation of "the right to property" must be thought of
alongside *Plessy*'s interpretation of "equal protection," I want to offer that
the valorization of process as justice and the turn to enshrine the principle
of equality as a constitutional standard are multiple sides of the same coin.
The members of the *Plessy* majority sought above all to realize the "intent"
of the Fourteenth Amendment, however morally agnostic or politically
noxious their own personal motives; they sought to give effect to the "letter
of the law" and to heed the "plain meaning" of its words, at least to the extent that the law spoke in the morally neutral language of "equality." I presume that the members of the *Plessy* majority possessed this much in the
way of methodological integrity, though it is precisely that safe presumption that leads me to want to substitute a provocation for a conclusion: if the
rhetoric of equality can be invoked (and with legitimacy) to maintain as
patent an inequality as racial segregation, then it seems entirely within reason to shift our scorn away from those who put this rhetoric to such ends
and toward the very idea of equality.

PRINCIPLE AND HISTORY

In his recent critique of liberalism, *The Trouble with Principle*, Stanley Fish
singles out the majority opinion in *Plessy* as not only an exemplary equal
protection case—"exemplary" in the sense that the Court evaded the pitfalls of racial history in pursuit of the impartial designs of the procedural republic—but a paradoxically bold expression of liberal conceit. The crux of

the Court's liberalism lay in its interpretation of the plaintiff's claim that the Louisiana railway law "stamps the colored race with a badge of inferiority" (about which I have already said a great deal). "If this be so," said the Court, "it is not by reason of anything found in the act but solely because the colored race chooses to put that construction on it" (*Plessy*, 551). For Fish, the key phrase here is "in the act," which means "in the act *itself*," or the act as it is abstracted from "the history that gave rise to it or the intentions of those who performed it."[6] This abstraction of the Louisiana law from its history effectively drains "the act" of the significance imputed to it by the plaintiffs; the law "becomes unreadable, or (it is the same thing) it becomes readable in any direction you like" (*Trouble with Principle*, 5). Few, I propose, either then or now, would disagree with the claim that the statute was expressly designed by whites to maintain the subordinate status of blacks, but the Court drained the legislation of this substantive moral content in an effort to render it entirely formal; henceforth, the Court could do its work under the cover of a neutral principle. And ironically, it is Justice Harlan who, in his dissent, provided the clearest description of this principle: "It was said in argument that the statute of Louisiana does not discriminate against either race, but prescribes a rule applicable alike to white and colored citizens" (*Plessy*, 556–57). Fish labels this "the principle of nondiscrimination" (*Trouble with Principle*, 5).

The trouble with nondiscrimination is that it transformed Homer Plessy, Attorney General John Ferguson, and anyone else who sought to either challenge or exercise this rule from persons endowed with histories and interests into fungible units of exchange—into "parties" assumed to have no histories (which is tantamount to having no race) and equal in all respects, for they confronted each other shorn of reference to class, economic power, differential access to institutions outside the courts, legislative intent, and so on.[7] The "trouble with principle," further, is that it evacuates the law more generally of both its history and its substantive moral content. A principle is an abstraction much like any other; and, as is often the case with legal abstractions (e.g., formal equality, rights, duties), we "forget" that they are abstractions and then repress the knowledge that we have forgotten. "At that point," Peter Boyle notes, "we imagine ourselves actually to be living in a world of rights-holders, legal subjects and formal equality."[8] However, principles spur a unique type of amnesia, about which Fish lends further caution: "A neutral principle that facilitates the forgetting of history is repeating the forgetting that allowed it to emerge as a neutral principle. Neutral principles, if they are to deserve the name, must be presented *as if they came first, as if they were there before history,* even if the inhabitants of history were slow to recognize them" (*Trouble with Principle,* 6, emphasis mine). Equality is one such principle—and the counterfactual (it should by now be clear) one such form of forgetting.

Equality is the proposition in law and morals that people who are alike should be treated alike. It promises a moral standard against which subsequent legal conclusions can be measured. Yet the specific idea that equality precedes history is simply a version of the idea that all liberties flow from the principle of equality; and this idea—that the substantive right of persons to be treated with human respect derives from an antecedent judgment that all persons are equal—is an invention of the victors in the Civil War.[9] When the drafters of the Constitution sought to define the relationship between the central government and the people, they spoke of a "bill of rights;" when the architects of Reconstruction sought to redefine the relationship between the states and the people they spoke in a language of "equality."[10] Reconstruction was certainly revisionist but not in the way that this shift in language implies (not, i.e., at the level of rights); for Congress passed the Reconstruction Amendments with the express purpose of extending rights to the recently emancipated (such as the right to vote or the right to due process). The Fourteenth Amendment was as much a part of this emergent rights discourse as the Thirteenth and the Fifteenth; the only difference was the rather irrepressible one of language. The framers of the Fourteenth, having triumphed in the war against slavery, enacted the equal protection clause to transform radically national notions of racial justice.

Those notions and their corresponding rights are the forgotten moral and legal substance of the equal protection clause. The ideal (or standard) of equality is not. Subsequent interpreters of the clause have forgotten that substance for the sake of the "principle" of equality. The victors in the Civil War, by framing these rights in a language of equality, gave to the latter the appearance of a separate and independent norm. They distorted the substance of decision making, for their chosen language added to constitutional jurisprudence the additional (and unnecessary) step of transforming simple statements of rights into putatively foundational statements of equality. Equality, in this sense, in the thinking of Peter Westen, is nothing more than a formality, one that is entirely circular and tautological in its effect and, thus, superfluous to the workings of the law: "Equality is an empty vessel with no substantive moral content of its own. Without moral standards, equality remains meaningless, a formula that can have nothing to say about how we should act. With such standards, equality becomes superfluous, a formula that can do nothing but repeat what we already know. . . . It is a 'form' for stating moral and legal propositions whose substance originates elsewhere, a 'form' of discourse with no substantive content of its own" (547, 577–58). Rights precede equality both logically and chronologically. In short, rights are substantive, and equality, not simply circular and tautological, but nothing short of an alibi.

My reference to equality as "form" and "alibi" revives a core concern of this book: the problem of the legal a priori, of how the law conceives its objects of scrutiny — or the possibility, if we extend this concern, when confronting one of the law's putatively immutable and determinate essences ("all men are created equal"), that equal protection jurisprudence may spring the old metaphysical traps of fugitive property. *The Fugitive's Properties* is fundamentally a book about how forms of the law are derived not from the stability of its objects of scrutiny — of property and notions of the person derived from property — but from fugitive domains of intangible value (i.e., labor, voice, ideas, feelings, principles). The "free market" in this conception is neither a function of the natural rights of man nor an effect of the inherent attributes of property; rather, the rules of private law (contract, property, tort), as everyone from Peter Gabel to Morton Horwitz has helped us to see, actually define the shape of the market, lend all apprehensible contour to property. Property is a conduit, a relation, not a thing. The law's purpose is to produce reliable principles of value that seem to emanate from the object — with the consequence that the very conception of property as an object appears only at the end, not the beginning, of any legal deliberation. Equality is no different, in this regard, than property — the "badge of inferiority" no different than the "fugitive." It, too, is an effect, not a grounds, of deliberation — *post facto,* not a priori — and thus much closer to the pragmatist's conclusion than the ethicist's precondition.

PROCEDURE AND PRAGMATISM

Pragmatism is a school of thought devoted to understanding schools of thought — the systems and schemes whereby people develop ideas, form beliefs, and make decisions. It is a school of thought that develops alongside the struggle against slavery and segregation, yet one that (important for my concerns) takes all moral assertions (all claims to belief) to be gestures irredeemably superfluous. Pragmatism, that is, takes morality to be a function of the circumstances and troubles in which our lives happen to be embedded, takes morality as the sign not of transcendent truths but simply of substantive commitments. While it was not uncommon for abolitionists to appeal to natural law as a source for the larger principles that underlay the rules of state, it was no less common for pragmatists to dismiss such pursuit of foundational premises as quixotic. Perhaps oddly to some, then, I have been guided in many of my arguments by the insights of legal pragmatism and have drawn with particular fervor from the writings of Oliver Wendell Holmes, Jr.

Holmes, of course, writes from the position of the moral agnostic and claims that agnosticism for the law itself, conceiving the latter as a system of thought that arrives at—rather than reasons from—principle. His arguments on the semiotics of property and the workings of the common law reflect this moral agnosticism. Recall his words: "It is the merit of the common law that it decides the case first and determines the principle afterwards" ("Codes, and the Arrangement of the Law" [1870]); "the life of the law has not been logic; it has been experience" (*The Common Law* [1881]); "general propositions do not decide concrete cases" (*Lochner v. New York* [1905]). These phrases are all talismans within the Holmes corpus, and what I have termed his agnosticism suffuses each one; for each reflects the pragmatic axiom that object follows conception. The object, in this case, is principle; and the axiom that of Charles Sanders Pierce, Holmes's peer: "Consider what effects, which might conceivably have practical bearings, we conceive the object of our conception to have, then, our conception of these effects is the whole of our conception of the object."[11] There is no principle in advance of thought and argument, no property before legal deliberation, no concept of equality before the messy struggle to bring one's particular conception of equality to life.

Equality, fairness, rightness, legality, cruelty. For the antebellum moralist, these were keywords in the felt disparity between law and morality, a disparity that had historically made the world safer for commodified personhood than for universal freedom. These words captured a sense of what the law should be but wasn't. From the perspective of the antebellum jurist adjudicating the status of a fugitive slave—or, as in the case of Holmes, the postbellum legal scholar theorizing the mechanism of the law—this distinction was moot. The jurist will do what he believes is "right," but "rightness" will be, in effect, the complement he gives to the outcome of his deliberations (*Metaphysical Club,* 352). Again Menand: "We know an outcome is right not because it was derived from immutable principles, but because it was reached by following the correct procedures. . . . If the legal process was adhered to, the outcome is just. Justice does not preexist the case at hand; justice is whatever result just procedures have led to" (*Metaphysical Club,* 432). In late-nineteenth-century American jurisprudence, these, in short, were the rules of the game, rules that would prove the distinct inheritance of the twentieth. The rules of the game are constructed as the game is played, whether one means by that the construction of a good or the construction of a rights-bearing self. To that extent, it seems reasonable to conclude, in matters of property as well as matters of right, that there are no rules.

NOTES

NOTE: Once works have been cited here, they generally will be cited by short title in the text thereafter.

1. Harriet Beecher Stowe, *Uncle Tom's Cabin; or, Life among the Lowly* (1852; reprint, New York: Penguin, 1986), 609, 626.

2. *Courier* (Charleston), March 16, 1853, 2.

3. A paraphrase of Walter Benjamin: "The commodity attempts to look itself in the face. It celebrates its becoming human in the whore." See his "Central Park," *New German Critique* 34 (winter 1985): 42.

4. One argument of *The Fugitive's Properties* shall be that the "fugitive" became a money form in nineteenth-century American legal and literary culture—a "money" form in the sense of that term outlined in Georg Simmel's *The Philosophy of Money* (1900) as a paradoxical form that wed fugacity to absolute stillness. Simmel writes: "There is no more striking symbol of the completely dynamic character of the world than money. The meaning of money lies in the fact that it will be given away. When money stands still, it is no longer money according to its specific value and significance. The effect that it occasionally exerts in a state of repose arises out of an anticipation of its further motion. Money is nothing but the vehicle for a movement in which everything else that is not in motion is completely extinguished." But, Simmel notes further, money also possesses an arresting character that contravenes this tendency toward motion and flow: "As a tangible item, money is the most ephemeral thing in the external-practical world; yet its content is the most stable since it stands at the point of indifference and balance between all other phenomena in the world" (*Philosophy,* cited in Lawrence Weschler, *Boggs: A Comedy of Values* [Chicago: University of Chicago Press, 1999], 23).

5. William Goodell, *The American Slave Code—Its Theory and Practice; Its Distinctive Features Shown by Its Statutes, Judicial Decisions, & Illustrative Facts* (London: Clarke, Beeton, & Co., 1853), 18.

6. On "fictions of law," see 340n.37. My arguments throughout this book concerning the "person" and its various cognates (e.g., chattels personal) as "fictions of law" further those offered by Joan Dayan in her recent work on how legal disabilities are made indelible through time, e.g., through the fiction of "corruption of blood": "From the feudal *attainder,* the essence of which became corruption of blood, as punishment for crime; to the transport of blood to the British colonies and its incarnation as the black taint that legally inscribed slavery; to the disabilities of the post–Civil War, when slaves were reborn as criminals and translated into 'slaves of the state.' I take this circuit of stigmatization as a *historical residue* that turns metaphoricity into a way of knowing; that is, acknowledging history." See "Legal Slaves and Civil Bodies," in *Materializing Democracy: Toward a Revitalized Cultural Politics,* ed. Russ Castronovo and Dana Nelson (Durham, N.C.: Duke University Press, 2002), 53–94, 58.

7. William Blackstone's *Commentaries on the Laws of England* (1765; reprint, Portland, Me.: Thomas B. Wait & Co., 1807).

8. The Case of the Duchy of Lancaster, cited in Edmund Plowden, *Commentaries or Reports* (London: 1816), chap. 7, nos. 302 ff. The case is also cited in Ernst H. Kantorowicz, *The King's Two Bodies: A Study in Medieval Political Theology* (Princeton, N.J.: Princeton University Press, 1957).

9. Edmund Plowden quoted in Kantorowicz, *King's Two Bodies*, 7.

10. Claude Lefort, "The Permanence of the Theologico-Political?" chap. 11 in *Democracy and Political Theory*, trans. David Macey (Minneapolis: University of Minnesota Press, 1988), 243.

11. Ibid., 217, 242.

12. Frederic W. Maitland, "The Crown as Corporation" (1901), in *The Collected Papers of Frederic William Maitland*, ed. H. A. L. Fisher (Cambridge: Cambridge University Press, 1911), 3:249.

13. When I characterize Maitland's evasion as "agnostic," I intend that term in its narrow sense, as the legal historian in question seems here to suffer a temporary lapse of faith (or, better, a break with the articles of faith that suffuse his historical texts), seems to approach the position of those agnostics "who hol[d] that the existence of anything beyond and behind material phenomena is unknown and (so far as can be judged) unknowable" (*Oxford English Dictionary*, 2d ed.).

14. Thomas Paine, *Common Sense* (1776), reprinted in *Tracts of the American Revolution: 1763-1776*, ed. Merrill Jensen (New York: Bobbs-Merrill, 1967), 400-446, 409.

15. John Locke, *Two Treatises of Government: In the Former, the False Principles and Foundation of Sir Robert Filmer . . . , The Latter Is an Essay concerning the True Original, Extent, and End of Civil-Government* (1698; reprint, Cambridge: Cambridge University Press, 1988), 288.

16. C. B. Macpherson, *The Political Theory of Possessive Individualism* (Oxford: Oxford University Press, 1962), 3.

17. On the distinction between "chattels personal" and "freehold property" (or "realty"), see A. Leon Higginbotham, *In the Matter of Color: Race and the American Legal Process: The Colonial Period* (New York: Oxford University Press, 1978), 211-12. See also Thomas D. Morris, *Southern Slavery and the Law, 1619-1860* (Chapel Hill: University of North Carolina Press, 1996), 61-80.

18. Francis Lieber, handwritten piece entitled "Is There Any Insult to the South in Slavery Being Excluded from California," 1849, Lieber Papers, Huntington Library, San Marino, Calif.

19. Albert Taylor Bledsoe, *An Essay on Liberty and Slavery* (Philadelphia: J. B. Lippincott & Co., 1856), 89, quoted in Morris *Southern Slavery*, 62.

20. E. N. Elliot, *Cotton Is King, and Pro-Slavery Arguments* (1860; reprint, New York: Negro Universities Press, 1969), vii, quoted in Morris, *Southern Slavery*, 62.

21. Otto Friedrich von Gierke, *Political Theories of the Middle Ages* (1902; reprint, Cambridge: Cambridge University Press, 1951), xxvi, cited in John Dewey, "The Historic Background of Corporate Legal Personality," *Yale Law Journal* 35, no. 6 (April 1926): 655-73, 658.

22. Arthur W. Machen, Jr., "Corporate Personality," *Harvard Law Review* 24, no. 4 (February 1911): 253-267, 257.

23. *Trustees of Dartmouth College v. Woodward*, 17 U.S. (4 Wheat.) 518, 634-35 (1819).

24. Machen, "Corporate Personality," 257. When Machen says that a corporation is a

"fictitious person" he means that it is fictive in the sense derived from its Latin root, *fingère*, to fashion or form (not to feign or counterfeit).

25. Mark Tushnet, *The American Law of Slavery, 1800–1860* (Princeton, N.J.: Princeton University Press, 1981), 57; *Santa Clara v. Southern Pacific Railroad*, 118 U.S. 394 (1885) (C.C.D. Cal. 1883).

26. Argument for Defendant at 10, *San Mateo v. Southern Pac. R. R.*, 116 U.S. 138 (1885) (collected in Union List of Cases and Points/Records and Briefs in New York State Law Libraries, comp. Joan T. White and Dawn M. Tybur, 3d ed. (Buffalo, N.Y.: Hodgson et al., 1987)).

27. Reverend Isaac W. Brinckerhoff, *Advice to Freedmen* (New York: AMS Press, 1864), quoted in Saidiya V. Hartman, *Scenes of Subjection: Terror, Slavery, and Self-Making in Nineteenth-Century America* (New York: Oxford University Press, 1997), 125–26.

28. Karl Marx, *Das Kapital*, vol. 1 (1867), in *The Marx-Engels Reader*, trans. Robert C. Tucker (New York: W. W. Norton & Co., 1978), 313.

29. Guyora Binder and Robert Weisberg, *Literary Criticisms of the Law* (Princeton, N.J.: Princeton University Press, 2000), 527. Much of what I have to say in the paragraphs that follow in the text regarding transcendent abstraction and relative autonomy is derived from Binder and Weisberg's succinct analysis of the various fields of law and literature scholarship.

30. See Peter Gabel, "Reification in Legal Reasoning," *Research in Law and Sociology* 3 (1980): 25–51; Isaac D. Balbus, "Commodity Form and Legal Form: An Essay on the 'Relative Autonomy' of the Law," *Law and Society Review* 11 (1977): 571 ff.; Roberto Unger, "The Critical Legal Studies Movement," *Harvard Law Review* 96 (1983): 561, 580.

31. I discuss *Uncle Tom's Cabin* and the Fugitive Slave Law as they relate to this homology between legal form and commodity form in chap. 2.

32. William James, "The Consciousness of Self," in *The Principles of Psychology* (New York: H. Holt & Co., 1890).

33. The book's method is intended to coax readers to reconceive extant models of interdisciplinary scholarship—in particular, it is meant to revise the models of causation, agency, and evidence in the law and literature scholarship currently considered the state of the art (I have in mind here the formalism of Wai Chee Dimock's *Residues of Justice: Literature, Law, and Philosophy* [Berkeley: University of California Press, 1997] and the historical realism of Brook Thomas's *American Literary Realism and the Failed Promise of Contract* [Berkeley: University of California Press, 1997]).

34. Steven Knapp, "Collective Memory and the Actual Past," in *Literary Interest: The Limits of Anti-Formalism* (Cambridge, Mass.: Harvard University Press, 1993): 106–36, 116.

35. Fredric Jameson in Knapp, 118. See Fredric Jameson, *The Political Unconscious: Narrative as a Socially Symbolic Act* (Ithaca, N.Y.: Cornell University Press, 1981), 17–20. E. P. Thompson also points to the "extraordinary coincidence" between Methodist theology and utilitarian philosophy in his *The Making of the English Working Class* (New York: Vintage Books, 1966), 365.

36. *The Fugitive's Properties*, like much of current literary criticism, is concerned with the literariness of the economic, metaphoric conceptions of property, and aesthetic resolutions of the legal conundrum of the slave's and the corporation's personhood. See, especially, Walter Benn Michaels's *The Gold Standard and the Logic of Naturalism: American Literature at the Turn of the Century* (Berkeley: University of California Press, 1987). Of particular interest to me in Michaels's study is his tendency to reduce the market to writing, which, "intrinsically different from itself, neither material nor ideal," provides a structure of inter-

nal difference that absorbs within its logic the forms central to the turn-of-the-century economy: money (which "cannot be reduced to the thing it is made of and still remain the thing it is"), the commodity ("whose identity involves something more than its physical qualities"), and the corporation (which, as it cannot "be reduced to the men and women who are its shareholders," points to the more general problem of "the relations of bodies to souls, the problem of persons" (21). The slave's personhood and the institution of slavery play incidental roles in the *Gold Standard*'s narrative, and as regards the text's consequent conception of capitalism remain just that.

The wider field of economic criticism to which *The Fugitive's Properties* bears some relation includes Bill Brown, *The Material Unconscious: American Amusement, Stephen Crane, and the Economies of Play* (Cambridge, Mass.: Harvard University Press, 1996); Ann Fabian, *Card Sharps and Bucket Shops: Gambling in Nineteenth-Century America* (New York: Routledge, 1999); Kurt Heinzelman, *The Economics of the Imagination* (Amherst: University of Massachusetts Press, 1980); Catherine Gallagher, *Nobody's Story: The Vanishing Acts of Women Writers in the Marketplace, 1670–1820* (Berkeley: University of California Press, 1995); Lorna Hutson, *The Usurer's Daughter: Male Friendship and Fictions of Woman in Sixteenth-Century England* (New York: Routledge, 1994); and Marc Shell, *The Economy of Literature* (Baltimore: Johns Hopkins University Press, 1978), and *Money, Language, and Thought: Literary and Philosophical Economies from the Medieval to the Modern Era* (Berkeley: University of California Press, 1982).

37. For the most eloquent articulation of New Historicist method (and those dimensions relevant to *The Fugitive's Properties*), see Catherine Gallagher and Stephen Greenblatt, *Practicing New Historicism* (Chicago: University of Chicago Press, 2000), esp. the introduction and "Counterhistory and the Anecdote." The reference to Pound's "method of Luminous Detail" appears on p. 15.

38. Joel Fineman, "The History of the Anecdote: Fiction and Fiction," in *The New Historicism*, ed. H. Aram Veeser (New York: Routledge, 1989), 49–76, 72n. 34.

39. For an especially trenchant critique of New Historicist's "structure," see Fredric Jameson's "Immanence and the New Historicism," in *Postmodernism, or the Cultural Logic of Late Capitalism* (Durham, N.C.: Duke University Press, 1991): 181–217.

40. Oliver Wendell Holmes, "Codes, and the Arrangement of the Law," *American Law Review* 5, no. 1 (1870): 1–13, 2.

41. Aristotle, *Physics*, bk. 2 in *Aristotle: Selected Works*, trans. Hippocrates G. Apostle and Lloyd P. Gerson (Grinnell, Iowa: Peripatetic Press, 1982), 198a.14.

CHAPTER ONE

1. Economy and interest are commonly, and readily, ranked as the totalizing figures of Marxism and liberalism, respectively. Foucault's work, especially his query into sources of power other than the state (and sovereignty), *Discipline and Punish: The Birth of the Prison* (New York: Vintage Books, 1979), and his investigation into sexuality as one of power's "intentional and nonsubjective" fields of play, *The History of Sexuality* (New York: Random House, 1978), vol. 1, are taken as the foundation of his critique of Marxism and the crux of the corresponding shift in emphasis from capitalist domination to a "techniques" of power. See Foucault's reconsideration of his own thoughts on the matter of law and interest in "Governmentality," in *The Foucault Effect: Studies in Governmentality*, ed. Graham Burchell, Colin Gordon, and Peter Miller (Chicago: University of Chicago Press, 1991): 87–104.

2. *Brett v. Ebel*, 29 A.D. 256, 51 N.Y.S. 573 (1st Dep't 1898).

3. *Peabody v. Norfolk*, 98 Mass. 452, 459–60 (1868). *Peabody* represents only the first

American case. The earliest trade secret case in Anglo-American law is *Newberry v. Janes* (2 Mer. 445, 35 Eng. Rep. 1011 [1817]), which passes through the common law courts of early-nineteenth-century England.

4. *Chicago Board of Trade v. Christie Grain and Stock Co.,* 198 U.S. 236 (1905). Henry Crosby Emery, *Speculation on the Stock and Produce Exchanges of the United States,* in Columbia Studies in History, Economics, and Public Law (1896; reprint, New York: AMS Press, 1968), 7, 8, 9, 12. The farmers' jibe at property as evanescent as the wind sustains a symbolism as old as the Dutch reference to *windhandel* (the wind trade), which term was used to describe the hyperinflation and rampant abstraction of the *tulpenwoerde,* or Dutch tulip speculation of the 1630s.

5. See Ann Fabian's superb analysis of "the miraculous fertility of speculative capitalism" in the nineteenth century and the intimacies emergent capitalist institutions shared with denigrated practices such as gambling: *Card Sharps and Bucket Shops: Gambling in Nineteenth-Century America* (New York: Routledge, 1999), 153–62, 188–200.

A "credit economy" is no longer an avenue for goods but is "a vent for accumulated money values and a source of supply of capital" (and, in this characteristic, a credit economy differs from a money economy, whose distinctive feature "is the ubiquitous resort to the market as a vent for products and a source of supply of goods" and from a natural economy, which is identified, simply, by a premarket, subsistence mode of agriculture). The credit financier manipulates not consumable commodities but "putative" value, or "earning capacity," in "an interminable process of valuation and revaluation" (Thorstein Veblen, *The Theory of Business Enterprise* [1904; reprint, New York: Charles Scribner's Sons, 1936], 23, 88, 131–33, 135–36, 150–54, 275). "With value putative and immaterial, an interminable and shifting process of valuation, the distinction between credit and capital vanishes, and all business activity becomes in some respect 'speculative,' a matter of inferring distant and future trends and needs" (Howard Horwitz, "'To Find the Value of X': *The Pit* as a Renunciation of Romance," in *American Realism: New Essays,* ed. Eric J. Sundquist [Baltimore: Johns Hopkins University Press, 1982], 217, 215–37. Horwitz's essay provides a more sustained analysis of speculative market practices and realist economic and literary principles than I can venture here.)

6. In *Santa Clara,* the U.S. Supreme Court took as its task the determination of whether the equal protection clause of the Fourteenth Amendment barred California from taxing corporate property—in this case, railroad property—differently from individual property. Beginning with the case of *Dartmouth College v. Woodward* (17 U.S. [4 Wheat.] 518 [1819]), corporations had been protected as "invisible," "intangible," and "artificial beings," "mere creature[s] of law" taken to exist "only in contemplation of law. "In the opinion and words of the *Dartmouth* court, "Among the most important [characteristics of a corporation] are immortality, and, if the expression may be allowed, individuality; properties, by which a perpetual succession of many persons are considered the same, and may act as a single individual. They enable a corporation to manage its own affairs, and to hold property. . . . It is chiefly for the purpose of clothing bodies of men, in succession, with these qualities and capacities, that corporations were invented" (634). The state, then, when it chartered a corporation, fashioned an immortal individuality (or artificial personhood), one that permitted a collection of moral individuals (or natural persons) to act singularly and manage the corporate individual's property for a time. The *Santa Clara* case would invert this relation. Corporations, both the defendant's lawyers and the court averred, were "natural" persons under law. (See the comments to this effect of John Norton Pomeroy, cited in the introduction, 12.) Corporations were natural persons as "persons" were construed within the mean-

ing of the Fourteenth Amendment, particularly the "privileges and immunities," "due process," and "equal protection" provisions of sec. 1 of that amendment, which extended a formal equality to the recently freed slaves.

Kenneth J. Vandevelde, "The New Property of the Nineteenth Century: The Development of the Modern Concept of Property," *Buffalo Law Review* 29, no. 2 (1980): 325-67.

7. Arthur Machen has argued, in his authoritative essay on corporate personality, that as "a corporation is not a rational being, is not capable of understanding the law's commands, and has no will which can be affected by threats of legal punishment, it follows . . . that a corporation is not a real person"; it is merely "personified," i.e., endowed with certain rights and duties "for the sake of convenience" ("Corporate Personality," *Harvard Law Review* 24 [1911]: 253-67, 265). John Dewey, "The Historical Background of Corporate Legal Personality," *Yale Law Journal* 35 (1926): 655-73.

8. I mean no conceptual sloppiness or lapse in methodological rigor in my reference (here and subsequently in the text) to "things." As Martin Heidegger maintains in "The Origin of the Work of Art" (in *Basic Writings,* ed. David Farell Krell [San Francisco: Harper Collins, 1993], 143-212, originally published as *Der Ursprung des Kunstwerkes,* ed. H. G. Gadamer [Stuttgart: P. Reclam, 1960]), all artworks share a thingly [*dinglich*] quality with the brute matter of the world: "There is something stony in a work of architecture, wooden in a carving, colored in a painting, spoken in a linguistic work, sonorous in a musical composition." What makes the artwork a "work" and not merely a "thing," however, is "something else over and above the thingly element"—its "origin." Efforts in the West to conceptualize the thing can be reduced, Heidegger perceives, to three interpretive schemes, all of which find their origin in ancient ontology.

According to the first explanation, a block of granite, as just one example, possesses certain characteristics (hardness, heaviness, bulkiness, shapelessness) that we consider proper to the stone itself. These are its "properties." In our common understanding, the thing "is that around which the properties have assembled." The Greeks, Heidegger notes, are supposed to have called the core of the thing *to hypokeimenon,* the ground that is always already there; and in Roman-Latin thought *hypokeimenon* would be translated, infelicitously, as *subiectum,* substance. Similarly, the Greek term for properties, *ta symbebēkota,* will translate, again erroneously, as *accidens.* On account of the translation—i.e., the reinterpretation—Greek thing-structure finds itself subsumed beneath and made a mere variation of all "sentence structure," of the simple propositional-structure between subject (*subiectum*) and predicate, between substance and the accidents in which the thing's traits are stated of it. Thus, it has become part of our "natural outlook" on things to define "the thingness of the thing as the substance with its accidents . . . [to] transpos[e a] propositional way of understanding things into the structure of the thing itself." Evidence to support Heidegger's claim that translation weakens the Greeks' structure for thinking about the thing can be found in Aristotle's *Topics* and the definition of "property" found therein.

Property, Aristotle maintains, protects two distinct forms of identity, those that always signify essence, and those that do so only contingently. That form "which signifies the essence of a thing" he calls "definition," while "the other part" covers "property" (*Topics,* in *The Basic Works of Aristotle,* trans. Hippocrates G. Apostle and Lloyd P. Gerson [Grinnell, Iowa: Peripatetic Press, 1982], 1.4.19-23). A property of a thing is an attribute "which does not reveal the essence of that thing but belongs to that thing and is convertible with it as a predicate" (1.5.17-19). Aristotle clarifies with the following example: "To be sleeping is not a property of man, even if it happens that during a certain time, T, sleeping belongs only to man. But even if one were to call a thing such as this 'a property,' he would have to say that it is a property not without qualification but during a certain time, or in relation to some

other thing, etc. . . . [If] something is asleep, there is no necessity for it to be a man"
(1.5.23–30). In sum, to sleep might offer a definition of "animal," but it is only ever a relative
property of "man." Property, then, is not distinguished from definition by its failure to "signify the essence of a thing." Property is, rather, only ever a provisional claim on essence. The
structure of this first interpretation of thing "keeps the thing at arm's length from us" (Heidegger, 152), and its translation reveals a "rootlessness of Western thought" (149) that opens
the possibility of a second definition of thing quite at odds with the first.

The second interpretation to which Heidegger refers sees the thing not as an assemblage
of properties detached from a ground or core but as an "undistorted presenc[e]," or *ais-
thēton,* "that which is perceptible by sensations in the senses belonging to sensibility" (151).
The thing in this consideration "move[s] us bodily" (151) and is conceived of as a totality, as
the unity within the mind of a manifold of sense impressions. This second concept of the
thing "makes it press too physically upon us" (152), with the ultimate cost to the thing itself
that it "vanishes" (152). Finally, in the third interpretation of the thing, *dinglich* appears to
be independent of either propositional thinking or sensation. Here, a thing consists in its
matter [*hyle*], which presupposes in its exclusion form [*morpē*]. "What is constant in a thing,
its consistency, lies in the fact that matter stands together with a form. The thing is formed
matter" (152). The remainder of "The Origin of the Work of Art" elaborates on the proposition that these three interpretations of thing and *dinglich* share an origin in a particular
kind of human activity—involvement with tools and equipment. Heidegger continues and
elaborates his discussion of how tools bring about the "thingly" (i.e., for him, serviceable,
helpful, usable, and handy, as well as substantial, material, and extended) character of the
world in secs. 15–18 of *Being and Time* (originally *Sein und Zeit*), trans. Joan Stambaugh
(Albany: State University of New York Press, 1996), 62–83.

9. J. W. Ehrlich, *Ehrlich's Blackstone* (San Carlos, Calif.: Nourse Publishing, 1959), 122.
Ehrlich's text condenses Blackstone's multivolume *Commentaries,* which were published,
sequentially, in the years 1765, 1766, 1768, and 1769. James Kent's *Commentaries on American Law* (1st ed., 4 vols., 1826–30) and Joseph Story's *Commentaries on the Constitution*
(1833) attempt to clarify the common law fundaments of American law.

In Blackstone's taxonomy of property, all hereditaments are of two kinds: corporeal and
incorporeal. Corporeal hereditaments are "substantial and permanent objects" (*Ehrlich's
Blackstone,* 123) and can be "always seen, always handled" (125). Passed "from hand to
hand" (125), they are objects of "the senses" (of sight and touch, specifically) that can be "delivered into bodily possession" (125). "Annexed" to these reified and sensuous properties
are incorporeal hereditaments, or rights of inheritance and benefit that issue out of things
corporate; "a sort of accidents," Blackstone claims, that are "collateral" to things such as
land, houses, or goods. These incorporeal properties "inhere in and are supported by [the]
substance" of corporeal things "but [are] not the thing itself" (125). "Appurtenant" and
"appendant" to sensuous property, incorporeals are "invisible" (125) and exist only "in the
mind's eye" (126), "neither capable of being shown to the eye, nor of being delivered into
bodily possession" (125). And while corporeal hereditaments can be exchanged and "delivered over from hand to hand," incorporeals are only subject to exchange by law, in writing,
in "a kind of invisible, mental transfer" (126). Rents (compensation for the possession of a
corporeal hereditament), ways (the right to traverse another's land), commons (the profit
one has in the corporeal hereditament of another), and advowsons (a right of presentation
to a church, a patronage) are examples of incorporeal hereditaments. Incorporeal hereditaments are, ostensibly, the spiritual correlates to tangible property. Yet, insofar as incorporeals cannot exist independent of and are always tethered to sensuous "thingy" property, they
are, inescapably, "thingy" (i.e., alienable, transferable, exchangeable) themselves. In Black-

stone's taxonomy, all properties, from tangible and sensuous parcels of land to those possessions that have "only a mental existence" "in the mind's eye," share the quality of "thingness"—i.e., all property is fungible.

Blackstone's perception of things as the fulcrums of property fosters the further belief that the concept of property rests inevitably and securely in the "nature" of things. Common law's property was based on a taxonomy of things, with the nature of each thing determining its treatment at law. As a consequence, the recognition of some thing as the object of property rights offers a premise from which the owner's control over that thing can be deduced with certainty (Vandevelde, "New Property," 328–29). Courts use this concept of property as serviceable and inevitable "to fix the boundaries of dominion between private individuals and between individuals and the state" (Vandevelde, "New Property," 329). See Vandevelde ("New Property," 330–33) for a discussion of the pressure the ineradicable "thingyness" Blackstone's physicalist conception of property places on postbellum dephysicalized notions of property as rights *simpliciter.*

10. Within antebellum fictions of possession, the right to property confers on an owner "the power to prevent any use of his neighbor's land that conflicted with his own quiet enjoyment" (Morton J. Horwitz, *The Transformation of American Law, 1780–1860* [Cambridge, Mass: Harvard University Press, 1977], 31).

11. Morton J. Horwitz, *The Transformation of American Law, 1870–1960: The Crisis of Legal Orthodoxy* (Oxford: Oxford University Press, 1992), 145.

12. Martin J. Sklar, *The Corporate Reconstruction of American Capitalism, 1890–1916: The Market, the Law, and Politics* (Cambridge: Cambridge University Press, 1988), 49.

13. *Chicago, M. & St. P. Ry. v. Minnesota,* 134 U.S. 418 (1890). For a sustained discussion of the impact of the first *Minnesota Rate Case,* see John R. Commons, *Legal Foundations of Capitalism* (New York: Macmillan, 1924).

Justice Swayne's reconfiguration of property as exchange value aspired to (yet fell short of) a revolution in legal thought, since, as Karl Marx had pointed out decades earlier, to permit one commodity to substitute for another, to make commodities appear equal, of commensurate value, exchangeable, their material [*stofflichen*] character must be sufficiently evacuated yet nonetheless residual. Value in the market assumes a "use" subordinate to (and not, as Swayne had proposed, in place of) "exchange." The reconception of property as abstraction *tout court* is merely a recognition of the abstraction inherent in property in capitalist exchange. What is more, this recognition of the immateriality and abstraction of commodities in the final decade of the nineteenth century came as no surprise to Anglo-American property law. For, from the moment of the passage of the Statute of Anne in 1710, which recognized authors as well as booksellers as persons with standing under law, abstraction served as the source of unending difficulties in intellectual property law. In the face of incontrovertible evidence of the abstractness of literary property, courts seemed intent to determine the precise "nature" of literary accomplishment.

Some interpreters of the history of copyrights have held that, before the Statute of Anne, licensing acts such as King Philip and Queen Mary's charter of the Stationers' Company (May 4, 1557) presumed intellectual property and, hence, represented some legal investment in printers as "source" and "originator" of literary property in the books they produced and reproduced. For the strongest cases presumptive of property before 1710, see Frank Arthur Mumby, *Publishing and Bookselling* (London: Cape, 1930), 169–71; and Joseph Loewenstein, "For a History of Literary Property: John Wolfe's Reformation," *English Literary Renaissance* 18 (1988): 389–412. Few hold to the view of a literary property in advance of the Statute of Anne, especially since the persuasive refutation of Mark Rose in his *Authors and Owners: The Invention of Copyright* (Cambridge, Mass.: Harvard University Press, 1993),

9–25, 31–48. See also Catherine Gallagher, *Nobody's Story: The Vanishing Acts of Women Writers in the Marketplace, 1670–1820* (Berkeley: University of California Press, 1994), 63n. 27. I thank Catherine Gallagher for suggesting a genealogy of abstraction in the law of property that would lead back to the Statute of Anne.

14. *Slaughterhouse Cases,* 83 U.S. (16 Wall.) 36, 127 (1873).

15. Horwitz, *Transformation of American Law, 1780–1860,* 151.

16. Charles Sellers, *The Market Revolution: Jacksonian America, 1815–1846* (New York: Oxford University Press, 1991), 51.

17. Jeremy Bentham, "Property," in *Property: Mainstream and Critical Positions,* ed. C. B. Macpherson (Toronto: University of Toronto Press, 1978), 51–52.

18. Oliver Wendell Holmes, *The Common Law* (1881; reprint, Boston: Little, Brown & Co., 1923), 1.

19. Oliver Wendell Holmes, "The Path of the Law," in *Collected Legal Papers* (1897; reprint, New York: Harcourt, Brace & Co., 1920), 167–202, 180. Harriet Beecher Stowe, *A Key to "Uncle Tom's Cabin"* (Boston: J. P. Jewett & Co., 1854), 82.

20. Horwitz, *The Transformation of American Law, 1870–1960,* 35, 48–49. The very doctrine of contract seems perpetually caught "between the commitment to objectivity expressed as reliance on 'manifestation' and the commitment to subjectivity expressed as reliance on 'intent,'" Clare Dalton has argued. The Progressivist doctrine of objectification replaces the unknowable and possibly idiosyncratic intentions of the contracting parties with "that stubborn anti-subjectivist, the 'reasonable man'" ("An Essay in the Deconstruction of Contract Doctrine," in *Interpreting Law and Literature: A Hermeneutic Reader,* ed. Sanford Levinson and Steven Mailloux [Evanston, Ill.: Northwestern University Press, 1988], 305, 313).

21. Ferdinand de Saussure, *Course in General Linguistics,* ed. Charles Bally and Albert Sechehaye, trans. Wade Baskin (New York: Philosophical Library, 1959).

22. This paragraph summarizes the assessments of Mark Tushnet on analogy and legal codification (*The American Law of Slavery, 1810–1860: Considerations of Humanity and Interest* [Princeton, N.J.: Princeton University Press, 1981], 41).

23. Oliver Wendell Holmes, "Codes, and the Arrangement of the Law," *American Law Review* 5, no. 1 (1870): 1–13, 2. On how unspoken preferences deny the claims of the legal system to logical or "mathematical" certainty, see Horwitz, *The Transformation of American Law, 1780–1860,* 56.

24. Steven J. Burton, "Rhetorical Jurisprudence: Law as Practical Reason" (unpublished manuscript), 69, quoted in Stanley Fish, "The Law Wishes to Have a Formal Existence," in *There's No Such Thing as Free Speech: And It's a Good Thing, Too* (New York: Oxford University Press, 1994), 141–179, 171, originally in *The Fate of Law,* ed. Austin Sarat and Thomas R. Kearns (Ann Arbor: University of Michigan Press, 1991).

25. Stanley Fish, "The Law Wishes to Have a Formal Existence," 156.

26. Guyora Binder and Robert Weisberg, *Literary Criticisms of the Law* (Princeton, N.J.: Princeton University Press, 2000), 39. See also H. Jefferson Powell, "The Original Understanding of Original Intent," *Harvard Law Review* 98 (1985): 885.

27. Abraham Lincoln, "'House Divided' Speech at Springfield, Illinois" (June 16, 1858), in *Abraham Lincoln: Speeches and Writings, 1832–1858,* ed. Don E. Fehrenbacher (New York: Library of America, 1989), 436.

28. The court cases relating to those property rights are, for photographic images, *Burrow-Giles Lithographic Co. v. Sarony,* 111 U.S. 53 (1884); for published dramatic and literary material, *Stowe v. Thomas,* 23 Fed. Cas., 201(1853); *London v. Biograph Co.,* 231 F. 696 (2d. Cir. 1916); and *Nichols v. Universal Pictures Corp.,* 45 F. 2d. 119 (2d. Cir. 1930); for "picto-

rial illustrations," *Bleistein v. Donaldson Lithographing Co.,* 188 U.S. 239 (1903); for "grace-ful movements," *Fuller v. Bemis,* 50 F. 926 (1892); for facial expressions (in look-alike cases), *Chaplin v. Amador,* 93 Cal. App. 358 (1928); and for vocal "style" and "captured perfor-mance" (in sound-alike cases), *Gardella v. Log Cabin Products,* 154 F. 2d. 464 (2d. Cir. 1946); and *Ferris v. Frohman,* 223 U.S. 424 (1912).

29. The first American copyright statute, passed on May 31, 1790, specified certain rights to intellectual property covered broadly at the Constitutional Convention three years earlier. The Constitution authorized Congress "to promote the Progress of Science and use-ful Arts by securing for limited Times, to Authors and Inventors, the exclusive Right to their respective Writings and Discoveries" (art. 1, sec. 8, clause 8). The 1790 law extended pro-tections, not generally to "Writings," but specifically to "maps, charts, and books" and guar-anteed such protections for a span of fourteen years (Act of May 31, 1790 [1 U.S. St. 124]). Over the intervening century and on numerous occasions, this law was found anachronistic and of weakened applicability as regarded various communications technologies. The fed-eral legislature, as a result, expanded the 1790 law's bundle of entitlements to include new forms of aesthetic labor: prints and engravings in 1802 (Act of April 29, 1802 [2 U.S. St. 1 71]); musical compositions in 1831 (Act of February 3, 1831 [4 U.S. St. 436]); dramatic com-position and theatrical performance in 1856 (Act of August 18, 1856 [11 U.S. St. 1 38]); and, finally, paintings, drawings, statuary, models, and designs in 1870 (Act of July 8, 1870 [16 U.S. St. 212]). The courts defined, with increasing specificity, the nature of the rights in the copyright bundle originally contrived under the 1790 law's admittedly vague protection of "maps, charts, and books," a sequence of clarifications that possessed the dual effect of, on the one hand, holding legal assertions of broad claims to ownership (in ideas, in sentiments, in concepts) in abeyance, while, on the other hand, dedicating to the public rights in the copyrighted work not expressly or specially covered by the language of the statutes themselves.

30. Samuel Warren and Louis Brandeis, "The Right to Privacy," *Harvard Law Review* 4, no. 5 (1890): 193-220. Significant clarifications of the privacy right appear in the follow-ing essays: Wilbur Larremore, "The Law of Privacy," *Columbia Law Review* 12 (1912): 693-708; William L. Prosser, "Privacy," *California Law Review* 48 (1960): 383-423; Alan F. Westin, *Privacy and Freedom* (New York: Atheneum, 1967); Richard Posner, "Privacy, Secrecy, and Reputation," *Buffalo Law Review,* vol. 28 (1979), and "The Right to Privacy," *Georgia Law Review* 12, no. 3 (1978): 392-422; Ruth Gavison, "Privacy and the Limits of Law," *Yale Law Journal* 89, no. 3 (1980): 421-71; and Robert C. Post, "Rereading Warren and Brandeis: Privacy, Property, and Appropriation," *Case Western Reserve Law Review* 41 (1991): 647-80.

31. See Jane Gaines, *Contested Culture: The Image, the Voice, and the Law* (Chapel Hill: University of North Carolina Press, 1991), 119-20, and passim.

32. *White-Smith Music Company v. Apollo Co.,* 28 S. Ct. 319 (1908), 209 U.S. 1. For an account of the pressures the player piano places on turn-of-the-century mechanical repro-duction and performance, see Jean Thomas Allen, "The Industrialization of Culture: The Case of the Player Piano," in *The Critical Communications Review,* vol. 3, *Popular Culture and Media Events,* ed. Vincent Masco and Janet Wasko (Norwood, N.J.: Ablex, 1985), 93-108, as well as, "Copyright and Early Theater, Vaudeville, and Film Competition," in *Film before Griffith,* ed. John Fell (Berkeley: University of California Press, 1983), 176-87, in which Allen deals further with the player piano's effect on the drive to codify property in-terests in the face of vaudeville's nebulously defined and infringing performance practices.

33. *Stern v. Rosey,* 17 App. D.C. 562 (1901), quoted in *White-Smith,* 321.

34. The Sound Recording Act of 1971 makes it possible to grant copyright in mechani-

cally reproduced forms. This act repealed the 1909 U.S. Copyright Act (Act of March 4, 1909), under whose provisions the right to reproduce on a phonographic record or a piano roll accompanied the copyright in the written musical composition. The Copyright Act of 1909 overturned the Supreme Court's decision in *White-Smith Music Co. v. Apollo Co.* (1908) and repealed all extant nineteenth-century copyright laws.

35. The 1909 Copyright Act was enacted "before sound motion pictures, radio, television, and computers" and therefore modeled its protections on the book; "it was not relevant to modern communications" (Kenneth P. Norwick and Jerry Simon Chasen, *The Rights of Authors, Artists, and Other Creative People: The Basic ACLU Guide to Author and Artist Rights* [Carbondale: Southern Illinois University Press, 1992], 5 – 6). On copyright's aporia and on the belatedness of its property protections in the face of novel technologies, see Jane Gaines, "Bette Midler and the Piracy of Identity," in *Music and Copyright*, ed. Simon Frith (Edinburgh: Edinburgh University Press, 1993), 86 – 98; and Melville Nimmer, *Cases and Materials on Copyright and Other Aspects of Entertainment Litigation — Including Unfair Competition, Defamation and Privacy*, 3d ed. (Saint Paul, Minn.: West Publishing, 1985), 215.

36. The cases from which the quotes are taken are, respectively, *Shirley Booth v. Colgate-Palmolive Co., 362* F. Supp. 343 (SDNY 1983); and *Bette Midler v. Ford Motor Co.,* 849 F. 2d. 460 (1981).

37. *Gardella v. Log Cabin Products, Inc.,* 89 F. 2d 871 (2d. Cir. 1937).

38. Carol Rose, "Seeing Property," in *Property and Persuasion: Essays on the History, Theory, and Rhetoric of Ownership* (Boulder, Colo.: Westview Press, 1994), 270 – 71.

39. Warren and Brandeis's "The Right to Privacy" is motivated, on its authors' confession, by the growing "feeling" that the law must afford "some remedy for the unauthorized circulation of portraits of private persons" (195). It is worthy of note that the essay's attempts to reclassify the person under law and its further aspiration to clarify the law's precise investments in "solitude and privacy" and "mental pain and distress" represent legal investments in the person harmonious with what in the scientific and cultural arena gets expressed as an increased interest in the importance of "sensations." Of particular value as documents of the late-nineteenth-century discourse of sensations are the writings of S. Weir Mitchell: *Wear and Tear; or, Hints for the Overworked* (Philadelphia: J. B. Lippincott Co., 1871), "Nervousness and Its Influence on Character," in *Doctor and Patient* (1887; reprint, Philadelphia: J. B. Lippincott Co., 1904), 6 – 13, 115 – 20, and "The Evolution of the Rest Treatment," *Journal of Nervous and Mental Disease* 31, no. 6 (June 1904): 368 – 73.

Warren and Brandeis's proposition that the "intense . . . emotional life" and "heightening of sensations" derive from the "advance of civilization" finds its most sustained elaboration in the work of George M. Beard, who coined the word "neuresthenia" to describe a ubiquitous and apparently national late-nineteenth-century state of nervousness (*American Nervousness* [New York: Putnam, 1881]): "American nervousness is the product of American civilization."

40. Justice Brandeis would soon be faced with the challenge of putting the theories he advanced in "The Right to Privacy" into jurisprudential "practice." Brandeis and Holmes provided the only two dissents (and their most important defenses of the right to privacy) in *Olmstead v. United States* (277 U.S. 438 [1928]), a case in which the U.S. Supreme Court held that wiretapping was not a search or seizure within the meaning of the Fourth Amendment. Holmes condemned the government for engaging in the "dirty business" of illegal wiretapping and reminded the members of the other branches of the federal government that "we have to choose, and for my part I think it a less evil that some criminals should escape than that the government should play an ignoble part" (469 – 71). Brandeis was far less

gentle in his rebuke, offering this windy jeremiad on "the pursuit of happiness": "The makers of our Constitution undertook to secure conditions favorable to the pursuit of happiness. They recognized the significance of man's spiritual nature, of his feelings and of his intellect. They knew that only a part of the pain, pleasure and satisfactions of life are to be found in material things. They sought to protect Americans in their beliefs, their thoughts, their emotions and their sensations. They conferred, as against the government, the right to be let alone—the most comprehensive of rights and the right most valued by civilized man" (478-79).

41. James Shamus, "Narrative Rights," paper presented to the Department of English, University of California, Berkeley, October 1997.

42. I will not rehearse here the poststructuralist critique of voice and the metaphysics of presence. Jane Gaines has already considered the limitations of the poststructuralist critique in her own work on intellectual property: "Jacques Derrida's insight about the voice as direct line to the soul and hence measure of authenticity and veracity works only in relation to a writing/speech dichotomy in which writing plays the secondary, supporting role. The sound/image dichotomy that informs the development of mimetic technologies in Western culture, however, is not a relation of surrogacy but one of a hierarchy defined by the model of the socialized body. In this hierarchy, eye is over ear and the body is higher than the voice" (*Contested Culture,* 126). I am largely in agreement with Gaines's reading of voice in poststructuralist theory and intellectual property law.

43. Margaret Jane Radin, "Market-Inalienability," *Harvard Law Review* 100, no. 8 (1987): 1849-1937. In "Market-Inalienability" and an earlier, related essay ("Property and Personhood," *Stanford Law Review* 34, no. 4 [1982]: 957-1015), Radin defines inalienables and inalienability in terms that are of a piece with traditional liberal theories of property and personhood, theories that respect a perceived "metaphorical wall" between persons and properties, the internal and the external, subject and object, nonmarket refuges and market domains. This liberal line of thinking runs through the writings of Immanuel Kant and G. W. F. Hegel, the former of whom notes, rather famously, that "man cannot dispose over himself because he is not a thing . . . [that] in so far as he is a person he is a Subject in whom the ownership of things can be vested, and if he were his own property, he would be a thing over which he could have ownership. But a person cannot be a property and so cannot be a thing that can be owned, for it is impossible to be a person and a thing" (*Lectures on Ethics,* rev. ed. J. Macmurry, trans. L. Infield [New York: Century, 1930], 165). In line with Kantian metaphysical presumptions, the law, Radin notes, respects and protects two distinct categories of inalienables as intimately tied to the person. It protects what are called "market inalienables" for reasons of ethics and public policy, refusing, by and large, to make infants the subjects of market trading, and similarly, considering prostitution an illegal form of market exchange on the grounds that sexuality approaches "nonmonetized sharing" when considered along a continuum stretching between fungible "goods" and nonfungible "acts." "Personal property" makes up the second category of inalienables and includes objects people feel "are almost a part of themselves" (i.e., a wedding ring, an heirloom, a portrait of a beloved). By and large, the law considers personal property noncommodifiable for reasons that its "loss causes pain" (Radin, "Property and Personhood," 958-59).

There are three liberal theories of property: the personality theory of G. W. F. Hegel (*The Philosophy of Right*), the labor-desert theory of John Locke (*Second Treatise of Government*), and the utilitarian theory of Jeremy Bentham (*Principles of Morals and Legislation*). Valorizations of inalienability within property law correspond, by and large, to the methodological and philosophical principles of the first.

That said, common law and moral philosophy share a syntax of perception and probability, an inductive structure for thinking about property that reads as follows: (1) properties are the focal points of rights of ownership, which in turn find their necessary anchor in persons ("a person [is] he . . . in whom the ownership of things can be vested"); (2) ownership is characterized by powers of disposal, abandonment, gift, and transfer; (3) these powers are only exercised on "thing[s] external by nature"; (4) things "external" are things *tout court,* and things that are not external are, to cite Hegel, aspects of "personality as such"; (5) fungibility, transferability, and exchangeability are deep indicators of externality; (6) property, it follows, needs "thingness." So inexorable is the movement from property to things (so inescapable the probability that a property will be a thing), that we often permit ourselves to think through the above process in reverse: (1) immateriality, evanescence, and lack of "thingness" indicates inalienability from the person; (2) inalienability wards off the potential further conception of aspects of personhood as fungible, as subject to exchange and the vicissitudes of market measures of value; (3) the impossibility of exchange is tantamount to the impossibility of ownership; (4) without ownership, there is no property; and (5) lack of thingness, it follows, annuls the possibility of property.

The back and forth between perception and inference buttresses the metaphorical wall that distinguishes inalienables from alienables, personality from property, and nonmarket niches from the market itself in liberal theories of property. Two centuries after the publication of the *Commentaries,* we still tend to think of property in terms of markets, exchange, and alienability, while preserving for personhood market refuges, embeddedness, and the moral protections of identity. Thus, goods, services, even labor exist in the market, while, for reasons of public policy and the ethical protection of deep markers of personality, we prohibit monetary exchange in sexual acts and powers of childbirth ("Market-Inalienability," 1921–36) Or, more complexly, we permit images of ourselves and our writings to circulate within the marketplace, while protecting the face itself or ideas and imagination as its respective inalienable personal analogs.

44. Harriet Beecher Stowe, *Uncle Tom's Cabin; or, Life among the Lowly* (1852; reprint, New York: Penguin, 1986), 622,624.

45. Walter Benn Michaels, *The Gold Standard and the Logic of Naturalism* (Berkeley: University of California Press, 1987), 101–12.

46. *Pavesich v. New England Life Insurance Co.,* 122 Ga. 190, 201–2, 219–20; 50 S.E. 68 (1905), 73, 80, cited in Robert Post, "Rereading Warren and Brandeis: Privacy, Property, and Appropriation," *Case Western Law Review* 41 (1991): 647–80, 671.

47. Legal rhetoric can here be taken to follow the outlines of rhetoric at large. As Aristotle notes in the *Rhetoric,* the words of any metaphoric technology "ought to set the scene before our eyes; for events ought to be seen *in progress* rather than in prospect." Metaphors enact progress (which, in Aristotle's use of the term, respects the meaning of the original Latin *progressus,* advance, a form of the verb *progredi,* to go forth). Metaphors move us into the world. They are the means by which we "get hold of new ideas"; for, through them, as Kenneth Burke maintains, we make "analogical extensions" into a world that "without metaphor would be . . . without purpose." Or, as Northrop Frye would note more recently, metaphor captures a "sense of identity of life or power or energy between man and nature." We secure our "power over nature," Frye proposes, through the quite simple metaphoric assertion "this is that." See Aristotle, *Rhetorica,* trans. W. Rhys Roberts (Oxford: Clarendon Press, 1963), 3.1410b.32; Kenneth Burke, *Permanence and Change: An Anatomy of Purpose,* 3d ed. (Berkeley: University of California Press, 1984), 194; and Northrop Frye, *The Great Code: The Bible and Literature* (New York: Harcourt Brace Jovanovich, 1982), 7–8.

48. *Mercury* (Charleston), 30 January 1860, quoted in Geneva Southall, *Blind Tom: The Post-Civil War Enslavement of a Black Musical Genius* (Minneapolis: Challenge Productions, 1979), 20.

49. Ricky Jay, *Learned Pigs and Fireproof Women* (New York: Villard Books, 1987), 80-81. The court battles over guardianship of Tom and ownership of the copyrights to his compositions are detailed in Arthur R. La Brew's *Free at Last: Legal Aspects concerning the Career of Blind Tom Bethune, 1849-1908* ([Detroit]: Arthur R. La Brew, 1976).

50. Letter, *Observer* (Fayetteville), May 19, 1862, quoted in Oliver Sachs, *An Anthropologist on Mars* (New York: Vintage, 1995), 188.

51. *Times-Picayune* (New Orleans), February 5, 1861, quoted in Southall, *Blind Tom*, 27-28; Edward Seguin, *Extraordinary People: Understanding "Idiot Savants"* (New York: Harper & Row, 1989).

52. Rebecca Harding Davis, "Blind Tom," *Atlantic Monthly* (November 1862), reprinted in *A Rebecca Harding Davis Reader: "Life in the Iron-Mills," Selected Fiction, and Essays,* ed. Jean Pfaelzer (Pittsburgh: University of Pittsburgh Press, 1995), 104-111, 110.

53. *London Times,* August 18, 1866, quoted in Geneva Southall, *The Continuing Enslavement of Blind Tom, the Black Pianist-Composer (1865-1887)* (Minneapolis: Challenge Productions, 1983), 51.

54. *Dundee Advertiser* [n.d.]; *Daily Herald* (Glasgow), January 2, 1867; reprinted in *The Marvelous Musical Prodigy, Blind Tom, the Negro Boy Pianist: Songs, Sketches of the Life, Testimonials from the most Eminent Composers, and Opinions of the American and English Press* (Baltimore: Sun Book and Job Printing Establishment, n.d.), Bancroft Library, University of California, Berkeley.

55. Willa Cather, "Blind Tom," *Journal,* May 18, 1894, 6, reprinted in *The World and the Parish: Willa Cather's Articles and Reviews, 1893-1902,* ed. William M. Curtin (Lincoln: University of Nebraska Press, 1970), 1:166.

56. *Sun* (Baltimore), 1859, quoted in Jay, *Learned Pigs,* 75, 77.

57. The distinction between imitation and duplication is offered as a fundamental analytic within intellectual property law by R. Goldstein and A. Kessler in their essay "The Twilight Zone: Meandering in the Area of Performers' Rights," *UCLA Law Review* 9 (1962): 819-61.

58. *Argus* (Albany), January 1866; in *Marvelous Musical Prodigy,* 24-25.

59. I use the enigmatic term "romanticism," which carries with it connotations of authorial will, interiority, and aesthetic genius, for it calls to mind in this particular instance several significant elements of the opposition offered by Friedrich Kittler between the "romantic" discourse network of 1800 and the "modern" discourse network of 1900. The "romantic" discourse network depends on relays that link hand, eye, and letter in the act of writing by hand and fabricates a self possessed by means of a romance of handwriting's irreproducibility (a metaphysical fantasy in which the handmade mark, enabled by the ostensibly nontechnological pen, betrays a nostalgia for the individual). The relays that posit the circular translation of mind to hand to eye privilege transformations from the inward and invisible to the outward and visible and physical and are, thus, biased toward a continuous transition from nature to culture and, in turn, a circular reciprocation from the self that writes to the writing of the self and back. See *Discourse Networks, 1800/1900* (Stanford, Calif.: Stanford University Press, 1990). Elsewhere ("Gramophone, Film, Typewriter," *October* 41 [summer 1987]: 101-18), Kittler clarifies that writing's monopoly over the optical and acoustical imprints of the body—a monopoly maintained under the romantic discourse network of 1800 in the form of handwriting and print—ceased on the introduction of the type-

writer, for, it and other forms of mechanical reproduction deemphasized handwriting's bias toward the visual. Kittler cites Angelo Beyerlen, one of the earliest investors in the typewriter:

> In writing by hand the eye must continually observe the place where the writing goes and this place only. It must supervise the emergence of every written sign, must measure, keep in line, in short, lead and guide the hand in the execution of every movement. . . . It must attend to the creation of each written line, must measure, direct, and, in short, guide the hand through each movement. For this, the written line, particularly the line being written, must be visible. . . . By contrast, after one presses down briefly on a key, the typewriter creates in the proper position on the paper a complete letter, which not only is untouched by the writer's hand but is also located in a place entirely apart from where the hands work. Why should the writer look at the paper when everything there occurs dependably and well as long as the keys on the fingerboard are used correctly?
>
> The spot that one must constantly keep in view in order to write correctly by hand — namely, the spot where the next sign to be written *occurs* — and the process that makes the writer believe the hand-written lines must be seen are precisely what, even with "view typewriters," *cannot* be seen. . . . The spot that must be seen is always visible, but not at the instant when visibility is believed to be required. (Angelo Beyerlen quoted in Richard Herbertz, "Zur Psychologie des Maschinenschreibens," *Zeitschrift für angewandte Psychologie* 2 [1909]: 551–61, 559; Kittler, *Discourse Networks*, 12)

Clearly, Kittler's work on technologies of inscription leans heavily on Walter Benjamin's foundational essay "The Work of Art in the Age of Mechanical Reproduction" (in *Illuminations: Essays and Reflections*, ed. Hannah Arendt, trans. Harry Zohn [New York: Schocken Books, 1969], 217–51). It goes without saying, furthermore, that Tom's secondi anticipate the calculations of the machine while harking nostalgically for an artisan's romance with the handmade and the nontechnological ("the personal reaction of an individual upon nature"), appearing blindly indifferent yet committed to the "ascesis that knows only black letters on white paper" (Kittler, *Discourse Networks*, 117).

60. Walter Benjamin, "The Storyteller," in *Illuminations*, ed. Arendt, 108.

61. I mean "crisis" in the sense of a "vitally important or decisive stage in the progress of anything; a turning-point; [and] a state of affairs in which a decisive change for better or worse is imminent" (*Oxford English Dictionary*, 2d ed.).

62. It may stretch a point — the point, specifically, that blackness is here exemplary for the fetishism of the commodity form, the immutability of value ("a part of his nature, as much so as the color of his skin") — to note that fetishism comes from the Portuguese *fetisso*, or *fetiço*, a word that came into parlance as a trading term descriptive of the "small wares" and "magic charms" used for barter between West Africans and Europeans. White merchants secured their commercial transactions by taking oaths on African *fetisso*, which act of devotion proved idolatrous both to their religion and to their rational economic principles. European capital became, by asseveration, magical, a mask for black objects in a white society, ghostly presences, or "gespenstige Gegenständlichkeit" as Marx describes fetishes in *Das Kapital: Kritik der politischen Ökonomie* (in Karl Marx and Friedrich Engels, *Werke* [Hamburg, 1890; reprint, Berlin: Dietz, 1984], 23:52).

The notion of *fetisso* as a type of contraband African goods in Western economies retained a measure of significance till well into the nineteenth century, when, as just one example, the lexicographer Emile Littre imagined fetishes as "les objects qu'adorent les negres." See Emily Apter, introduction to *Fetishism as Cultural Discourse*, ed. Emily Apter and William Pietz (Ithaca, N.Y.: Cornell University Press, 1993), 5–6; and William Pietz, "Fetishism and Materialism," 129–43, in the same volume. See also Pietz, "The Problem of the Fetish," pt. 1, *Res* 9 (1985): 5–17; pt. 2, *Res* 13 (1987): 23–45; and pt. 3, *Res* 16 (1988): 105–23.

It may stretch the above point even further to note a telling wrinkle in one particular reading of *Das Kapital.* Thomas Keenan perceives within Marx's discussion of the conditions of exchange a rhetorical economy consisting of four tropes. For the transfer of property to occur, for the symmetries of an exchange to have value, the rhetorical tropes of metaphor, synecdoche, prosopopoeia, and catachresis must make up the logic of exchange. Metaphor provides a principle of resemblance, an axis of similarity. Synecdoche, in advance of metaphor, reduces manifold and diverse uses to a common something on which exchange can be based, permits one "part" of the thing to stand in for the "whole." The metaphorical abstraction is recomposed by means of prosopopoeia, or personification, a projection through which producer-exchangers reanimate commodities with a life [*überleben*] or animation erased by the act of abstraction itself: "Our use-value may be a thing that interests men. It is no part of us as objects. What, however, does belong to us as objects, is our value. . . . In the eyes of each other we are nothing but exchange-values." And, finally, since there is in theory no one particular or common use for which an abstraction can substitute, no common trait, the abstraction is in fact a substitution for nothing, which looks like "the positing of an improper name . . . for something that has no name at all of its own," i.e., catachresis. See Keenan's "The Point Is to (Ex)change It: Reading *Capital,* Rhetorically," in *Fetishism as Cultural Discourse,* ed. Apter and Pietz, 152–85.

63. Jessica Litman, "The Public Domain," *Emory Law Journal* 39, no. 4 (1990): 965–1023, 971–72. Justice Joseph Story expresses the peculiar claims intellectual property makes on the spirit of the law in his opinion in the case of *Folsom v. Marsh* (1841): "Patents and copyrights approach, nearer than any other class of cases belonging to forensic discussions, to what may be called the metaphysics of the law, where the distinctions are, or at least may be, very subtle and refined, and sometimes, almost evanescent" (9 F. Cas. 342 [CCD Mass. 1841] [No. 4901], 344).

64. Carol Rose, "Possession as the Origin of Property," *University of Chicago Law Review* 52 (1985): 73–88, 83–85.

65. Mark Rose, *Authors and Owners: The Invention of Copyright* (Cambridge, Mass.: Harvard University Press, 1993), 7.

66. Murphy's metaphorical synthesis of literary property and real estate reads:

> I thought of a sudden that I was hurried away to the realms of *Parnassus.* . . . The greatest part of these regions is portioned out by *Apollo* into different tenures, some of them conveyed to the person for ever, others for life, and many for a shorter duration. There are mansion-houses built on many of these estates, and the great genius's, who have made a figure in the world, have here fixed their residence. . . . The ancient Patriarchs of Poetry are generous, as they are rich: a great part of their possessions is let on lease to the moderns. *Dryden,* besides his own hereditary estate, had taken a large scope of ground from *Virgil.* Mr. *Pope* held *by copy* near half of *Homer*'s rent-roll. Mr. *Dryden* spent most of his time in writing Prefaces and Dedications to the great men of *Parnassus:* Mr. *Pope* was retired to his own house, on the banks of the river already mentioned. His grounds were laid out in the most exquisite taste. . . . The great *Shakespeare* sat upon a cliff, looking abroad through all creation. His possessions were very near as extensive as *Homer*'s, but in some places, had not received sufficient culture. But even there spontaneous flowers shot up, and in the *unweeded garden, which grows to seed,* you might cull lavender, myrtle, and wild thyme . . . *Aristotle* seemed to lament that *Shakespear* had not studies his Art of Poetry, but *Longinus* admired him to a degree of enthusiasm. *Otway, Rowe,* and

Congreve had him constantly in their eye. Even *Milton* was looking for flowers to trans-plant into his own Paradise. (Arthur Murphy, *Gray's-Inn Journal,* 11 November 1752, quoted in Rose, *Authors and Owners,* epigraph, xiii)

67. I thank Harry Berger for discussing with me the dynamic of metaphor and metonymy in the law—and for sharing his phenomenal written reflections on the topic, "Metaphor and Metonymy, and the End of the Middle Ages" (Literature Board, University of California, Santa Cruz, photocopy), 4.

68. Mark Rose, "The Author as Proprietor: *Donaldson v. Becket* and the Genealogy of Modern Authorship," *Representations* 23 (1988): 51–85, 75.

69. *Bleistein v. Donaldson,* 188 U.S. 239, 250 (1903); 23 S.Ct. 298, emphasis mine.

70. The quoted material is from, respectively, *Jefferys v. Boosey,* 4 H.L. Cas. 814 (1854), 869; Frank Hargrave, *Argument in Defense of Literary Property* (1774), quoted in *Jefferys v. Boosey,* 867; *White-Smith Music Co. v. Apollo Co.,* 28 S. Ct. 319 (1908), 320; *Shirley Booth v. Colgate-Palmolive,* 362 F. Supp. 343 (S.D.N.Y. 1973), 345; and *Midler v. Ford Motor Co.,* 849 F. 2d. 460 (1981), 463.

71. Marxist analyses of the law and readings in rhetorical jurisprudence share a distaste for the propensity of legal writing to animate tropes while at the same time denying its own rhetoricity. The result makes for telling intimacies between the positions of the French legal theorist Bernard Edelman and the American legal scholar Peter Goodrich, offered respectively:

The juridical fiction is that property is a concept of law. . . . Through its own function-ing this fiction permits the transition from the invisible—"intelligence," "creation," "ge-nius"—to the visible—real estate, the "tangible," the "true," the transition from the im-material to the material. The functioning of the fiction denounces its role. It is a matter of giving to the *invisible*—the thought of man—*the character of the visible*—private property. People knew already, without knowing it, even though it was impossible for them not to know, that the invisible was what is the visible, since it presents itself in the visible. Such, then, is the effectivity of the fiction. (Bernard Edelman, *Ownership of the Image: Elements for a Marxist Theory of Law,* trans. Elizabeth Kingdom [London: Rout-ledge & Kegan Paul, 1979], 40)

In reading the law, it is constantly necessary to remember the compositional, stylistic and semantic mechanisms that allow legal discourse to deny its historical and social gen-esis. It is necessary to examine the silences, absences and empirical potential of the legal text and to dwell on the means by which it appropriates the meaning of other discourses and of social relations themselves, while specifically denying that it is doing so. (Peter Goodrich, *Legal Discourse: Studies in Linguistics, Rhetoric, and Legal Analysis* [New York: St. Martin's Press, 1987], 204)

72. Kenneth Burke, *A Grammar of Motives* (1945; reprint, Berkeley: University of Cali-fornia Press, 1969), 506.

73. Karl Marx and Friedrich Engels, *The Holy Family; or, Critique of Critical Criticism: Against Bruno Bauer and Company* (Moscow: Progress Publishers, 1975), 152; Wai Chee Di-mock, *Residues of Justice: Literature, Law, Philosophy* (Berkeley: University of California Press, 1997), 60.

74. In "Icon, Index, and Symbol," Charles Sanders Pierce defines an index as a sign "physically connected with its object" (in *Collected Papers of Charles Sanders Peirce: Ele-ments of Logic,* ed. Charles Hartshorne and Paul Weiss [Cambridge, Mass: Belknap Press, Harvard University Press, 1960], 2:156–73, 168). An index is a "pointing finger" with "ex-

clusive reference to objects of experience," which would "lose the character which makes it a sign if its object were removed" (2:170). "A sundial or a clock *indicates* the time of day. . . . A rap on the door is an index. . . . A weathercock is an index of the direction of the wind" (2:161). To this list, Pierce adds: "Letters are similarly used by lawyers and others. . . . [Indices are] so far approximate to reality as to have a certain degree of fixity, in consequence of which they can be recognized and identified as individuals. . . . Lawyers and others who have to state a complicated affair with precision have recourse to letters to distinguish individuals" (2:161, 171–72). In place of "complicated affair" I would substitute, for purposes of the current chapter, "insubstantial phenomena." Indices, he adds, are distinguished by three characteristic marks: "First . . . they have no significant resemblance to their objects; second . . . they refer to individuals, single units, single collections of units . . . ; third . . . they direct the attention to their objects by blind compulsion" (2:172). He concludes, in an echo of both Burke and Jakobson on metonymy, that, "psychologically, the actions of indices depend upon association by contiguity, and not upon association by resemblance or upon intellectual operations" (2:172).

75. This formulation is as much a truism as the one that precedes it.

The scholarship on intellectual property is too comprehensive and too broad methodologically, theoretically, and politically adequately to be surveyed here. The current study is influenced, in the main, by recent work that attempts to deconstruct the human subject as the solitary origin of any given textual production; the enduring person in whom rights over any given production can be vested. For deconstructions of the "romantic" mold of authorship in the fields of literary and legal studies, see Roland Barthes, "The Death of the Author," in *Image, Music, Text*, trans. Stephen Heath (1968; reprint, New York: Hill & Wang, 1977): 142–48; Michel Foucault, "What Is an Author?" in *The Foucault Reader*, ed. Paul Rabinow (New York: Pantheon, 1984): 101–20; Peter Jaszi, "Toward a Theory of Copyright: The Metamorphoses of 'Authorship,'" *Duke Law Journal* 1991 (1991): 455–502; Rose, *Authors and Owners;* Robert H. Rotstein, "Beyond Metaphor: Copyright Infringement and the Notion of the Work," *Chicago-Kent Law Review* 68, no. 2 (1993): 725–804; Jeremy Waldron, "From Authors to Copiers: Individual Rights and Social Values in Intellectual Property," *Chicago-Kent Law Review* 68, no. 2 (1993): 841–87; Martha Woodmansee, *The Author, Art, and the Market: Rereading the History of Aesthetics* (New York: Columbia University Press, 1994).

76. See Bernard Bosanquet's "The Principle of Private Property" for an expression of the person as continuing character structure typical of thinking of the period: "Private property . . . is the unity of life in its external or material form; the result of past dealing with the material world, and the possibility of future dealing with it; the general or universal means of possible action and expression corresponding to the moral self that looks before and after" (in *Aspects of the Social Problem* [New York: Macmillan & Co., 1895], 308–18, 311).

77. *Trustees of Dartmouth College v. Woodward*, 17 U.S. (4 Wheat.) 518 (1819) 634.

78. George Puttenham, *The Arte of English Poesie* (1589), ed. Gladys Doidge Wilcock and Alice Walker (Cambridge: Cambridge University Press, 1936), 239.

79. Michel Foucault, personal communication, in Hubert L. Dreyfus and Paul Rabinow, *Michel Foucault: Beyond Structuralism and Hermeneutics*, 2d ed. (Chicago: University of Chicago Press, 1983), 187.

80. Friedrich Nietzche, *The Genealogy of Morals* (New York: Vintage Books, 1969), 57–58.

81. Immanuel Kant, *The Metaphysical Elements of Justice*, trans. John Ladd (Indianapolis: Bobbs-Merrill, 1965), 98.

82. *Dred Scott v. Sandford*, 60 U.S. (19 How.) 691 (1856), at 700. Don E. Fehrenbacher provides a thorough provenance of the Emersons' and John Sanford's ownership of the

Scotts in *Slavery, Law, and Politics: The Dred Scott Case in Historical Perspective* (New York: Oxford University Press, 1981), 121–50. See also Fehrenbacher, *The Dred Scott Case: Its Significance in American Law and Politics* (Oxford: Oxford University Press, 1978), 239–49.

83. The defendant's last name, Sanford, was misspelled in the official Supreme Court report.

84. Fehrenbacher, *Dred Scott Case*, 252; *Rachel v. Walker*, 4 Missouri 350 (1836); the appeal of the original *Scott v. Emerson* case was handed down on January 12, 1850.

85. *Scott v. Emerson*, 15 Missouri 576 (1852). On fluctuations in slave value, see Robert William Fogel and Stanley L. Engerman, *Time on the Cross: The Economics of American Negro Slavery* (New York: W. W. Norton & Co., 1974), 52–58, 67–78; and Gavin Wright, *The Political Economy of the Cotton South* (New York: Norton, 1978).

86. The U.S. Supreme Court did not contend with the issue of reversion until the case of *Strader v. Graham* (10 Howard 82 [1851]), a case that involved slave musicians taken briefly into Ohio for performances who later fled from Kentucky to Canada. In that case, Chief Justice of the Supreme Court Roger B. Taney lent a federal stamp of approval to the doctrine of reversion (according to which the laws of Ohio might have had an effect on the status of the slaves while they were in Ohio, but on their return in restraint to Kentucky their status, in Taney's words, "depended altogether upon the laws of that State and could not be influenced by the laws of Ohio" [*Strader* quoted in Fehrenbacher, *Slavery, Law, and Politics*, 136]).

For a discussion of early conflict of law cases in nineteenth-century disputes over slavery (in trial courts, appeals courts, and state supreme courts), see Robert Cover, "Conflict of Law," in *Justice Accused: Antislavery and the Judicial Process* (New Haven, Conn.: Yale University Press, 1975), 83–99; and David Brion Davis, "Antislavery and the Conflict of Laws," in *The Problem of Slavery in the Age of Revolution, 1770–1823* (Ithaca, N.Y.: Cornell University Press, 1975), 469–522. There is now a voluminous literature of choice of law (the contemporary term for nineteenth-century conflict-of-law theory), and nearly all this work focuses its attentions on two treatises on the conflict of laws: Samuel Livermore, *A Dissertation on the Questions Which Arise from the Contrariety of the Positive Laws of Different States and Nations* (New Orleans: B. Levy, 1828); and Joseph Story, *Commentaries on the Conflict of Laws, Foreign and Domestic* (Boston: Hilliard, Gray, & Co., 1834).

87. In *Somerset v. Stewart* (Howell State Trials [1772] 1), Lord Mansfield ordered the release of the slave Somerset, who had been taken from Virginia to England and then consigned to a slave ship for sale in Jamaica. Mansfield defends his ruling on the grounds that the law of the realm did not authorize imprisonment aboard a departing ship.

88. Notably, in America, in the midcentury spirit of accommodation, "sojourning" and "domicile" provided a rather intricate weave in the legal quilt of compromise, the very terms of reciprocity and respect in the largely turbulent scrimmage over the recognition of southern slave property within northern jurisdictions. See Davis, "Antislavery and the Conflict of Laws," 480–86, for a general overview of the *Somerset* case. And for a sustained analysis of the specifics of the case, as well as its relation to the economics of English slavery, the Atlantic slave trade, and revolutionary American politics, see A. Leon Higginbotham, Jr., *In the Matter of Color: Race and the American Legal Process: The Colonial Period* (New York: Oxford University Press, 1978), 333–70.

The description of the conveyance of living property as a "fraudulent shuffling backwards and forwards" appears in the fugitive slave case *Butler v. Delaplaine*, 7 Serg. & Rawle 378 (Pa. 1821), reprinted in *The Founder's Constitution*, ed. Kurland and Lerner, 4:535.

89. *Scott v. Emerson*, 15 Missouri 576 (1852), 582–87. Story, *Commentaries*, 31–33.

90. The rights of citizenship denied in the *Dred Scott* decision but formally overturned with the passage of the Civil Rights Acts in 1875 include (1) the right to make and enforce contracts, (2) broad rights of usufruct with regards to real and personal property, and (3) the "full and equal benefit to all laws and proceedings for the security of property and person" (Civil Rights Act, *Congressional Globe,* 39th Cong., 1st sess., 476).

91. Judith M. Shklar, "Political Theory and the Rule of Law" (1985), quoted in H. N. Hirsch, *A Theory of Liberty: The Constitution and Minorities* (New York: Routledge, 1992), 32. The work of Montesquieu of greatest relevance to debates concerning the notion of limited government is *The Spirit of the Laws,* ed. Anne M. Cohler, Basia Carolyn Miller, and Harold Samuel Stone (Cambridge: Cambridge University Press, 1989), esp. bk. 12.

92. John Adams cited in Zoltán Haraszti, *John Adams and the Prophets of Progress* (Cambridge, Mass.: Harvard University Press, 1952), 219.

93. On the "rhetoric of antirhetoric," of the desire to minimize the aesthetic dimension, see Paolo Valesio's *Novantiqua: Rhetorics as a Contemporary Theory* (Bloomington: Indiana University Press, 1980), 41-60.

94. Robert Post, "Theories of Constitutional Interpretation," in *Law and the Order of Culture,* ed. Robert Post (Berkeley: University of California Press, 1991): 13-41, 14.

The legal methodology for which the majority opinion in *Dred Scott* stands exemplary, the "plain meaning" mode of interpretation, would fall, in Post's taxonomy, under what he describes as a "historical" form of interpretation, "a form of interpretation that attempts to construe the Constitution to reflect the original intent of its Framers" ("Constitutional Interpretation," 18). Alongside the historical stand the "doctrinal," which describes that form of interpretation "that strives to implement the Constitution through the articulation of explicit doctrinal rules," and the "responsive," which "reads the Constitution in a manner designed to express the deepest contemporary purposes of the people" (18). Stanley Fish seconds Post's taxonomy in "The Law Wishes to Have a Formal Existence," where the essay's title means, first, that "the law does not wish to be absorbed by, or declared subordinate to, some other—nonlegal—structure of concern," and, second, that "the law wishes in its distinctness to be perspicuous; i.e., it desires that the components of its autonomous existence be self-declaring and not be in need of piecing out by some supplementary discourse" (141).

For a *bravura* interpretation of the Constitution as a work of literature, see Robert A. Ferguson, "'We Do Ordain and Establish': The Constitution as Literary Text," *William and Mary Law Review* 29, no. 1 (1987): 3-25.

95. Henry Paul Monhagen, "Stare Decisis and Constitutional Adjudication," *Columbia Law Review* 88 (1988): 725. We would be wise, from here forward, to consider "consent" in the positive law as it is most broadly construed, as an expression of "political, moral, or social theory that casts society as a collection of free individuals and then seeks to explain or justify outcomes by appealing to their voluntary actions, especially choice and consent." It seems safe to take the pitfalls of such a broad definition as a given. Don Herzog, *Happy Slaves: A Critique of Consent Theory* (Chicago: University of Chicago Press, 1989), 1.

96. Robert Cover, *Justice Accused: Antislavery and the Judicial Process* (New Haven, Conn.: Yale University Press, 1975), 132.

97. For a discussion of the "elevation of formal stakes" that heightened respect for the formal restraints of law and led traditionally antislavery as well as proslavery jurists to rule in favor of slavery's property rights, see Cover, "Judicial Responses," in *Justice Accused,* 226-56, esp. 229-32.

98. Against his express declarations, Taney's language in these passages, his emphasis on the transparent heterogeneity of the framer's homogeneous "person," reflects a judicial

presentism (and positivism) characteristic of much modern American legal interpretation—a sense of an imposition without a present justification, which, in Stanley Fish's assessment, so identifies lexical repetition with self-justification as to thoroughly mystify the foundations of the law's authority (*Doing What Comes Naturally: Change, Rhetoric, and the Practice of Theory in Literary and Legal Studies* [Durham, N.C.: Duke University Press, 1989], 87, 328–31). Taney's interpretation reflects a tendency within American legal thought to justify court decisions through reference to two particular myths; myths encoded, Fish claims, in the key phrases "the intent of the founding fathers" and "the plain meaning of the words." Within literary studies alone there is an abundant literature on the sometimes oceanic political waves and sometimes microscopic textual ripples triggered by those words "intent" and "plain meaning"—far too abundant, in fact, to be adequately summarized here. A fair sampling of that work would range from the positivistic to the deconstructive (often regarded in legal hermeneutics as "skeptical"). On the positivist side, the scholarly exemplar, Richard Posner, argues that practical legal interpretation is an unproblematic activity—an interpretive practice, when at its best, not in the slightest bit worried about textual indeterminacy or vexed by a sense of the ultimate irretrievability of original and authentic meaning ("intent"), for, as he puts the matter, admittedly artlessly, "law is coercion rather than persuasion" (*Law and Literature: A Misunderstood Relation* [Cambridge, Mass.: Harvard University Press, 1988], 249). James Boyd White, though at odds with Posner on the place (in the latter's case, the centrality) of economic analysis in the law and though he brooks no quarter for Posner's aesthetic disinterestedness, agrees with his central thesis that the law is a value-free domain of authority that resolves all textual indeterminacy and ambivalence into the coherence of legal "tradition." See his *Heracles' Bow: Essays on the Rhetoric and Poetics of the Law* (Madison: University of Wisconsin Press, 1985); as well as Owen Fiss, "Objectivity and Interpretation," *Stanford Law Review* 34 (1982): 739. For a strenuous critique of positions that take the *nomos,* or normative universe, of law as a realm distinct from narrative (i.e., rhetoric, persuasion, literary hermeneutic), see Robert Cover, "Nomos and Narrative," in *Narrative, Violence, and the Law: The Essays of Robert Cover,* ed. Martha Minow, Michael Ryan, and Austin Sarat (Ann Arbor: University of Michigan Press, 1992), 95–172. See also the essays collected in *Interpreting Law and Literature,* ed. Sanford Levinson and Steven Mailloux (Evanston, Ill.: Northwestern University Press, 1988), esp. Stanley Fish, "Fish vs. Fiss" (originally published in *Stanford Law Review* 36 [1984]: 1325), and Clare Dalton, "An Essay in the Deconstruction of Contract Doctrine" (originally published in *Yale Law Journal* 94 [1985]: 997). Victoria Kahn provides an indispensable synopsis of the debates regarding law and rhetoric in "Rhetoric and the Law," *Diacritics* 19, no. 2 (1989): 21–34.

99. Chief Justice John Marshall, writing in *McCulloch v. Maryland,* 17 U.S. (4 Wheat.) 316 (1819) at 407.

100. Benjamin Franklin, *A Dissertation on Liberty and Necessity, Pleasure and Pain* (New York: Lawrence C. Wroth, 1724), 19–20, quoted in Norman Jacobson, *Pride and Solace: The Functions and Limits of Political Theory* (Berkeley: University of California Press, 1978), 64. Franklin's mathematics, which is simply a variation of the then-novel concept of checks and balances, expresses what Albert O. Hirschman calls "the principle of countervailing passion"—a distinct inheritance of the thinking of Spinoza, Machiavelli, and Helvétius. This principle, Hirschman argues, was used by the Founding Fathers "as an important intellectual tool for the purposes of constitutional engineering." See *The Passions and the Interests: Political Arguments for Capitalism before Its Triumph* (Princeton, N.J.: Princeton University Press, 1977), 20–31.

101. Thomas Paine, "Common Sense" (January 9, 1776), in *Tracts of the American Revolution, 1763–1776,* ed. Merrill Jensen (Indianapolis: Bobbs-Merrill, 1967), 407–8.

102. John C. Calhoun, *Disquisition on Government* (Indianapolis: Bobbs-Merrill, 1953), quoted in Jacobson, *Pride and Solace,* 64.

103. Frank M. Coleman, *Hobbes and America: Exploring the Constitutional Foundations* (Toronto: University of Toronto Press, 1977).

104. William Outhwaite, Tom Bottomore, et al., eds., *The Blackwell Dictionary of Twentieth-Century Social Thought* (Oxford: Blackwell Publishers, 1994), 321–22.

105. Hannah Arendt, *On Revolution* (1963; reprint, New York: Penguin, 1990), 159. For a further account of the absolutist state that credits it with playing a significant and instrumental role in the creation of the preconditions of capital, see Nicos Poulantzas, *Political Power and Social Classes,* trans. Timothy O'Hagan et al. (London: Verso, 1978).

106. Thomas Hobbes argues, in *Leviathan,* for an integrated notion of authority, obligation, and the sovereign—which argument is elaborated in the nineteenth century by such authorities on jurisprudence as Jeremy Bentham and John Austin in theories of positive law. See Thomas Hobbes, *Leviathan; or, The Matter, Forme, and Power of a Common-Wealth Ecclesiasticall and Civill* (1651), ed. Richard E. Flathman and David Johnston (New York: W. W. Norton & Co., 1997); Jeremy Bentham, *Of Laws in General* (ca. 1780–82), ed. H. L. A. Hart (London: Athlone, 1970); and John Austin, *The Province of Jurisprudence Determined and the Uses of the Study of Jurisprudence* (1861; reprint, London: Weidenfeld & Nicolson, 1955).

107. Outhwaite, Bottomore, et al., eds., *Blackwell Dictionary,* 334. For Hobbes, an antecedent moral domain was immanent within the modern political sphere, and the presumption of morality in advance of politics made it possible to think of the latter as a secondary, auxiliary order, founded on contractual obligation. Justification for the monarchical despotism Hobbes championed, then, argues Wai Chee Dimock, "must be derived . . . from a prior morality, a morality inhering in the consent of those who voluntarily agreed to its terms, those who voluntarily entered into contract" (*Residues of Justice,* 184). Typical of Hobbes's thinking is the assertion, made in *De homine,* that "whatsoever is good, is good for someone or other. . . . For the nature of good and evil follows from the nature of circumstances" (*De homine,* in *Man and Citizen,* ed. Bernard Gert [Indianapolis: Hackett, 1991], 47)—a logic in which the political finds its condition of possibility "in the realm of private judgement, private volition" (Dimock, *Residues of Justice,* 184).

108. Michael Rogin, *"Ronald Reagan," the Movie and Other Episodes in Political Demonology* (Berkeley: University of California Press, 1987), 298.

109. Outhwaite, Bottomore, et al., eds., *Blackwell Dictionary,* 322. Man, contends Norman Jacobson, in his reading of Hobbes's *Leviathan, Pride and Solace,* "dare not act for fear of retribution by a sovereign power which stands above the laws and which is their creator. Public life is to be organized about the fear of death" (*Pride and Solace,* 62).

110. It is on these grounds of "covenant" that certain minor partisans in the American revolutionary debate—such as Josiah Tucker, in his *A Treatise concerning Civil Government* (1781)—take talk of "inalienable rights" as pure political nonsense. On Tucker, see J. G. A. Pocock, *Virtue, Commerce and History: Essays on Political Thought and History, Chiefly in the Eighteenth Century* (Cambridge: Cambridge University Press, 1985), 114, 119–21.

111. "Lyberties . . . depend on the Silence of the Law. In cases where the Soveraign has prescribed no rule, there the Subject hath the Liberty to do, or forbeare, according to his own discretion" (Hobbes, *Leviathan,* 120).

112. Mary Poovey, *History of the Modern Fact: Problems of Knowledge in the Sciences of Wealth and Society* (Chicago: University of Chicago Press, 1998), 104. See also Hanna Fenichel Pitkin, "Hobbes's Concept of Representation," *American Political Science Review* 68 (1964): 328–40, 902–18.

113. Frank M. Coleman, *Hobbes and America: Exploring the Constitutional Foundations* (Toronto: University of Toronto Press, 1977), 57.

114. Hobbes, *Leviathan*, 88. For an excellent use of *Leviathan* to open up the issue of political representation, see Hanna Pitkin, *The Concept of Representation* (Berkeley: University of California Press, 1967); for an extension of Pitkin's insights to the dramatic, see Jean-Christophe Agnew, *Worlds Apart: The Market and the Theater in Anglo-American Thought, 1550-1750* (Cambridge: Cambridge University Press, 1986), 101-48.

For a "Naturall Person," in this early-modern statement of market measures of the self, words and actions are "owned" by those who are their ostensible performative "origin," in a closed loop of possession whose reciprocity affords, in the end, status as *"Naturall."* Contrarily, beneath the category of "Artificiall person" fall the functionary, the fraud, the stage actor (and, later, in its late-nineteenth-century expression, the corporation), those whose relation to their words and actions follow the lineaments of ownership to land—whose possession and dominion are not only transferable but may in fact lie elsewhere. Beyond Hobbes's peculiar formulation, "person" signifies a "character sustained or assumed in a drama ... or in actual life; part played ... function, office, capacity; guise, semblance," as well as an "individual human being ... emphatically, as distinguished from a thing" (*Oxford English Dictionary*, 2d ed.). No doubt *Leviathan's* conception of "person" expresses the multiplicity of the term's Latin root *persōna*, which is defined as "a mask used by a player, a character ... (*dramatis personae*)"— of, in *Leviathan's* terms, a "disguise ... Mask or Visard," an "outward appearance ... counterfeited on the Stage" (88)—but also includes within its range of meanings "a being having legal rights, a juridical person" (*Oxford English Dictionary*, 2d ed.). "Person" in Hobbes's dissection takes on the dual resonances of the "Naturall" and the "Artificiall" for reasons that seem immanent to the etymological root of *persōna* itself, which multiple sources take to derive from *persōnāre*, to represent, while noting, in addition, phonetic resemblance to *persōnāre*, to sound through. *Persōnāre* emphasizes artifice, the qualities of character (L. *character*, which, taken from the Greek term for impressing instrument, doubles graphic sign with countenance ["by characters graven on the brows" (Marlowe, *Tamburlaine*, I.1.ii); "I will beleeve thou hast a mind that suites with this thy faire and outward character" (*Twelfth Night*, I.ii.51)]). *Persōnāre*, in contrast, emphasizes authenticity, authentication, and authorship, a glimpse at the "real" authority behind any action or utterance ("Of Persons Artificiall, some have their words and actions *Owned* by those whom they represent. And then the Person is the *Actor;* and he that owneth his words and actions, is the Author: In which case the Actor acteth by Authority"; "[Under] license from him whose right it is" [Hobbes, *Leviathan*, 89]).

The fungibility of Hobbes's "person" is an index of this traffic from the dramatic to the juridical. *Persōna's* profuseness signifies the duplicity of all masking, which Hanna Arendt, in her analysis of metaphors of revolution as unmasking, calibrates as follows: "[The mask] had to hide, or rather to replace, the actor's own face and countenance, but in a way that would make it possible for the voice to sound through" (*On Revolution*, 106). It was on account of the twofold understanding of a mask through which a voice sounds, by way, in short, of the metaphor's appositeness as counterfeit and ego, commodity and inalienable, property and personhood, that "persona" migrated from the sphere of the dramatic into legal rhetoric and terminology (*On Revolution*, 106-7). The persona or mask affixed to the actor's face by the exigencies of the play drifts, through the aid of metaphor, to cover "the 'person,' which the law of the land can affix to individuals as well as to groups and corporations, and even to 'a common and continuing purpose.'" The legal persona is a "right-and-duty-bearing person" independent, in the words of an Arendt source, of "the natural Ego" (Gierke in Arendt, *On Revolution*, 107). "Persona" is a trope for the dialectic between the creation of law and the law's aporia, the legally rationalized and the legally unthought, a figure for the reciprocity between *persōnāre* and *persōnāre*, artifice and authenticity, estimable sign and superfluous sound. In short, persona signifies the intimacy of (inalienable) personhood with (transferable) property, confounds the segregation between agency and inscription. Again Arendt: "It was as though the law had affixed to him the part he was expected to play on the public scene, with the provision, however, that his own voice would be able to sound through" (107). Within Hobbes's theory of person, then, a theory that has exerted and continues to exert, whether explicitly or implicitly, a controlling force on the way Westerners think about legal personality, property, and representation, one finds designs useful to the constitutional framers's difficult purposes — articulations of ownership through personhood, possession in persons, and representation as artifice and authenticity.

115. I apologize to readers schooled in seventeenth-century English political theory, as well as those acquainted with nineteenth-century American jurisprudence. The Americanist and nineteenth-century contours of this project warrant this rather pedantic overview of the concepts of sovereignty and positive law. Yet, the pedestrian contours of my analysis are redeemed, arguably, by Michel Foucault's characterization of modern government as "power organized around the management of life rather than the menace of death" (*History of Sexuality*, 1:147). According to Lora Romero, Foucault "concedes that the modernity of the genocidal might seem to suggest that the life-destroying power of the sovereign not only survived his decapitation but actually escalated in the nineteenth and twentieth centuries" (*Home Fronts: Domesticity and Its Critics in the Antebellum United States* [Durham, N.C.: Duke University Press, 1997], 38–39).

116. For stunning assessments of race and ideology that take into account the Constitution's silence with regards to race, see Barbara J. Fields, "Slavery, Race and Ideology in the United States of America," *New Left Review* 181 (1990): 95–118, esp. 99–101, and "Ideology and Race in American History," in *Region, Race and Reconstruction: Essays in Honor of C. Vann Woodward*, ed. J. Morgan Kousser and James M. McPherson (New York: Oxford University Press, 1982): 143–77.

117. The Constitution presupposes race in its exclusion when, on the matter of representation, the document designates "free Persons" to include "those bound to Service for a Term of Years, and excluding Indians not taxed, three fifths of all other Persons" (art. 1, sec. 2, clause 3, in *The Founder's Constitution*, (2:86).

118. Throughout this chapter I advance readings consistent with Orlando Patterson's rebuttal of the fallacy that the slave is an individual dispossessed of legal personality. See "The Idiom of Power," in *Slavery and Social Death: A Comparative Study* (Cambridge, Mass.: Harvard University Press, 1982), 17–43. The fallacy has become so much of a commonplace as to pepper even the sophisticated and measured analyses of a literary critic such as Priscilla Wald, who, in her work *Constituting Americans: Cultural Anxiety and Narrative Form* (Durham, N.C.: Duke University Press, 1995), equates "personhood" with "citizenship." Her text reads:

> [Native Americans and the descendants of Africans] represented human beings who had not consented to the laws by which they were bound, human beings, i.e., excluded not only from citizenship, but also from certain basic natural rights and thereby from the personhood defined by those rights. . . . Those deprived of natural rights . . . embodied — or disembodied — a challenge to the conception of personhood articulated in the founding texts. . . . Embodying the alienability of natural rights — and the consequent denial of the personhood defined by those rights — the disenfranchised pointed to the power of government to violate its sacred trust. (17, 19)

As a consequence, slaves (and Native Americans) are figured (erroneously, I would propose) as "a visible symbol of legal nonpersonhood" (Wald, *Constituting Americans*, 43).

119. See Adam Smith on the inefficiency of slave labor relative to the labor of free men: *An Inquiry into the Nature and Causes of the Wealth of Nations* (London: George Routledge & Sons, 1776) 301–2.

Thomas Jefferson reports, in an account of the meetings of the Committee of the Continental Congress appointed to draw up the articles of confederation, that one committee member, Mr. Benjamin Harrison, proposed, in compromise, "that two slaves should be counted as one freeman. He affirmed that slaves did not do so much work as freemen; and doubted if two effected more than one. That this was proved by the price of labor. The hire of a labourer in the Southern colonies being from 8 to £12, while in the Northern it was generally £24" (Continental Congress, Taxation and Representation, July 12, 1776, in Jefferson *Autobiography* (1821), in *Works* 1:43–57, reprinted in *The Founder's Constitution,* ed. Kurland and Lerner, 2:87.

120. Debt is defined by the *Oxford English Dictionary* (2d ed.) as a "liability or obligation to pay or render something; the condition of being under such obligation" and comes from the Latin *debitum* (past participle of *debere*, to owe; *de*, from, and *habere*, to have). This quite simple definition accentuates responsibility and a temporality that assumes both the costs of past volition (incurred liability) and a moral economy of present blame: "He is become a voluntary debitor . . . in a debt of honour" (Daniel Evance, *Noble Order* [1646]); "He . . . is obliged to pay debts of Honour, i.e., all such as are contracted by Play" (Bishop George Berkeley, *Alciphron*, I.98 [1732]). My aim in drawing attention to a rhetoric of indebtedness should be clear; however, I leave a more thorough handling of debt to chap. 2, in which I discuss the Fugitive Slave Law of 1850, whose repetition of the 1793 act's terms of debt reflects the need, in the face of a midcentury intensification of abolitionist assaults on suspect property rights heretofore protected behind the ramparts of law, to figure a person within legislative documents at the precise moment when the security of property-in-persons is subject to greatest question, an almost paranoid counterinvestment in willfulness when the legal usurpation of will finds itself subject to heightened (if not its most trenchant) scrutiny.

In one of many deft readings of legal and literary texts, Saidiya Hartman proposes that it was emancipation that "instituted indebtedness," that freedman's primers in the vein of Isaac Brinckerhoff's *Advice to Freedmen* (New York: AMS Press, 1864) fashioned the emancipated as sovereign individuals through a calculus of blame and responsibility, through an enumeration of debt that "mandated that the formerly enslaved both repay [an] investment of faith and prove their worthiness." She clarifies:

> The temporal attributes of indebtedness bind one to the past, since what is owed draws the past into the present, and suspend the subject between what has been and what is. In this regard, indebtedness confers durability, for the individual is answerable to and liable for past actions and must be abstinent in the present in the hopes of securing the future. . . . [The] transition from slavery to freedom introduced the free agent to the circuits of exchange through this construction of already accrued debt, an abstinent present, and a mortgaged future. In short, to be free was to be a debtor—i.e., obliged and duty-bound to others. (*Scenes of Subjection: Terror, Slavery, and Self-Making in Nineteenth-Century America* [New York: Oxford University Press, 1997], 125–63, esp. 130–34)

I am loath to dismiss even the least significant thread in Hartman's formulation; for, as she persuasively argues, freedman's primers accentuated the attenuation of debt's reciprocity along a temporal trajectory imagined to stretch from bondage to emancipation. Yet, the constitutional rhetoric of a coeval indebtedness—of an enslavement founded on contractual obligation and debt—seems to warrant our scrutiny, since, as the historian Thomas Haskell has argued, the institution of slavery was itself characterized by and as a crisis in the "norm[s] of promise keeping" that typify market capitalism, i.e., as a crisis in contract (Thomas Haskell, "Capitalism and the Origins of the Humanitarian Sensibility, Part I," *American Historical Review* no. 1 [April 1985], 339–61, and "Capitalism and the Origins of the Humanitarian Sensibility, Part II," *American Historical Review* no. 2 [June 1985], 547–66). As Haskell conceives of slavery, it signifies a reversion to "older" forms of "the ownership of persons" from within a culture ostensibly dedicated to contract. Market capitalism's code of contract centers on the legal exchange of promises and emerges in lieu of a code of status, custom, and traditional authority. Contract, or the making ("I will") and keeping ("I must") of promises, presupposes "a power over circumstance and . . . a standing security for the future delivery of one's will" (Mark Seltzer, *Bodies and Machines* [London: Routledge, 1992], 73). Contract's subject bears a protected right in his property ("a power over circumstance") that allows him assuredly to make and abjure his willfulness. The task of contract, to cite Nietzsche, is "to breed an animal with the right to make promises" (*The Genealogy of Morals* [New York: Vintage Books, 1969], 57–58.). Contract, in this view, protects the radical freedom of the individual—a freedom enclosed within "the *principle of identity and self-identity* over time and circumstance" (Seltzer, *Bodies and Machines,* 73). Contract produces identity because it requires that you be tomorrow who you promise you will be today (that you remain all powerful "over [your] circumstance"). Promise keeping requires, in the words provided in Nietzsche's *Genealogy,*

> a desire for the continuance of something desired once, a real *memory of the will:* so that between the original "I will," "I shall do this" and the actual discharge of the will, its *act,* a world of strange new things, circumstances, even acts of will may be interposed without breaking this long chain of will. But how many things this presupposes! To ordain the future in advance in this way, man must first have learned to distinguish necessary events from chance ones, to think causally, to see and anticipate distant eventualities as if they belonged to the present, to decide with certainty what is the goal and what [are] the means to it, and in general be able to calculate and compute. Man himself must first of all have become *calculable, regular, necessary,* even in his own image of himself, if he is to be able to stand security for *his own future,* which is what one who promises does! (57–59)

By the terms established here, slavery, which exempts slaves from standing secure over their property, violates the model of contract, for the law of slavery (the civil law of markets and contracts) is structured to incapacitate slaves from making and keeping their promises. To speak figuratively for a moment, the chains of the vassal substitute contract's "long chain of will"—hence the alarm of the debtor slave.

The ruse of the debtor slave arises, in part, out of the difficulties, at midcentury, of distinguishing the law of contract from the law of property (a fact of codification and institutionalization too far afield of the current study to warrant exploration). Property was tightly wed to the right to make contracts in antebellum jurisprudence. Contract law played "a very small part in the legal scheme" of the late eighteenth as well as pre–Civil War nineteenth century, P. S. Atiyah observes, amounting to little more than "an appendage to the law of property" (*The Rise and Fall of Freedom of Contract* [New York: Oxford University Press, 1979], 102). For an example of the intimacies between contract and property in early-nineteenth-century Anglo-American law, see John Joseph Powell, *Essay upon the Law of Contracts and Agreements* (Walpole: Thomas & Thomas, 1802), esp. i–viii ("On the Primitive State of Property"). The following studies of contract touch on a nineteenth-century American contract doctrine yoked to (and largely indistinguishable from) the law of property: Richard T. Ely, *Property and Contract in Their Relations to the Distribution of Wealth* (New York: Macmillan Co., 1914); E. Allen Farnsworth, *Contracts* (Boston: Little, Brown, 1982); Brook Thomas, *American Literary Realism and the Failed Promise of Contract* (Berkeley: University of California Press, 1997); Walter Benn Michaels, "The Phenomenology of Contract," in *Gold Standard,* 115–36.

121. In no way should the decision to bracket concerns of property and foreground the rhetoric of persons be taken as evidence of a desire to evacuate the specifically racial violence fomented by the *Dred Scott* decision (willful denial that slaves were, whatever the law's express content, de facto treated, barbarously, as property, as, simply, devoid of sentiment).

As a matter of local jurisprudence, slaves were, generally, considered to be persons under criminal law, but property at the civil bar. Mark Tushnet provides an excellent discussion of local magistrates and the effort to develop a rigid separation between slave and market relations, workable, discrete economies of sentiment and law, humanity and interest. See *The American Law of Slavery, 1810–1860: Considerations of Humanity and Interest* (Princeton, N.J.: Princeton University Press, 1981). For an early and formative study of the antinomies of passion and interest, see Albert O. Hirschman, *The Passions and the Interests: Political Arguments for Capitalism before Its Triumph* (Princeton, N.J.: Princeton University Press, 1977).

As a matter of constitutional jurisprudence, abolitionists as well as slavery's apologists were often found in agreement that the fugitive slave clause dictated a return of runaway slaves, a moment of interpretive parity that would foment the antislavery anticonstitutionalism and nomian insularity of William Lloyd Garison and Wendell Phillips, and fire Taney's commitment to constitutional authority; while, at the same moment, Taney's proslavery constitutionalism would find itself in conjunction with Frederick Douglass's antislavery constitutionalism, both assured of the document's self-enclosed authority. Here is Douglass, elder statesman, long after Taney and long before Fehrenbacher: "The Constitution of the United States not only contained no guarantees in favor of slavery, but, on the contrary, was in its letter and spirit an anti-slavery instrument, demanding the abolition of slavery as a condition of its own existence as the supreme law of the land . . . [it] could not well have been designed at the same time to maintain and perpetuate a system of rapine and murder like slavery, especially as not one word can be found in the Constitution to authorize such a belief" (*Life and Times of Frederick Douglass* [1893; reprint, New York: Library of America, 1994], 705–6). See Cover, "Nomos and Narrative," 133–38.

122. Marcel Mauss, *The Gift: Forms and Functions of Exchange in Archaic Societies,* trans. Ian Cunnison (1925; reprint, New York: W. W. Norton & Co., 1967), 45, originally published as "Essai sur le don," in *Sociologie et anthropologie* (1923; reprint, Paris: Presses Universitaires de France, 1950), 145–279.

123. Gayle Rubin, "The Traffic in Women: Notes on the 'Political Economy' of Sex," in *Towards an Anthropology of Women,* ed. R. Reiter (New York: Monthly Review Press, 1975), 157–210, 172.

124. Lewis Hyde, *The Gift: Imagination and the Erotic Life of Property* (New York: Random House, 1983), 86.

125. Lorna Hutson's *The Usurer's Daughter: Male Friendship and Fictions of Women in*

Sixteenth-Century England (London: Routledge, 1994) makes excellent use of Mauss to discuss the economic as well as emotional resonances to "friendship," paying particular attention to the instrumental function of a code of "faithfulness" in another crisis within modern capital: the transformation from feudal to market modes of exchange.

126. Emphases added. Joseph Galloway, defender of British sovereignty over the American colonies, attributes this maxim to Tully. The translation is Galloway's. See his, "A Candid Examination of the Mutual Claims of Great Britain and the Colonies" (February 1775), in *Tracts of the American Revolution,* ed. Jensen, 353.

127. Fish, "The Law Wishes to Have a Formal Existence," 142.

128. "Debt" appears, in this respect, a term very much like "sexuality," a term, as Hortense Spillers maintains, of "implied relationship and desire in the context of enslavement" and, thus, a term demanding the most cautious use in our critical attempts to comprehend the obligations and responsibilities of what the antebellum layperson understood to be "property." See Spillers, "Mama's Baby, Papa's Maybe: An American Grammar Book," *Diacritics* 17 (1987): 65–81.

129. The effects of the law's rhetoricity—an *autopoesis* personified in this instance in the image of the slave's gift of his or her own personhood—are, according to Stanley Fish, both the law's most pragmatic feature and the instrument of its great success:

> The law is continually creating and recreating itself out of the very materials and forces it is obliged, by the very desire to be law, to push away. The result is a spectacle that could be described (as the members of the critical legal studies movement tend to do) as a farce, but I would describe it differently, as *a signal example of the way in which human beings are able to construct the roadway on which they are traveling, even to the extent of "demonstrating" in the course of building it that it was there all the while.* The failure of legal positivists and natural law theorists to find the set of neutral procedures or basic moral principles underlying the law should not be taken to mean that the law is a failure, but rather that it is an amazing kind of success. The history of legal doctrine and its applications is a history neither of rationalistic purity nor of incoherence and bad faith, but an almost Ovidian history of transformation under the pressure of enormously complicated social, political, and economic urgencies, a history in which victory—in the shape of keeping going—is always being wrested from what looks like certain defeat, and wrested by means of stratagems that are all the more remarkable because, rather than being hidden, they are almost always fully on display. ("The Law Wishes to Have a Formal Existence," 156, emphasis mine)

I would draw your attention to the final sentence here ("victory—in the shape of keeping going—is always being wrested from what looks like certain defeat"), for, echoing George Puttenham's *The Arte of English Poesie,* it merely places the work of metaphor before the vicissitudes of history: "There is a kind of *wresting* of a single word from his owne right signification, to another not so naturall, but yet of some affinitie or conveniencie with it" (178, emphasis mine).

Also, for a more pointed discussion of the Constitution as a self-perpetuating machine, see Michael Kammen, *A Machine That Would Go of Itself* (New York: Knopf, 1986).

130. Eric Cheyfitz, *The Poetics of Imperialism: Translation and Colonization from "The Tempest" to "Tarzan"* (Oxford: Oxford University Press, 1991).

131. Henry Peacham, *The Garden of Eloquence* (1577; reprint, Menston: Scolar Press, 1971), 1–2.

132. Abraham Fraunce, *The Arcadian Rhetoric,* ed. Ethel Seaton (1588; reprint, Oxford: Basil Blackwell, 1950), 3.

133. Puttenham, *The Arte of English Poesie,* 178.

134. In "The Judicial Opinion as Literary Genre," Robert Ferguson conveys the "directed or selective sense of history" through which the judicial opinion obscures its own arbitrariness (215). Legal precedent, Ferguson suggests, restructures the present in accordance with a presumed (created) past. Ferguson's essay appears in *Yale Journal of Law and Humanities* 2 (1990): 201–19.

135. In "The Force of Law: The 'Mystical Foundation of Authority,'" Jacques Derrida takes up the tendency within American legal thought to justify court decisions through reference to two particular myths: "the intent of the founding fathers" and "the plain meaning of the words." Derrida's contribution to the extended debates on legal positivism engage and build on Walter Benjamin's "Critique of Violence," attempting to strip away the law's pretension to be other than politics by demonstrating the contamination of one form of violence (the mythic, founding violence that institutes and positions law, *die rechtsetzende Gewalt,* "law making violence") by its ostensible antithesis (the violence that conserves, maintains, confirms, and insures the permanence and enforceability of law, *die rechtserhatende Gewalt,* "law preserving violence"). The second form of violence, *die rechtserhatende Gewalt,* takes the form of an appeal to "precedent"—"the intent of the founding fathers" and "the plain meanings of the words"—which appeal, Stanley Fish maintains, defines the limit of the practical power of the legal system to preserve itself through the conflation of repetition with justification. See Jacques Derrida's "The Force of Law: The 'Mystical Foundation of Authority,'" *Cardozo Law Review* 11 (1990): 919; Walter Benjamin, "Critique of Violence," in *Reflections: Essays Aphorisms, Autobiographical Writings,* ed. Peter Demetz (New York: Schocken Books, 1978), 277–300, originally published as *Zur Kritiz der Gewalt,* in *Schriften* (Frankfurt am Main: Suhrkamp Verlag, 1955), vol. 1; and Stanley Fish's "The Law Wishes to Have a Formal Existence," 87.

136. Karl Marx, *The Eighteenth Brumaire of Louis Bonaparte* (1851–52), in *The Marx-Engels Reader,* ed. Robert C. Tucker (New York: W. W. Norton & Co., 1978), 594–617, 594, 597, originally published as *Der achtzehnte Brumaire des Louis Bonaparte,* in *Werke* (Berlin: Dietz Verlag, 1960), vol. 8.

137. Karl Marx, *The Class Struggles in France, 1848–1850,* in *The Marx-Engels Reader,* ed. Tucker, 586–93, 591.

138. Andrew Parker, "Unthinking Sex: Marx, Engels, and the Scene of Writing," *Social Text* 29, no. 9 (1991): 28–45, 31–32. Subsequent observations in the text regarding *Brumaire*'s theatrical rhetoric are taken from Parker's essay.

139. Brook Thomas, "Narratives of Responsibility and Blame in Nineteenth-Century United States Law and Literature," *Narrative* 5, no. 1 (1997): 16. See also Jacques Derrida, *Specters of Marx: The State of the Debt, the Work of Mourning, and the New International,* trans. Peggy Kamuf (New York: Routledge, 1994), 108; and Jeffrey Mehlman, *Revolution and Repetition: Marx/Hugo/Balzac* (Berkeley: University of California, 1977), 34.

140. Karl Marx, *Eighteenth Brumaire,* 75, cited in Parker "Unthinking Sex," 32.

141. Adam Smith quoted in Parker, "Unthinking Sex," 33.

142. See Edward Said's "On Originality," in *The World, the Text, and the Critic* (Cambridge, Mass.: Harvard University Press, 1983), 126–39, 133, 135.

143. James Weldon Johnson, *Black Manhattan* (1930; reprint, New York: Atheneum, 1972), 87.

144. Robert P. Nevin, "Stephen C. Foster and Negro Minstrelsy," *Atlantic Monthly* 20, no. 121 (November 1867): 608–16.

145. Nevin incorrectly names the founder of blackface minstrelsy "W. D. Rice." The actor was actually "T. D. Rice"—Thomas Danforth Rice.

146. Eric Lott, *Love and Theft: Blackface Minstrelsy and the American Working Class* (Oxford: Oxford University Press, 1993), 19, 43.

147. David Roediger, *The Wages of Whiteness: Race and the Making of the American Working Class* (London: Verso, 1991), 95.

148. George Rawick, *From Sundown to Sunup: The Making of the Black Community* (Westport, Conn.: Greenwood Publishing Group, 1972), 132–33.

CHAPTER TWO

1. Oliver Wendell Holmes, Jr., *The Common Law* (1881; reprint, Boston: Little, Brown & Co., 1923), 69. I have chosen to open with this one of Holmes's many aphoristic and "poetic" sketches of the law not because it bears any direct relation to the texts under scrutiny in this chapter but because it exemplifies the argumentative scheme that characterizes *The Common Law* and much of Holmes's writing in general. Morton Horwitz (far more widely read than most in Holmes's oeuvre) describes Holmes's method as follows: "The typical structure of argument in *The Common Law* for Holmes is to identify two intellectual extremes or poles in a particular field of law, to show why some small group of cases falls within one or the other extreme, and then to demonstrate that the rest of the cases—most of the significant everyday stuff of the law—falls on the continuum between the extremes. The problem of the legal thinker was how to locate legal problems on the spectrum between the extremes." See Morton J. Horwitz, *The Transformation of American Law, 1870 –1960: The Crisis of Legal Orthodoxy* (New York: Oxford University Press, 1992), 129.

"Common law" names that nebulous body of law and juristic theory distinguished from Roman law, canon law, equity law, and ecclesiastical law. Generally, the common law is distinguished from the laws created by legislatures and "comprises the body of those principles and rules of action, relating to the government and security of persons and property, which derive their authority solely from usages and customs of immemorial antiquity." In the United States, "the phrase designates that portion of the common law of England (including such acts of parliament as were applicable) which had been adopted and was in force here at the time of the Revolution. This, so far as it has not since been expressly abrogated, is recognized as an organic part of the jurisprudence of most of the United States." For a complete definition of the common law, see *Black's Law Dictionary* (Saint Paul, Minn.: West Publishing, 1968), 345–46.

2. "Fancy," notes Martha Nussbaum in *Poetic Justice: The Literary Imagination and Public Life* (Boston: Beacon Press, 1995), names the ability "to imagine nonexistent possibilities, to see one thing as another and one thing in another, to endow a perceived form with a complex life" (4); and, labeled unscientific and irrational by some formidable legal thinkers, fancy has been institutionally abhorred throughout much nineteenth- and twentieth-century American jurisprudence.

3. Holmes, *Common Law*, 100. Lauren Berlant is to be thanked for bringing into focus for me the connection between Holmes's figures of error and the dynamics of capitalism and culture that I emphasize in other parts of this chapter.

4. Production is always production for exchange; any notion of production for use is essentially of no use either to nineteenth-century industry or to classical political economy. Catherine Gallagher, "Review Article," *Criticism* 29, no. 2 (1987): 235. The notion of production for use, notes Mark Seltzer, is essentially a residue of the methodological move "to 'periodize' the fall into consumer culture," which takes the general form "of a standard, and remarkably portable, story of a fall from production to consumption (or from industry to luxury, or from use to exchange, etc.)." At times, he acerbically adds, this narrative of the fall "seems as crude as the claim that people grew things in the first half of the nineteenth

century and ate them in the second half" (*Bodies and Machines* [New York: Routledge, 1992], 60).

5. Hannah Arendt, *The Human Condition* (1958; reprint, Chicago: University of Chicago Press, 1989), 182.

6. Jeremy Bentham, *Usury Laws: Their Nature, Expediency, and Influence* (New York: Society for Political Education, 1881), 9.

7. According to the *Oxford English Dictionary* (2d ed.), the difference between "interest" and "usury" approaches the modern distinction between "simple interest" and "compound interest." The entry under "interest" (med. L., *interesse*) reads:

> *Simple interest* is the interest paid on the principal as lent. *Compound (compounded) interest* (interest upon interest), is the interest eventually paid on a principal periodically increased by the addition of each fresh amount of interest as it becomes due and remains unpaid. Interest in this sense was formerly called usury, a name still applied when interest is charged at a rate beyond what is considered legitimate or just. In med. L. *interesse* (Interest) differed from *usura* (Usury) in that the latter was avowedly a charge for the use of money, which was forbidden by the Canon Law; whereas originally "*interesse* refers to the compensation which under the Roman Law, was due by the debtor who had made default. The measure of compensation was *id quod interest,* the difference between the creditor's position in consequence of the debtor's laches [sitting on his rights] and the position which might reasonably have been anticipated as the direct consequence of the debtor's fulfilment of his obligation." This compensation was always permissible when it could be shown that such loss had really arisen (*damnum emergens*). At a later period, *lucrum cessans*—loss of profit through inability to reinvest—was also recognized as giving a claim to *interesse;* both cases appear to be included in the formula *damna et interesse.* The *interesse* was originally a fixed sum specified in the contract; but a percentage reckoned periodically, so as to correspond to the creditor's loss, was afterwards substituted (as sometimes in England in the first half of the 13th cent.).

8. Guyora Binder and Robert Weisberg, *Literary Criticisms of the Law* (Princeton, N.J.: Princeton University Press, 2000), 518. Binder and Weisberg draw on a wide range of "New Historicist" work to provide models of one particular method of law and literature scholarship, the "cultural criticism of law"—from Stephen Greenblatt on the reciprocity between economic and symbolic orders of culture, to Joyce Appleby on economic thought in seventeenth-century England. Much of what I have to say in the following two paragraphs derives from the conclusions that Binder and Weisberg draw from this work.

9. In the paragraph in text, I state some of the general concerns of this chapter, but in quite particular ways my argument takes its cue from the interpretive practice of that Renaissance New Historicism elaborated in Lorna Hutson's *The Usurer's Daughter: Male Friendship and Fictions of Woman in Sixteenth-Century England* (London: Routledge, 1994). Hutson traces a sixteenth-century Renaissance code of "faithful friendship" between men—a system of credit articulated through the exchange of gifts and services between a lord and his "fee'd man"—as an exchange of gifts that assures the "continewance" of good faith between creditors and debtors and that appears in Renaissance texts in the narrative forms of "fidelity," "trust," or "good faith." Concerned with the transformation from feudalism to capitalism, *The Usurer's Daughter* finds in the gendered tropes of Renaissance texts not only a wedding of the semiotic and the material, the emotional and the economic, but also a practical transformation of the conditions of exchange. Hutson proposes that the

economic implications of the literature of the period (particularly of Shakespeare's plays) are bound up with the transformation "of the media through which relations of service and exchange had hitherto taken place"—including the flexibility of legal procedure in the area of property transmission and credit relations. It is arguably the case, she proposes, that women's infidelity is expressive not of an eternal truth about men's imaginations or women's sexuality "but of a historically specific transition in socio-economic relations, in which Shakespeare's dramatic rhetoric is itself implicated" (2).

10. It is generally accepted that Stanley Jevons's *The Theory of Political Economy* (New York: Macmillan, 1871) heralds the start of the marginal revolution.

11. I take the phrase "random walk of value" from Burton Malkiel's book titled *Random Walk Down Wall Street* (1973; reprint, New York: W. W. Norton & Co., 1991).

Some might take my invocation of "the random walk of value" in this context as anachronistic; but I would seek haven in a recent cultural criticism on finance capital that has demurred from reading capitalism's "stages" as diachronic and successive, one that embraces instead an emphasis on the multiple and synchronic "internal stages" of every capitalist cycle. Fredric Jameson has recently noted this turn toward the synchronic in "Culture and Finance Capital," this "way in which capitalist development in each of [its] moment[s] replicates itself and reproduces a series of three moments." Those moments, understood sequentially, in accordance with the terms of Marx in *Das Kapital*'s (in *The Marx-Engels Reader*, trans. Robert C. Tucker [New York: W. W. Norton & Co., 1978]) classic formulation for profit, M-C-M', run as follows: (1) the phase of trade or "primitive accumulation," (2) the phase when money becomes capital, and (3) the speculative phase coincident with finance capital (*Critical Inquiry* 24, no. 1 [autumn 1997]: 246–65, 250). Inspired in part by works such as Giovanni Arrighi's *The Long Twentieth Century*, which replaces "stages" with the economic figure of the "spiral," a figure for discontinuous but expansive history, these interpretations of the speculative take a reprieve from one of Marxist cultural criticism's favorite subjects, production (or, rather, readings of speculation as a final extirpation of production from the calculus of profit). It is the finality of that narrative that proves anathema— the latent teleology, within much recent Marxist cultural criticism, of historical progression, of developmental narrative, of prophetic forecast; a teleology captured in accounts of finance capital as capitalism's "highest stage" (in echo of V. I. Lenin's *Imperialism: The Highest Stage of Capitalism* [1939; reprint, New York: International Publishers, 1988]) or as an incident of "late capitalism" (e.g., Ernest Mandel, *Late Capitalism*, trans. Joris De Bres [1975; reprint, London: Verso, 1978]), "as though this were the last stage conceivable, or as though the process [of producing profit] were some uniform historical progression" (Jameson, "Culture and Finance Capital," 249).

For examples of the new logic of finance capital, which carefully exfoliate the Marxist formula (M-C-M') while resisting Marxism's slip into periodization, see the following: Giovanni Arrighi, *The Long Twentieth Century: Money, Power, and the Origins of Our Times* (New York: Verso, 1994); Gilles Deleuze and Felix Guattari, *Anti-Oedipus: Capitalism and Schizophrenia* (Minneapolis: University of Minnesota Press, 1983); Jacques Derrida, *Specters of Marx: The State of the Debt, the Work of Mourning, and the New International*, trans. Peggy Kamuf (New York: Routledge, 1994), and *Given Time: I. Counterfeit Money*, trans. Peggy Kamuf (Chicago: University of Chicago Press, 1992), originally published as *Donner le temps* (Paris: Editions Galilée, 1991).

12. James Medbery, *Men and Mysteries of Wall Street* (New York: R. Worthington, 1878), 209.

13. William Fowler, *Ten Years on Wall Street* (New York: B. Franklin, 1870), 249.

14. The *Dictionary of American Regional English* defines the "cakewalk" as a "social en-

tertainment, once especially favored by Blacks, in which a cake was the prize awarded for the fanciest steps, or figures executed by those who walked or paraded around it. And in some descriptions, the cake is featured at the center of the room, and is the object around which the dancers parade" (ed. Frederick Cassidy [Cambridge, Mass.: Harvard University Press, 1985], 1:507). On the cakewalk craze of the turn of the century, see also Marshall Stearns and Jean Stearns, "Williams and Walker and the Beginnings of Vernacular Dance on Broadway," chap. 16 of *Jazz Dance: The Story of American Vernacular Dance* (New York: Macmillan, 1970), 121–23.

15. Harriet Beecher Stowe, *Uncle Tom's Cabin; or, Life among the Lowly* (1852; reprint, New York: Penguin, 1986), 118, 133, 624.

16. Harriet Beecher Stowe, *A Key to Uncle Tom's Cabin: Presenting the Original Facts and Documents upon Which the Story Is Founded. Together with Corroborative Statements Verifying the Truth of the Work* (Port Washington, N.Y.: Kennikat Press, 1853), 27–8.

Though widely divergent in methodology and political stance, much recent work on *Uncle Tom's Cabin*, in shared effort strenuously to reconfigure our sense of nineteenth-century conceptions of the "public" and the "private," domesticity and the market, and gender as a matter of public concern, has been keen to bridge Stowe's implicit critique of the market with the imaginative labors spawned by the Negro's putative "nervous organization": Elizabeth Ammons, "Heroines in *Uncle Tom's Cabin*," in *Critical Essays on Harriet Beecher Stowe*, ed. Elizabeth Ammons (Boston: Hall, 1980), 152–65, and "Stowe's Dream of the Mother-Savior: *Uncle Tom's Cabin* and American Women Writers before the 1920s," in *New Essays on Uncle Tom's Cabin*, ed. Eric Sundquist (Cambridge: Cambridge University Press, 1986), 155–95; Rachel Bowlby, "Breakfast in America: *Uncle Tom*'s Cultural Histories," in *Nation and Narration*, ed. Homi Bhabha (New York: Routledge, 1990) 197–212; Gillian Brown, *Domestic Individualism: Imagining Self in Nineteenth-Century America* (Berkeley: University of California Press, 1990); Ann Douglas, "Feminine Sentimentalism: The Bitterness of Harriet Beecher Stowe," in *Critical Essays*, ed. Ammons, 235–243, originally published in *The Feminization of American Culture* (New York: Avon Books, 1978); Leslie Fiedler, "Harriet Beecher Stowe's Novel of Sentimental Protest," in *Critical Essays*, ed. Ammons, 112–16; Philip Fisher, "The Sentimental Novel and Slavery," in *Hard Facts: Setting and Form in the American Novel* (Oxford: Oxford University Press, 1985); Theodore Hovet, "Modernization and the American Fall into Slavery in *Uncle Tom's Cabin*," *New England Quarterly* 54 (1981): 500; Bruce McConachie, "Out of the Kitchen and into the Marketplace: Normalizing *Uncle Tom's Cabin* for the Antebellum Stage, " *Journal of American Drama and Theater* 3 (1991): 5–28; Karen Sanchez-Eppler, "Bodily Bonds: The Intersecting Rhetorics of Feminism and Abolition," in *The New American Studies*, ed. Philip Fisher (Berkeley: University of California Press, 1991), 228–59; Jane Tompkins, "Sentimental Power: *Uncle Tom's Cabin* and the Politics of Literary History," in *Sensational Designs: The Cultural Work of American Fiction, 1790–1860* (New York: Oxford University Press, 1985), 122–46.

Many of the above studies remain alarmingly silent on the topic of race. For readings of Stowe's novel that pay acute attention to the theoretical and historical dimensions of race, see James Baldwin, "Everybody's Protest Novel," in *Notes of a Native Son* (Boston: Beacon Press, 1955), 13–23; Hortense Spillers, "Changing the Letter: The Yokes, the Jokes of Discourse, or, Mrs. Stowe, Mr. Reed," in *Slavery and the Literary Imagination*, ed. Deborah McDowell and Arnold Rampersad (Baltimore: Johns Hopkins University Press, 1989), 25–61; Robert Stepto, "Sharing the Thunder: The Literary Exchanges of Harriet Beecher Stowe, Henry Bibb, and Frederick Douglass," in *New Essays*, ed. Sundquist, 135–53; Kenneth W. Warren, "The Persistence of Uncle Tom and the Problem of Critical Distinction," in *Black and White Strangers: Race and American Literary Realism* (Chicago: University of Chicago Press, 1993), 71–108; Richard Yarborough, "Race, Violence, and Manhood: The Masculine Ideal in Frederick Douglass's 'The Heroic Slave,'" in *Frederick Douglass: New Literary and Historical Essays,* ed. Eric Sundquist (New York: Cambridge University Press, 1990), 166–88.

On sentimentalism, domesticity, and capitalism, see Nancy Cott, *The Bonds of Womanhood: "Woman's Sphere" in New England, 1780–1835* (New Haven, Conn.: Yale University Press, 1977); Karen Halttunen, *Confidence Men and Painted Women: A Study of Middle-Class Culture in America, 1830–1870* (New Haven, Conn.: Yale University Press, 1982); and Barbara Welter, *Dimity Convictions: The American Woman in the Nineteenth Century* (Athens: Ohio University Press, 1976).

And, finally, for readings that situate slavery and *Uncle Tom's Cabin* within the rival claims of "machine culture" and "market culture," see Seltzer, *Bodies and Machines,* 47–49; and Walter Benn Michaels, *The Gold Standard and the Logic of Naturalism: American Literature at the Turn of the Century* (Berkeley: University of California Press, 1987), 101–12.

17. Thomas Jefferson, *Notes on the State of Virginia* (1787), ed. William Peden (New York: W. W. Norton & Co., 1982), 139.

18. Charles Mackay, *Memoirs of Extraordinary Popular Delusions and the Madness of Crowds* (1841; reprint, Wells, Vt.: Fraser, 1932), 1–97, 629–31.

19. In essence, I am concerned in this chapter with the intersecting lines of flight between the aesthetic forms common to a literature of sentimentality and the affective circuits of finance capital. I will at times refer to a process by which "a logic becomes a chronologic," alluding in that phrase to the acts of translation in which the novel's sentimentality is turned into the festal whimsy of its theatrical and cinematic adaptations. This notion is very close to what Lauren Berlant, in her reading of *Show Boat's* sundry textual instances, has termed "the unfinished business of sentimentality," which she takes as that matrix of "adaptation, commodification, and affect" through which moments of slave sufferance "get turned into forms of modern entertainment." Of specific concern to Berlant is the "theory or account of history" preserved in melodramatic texts that traffic in the "semiotic substance of sentimentality." Texts such as *Show Boat* bear "an obsessive relation to futurity"—they "hold a wedge open for the future"—when the sublime objects of slave affliction are made the cornerstone of ever-evolving and utopian melodramatic narratives. The slave's suffering thus serves as a building block in a much broader cultural project that "stages the nation's recovery from the legacies of slavery, migration, urbanization, and industrialization." If I were to assimilate my interests to Berlant's vocabulary, I would say that I am quite literally interested in the "unfinished" business of sentimentality—in the achronicity of the moment of speculative valuation; in the ungainly reciprocities, incalculable dividends, and affective inflation of finance capital. See Berlant, "Pax Americana: The Case of *Show Boat,*" in *Cultural Institutions of the Novel,* ed. Deidre Lynch and William Warner (Durham, N.C.: Duke University Press, 1996), 399–402, passim.

20. Where I use the term "redundant," copyright scholars such as Timothy Brennan might be more inclined to use the technical term "nonrivalrous." Nonrivalrous possession describes what economists call "public goods," a possession whose redundancy and superfluity stands in sharp contrast to notions of consumption and ownership based in assumptions of scarcity: "The same meal cannot be consumed repeatedly, but a book can be re-read. . . . The very idea of nonrivalry itself is inconsistent with 'consumed' in the sense of being used up. Moreover, much of the information many of us possess in our bookshelves . . . is not consumed, in the sense of being ingested" (Timothy Brennan, "Copyright,

Property, and the Right to Deny," *Chicago-Kent Law Review* 68, no. 2 [1993]: 675–714, esp. 686). Another synonym for "redundant" would be "pyramiding," as it has been used by Walter Benn Michaels: "The art of finance is the production of money by 'pyramiding' and 'kiting' instead of investing. The financier recognizes in money a quirk of identity that makes it possible to transcend the limitations of any 'actual fact.' Money can be in two, three, even four places at one time. Seeing this quirk of identity as a principle of productivity, the financier makes ten or twelve times what he has to start with" (*Gold*, 67).

21. According to Thorstein Veblen, goodwill is defined as a business's established relations, reputation for upright dealing, and extended credit. It provides capital with a "nucleus" in the form of "virtual collateral"—a fund on the one hand "already employed" (and "to the full extent") in "the ordinary business of the concern," yet, on the other, and concurrently, "solvent," or capable of enabling the financier to carry on further traffic in vendible capital "without withdrawing any appreciable portion of his holdings from the lucrative investments in which they have been placed." Goodwill is capital's value and spirit, so much so that, "by virtue of the ubiquity proper to spiritual bodies, the whole of it may undividedly be present in every part of the various structures that it has created" (*The Theory of Business Enterprise* [New York: Charles Scribner's Sons, 1904], 117, 173).

A standard accounting textbook describes goodwill as "the most 'intangible' of the intangibles," adding to this definition echoes of Veblen's "value and spirit" that underscore the literariness of this form of capital. Goodwill, the textbook continues, "cannot be separated from the business as a whole . . . [and] because no objective transaction with outside parties has taken place, a great deal of subjectivity—even misrepresentation—might be involved." See Donald E. Kieso and Jerry J. Weygandt, *Intermediate Accounting* (New York: John Wiley & Sons, 1998), 601–6.

22. *Stowe v. Thomas,* 23 Fed. Cas. (2 Am. Law Reg. 210) 201, 202 (1853). Until the law came to recognize a "work" with protections independent of the physical manuscript, narrow and literal visions of the scope of copyright (such as in *Stowe*) prevailed. Prior to 1853, Peter Jaszi suggests, the "work" protected under copyright appeared disaggregable from the concrete manuscript that it shadowed. The work had yet to mature (as it would over proceeding decades) into the form it would finally take: its protected "expression" and its unprotected "idea." For a discussion of *Stowe* and the evolution of the concept of the "work," see Peter Jaszi, "Toward a Theory of Copyright: The Metamorphoses of 'Authorship,'" *Duke Law Journal* no. 2 (April 1991): 455–502, esp. 471–80.

For Eaton S. Drone, author of *A Treatise on the Law of Property in Intellectual Productions in Great Britain and the United States* (Boston: Little, Brown, & Co., 1879) and defender of a natural right in "intellectual labor" (or labor "without material substance"), as publication and dissemination are immanent to the creation of literary value, the scope of property is far greater than the limited and physical contours of the book: "It is the peculiarity of literary property that only by the multiplication of copies can it have any value to its owner; by publication alone can the author secure the reward of his labor. Without this, his toil is without fruit, his property without value" (13). The *Stowe* opinion thus reflects judicial literalism in the extreme: "Literary property, as has been shown, is not in the language alone; but in the matter of which language is merely a means of communication. . . . That which constitutes the essence and value of a literary composition, which represents the results of the author's labor and learning, may be capable of expression in more than one form of language different from that of the original. . . . The translation is not in substance a new work. It is a reproduction in a new form of an existing one" (451–52). Drone's formulation ultimately prevailed in the mature conceptions of the work.

23. See chap. 1 for discussion of William Blackstone's *Commentaries on the Laws of England* (1765), which conceives common law property rights as rights of "sole and despotic dominion" over things.

24. *Publici juris:* of public right. "This term, as applied to a thing or right, means that it is open to or exercisable by all persons. It designates things that are owned by 'the public'; i.e., the entire state or community, and not by any private person. When a thing is common property, so that any one can make use of it who likes, it is said to be *publici juris;* as in the case of light, air, and public water" (*Sweet's Law Dictionary,* quoted in *Black's Law Dictionary,* 1397).

25. Meredith L. McGill, "The Matter of the Text: Commerce, Print Culture, and the Authority of the State in American Copyright Law," *American Literary History* 9, no. 1 (1997): 21–59, esp. 50–51.

The first American copyright statute, passed on May 31, 1790, specified certain rights to intellectual property covered broadly at the Constitutional Convention three years earlier. The Constitution authorized Congress "to promote the Progress of Science and useful Arts by securing for limited Times, to Authors and Inventors, the exclusive Right to their respective Writings and Discoveries" (art. 1, sec. 8, clause 8). The 1790 law extended protections not generally to "Writings" but specifically to "maps, charts, and books" and guaranteed such protections for a span of fourteen years (Act of May 31, 1790 [1 U.S. St. at L. 124]). Over the intervening century, and on numerous occasions, this law was found to be anachronistic and of weakened applicability as regarded various communications technologies. The federal legislature, as a result, expanded the 1790 law's bundle of entitlements to include new forms of aesthetic labor: prints and engravings in 1802 (Act of April 29, 1802 [2 U.S. St. at L. 1 71]); musical compositions in 1831 (Act of February 3, 1831 [4 U.S. St. at L. 436]); dramatic composition and theatrical performance in 1856 (Act of August 18, 1856 [11 U.S. St. at L. 1 38]); and, finally, paintings, drawings, statuary, models, and designs in 1870 (Act of July 8, 1870 [16 U.S. St. at L. 212]).

Over the century following ratification of the Constitution's copyright protections (from 1790 to, roughly, the publication of Warren and Brandeis's "The Right to Privacy" in 1890), courts developed the idea that in order to carry through on the "limited Times" language of the Constitution's copyright clause, their decisions necessarily had to eviscerate any related common law literary rights. Courts tended to limit the scope of copyright in decisions that expressed a rationale that ran (on the face of it) contrary to the conception of intellectual property rights as "monopoly grants" in aesthetic labor (a rationale that held a particularly fervent sway in three pivotal nineteenth-century copyright cases: *Wheaton v. Peters* [1834]; *Stowe v. Thomas* [1853]; and *Baker v. Selden* [1879]). These judicial opinions, though at variance in the specific rights and properties they protected, held to a single line of reasoning: that since the Constitution and acts of Congress expressed copyright in terms of specific rights, all other literary rights, whether protected at common law or not, must pass into the public domain upon the vesting of statutory copyright. Such reasoning produced twin though antagonized effects. On the one hand, courts emphasized and protected the clear and well-honed results of intellectual effort (protecting specific volumes in an anthology but not the particular works anthologized [*Wheaton v. Peters*]; exact copies of a book but not subsequent translations [*Stowe v. Thomas*]; copies of the books in which a system or process is explained but not the system itself or the forms through which it is calculated [*Baker v. Selden*]). On the other hand, the courts also managed to nurture not authors themselves (not authors exclusively) but a public domain, or "commons," an arena of unprotectable or uncopyrightable material, the culture's repository for the raw material of authorship.

26. McGill, "The Matter of the Text," 50. Recall here the arguments of Samuel Warren and Louis Brandeis in "The Right to Privacy," where it is claimed that privacy falls beneath the purview of those protections that precede the act of going into print.

27. Jessica Litman, "The Public Domain," *Emory Law Journal* 39, no. 4 (1990): 965–1023, 977. Litman portrays the public domain neither as the "public's toll" for conferring private property rights in works of authorship nor as the realm of material undeserving of property rights. The public domain represents, in her view, a device necessary to the workings of a system of authorship that is based on the necessarily apparitional notion of "originality." Anglo-American copyright law is rooted in a vision of authorship as ineffable creation from nothing (textual creation of "Aphrodite from the foam of the sea")—a vision that, if taken seriously, would require either that we not grant authors copyrights without first "dissecting their creative process to pare elements adapted from the works of others from the later authors' recasting of them" or that we oblige authors to solicit the permission of their predecessors (1023). Barring either of those impossible scenarios, the public domain enters as a crucial device in an otherwise unworkable system, for it reserves the raw material of authorship (e.g., *scènes à faire*, plots, clichés, common devices, and details) to the commons, thus fostering the translation and recombination inherent to all creative activity. In sum, Litman endorses a wide and thriving public domain, since a public domain that is capacious and ravenous for form is the very monster that makes literary production possible. For a defense of the alternative view of the public domain as the "public's toll," see M. William Krasilovsky, "Observations on Public Domain," *Bulletin of the Copyright Society of the USA* 14 (1967): 205, 210–18; and L. Ray Patterson, "Free Speech, Copyright, and Fair Use," *Vanderbilt Law Review* 40 (1987): 1, 7. Finally, Benjamin Kaplan offers a defense of the "matter unmerited" posture in *An Unhurried View of Copyright* (New York: Columbia University Press, 1967), 45–46.

28. Melville B. Nimmer and David Nimmer, *Cases and Materials on Copyright and Other Aspects of Entertainment Litigation Including Unfair Competition, Defamation, Privacy*, 4th ed. (Saint Paul, Minn.: West Publishing, 1991), 13.03 (B), at 13.62.2, quoted in Robert H. Rotstein, "Beyond Metaphor: Copyright Infringement and the Fiction of the Work," *Chicago-Kent Law Review* 68 (1993): 725–804, 767.

Stowe v. Thomas offers an early installment in what, by the 1940s, will be referred to within intellectual property circles as *scènes à faire* doctrine, a starting point in copyright protection that refers to material that copyright does not protect because of its obviousness and conventionality. *Scènes à faire* doctrine is close to, but not the same as, the merger doctrine—the notion that in some cases an idea and its expression merge because there are so few ways of expressing that idea, and so even the expression is not entitled to copyright protection. The case of *Nicholas v. Universal Pictures Corp.*, a case that concerns the pilfered particulars of a play titled *Abie's Irish Rose*, provides a cornerstone in the unfolding public domain principles that will be termed *scènes à faire*. In the case in which someone (Universal Pictures) writes a play (*The Cohens and the Kelleys*) about a marriage between a member of an Irish Catholic family and a member of a Jewish family, endows both the betrothed with stereotypical traits, makes both families hostile to the marriage—and adds all the particulars that go into fleshing out these matters—said particulars go unprotected because *anyone* writing such a play would probably include them, and so to grant property in the particulars would almost be tantamount to granting property in the plot (it would be akin, in short, to granting only one of the many authors of cop shows right to a scene in which the principals eat doughnuts). Judge Learned Hand offered the most famous judicial pronouncement on the issue:

If *Twelfth Night* were copyrighted, it is quite possible that a second comer might so closely imitate Sir Toby Belch or Malvolio as to infringe, but it would not be enough that for one of his characters he cast a riotous knight who kept wassail to the discomfort of the household, or a vain and foppish steward who became amorous of his mistress. These would be no more than Shakespeare's "ideas" in the play, as little capable of monopoly as Einstein's Doctrine of Relativity, or Darwin's theory of the Origin of Species. It follows that the less developed the characters, the less they can be copyrighted; that is the penalty an author must bear for marking them too indistinctly. (*Nicholas v. Universal Pictures Corp.*, 45 F. 2d 119, 121 [282 U.S. 902 (1930)])

The phrase *scènes à faire* is applied to these sorts of common details by Judge Leon Yankwich in the case of *Cain v. Universal Pictures Corp.* (1942).

The following are key cases in the elaboration of *scènes à faire* doctrine: *London v. Biograph*, 231 F. 696 (2d Cir. 1916); *Cain v. Universal Pictures Co.*, 47 F. Supp. 1013 (S.D. Cal. 1942); *Schwarz v. Universal Pictures Co.*, 85 F. Supp. 270 (S.D. Cal. 1945); *Atari, Inc., v. North Am. Philips Consumer Elecs. Corp.*, 672 F. 2d. 607 (7th Cir. 1982); *Berkic v. Crichton*, 761 F. 2d 1289 (1985). Thanks go to Simon Stern for clarifying for me the tenets of *scènes à faire* doctrine.

29. Paul de Man, "Conclusions: Walter Benjamin's 'The Task of the Translator,'" in *The Resistance to Theory* (Minneapolis: University of Minnesota Press, 1986), 97.

30. Justice Noah H. Swayne (dissent), *Slaughterhouse Cases*, 83 U.S. (16 Wall.) 36, 127 (1873).

31. A. L. Corbin, "Taxation of Seats on the Stock Exchange," *Yale Law Journal* 31 (1922): 429.

32. *Eaton v. Boston, Concord & Montreal R.R.*, 51 N.H. 504, 511 (1872).

33. John R. Commons, *Legal Foundations of Capitalism* (New York: Macmillan, 1924), 16.

34. *Thompson v. Androscoggin River Improvement Co.*, 54 N.H. 545, 522 (1874). See also *Pumpelly v. Green Bay Co.*, 80 U.S. (13 Wall.) 166 (1871), in which the U.S. Supreme Court challenges the prevailing idea that a taking constitutes either physical trespass or appropriation of title; instead, it stands "for the increasingly prevalent proposition that all restrictions on the use of property that diminished its market value were takings in the constitutional sense" (Horwitz, *The Transformation of American Law, 1870–1960*, 148).

35. Adam Smith's *An Inquiry into the Nature and Causes of the Wealth of Nations* (1776; reprint, London: George Routledge & Sons, 1889).

I do not mean to suggest here that, in *Wealth*, Smith resolves private vices and the fear of overexpropriation through figures of public interest in some originary or foundational way—he is not the first, though he may be considered the most authoritative exponent. Insofar as medieval culture possessed a signature prejudice against the unlimited lust for gain—captured, to cite just one example, in Saint Augustine's consideration of the *appetitus divitarum infinitus* as one of the three principal sins, alongside the craving for power (*libido dominandi*) and sexual lasciviousness—the need for such resolution has born a distinct impress on early-modern as well as modern philosophical and economic thought. Resolutions similar to Smith's can be found in Giambattista Vico's *Scienza nuova*, an early document to figure the metamorphosis of destructive "passions" into "virtues." Moreover, Bernard Mandeville's argument in *The Fable of the Bees* (1714) that the private vices of avarice, prodigality, pride, and luxury produced public benefits has often been regarded as a precursor to everything from Smith's laissez-faire economics and the "marginal utility analysis" of Simon Nelson Patten (who argues that the consumer's splurges lead to the common good of all), to that late-twentieth-century theory of consumption termed, again beneficently, "trickle-down economics." For Patten's weave of eighteenth-century utilitarianism with concern for the morality of consumption, see "The Effect of the Consumption of Wealth on the Economic Welfare of Society," in *Science Economic Discussion,* ed. Richard T. Ely (New York: Science Co., 1886), 123–35, *The Stability of Prices* (Baltimore: American Economic Assoc., 1889), and *The Consumption of Wealth* (Philadelphia: T. & J. W. Johnson, 1889).

For discussions of the broad intellectual tradition to which Smith belongs, with particular attention paid to the emergent market dynamics for which his thinking proved exemplary, see Albert O. Hirschman, *The Passions and the Interests: Political Arguments for Capitalism before Its Triumph* (Princeton, N.J.: Princeton University Press, 1977), 69–112, and *Shifting Involvements: Private Interest and Public Action* (Princeton, N.J.: Princeton University Press, 1982); Joyce Appleby, *Capitalism and a New Social Order: The Republican Vision of the 1790s* (New York: New York University Press, 1983), 27–38; John Dwyer, *The Age of the Passions: An Interpretation of Adam Smith and Scottish Enlightenment Culture* (Edinburgh: Tuckwell Press, 1998); Michael Fry, ed., *Adam Smith's Legacy: His Place in the Development of Modern Economics* (London: Routledge, 1992); E. G. Hundert, *The Enlightenment's Fable: Bernard Mandeville and the Discovery of Society* (Cambridge: Cambridge University Press, 1994); Ronald L. Meek, *Smith, Marx, and After: Ten Essays in the Development of Economic Thought* (London: Chapman & Hall, 1977); Jerry Z. Muller, *Adam Smith and His Time and Ours: Designing the Decent Society* (New York: Free Press, 1993); and Patricia H. Werhane, *Adam Smith and His Legacy for Modern Capitalism* (Oxford: Oxford University Press, 1991).

36. Smith, *Wealth,* 260, 269. "He generally, indeed, neither intends to promote the public interest, nor knows how much he is promoting it" (345). This causal unknown is the very "moral" hub of Smith's moral economy, foregrounding a concern with unintended but realized effects that stands in sharp contrast with the intended but unrealized effects that are the central concern of many within the same intellectual tradition, from Albert O. Hirschman to Thomas Haskell.

37. Thorstein Veblen, a renowned and staunch critic of the "invisible hand" agenda, would concede that emulation is probably "the strongest and most alert and persistent" of economic motives proper:

> The currently accepted legitimate end of effort becomes the achievement of a favorable comparison with other men; and therefore the repugnance to futility to a good extent coalesces with the incentive to emulation. It acts to accentuate the struggle for pecuniary reputability by visiting with a sharper disapproval all shortcoming and all evidence of shortcoming in point of pecuniary success. Purposeful effort comes to mean, primarily, effort directed to or resulting in a more creditable showing of accumulated wealth. Among the motives that lead men to accumulate wealth, the primary, both in scope and intensity, therefore, continues to belong to this motive of pecuniary emulation. (*The Theory of the Leisure Class: An Economic Study of Institutions* [1899; reprint, New York: New American Library, 1953], 40)

38. Smith proposes two distinct objectives for political economy in the introduction to bk. 4 of *Wealth:* "First, to provide a plentiful revenue or subsistence for the people, or more properly to enable them to provide such a revenue or subsistence for themselves; and secondly, to supply the state or commonwealth with revenue sufficient for the public services. It proposes to enrich both the people and the sovereign" (323).

39. "Naive property" (a term that I have taken from Timothy Brennan) describes "the general conventional understanding regarding the ability to own, use, and sell land, physical objects, and other tangible goods." In the current chapter, "naïveté" shall stand in for the layman's intuition regarding property rights, the ancillary and muddled imagery of ownership buried, Brennan contends, in common law conceptions of property law—specifically, in the common law tradition that suggests that "property law evolved from the 'bottom-up' to facilitate the interactions among individuals as economic and social needs arose." Naive property rights are inherent in the workings of society and stand in contrast to statutory rights (e.g., copyright, patent, corporate law), rights that, from the vantage of common law tradition, seem to have been "created to further some efficiency or wealth interest." See Brennan, "Copyright, Property, and the Right to Deny," esp. 682–83.

40. This tale of "public gains borne of private interests" has recently been advanced with greatest vigor and rigor by Richard Posner, the law-and-economics defender of neoclassical political economy, in *Economic Analysis of Law* (Cambridge, Mass.: Harvard University Press, 1981). See also Gary Becker, *The Economic Approach to Human Behavior* (Chicago: University of Chicago Press, 1976); and Richard Epstein, *Takings* (Cambridge, Mass.: Harvard University Press, 1985), for the case presumptive "security" as a necessary adjunct to investment in (or the careful use of) property. Some challenges to the notion that private property offers the best and most efficient means of managing resources for the public good are offered in Carol Rose, "The Comedy of the Commons: Custom, Commerce, and Inherently Public Property," in *Property and Persuasion: Essays on the History, Theory, and Rhetoric of Ownership* (Boulder, Colo.: Westview Press, 1994), 105–62, originally published in *University of Chicago Law Review* 53 (1986): 711–81; and Duncan Kennedy and Frank Michelman, "Are Private Property and Freedom of Contract Efficient?" *Hofstra Law Review* 8 (1979–80): 711.

41. Maurice Godelier defines economics as the analysis of rational behavior or "the science which studies human behavior as a relationship between ends and scarce means which have alternative uses." Economics is a theoretical investigation aimed at discovering "the conditions under which it is possible to attain a certain objective, taking into account a certain set of constraints" (*Rationality and Irrationality in Economics,* trans. Brian Pierce [New York: New Left Books, 1972], 12–13).

It is at the crossroads of the public and the private—in the circumstance of private property's antithesis and necessary purlieu, public property, or "the commons"—where classical economy's relentlessly happy outcome turns sour and comedy generates tragedy. By the very logic that sanctions acquisitiveness, public property makes return on investment uncertain and unpredictable, and leads those with access to the commons to care little for its development. "No one wishes to care for things that may be taken away tomorrow, and no one knows whom to approach to make exchanges" (Rose, *Property and Persuasion* 106). Garret Hardin ("The Tragedy of the Commons," *Science* 162 [1968]: 1243–48) memorably figures the precariousness of public ownership in his fable of the herdsman on the commons, that rational being who "seeks to maximize his gain" through measures of the common's utility in relation to his desired profit. "Adding together the component utilities, the rational herdsman concludes that the only sensible course for him to pursue is to add another animal to his herd. And another; and another" (1244). Each herdsman with access to the commons reaches this same conclusion, and together the community is "locked into a system that compels . . . increase . . . without limit—in a world that is limited" (1244). "Ruin is the destination toward which all men rush, each pursuing his own best interest in a society that believes in the freedom of the commons" (1244). Freedom of this sort, Hardin warns, "brings ruin to all" (1244). In sum, when the will to accumulate advances against common resource, econ-omy remorselessly generates tragedy—the "tragedy of the commons."

42. This is the argument posed by Albert O. Hirschman in *The Passions and the Inter-ests*. Smith's *Wealth*, Hirschman contends, secures the final intellectual stakes in the histor-ical transformation of dangerous and potentially destabilizing "passions" (i.e., avarice, greed, covetousness) into constant and persistent "interests" in accumulation, also known as the "interests-versus-passions thesis" or, in short, the supposition that an interest in ac-cumulation acquires the task, within a modern abstract and global market, "of holding back those passions that had long been thought to be much less reprehensible" (41–42, 55, 59–63). The historical process that achieves something of an apotheosis in *Wealth* had ear-lier been advanced through the contributions of everyone from Helvéticus, Vico, and Man-deville, to Machiavelli, Montesquieu, and Stewart.

43. Jeremy Waldron, "From Authors to Copiers: Individual Rights and Social Values in Intellectual Property," *Chicago-Kent Law Review* 68, no. 2 (1993): 841–87, 842.

Richard Posner and William Landes, in their economic analysis of copyright law, offer an "efficiency" solution to the conundrum of authorship:

> Copyright holders might . . . find it in their self-interest, ex ante, to limit copyright pro-tection. To the extent that a later author is free to borrow material from an earlier one, the later author's cost of expression is reduced; and, from an ex ante viewpoint, every au-thor is both an earlier author from whom a later author might want to borrow material and the later author himself. In the former role, he desires maximum copyright protec-tion for works he creates; in the latter, he prefers minimum protection for works created earlier by others. *In principle, there is a level of copyright protection that balances these two competing interests optimally.* ("An Economic Analysis of Copyright Law," *Journal of Legal Studies* 18 [June 1989]: 325–63, 333, emphasis mine)

44. Susan Stewart's thoughts on "literary property" possess a pliancy that makes them applicable, in this instance, to the *Stowe* court's personification of the public domain in the fugitive slave:

> The subjection of speech to the demands of the absolutist state, and the rectification of crimes of speech by the suffering of the body, evolves into a new view of speech as intel-lectual property—a property whose dramatic separation from its site of production is best illustrated by the status of the debate regarding its ownership. . . . But once writing is considered as property, it is severed from the provenance of its authorial location and hence *freed from that bond at the very moment of its attachment;* in fact, what happens is the textualization of the authorial location, the site of the author as a site of a textual sys-tem, a place of quotation already located within a system of quotation. (*Crimes of Writ-ing: Problems in the Containment of Representation* [Oxford: Oxford University Press, 1991], 15–16, emphasis mine)

She continues:

> This "property," which must transcend its materiality and, in order to be recognized, must by definition be shared, thus becomes surrounded by a discourse of genealogy, in-heritance, derivation, production, and reception—*a merger of the attributive systems for persons as well as the attributive system for things.* . . . Furthermore, the oxymoron of "lit-erary property" continually appears as the site in which the law works out all that it is *not* as a form of writing: the unlocalizable, the excess of the signifier, the nondeclarative in syn-

tax. The idealized conditions of codification—authority, genealogy, precedence, application, specificity, and transcendence—are established as qualities of a literary realm that
it becomes the task of the law as writing that is *other* to regulate. (15-16, emphasis mine)

45. Karl Marx, *Grundrisse: Foundations of the Critique of Political Economy,* trans. Martin Nicolaus (1973; reprint, New York: Penguin Books, 1993), 165. Marx's excursus on
money finds an echo in the writings of Marshall McLuhan, who assesses money's multilin-
gual character less rigorously: "'Money talks' because money is a metaphor, a transfer, and
a bridge . . . [a] translator or reducer of multiple things to some common denominator"
(McLuhan, "Media as Translators" and "Money: The Poor Man's Credit Card," both in *Understanding Media: The Extensions of Man* (1964; reprint, Cambridge, Mass: MIT Press,
1995), 56-61, 131-44, respectively, esp. 136 and 143. On the mouth as "the original purse of
economy," dispenser of a poesy that compensates for the original insufficiency of economy
itself, see Kurt Heinzelman, "The Mouth-Tale of the Giants," in *The Economics of the Imagination* (Amherst: University of Massachusetts Press, 1980), 3-34.

46. See de Man, "Conclusions," 83; Marc Shell, "Language and Property: The Economics of Translation in Goethe's *Faust,"* in *Money, Language, and Thought: Literary and
Philosophical Economies from the Medieval to the Modern Era* (Berkeley: University of Cali-
fornia Press, 1982), 84-130, and his introduction to *The Economy of Literature* (Baltimore:
Johns Hopkins University Press, 1978), 1-10, esp. 4-5, 85n. 4,; as well as Eric Cheyfitz's
"The Foreign Policy of Metaphor" and "Translating Property," both in *The Poetics of Im-
perialism: Translation and Colonization from "The Tempest" to "Tarzan"* (Oxford: Oxford
University Press, 1991), 22-58.

47. Bill Brown, *The Material Unconscious: American Amusement, Stephen Crane, and
the Economies of Play* (Cambridge, Mass.: Harvard University Press, 1996), 96.

48. *Board of Trade of the City of Chicago v. Christie Grain and Stock Co.,* 198 U.S. 236,
246 (1905). Ann Fabian, *Card Sharps and Bucket Shops: Gambling in Nineteenth-Century
America* (New York: Routledge, 1999), 156.

49. *Chicago,* 245.

Bucket shops came about with the introduction of the "ticker" to official exchange transactions (i.e., the disclosure of the latest stock prices by means of the telegraph); and the
board sued to protect its right to sell and trade to speculators the subtle price differences between lots of agricultural produce through its intermediary, the Western Union Telegraph
Company. Counsel for the plaintiff described the contract between the Board of Trade and
the telegraph companies as follows:

> The quotation of the prices continuously offered and accepted in these pits during busi-
> ness hours are collected at the plaintiff's expense and handed to the telegraph compa-
> nies, which have their instruments close at hand, and by the latter are sent to a great
> number of offices. The telegraph companies all receive the quotations under contract not
> to furnish them to any bucket shop or place where they are used as a basis for bets or il-
> legal contracts. To that end, they agree to submit applications to the Board of Trade for
> investigations and to require the applicant, if satisfactory, to make a contract with the
> telegraph company and the Board of Trade, which, if observed, confines the information
> within a circle of persons all contracting with the Board of Trade. (245-46)

This limitation of information to a previously contracted circle of parties was read, by opposing counsel, as an illegal restriction of access to information in the wake of its "publication," which under statutory copyright preserved the benefit of market exchange and going
into print—in short, the bucket shops accused the board of censorship.

50. The case presumptive "corporeal substance" was made in *Wheaton v. Peters* and upheld in *Stowe v. Thomas,* where the court drew a distinction between immaterial public "conceptions" and the material "body of the book." In *Wheaton,* the U.S. Supreme Court refused renewal of the plaintiff's original copyright on the grounds that going into print made the products of mental effort (of interiority) public property and, consequently, made texts excessive to the bounds and protections of private property.

51. *Millar v. Taylor,* 4 Burr., 2303, 2361, 98 Eng. Rep. 201 (1769). "James Thomson wrote 'The Seasons' which appeared in 1727-1729. In 1729 Millar purchased the 'copy' from Thomson. Millar registered the book with the Stationers' Company as his property and printed and published it. Thomson dies in 1748. In 1763 Taylor printed and sold an addition [*sic*] of the same book without license of Millar. By this date the period of protection prescribed by the Statute of Anne, 8 Anne, c. 19 (1710), had expired. Millar commenced an action on the case claiming damages of £200. Upon a special verdict, King's Bench held for the plaintiff" (Benjamin Kaplan and Ralph S. Brown, Jr., *Cases on Copyright, Unfair Competition, and Other Topics Bearing on the Protection of Literary, Musical, and Artistic Works,* 2d ed. [Mineola, N.Y.: Foundation Press, 1974], 27n. c). *Chicago,* 241, 243.

52. *Chicago,* 250. Holmes drew on the authority of his own recent ruling in *Bleistein v. Donaldson Lithographing Company* (188 U.S. 239 [1903]):

It is obvious . . . that the plaintiffs' case is not affected by the fact, if it be one, that the pictures represent actual groups—visible things. They seem from the testimony to have been composed from hints or descriptions, not from sight of a performance. But even if they had been drawn from the life, that fact would not deprive them of protection. The opposite proposition would mean that a portrait of Velasquez or Whistler was common property because others might try their hand on the same face. Others are free to copy the original. They are not free to copy the copy. . . . The copy is the personal reaction of an individual upon nature. Personality always contains something unique. It expresses its singularity even in handwriting, and a very modest grade of art has in it something irreducible, which is one man's alone. That something he may copyright unless there is a restriction in the words of the act. (249-50)

53. The board's defense pivoted on the analogy between prices and "market news," an analogy that not only tilted the market in the direction of intellectual property (as metaphor for fiscal transaction) but anticipated arguments soon to be made for a property right in news itself. The watershed in this debate, *International News Service v. Associated Press* (248 U.S. 215 [1918]), which adjudicated the question of whether a news service had the right to prohibit others from selling news it had gathered, concluded on the same note as the earlier price and translation disputes: public domain versus private dominion. Justice Warren Brandeis, writing for the court, echoed the *Stowe* court's defense of information's ultimate unreclaimability: "The general rule of law is, that the noblest of human productions— knowledge, truths ascertained, conceptions, and ideas—become, after voluntary communication to others, free as the air to common use. Upon these incorporeal productions the attribute of property is continued after such communication only in certain classes of cases where public policy has seemed to demand it" (250). Justice Oliver Wendell Holmes, though a dissenter in the case, would take the position that statute afforded marginal protections when those protections were in the interest of public policy but would stop short of the claim that property's status as mere juridical fiction lent all valuable rights and interests the protective stamp of "property." More radical defenders of marketability-as-property would strike just such a tautological pose ("property is everything which has exchangeable

value" [*Minnesota Rate Case* (1890)]; "'property' has ceased to describe any *res*" [A. L. Corbin (1922)]), in a reconception of property as every species of valuable right and interest that, as many critics charged, threatened to engulf all legal relations. Holmes curtailed the threat: "Property, the creation of law, does not arise from value, although exchangeable — a matter of fact. Many exchangeable values may be destroyed intentionally without compensation. Property depends upon exclusion by law from interference" (246). Though in disagreement on the question of whether public policy should dictate whether news enjoyed status as property, Holmes and Brandeis together offered a strategy that afforded jurists the power to conclude that, while some valuable interests were property and some were not, the basis for distinguishing them was not to be sought in the property itself; rather, it was to be rooted in the prevailing principles of public policy and advanced in the prevailing interest of the "public good."

54. In the wake of the South Sea Bubble of 1720, Alexander Baring, Lord Ashburton, a member of the banking family, struck a dissonant chord between laissez faire economic policy and a moral repugnance for speculation that anticipates, in many respects, Holmes's defense of capitalism's fetish for waste: "The evil [of speculation] was certainly one that deserved to be checked; though he hardly knew how the check could be applied. The remedy would be worse than the disease, if, in putting a stop to this evil, they put a stop to the spirit of enterprise. That spirit was productive of so much benefit to the community, that he should be sorry to see any person drawing a line, discriminating between fair enterprise and extravagant speculation" (quoted in Edward Chancellor, *Devil Take the Hindmost: A History of Financial Speculation* [New York: Farrar, Straus, Giroux, 1999], 109–10).

55. "Credit, or belief, involves the very ground of aesthetic experience, and the same medium that seems to confer belief in fiduciary money (bank notes) and in scriptural money (created by the process of bookkeeping) also seems to confer it in literature. That medium is writing" (Shell, *Money, Language, and Thought,* 7).

56. Stephen A. Siegel, "Understanding the *Lochner* Era: Lessons from the Controversy over Railroad and Utility Rate Regulation," *Virginia Law Review* 70 (1984): 187–263, 244.

57. This quite standard critique of intrinsic value appears in chap. 4 ("Of the Principles on Which Courts of Equity Refuse to Interfere in Cases of Contracts or Agreements") of John Powell's *Essay upon the Law of Contracts and Agreements* (1790; reprint, Walpole, N.H.: David Newhall, 1802), 2:229.

58. Morton J. Horwitz, *The Transformation of American Law, 1780–1860* (Cambridge, Mass.: Harvard University Press, 1977), 181.

59. Ibid., 161.

60. *Lochner v. New York*, 198 U.S. 45 (1905). I thank Robert Post for insisting on the relevance of *Lochner* and the "marginal revolution" to the speculative economy I here seek to explore.

61. *Jacobson v. Massachusetts*, 197 U.S. 11 (1905), in *Lochner,* 67.

According to Holmes, who penned his own dissent in the case, the court had an established history of extending to states the power to regulate myriad dimensions of life, a power that legislators and citizens alike might find "injudicious" if not downright "tyrannical" — those "Sunday laws and usury laws" of ancient provenance, defenses of state vaccination laws, "prohibition[s] of lotteries" as well as of sales of stock on margin (*Lochner,* 75). These laws, Holmes added, might embody convictions and prejudices judges would be likely to share, yet, by the same token, they might just as likely not; and it was that very signifying fluidity that it was precisely the task of the law to preserve. "[The law] is made for people of fundamentally differing views, and the accident of our finding certain opinions natural and familiar or novel and even shocking ought not to conclude our judgement upon the question whether statutes embodying them conflict with the Constitution of the United States" (*Lochner, 76*).

62. On the "marginal revolution" in legal and economic thought, see Siegel, "Understanding the *Lochner* Era." 243–46; Phyllis Deane, *The Evolution of Economic Ideas* (Cambridge: Cambridge University Press, 1978), 93–114; Ellen Frankel Paul, *Moral Revolution and Economic Science* (Westport, Conn.: Greenwood Publishing, 1979), 219–79; and Joseph A. Shumpeter and Elizabeth Boddy Schumpeter, *History of Economic Analysis* (1954; reprint, New York: Oxford University Press, 1996), 909–44.

63. The quoted material is from Horwitz, *The Transformation of American Law, 1780–1860,* 35.

Pivotal cases in the "*Lochner* era" include *Allgeyer v. Louisiana* (1897), *Adair v. United States* (1908), *Coppage v. Kansas* (1915), *Adkins v. Children's Hospital* (1923), and *West Coast Hotel v. Parrish* (1937), this last of which overturned the *Lochner* ruling. In these cases, the Court struck down laws regulating labor on the grounds that such laws were unconstitutional and "an arbitrary interference with personal liberty and private property without due process of law"—violations, in short, of a fundamental "right to private property" and "right of free contract" (*Lochner,* 57, 63).

In the argument of Wai Chee Dimock, as well as a host of constitutional scholars, the *Lochner* era marks the transformation of the "subjective" into a basis for "substantive due process" in turn-of-the-century jurisprudence. Beginning with the *Slaughterhouse Cases* in 1873, the Supreme Court worked out a "substantive" interpretation of the Fourteenth Amendment that, over the coming decades, gave sanction to judicial review of federal and state regulations. Following a nominalist epistemology, the Court deployed the "substantive" as a form of attribution, according evidentiary weight to one set of rights: the right to private property, the right of free contract. That act of naming, Dimock writes, "must consign to insubstantiality that which is not [so attributed]." The *Lochner*-era rulings on labor enable the migration of the "substantive" from labor itself to its more ethereal correlate, "contract," the final result of which is that the set of rights associated with the latter "come to appear as solid, as self-evident, and as objective as things, as if they literally had materialized into moral furniture." The substantive's shift in reference would thus seem the cause of and alibi for Holmes's minoritized (and losing) opinion: "Within the adversarial language of rights, the substantive is the requisite name for the triumphantly subjective, the requisite name for the claim that has won out, that has beaten its opponent into insubstantiality" (*Residues of Justice: Literature, Law, Philosophy* [Berkeley, Los Angeles: University of California Press, 1996], 204–17).

64. Oliver Wendell Holmes, Jr., "Law in Science and Science in Law" (address to the New York State Bar Association, January 17, 1899), 19, 20.

65. Brook Thomas, *American Literary Realism and the Failed Promise of Contract* (Berkeley: University of California Press, 1997), 296.

66. Henry James, *A Small Boy and Others,* ed. Frederick W. Dupee (1913; reprint, New York: Criterion, 1956), 92–93.

67. Stephen A. Hirsch, "Uncle Tomitudes: The Popular Reaction to *Uncle Tom's Cabin,*" in *Studies in the American Renaissance,* ed. Joel Myerson (Boston: Twayne, 1978), 303–30.

68. Any list of theatrical "Tom shows" would need to begin with the following American and European versions: *Southern "Uncle Tom's Cabin"* (Dan Rice, 1854), *Uncle Tom's Cabin; or, Life in the South as It Is* (Joseph M. Field, 1854), *Uncle Tom's Cabin; or, Hearts and Homes* (Christy and Wood's Minstrels, 1853), *Uncle Dad's Cabin* (Charles White's Ethiopian Opera House, 1855), *Uncle Tom's Cabin; or, Freedom at the North and Service at*

the South (George Kunkel's Nightingale Ethiopian Opera Troupe, 1853); and, in Europe, *La Case de l'Oncle Tom* (MM. Dumanoir and D'Ennery, 1853), *The Slave Hunt, or, Legree's Bloodhounds! and the Happy Days of Uncle Tom* (London, 1856), *L'Oncle Tom* (Edmond Texier and L. De Wailly, 1853), *La Cabana de Tom, ó La Esclavitud de los Negros* (Don Ramon de Valladares, 1864), and *Onkel Tom's Hütte* (Therese von Megerle, 1853).

69. *Uncle Tom's Cabin* came to constitute its own corner of the early film industry—with "straight" attempts to remake *Uncle Tom's Cabin* (Vitagraph, 1910; Imp, 1913; Kalem, 1913; Universal, 1913; World Film Corporation, 1914; Famous Players-Lasky, 1918; Universal, 1927; Pathé Frères, 1929); the burlesques and rebuttals of *Uncle Tom Wins* (Edison, 1909), *When Do We Eat?* (Artcraft, 1918), *Uncle Tom's Caboose* (Universal, 1920), *Uncle Tom without the Cabin* (Paramount, 1919), *Uncle Tom's Gal* (Universal, 1925), *Uncle Tom's Uncle* (Pathé Frères, 1926), *Uncle Tom's Crabbin'* (Educational, 1927), *Topsy Turvey* (Paramount, 1927), *Topsy and Eva* (United Artists, 1927), *Uncle Tom's Bungalow* (Vitaphone, 1937); as well as the ubiquitous spin-offs of *The Barnstormers* (Biograph, 1905), *The Troubles of a Stranded Actor* (Lubin, 1909), *An Uncle Tom's Cabin Troupe* (Biograph, 1913), *The Open Road* (Reliance, 1913), *The Death of Simon Legree* (Universal L-Ko Comedy, 1915), *Girl in the Show* (MGM, 1929), *Dimples* (Fox, 1936), *Everybody Sing* (MGM, 1938), *Can This Be Dixie?* (Fox, 1936), *The Dolly Sisters* (Fox, 1945), and *Naughty Nineties* (Universal, 1945).

70. I shall henceforth refer to Porter's *Uncle Tom's Cabin; or, Slavery Days* by its subtitle so as to distinguish it from both Stowe's novel and Aiken's dramatization.

71. Marshall Stearns and Jean Stearns define juba as "any kind of clapping with any dance to encourage another dancer" (*Jazz Dance*, 29). See Saidiya V. Hartman, *Scenes of Subjection: Terror, Slavery, and Self-Making in Nineteenth-Century America* (New York: Oxford University Press, 1997), 70-76, for a discussion of juba and genealogy.

72. See the chapter entitled "Deep Play" in Bill Brown, *The Material Unconscious: American Amusement, Stephen Crane, and the Economies of Play* (Cambridge, Mass.: Harvard University Press, 1996)71, 94-96.

73. Hortense Spillers, "Changing the Letter," 25-61.

74. On the Castles, black dance, and the cakewalk, see Lewis A. Erenberg, *Steppin' Out: New York Nightlife and the Transformation of American Culture* (Chicago: University of Chicago Press, 1981), 150-52.

75. On discovery that Fletcher had been hired to teach the cakewalk to the Vanderbilts, Williams and Walker extend the following offer:

Dear Sir:

In view of the fact that you have made a success as a cake-walker, having appeared in a semi-public capacity, we, the undersigned world-renowned cake-walkers, believing that the attention of the public has been distracted from us on account of the tremendous hit which you have made, hereby challenge you to compete with us in a cake-walking match, which will decide which of us shall deserve the title of champion cake-walker of the world.

As a guarantee of good faith we have this day deposited at the office of the New York World the sum of $50. If you propose proving to the public that you really are an expert cake-walker we shall be pleased to have you cover that amount and name the day on which it will be convenient for you to try odds against us.

Yours very truly,

Williams and Walker

(Williams and Walker to Mr. And Mrs. William K. Vanderbilt [reprinted in Stearns and Stearns, *Jazz Dance*, 122-23].)

76. Charles W. Chesnutt, *The Marrow of Tradition* (1901), ed. Eric J. Sundquist (New York: Penguin Books, 1993).

77. The chalk-line walk, also known as the prize walk or walk-around, according to accounts Tom Fletcher attributes to his grandfather, often began with the construction of an impromptu stage on the plantation verandah. The walk contained "no prancing, just a straight walk on a path made by turns and so forth, along which the dancers made their way with a pail of water on their heads. The couple that was the most erect and spilled the least or no water at all was the winner." Taken up by members of the traveling minstrel shows, the walk, in a practice evocative of Shakespeare's Globe, was performed by troupes consisting entirely of men, "some of them putting on dresses and makeup and wigs to act as walking partners for others." By Fletcher's account, the introduction of "all sorts of improvisations [to] the Walk" (specifically the 1889 revue *The Creole Show*) transformed "the original . . . into a grotesque dance" (*100 Years of the Negro in Show Business,* ed. Thomas L. Riis [New York: DeCapo Press, 1984], originally published as *The Tom Fletcher Story: 100 years of the Negro in Show Business!* [New York: Burdge & Co., 1954], 19, 103). This transformation of the chalk-line walk into the cakewalk was the slave's doing, according to Lynne Fauley Emery: "The backward sway was added, and as the dance became more of a satire on the dance of the white plantation owners, the movement became a prancing strut" (*Black Dance: From 1619 to Today* [Princeton, N.J.: Princeton University Press, 1988], 208). Eric Sundquist locates the walk-around, originally (and I think erroneously) on the midcentury minstrel stage ("Charles Chesnutt's Cakewalk," in *To Wake the Nations: Race in the Making of American Literature* [Cambridge, Mass.: Harvard University Press, 1993], 271–454, 277).

78. Ex-slave's account of the cakewalk appear in Roscoe Lewis's Works Progress Administration–funded oral history of slavery, *The Negro in Virginia* (New York: Hastings House, 1940), 89–90. See also Emery, *Black Dance,* 87–101, for a discussion of the various prances and ceremonials layered over time into the plantation cakewalk.

79. Federal Writers' Project, *Slave Narratives: A Folk History of Slavery in the United States from Interviews with Former Slaves,* 17vols. (Washington, D.C.: Typewritten Records Prepared by the Federal Writers' Project, 1936–38), 16, pt.1:243, reprinted in Emery, *Black Dance,* 91.

80. Roger D. Abrahams, *Singing the Master: The Emergence of African American Culture in the Plantation South* (New York: Penguin, 1993), 96. For Abrahams's discussion of the cakewalk, see 96–101, and for his discussion of pantomimes of labor, see chap. 1 of the same volume, "Ain't You Gwine to the Shucking of the Corn?" (3–21). For a dazzling account of the slippery signification of an array of plantation amusements as both instruments of domination and informal enactments of subaltern practices of subversion, see Saidiya Hartman's "Innocent Amusements: The Stage of Sufferance," in *Scenes of Subjection,* 17–48.

81. Benjamin Franklin, *The Way to Wealth, as Clearly Shown in the Preface of an Old Pennsylvania Almanack, Intitled, Poor Richard Improved* (1758), vol. 3 of *The Complete Works . . . of the Late Dr. Benjamin Franklin . . .* (London: J. Johnson, 1806), 453–68.

82. The quote is from Sir James Stephen, *Digest of Criminal Law,* art. 223, quoted in Holmes, *Common Law,* 51.

83. See Lawrence M. Friedman, *A History of American Law* (New York: Simon & Schuster, 1973), which argues that (1) most common-law crime had been wiped out by the end of the nineteenth century by federal and state law (503), (2) there was a vast increase in the number of criminal laws on the books (508, 513), and (3) "the guilty mind" emerged as an object of legal scrutiny (513–24).

84. Oliver Wendell Holmes, Jr., "The Path of the Law," in *Collected Legal Papers* (New

York: Harcourt, Brace & Co., 1920), 171, originally published in *Harvard Law Review* 10 (1897): 457.

85. Oliver Wendell Holmes, Jr., "Codes, and the Arrangement of the Law," *American Law Review* 5, no. 3 (1870): 1–13, 3.

86. John Maynard Keynes, *The General Theory of Employment, Interest and Money* (New York: Harcourt, Brace, & Co., 1936), 147.

87. Thorstein Veblen, *The Theory of Business Enterprise* (New York: Charles Scribner's Sons, 1904), 150–51.

88. Ibid., 138, 153–54, 159. As Henry Crosby Emery outlines in *Speculation on the Stock and Produce Exchanges of the United States,* Columbia Studies in History, Economics, and Public Law (New York: Columbia University Press, 1896), the speculator's "good" is the contract, and speculation's places of business are the stock and produce exchanges that exist at the hubs between markets (i.e., the Chicago Board of Trade, the New York Stock Exchange). There, the speculator transacts through a series of contracts, the most common of which, the "future," a "contract to be fulfilled at some future time," guarantees a price for commodities based on present market conditions and expectations of future outcomes (32). The broker sells his commodity long before the results of the harvest—or before the shipment arrives—to protect himself against a future "fluctuation of prices" (33). The speculator takes the contract, buttressed by other contracts, on the hope and conjecture that "an anticipated difference in the present and future prices of the commodity in question leaves room for a possible profit" (33). Similar relations accrue in other speculative contracts. The "privilege" (or "option") grants one party the right, but frees him of the obligation, "to buy from or sell to the other party a certain amount of a certain commodity, at a certain price" (48). A "put" option is made with a view to a fall in price, and "enable[s] the seller to limit his risk of loss to a definite amount," while, conversely, a "call" option protects the reverse wager or the situation in which, for a consideration in cash, "one party acquires the right to receive from the other party, within a fixed period of time, a certain amount of a commodity at a stipulated price" (50). Futures and options wield the speculator chances of profit when he manages successfully to predict "differences in price in different markets," so, to reduce his risks against fluctuations of price within the same market, the speculative market affords a means of "hedging" his contractual obligations. Under a "hedge," for every trade transaction in the producers' market "a corresponding transaction of the opposite kind is made in the speculative market" (159–60). And, finally, when the speculator's capital falls short of the purchases and contracts he seeks to make, he can transact "on margin," putting up merely a percentage of the total value of the securities (or commodities, or shares) he seeks to purchase. When the speculator leverages "on margin," Emery notes, the "danger is correspondingly increased, since an unfavorable movement may 'wipe out' his margin altogether" (187). In short, the speculator on margin "is playing for higher stakes" (187).

The following hypothetical serves a specific purpose in Emery's *Speculation*—to illustrate the principle of "hedging"—and it shall serve our slightly different objective of demonstrating the broad practice of "recurring valuation" in credit economies:

> A New York merchant buys 100,000 bushels of No. 1 hard wheat at Duluth, and orders it shipped by vessel to Buffalo, to go thence to New York by canal. He does this not because he "wants the wheat for his own use," but as a merchant who believes that the Duluth price and the cost of getting the grain to New York, in view of known or apparent market conditions or of anticipated requirements abroad, will enable him to sell the grain in New York at a profit. With a more primitive view, he would ship his grain, wait until it arrived, look for a purchaser and, finding one, sell the wheat at the price current at date

of arrival—say three weeks after he bought it. If at a profit, well and good; but if the price had declined he would sustain a heavy loss, owing to the size of the shipment. Thus, when the world's requirements are for large available stocks, and the movement of grain must be in large lots, the future contract comes in to protect the handler. The New York merchant, therefore, sells 100,000 No. 2 spring, September delivery, at Chicago at the date of his Duluth purchase, in August. When the wheat reaches Buffalo the price has advanced and millers there want some No. 1 hard wheat. He sells them 25,000 bushels and buys 25,000 bushels of No. 2 spring wheat at Chicago, September delivery, to make good the original quantity purchased. By this time he has also sold at New York 100,000 bushels, September delivery, to an exporter and bought 100,000 bushels more at Chicago, relying on the 75,000 bushels on the way and his ability to get 25,000 bushels more before it is demanded, to keep his engagement. When the 75,000 bushels of No. 1 hard spring wheat reaches New York the price has declined fractionally, and the owner is enabled, in consequence, to purchase 25,000 at a slightly better price, relatively, than he had paid in Duluth, selling 25,000 bushels coincidently at Chicago for September delivery. He lost on his Duluth purchase and on the 25,000 and 100,000 bushel purchases at Chicago, and on the 25,000 bushel purchase at New York. But he made rather more than corresponding gains through his sale, spot delivery, of 25,000 bushels at Buffalo, including profits on his sales of 225,000 bushels for September delivery at Chicago and New York, so that he gains on sales of 250,000 bushels and loses on the purchases of 250,000. The transaction as a whole is not very profitable, but millers at home and abroad get wheat at the lowest market prices at dates of purchases, the grain is moved from Minnesota elevators to Buffalo and New York and the Glasgow mill, and the merchant whose sagacity, energy and foresight led him to aid in the undertaking, even when price conditions were unfavorable, is able to protect himself from excessive loss without depressing the price to the original holder, who represents the grower, and without having an incentive (not to mention the ability) to unduly advance the price to the consumer, as represented by the miller. (A. C. Stevens, "Futures in the Wheat Market," *Quarterly Journal of Economics* 2 [October 1887]: 50, quoted in quoted in Emery, *Speculation*, 160-61)

89. The account of Holmes's engagement with the ideas of custom and prophesy that I offer here is skeletal, at best, and can only take the most provisional account of Holmes's later abandonment of pure objectivity and acceptance of the uncertainty inherent in all inquiries into "states of mind" (a move toward the subjective meant to preserve the integrity of common law adjudication). For a masterful examination of the evolution in Holmes's thought over the period in question, see Morton J. Horowitz's "The Place of Justice Holmes in American Legal Thought," in *The Transformation of American Law, 1870-1960*, 109-43.

90. J. G. A. Pocock, *Virtue, Commerce, and History: Essays on Political Thought and History, Chiefly in the Eighteenth Century* (Cambridge: Cambridge University Press, 1985), 98.

91. The autonomy that attends the Greek *oikos* (a household productive unit inhabited by women, minors, and slaves) finds support in the very metaphysics of property Aristotle outlines in the *Topics*. Property, Aristotle maintains in that text, protects two distinct forms of identity: those that signify essence and those that do not (*Topics*, in *The Basic Works of Aristotle*, trans. Hippocrates G. Apostle and Lloyd P. Gerson [Grinnell, Iowa: Peripatetic Press, 1982]). That form "which signifies the essence of a thing" he calls "definition," while "the other part" covers "property" (1.4.19-23). A property of a thing is an attribute "which does not reveal the essence of that thing but belongs to that thing and is convertible with it

as a predicate" (1.5.17–19). Aristotle clarifies with an example: "To be sleeping is not a property of man, even if it happens that during a certain time, T, sleeping belongs only to man.
But even if one were to call a thing such as this 'a property,' he would have to say that it is a
property not without qualification but during a certain time, or in relation to some other
thing, etc. . . . [If] something is asleep, there is no necessity for it to be a man" (1.5.23–30).
To sleep might offer a definition of "animal," but it is only ever a relative property of "man."
Property, then, is not distinguished from definition by its failure to "signif[y] the essence of
a thing." Property is, rather, only ever a provisional claim on essence. William Blackstone
clarifies the common law effect of this rhetorical definition of property in his *Commentaries:*

> There are few, that will give themselves the trouble to consider the original and founda-
> tion of this right [in property]. Pleased as we are with the possession, we seem afraid to
> look back to the means by which it was acquired, as if fearful of some defect in our title;
> or at best we rest satisfied with the decision of the laws in our favour, without examining
> the reason or authority upon which those laws have been built . . . not caring to reflect
> that (accurately and strictly speaking) there is no foundation in nature or in natural law,
> why a set of words upon parchment should convey the dominion of land.

(William Blackstone, "Of the Rights of Things" (1765), in *Commentaries on the Laws of England* [Chicago: University of Chicago Press, 1979], 2:2)
    Property is always temporary and subject to "qualification"—an effect of the rank con-
tingency of "words upon parchment."
    The transformation of property from contingency to the security of essence, argues Eric
Cheyfitz, in his work *The Poetics of Imperialism,* entails the "translation" of property from
the metaphysical to the physical. Property in rhetoric consists of an economy of "signs" (that
which "does not reveal" the essence of a thing but is "convertible with it as a predicate").
Preoccupied by its signs, property is not essence pure and simple. Rather, it is "the sign of
essence," in the sense that "it is only through an elaboration of properties that we can define,
or indicate, a perpetually transcendent identity" (49). Yet property becomes substance itself
when the metaphysical becomes physical (when a system of "laws" clarifies "rights" in property). By turns, "those who own it and who in this system of property must inevitably
ground their identities on it become its shadow" (49–50). To be the shadow of property is
to bear the rights and privileges of identity (what Aristotle specifies as "what is peculiar to
anything" [1.4.19]). To be possessed by one's possessions is to be self-possessed; and those
who own nothing are denied even this "obscure visibility" (50). Cheyfitz summarizes the
paradox of property: "In the West, property, in that tangled space where the physical and
the metaphysical mix, is the very mark of identity, of that which is identical to itself: what we
typically call a 'self' or an 'individual,' indicating the absolute boundaries that are predicated
of this entity" (50). Property is individual, i.e., indivisible (Latin, sixth century, *individuus,*
from Greek *atomos,* not cuttable, not divisible)—"not divisible," incapable of possession by
any other than that "one" who bears "title." Property is in this instance the ground of autonomy. See entry on "Individual" in Raymond Williams, *Keywords: A Vocabulary of Culture
and Society* (New York: Oxford University Press, 1976), 133–36.
    92. Within an evolving republican vocabulary, Pocock explains, virtue could signify
many things at once: (1) "a devotion to the public good"; (2) "the practice, or the preconditions of the practice, of relations of equality between citizens engaged in ruling and being
ruled"; or (3), finally, on the presumption of citizenship as mode of action and of practicing
the active life, "that active ruling quality—practiced in republics by citizens equal with one

another and devoted to the public good—which confronted *fortuna* and was known to Renaissance Italians as *virtù*" (*Virtue, Commerce, and History*, 41–42).

93. "Every theory of corruption, without exception, is a theory of how intermediaries substitute their own good and profit for that of their supposed principals" (*Virtue, Commerce, and History*, 122).

94. David Hume, *A Treatise of Human Nature* (1739–40), ed. Ernest G. Mossner (New York: Penguin Books, 1985), 366.

95. Adam Smith, *The Theory of Moral Sentiments* (1759), ed. D. D. Raphael and A. L. Mackie (Indianapolis: Liberty Fund, 1984), 1.1.1.2. On the *dédoublement* that structures all acts of sympathy in Smith's *Moral Sentiments,* see David Marshall, *The Figure of Theater: Shaftesbury, Defoe, Adam Smith, and George Eliot* (New York: Columbia University Press, 1986), 170.

96. I have in mind here the writings of everyone from Bernard Mandeville, Sir James Stewart, and John Millar to Joseph Addison, Cato (a.k.a., John Trenchard and Thomas Gordon), and, most important, Adam Smith. Masterful accounts of this epistemological shift are offered by Joyce Appleby in *Economic Thought and Ideology in Seventeenth Century England* (Princeton, N.J.: Princeton University Press, 1980), and in her *Capitalism and a New Social Order: The Republican Vision of the 1790s.* Appleby also locates the rise of those arguments for economic liberalism (for the self-regulating market) that prove dominant in the nineteenth century in the debate over recoinage that took place in Britain in 1696. For the latter, see "Locke, Liberalism, and the Natural Law of Money," in *Liberalism and Republicanism in the Historical Imagination* (Cambridge, Mass.: Harvard University Press, 1992), 58–89.

97. Mary Poovey, *History of the Modern Fact: Problems of Knowledge in the Sciences of Wealth and Society* (Chicago: University of Chicago Press, 1998), xx.

Space does not permit and the demands of the chapter do not require a thorough explanation of why Smith seeks to locate the workings of the market in "human nature." Joyce Appleby and Mary Poovey offer explanations rooted in the same historical presumptions, and those explanations will here suffice as background to Smith's interest in human nature. According to the broader accounts of Appleby and Poovey, empirical observation was inadequate to explain the workings of the market as the market became a mechanism of which one could see no more than a tiny fraction. The market began, as a consequence, to figure as an abstraction, as "something that represented the aggregation of all market bargains condensed into a price, a number, a word" (Appleby, *Capitalism and a New Social Order,* 30). By the late eighteenth century, Smith explains in the opening of *Wealth,* "great manufactures" had begun to involve so many workmen "that it is impossible to collect them all in the same workhouse. We can seldom see more, at one time, than those employed in one single branch [of the operation]" (1.1.4; Poovey, *History of the Modern Fact,* 238). Myopia was thus the logical precursor to Smith's universals (i.e., human nature), abstractions (i.e., the market, society, *homo economicus*), and their combined effects (i.e., labor, national prosperity, the common good). Poovey explains: "Smith believed that creating abstractions was essential to the production of general knowledge, not simply because a single eye could not see all the workmen at the same time, but because what one needed to analyze was nowhere visible as such—nowhere, i.e., except in the writing of political economists such as Smith" (*History of the Modern Fact,* 239).

98. To Althusserian (as well as Lacanian) social theorists, *homo economicus,* or what I have called the "reunification of personality" in the liberal economic tradition, derives from a "logic of fantasy," a myth of historical genesis shared by capitalists and communists alike.

As Slavoj Žižek proposes, in "The King Is a Thing," capitalist accounts of "primitive accumulation" and communist tales of the emergence and the purpose of "the Party" share a particular "logic of fantasy" (*Emergences* 2 [1990]: 21–45). In the case of the latter, when the party is taken to embody the universality of all the disparate parts of the social (e.g., classes, groups, political structures), what it acquires is a kind of sublimity. Stalin's famous "vow of the Bolshevik Party to its leader Lenin" confirms the investment in this "sublime object": "We, the Communists, are people of a special mould. We are made of special stuff" (25). In the case of the former, as we have already seen, capitalism is taken to originate in the scrupulous moves of the "frugal man," who, rather than consume his surplus, employs it "in the support of domestic industry" (Smith, *Wealth*, 260). This diligent worker gradually becomes a capitalist, an owner of the means of production, and thus able to employ others who possess only their ability to work. Primitive accumulation would therefore seem to presuppose what it purports to explain: the notion of the capitalist ("It 'explains' the emergence of capitalism by presupposing the existence of an agent who 'acts like a capitalist' from the very beginning" [33]). The logic of fantasy, in both accounts, is a plot of undoing, a fiction of time travel. In this fiction, the "capitalist" is present as a gaze at its own conception; the ideological myth allows the capitalist to "jump into the past" and appear as its own cause. A similar plot applies in the case of the Leader's sublimity: "By conceiving of himself as an agency through which the People gives birth to itself, the Leader assumes the role of a *deputy from (of) the future,* he acts as a medium through which the future, not yet existing People organizes its own conception" (33).

Mary Poovey explains that capitalism's "origins" pose a problem of induction in the history of the modern fact—a problem witnessed in the "conjectural histories" of the mid-eighteenth century that attempted "to discover the origins of commercial society" in the face of a paucity of eyewitness accounts. In the work of Francis Hutcheson and George Turnbull, she notes, "assumptions about human nature and Providence filled the gaps where evidence was unavailable." For a more sustained address to the problem of induction see "From Conjectural History to Political Economy," chap. 5 of Poovey's *A History of the Modern Fact,* 214–63, esp. 218–49.

99. Aristotle, *The Politics,* trans. T. A. Sinclair (Harmondsworth: Penguin, 1962), 43.

100. James Fennimore Cooper, *The Chainbearer; or, The Littlepage Manuscripts* (New York: Burgess, Stringer, 1845), 1:171–72.

101. William Harbutt Dawson, *The Unearned Increment; or, Reaping without Sowing* (London: S. Sonnenschein & Co., 1910).

102. Henry Ward Beecher, *Lectures to Young Men, on Various Important Subjects* (New York: J. B. Ford, 1873).

103. Lydia Maria Child, *Letters from New York* (New York: C. S. Francis & Co., 1850), 48–49.

104. On the *windhandel* see 281n.4.

105. Oliver Wendell Holmes, Jr., to Harold Laski, November 5, 1926, in *Holmes-Laski Letters: The Correspondence of Mr. Justice Holmes and Harold J. Laski, 1916–1935,* ed. Mark DeWolfe Howe (Cambridge, Mass.: Harvard University Press, 1953), 893, quoted in Saul Touster, "In Search of Holmes from Within," *Vanderbilt Law Review* 18 (1965): 437. 448n. 26; and Holmes to Arthur Garfield Hays, April 20, 1928, in Mark Howe, *Justice Oliver Wendell Holmes: The Shaping Years, 1841–1870* (Cambridge, Mass.: Harvard University Press, 1957), 49, quoted in Touster, "In Search of Holmes," 448.

For an account of the effect of battle on Holmes's antislavery politics, see the first three chaps. ("The Politics of Slavery," "The Abolitionist," and "The Wilderness and After") of

Louis Menand's *The Metaphysical Club: A Story of Ideas in America* (New York: Farrar, Straus & Giroux, 2001), 3–69.

106. Oliver Wendell Holmes, Jr., to Charles Eliot Norton, April 17, 1864, quoted in Touster, "In Search of Holmes," 449.

107. Oliver Wendell Holmes, Jr., to Oliver Wendell Holmes, Sr., December 20, 1862, quoted in Touster, "In Search of Holmes," 462–63.

108. Oliver Wendell Holmes, Jr., to Harold J. Laski, September 18, 1918, 164; and Holmes to Laski, August 7, 1925, 772, both in *Holmes-Laski Letters,* ed. Howe.

109. Oliver Wendell Holmes, Jr., to Frederick Pollock, August 30, 1929, in *Holmes-Pollock Letters: The Correspondence of Mr. Justice Holmes and Sir Frederick Pollock, 1874–1932,* ed. Mark DeWolfe Howe (Cambridge, Mass.: Harvard University Press, 1961), 252–53.

110. Horwitz, *The Transformation of American Law, 1870–1960,* 116.

111. The theory of market equilibrium is of long and distinguished provenance and achieves its apotheosis in Adam Smith's "invisible hand," itself an assimilation of Newton's theory of equilibrium (the "invisible hand" is arguably the analogue of the "divine watchman"). The ideal of market efficiency Smith offers in *The Wealth of Nations* reflects a propensity toward quantification in moral philosophy with intellectual lineaments that run from Concordet's "mathematique social," Chastellux's "indices de bonheur," and Descartes's "esprit de geometrie" through to Kant's "mathematical sublime," Williams Petty's "political arithmetic," and Hobbes's esteem for "the Geometricians." Current proponents of "monetarism" resurrect the idea of efficient markets. See Milton Friedman, "In Defense of Destabilizing Speculation," in *Optimum Quantity of Money and Other Essays* (Chicago: Aldine Publishing, 1969), 285–91.

112. James Medbery, *Men and Mysteries,* 209.

113. Keynes, *General Theory,* 161–62.

114. Ibid., 155–56. In citing *The General Theory of Employment, Interest, and Money,* I want readers to be mindful that I am not making the argument that Stowe offers "Keynesian" methodology *avant la lettre.* I am not privileging Keynes alone when emphasizing the irrepressibility of passion in thinking on the economic—as earlier reference to Hume and Smith should make readily apparent. What such anachronistic citation means to say is that Keynes's discussion of the place of "optimistic and pessimistic sentiment" in market valuation is part of a long tradition of thought on the morality of finance. It is to say that passion and fancy coalesce in the *General Theory* as irrepressible elements in thinking on the economic.

115. A famous letter to the *Times* of London (July 12, 1845), written in response to the railway mania of the mid-1840s, reads: "There is not a single dabbler in script who does not steadfastly believe—first, that a crash sooner or later, is inevitable; and, secondly, that he himself will escape it. When the luck turns, and the crack play is *sauve qui peut,* or devil take the hindmost, no one fancies that the last mail train from Panic station will leave him behind. In this, as in other respects, 'Men deem all men mortal but themselves.'"

116. For an intersystemic analysis of poetic and economic systems, see Kurt Heinzelman, *The Economics of the Imagination* (Amherst: University of Massachusetts Press, 1980), esp. ix–xii, 3–13, 38–51. See also Shell's *Economy of Literature* and *Money, Language, and Thought.*

117. See n. 9 above, this chap., for more thorough elaboration of Hutson's argument that, within Shakespeare's dramatic rhetoric, the figure of women's infidelity bears specific economic implications in the transition from feudalism to capitalism. My formulation of the economic implications of blackness (and, specifically, of the figuration of the slave's wan-

tonness) paraphrases Hutson's framing of gender and the economic, but it follows, too, the formulations of Moishe Postone, who, in "Anti-Semitism and National Socialism," makes the case presumptive capital's necessary personifications (specifically, modern anti-Semitism as an imputation to "the Jew" of the more vexed characteristics of capitalism, i.e., abstractness, intangibility, universality, mobility). See Postone, "Anti-Semitism and National Socialism," in *Germans and Jews since the Holocaust,* ed. Anson Rabinbach (New York: Holmes & Meier, 1986), 302–14.

It deserves note, too, that much as Hutson, Patricia Parker, and other feminist critics have done for the Renaissance, eighteenth-century scholars have devoted considerable energies to tracking the economic implications of the female figures of public credit (and iconographic ancestresses such as Danaë and Fortuna) in the writings of the Augustan political journalists—Defoe, Steele, Addison, Mandeville. See the following: Nancy Armstrong, *Desire and Domestic Fiction: A Political History of the Novel* (New York: Oxford University Press, 1987); Terry Mulcaire, "Public Credit; or, The Feminization of Virtue in the Marketplace," *PMLA,* 114 (October 1999): 1029–42; Pocock, *Virtue, Commerce, and History,* 98–99; and Sandra Sherman, *Finance and Fictionality in the Eighteenth Century: Accounting for Defoe* (Cambridge: Cambridge University Press, 1996). Luce Irigaray's reading of vol. 1 of *Das Kapital,* "Women on the Market," deserves mention as theoretical prologema (if infrequently acknowledged) to much recent work on gender and speculation. See her *This Sex Which Is Not One,* trans. Catherine Porter and Carolyn Burke (Ithaca, N.Y.: Cornell University Press, 1985), 170–91, originally published as *Ce Sexe qui n'en est pas un* (Paris: Editions de Minuit, 1977).

118. Daniel Webster, "The Constitution and the Union" (speech), March 7, 1850, in *The Papers of Daniel Webster: Speeches and Formal Writings, 1834–1852,* ed. Charles M. Wiltse (Hanover, N.H.: University Press of New England, 1988), 2:529.

119. Joint Resolution of March 1, 1845, *Congressional Globe,* 28th Cong., 2d sess., 362–63; *U.S. Statutes at Large* 9 (1862): 797–98, quoted in *Papers of Daniel Webster,* ed. Wiltse, 529.

120. Daniel Webster, "Reception at New York," Niblo's Garden, 1837, in *Papers of Daniel Webster,* ed. Wiltse, 117–52.

121. Ibid., and "Address to Whig Convention," Springfield, Massachusetts, September, 1847, quoted in "The Constitution and the Union," 536, emphasis mine.

122. David Potter has provided what is simply the most formidable and compelling analysis of the Clay Compromise. See his "The Armistice of 1850," in *The Impending Crisis: 1848–1861,* ed. Don E. Fehrenbacher (New York: Harper & Row, 1976), 90–120; and James Ford Rhodes, *History of the United States from the Compromise of 1850,* vol. 1, *1850–1854* (New York: Harper & Brothers, 1893), 122. Clay's resolutions, *Congressional Globe,* 31st Cong., 1st sess., 244–45.

123. The rebuke of Thoreau, Parker, and others would seem to have borne little political fruit since the Republicans rode Webster's curious synthesis to electoral victory in the years running up to the Civil War. Abraham Lincoln perfected this strange political alchemy, in the reading of some: "Generally abhoring slavery, the canny prairie lawyer inspired Yankee moralists by opposing its further advance, reassured conservatives by acknowledging its constitutional right to exist where it was, and appealed to old-timer racism by endorsing white supremacy, black colonization, and reservation of the territories 'for the homes of free white people'" (Charles Sellers, *The Market Revolution: Jacksonian American, 1815–1846* [Oxford: Oxford University Press, 1991], 427).

124. Theodore Parker in Rhodes, *History of the United States,* 155. Ralph Waldo Emerson, "Address to the Citizens of Concord (On the Fugitive Slave Law)" (1851), and

"The Fugitive Slave Law" (1854), both in *Emerson's Antislavery Writings,* ed. Len Gougeon and Joel Meyerson (New Haven, Conn.: Yale University Press, 1995), 53-72, 73-89, respectively.

125. Frederick Douglass, "What to the Slave Is the Fourth of July?" speech delivered at Corinthian Hall, Rochester, New York (July 5, 1852), published in pamphlet form as *Oration, Delivered in Corinthian Hall, Rochester, July 5th, 1852,* and reprinted in *The Oxford Frederick Douglass Reader,* ed. William L. Andrews (Oxford: Oxford University Press, 1996), 108-30.

126. Whittier's lines read:

All else is gone; from those great eyes
    The soul has fled:
When faith is lost, when honor dies,
    The man is dead

His "thanks" are quoted in Rhodes, *History of the United States,* 280.

127. Lauren Berlant, "Poor Eliza," *American Literature* 70, no. 3 (1998): 635-68, 636.

128. The phrase "empire of love" is taken from Barbara Welter, "She Hath Done What She Could: Protestant Women's Missionary Careers in Nineteenth-Century America," *American Quarterly* 30, no. 5 (1978): 642-38.

129. Sellers, *The Market Revolution,* 32.

130. On the tension within the nineteenth-century discourse of domesticity between women's emotions and a masculine economics of the mind, see Brown, *Domestic Individualism,* 28-35.

131. "To details of subject matter and person": the "pure" law of contracts, according to Lawrence Friedman, is "blind to details of subject matter and person. It does not ask who buys and who sells, and what is bought and sold" (*Contract Law in America* [Madison: University of Wisconsin Press, 1965], 20-21). By means of those abstractions common to classical contract law, Brook Thomas has argued, the formalism implicit in nineteenth-century contract law becomes "a deliberate renunciation of the particular, a deliberate relinquishment of the temptation to restrict untrammeled individual autonomy or the completely free market in the name of social policy. The law of contract is, therefore, roughly coextensive with the free market" (*American Literary Realism and the Failed Promise of Contract* [Berkeley: University of California Press, 1997], 37).

132. Max Weber, *The Protestant Ethic and the Spirit of Capitalism* (New York: Scribner's, 1930). On mercantile Christianity and parsimonious visions of salvation and purgatory, see R. H. Tawney, *Religion and the Rise of Capitalism* (New York: Peter Smith, 1940). On the "extraordinary coincidence" between Methodist theology and utilitarian philosophy, see E. P. Thompson, *The Making of the English Working Class* (New York: Vintage Books, 1966), 365.

Miss Ophelia's impatience for shiftlessness finds echo in texts such as Richard Baxter's *Saints' Everlasting Rest* and *Christian Directory,* to choose just two examples: "Waste of time is . . . the first and in principle the deadliest of sins. The span of human life is infinitely short and precious to make sure of one's own election. Loss of time through sociability, idle talk, luxury . . . is worthy of absolute moral condemnation. . . . Time is infinitely valuable because every hour lost is lost to labor for the glory of God" (Baxter quoted in Weber, *Protestant Ethic,* 158-59). Calls such as Baxter's for efficiency and parsimony provide this brand of Lutheran Protestantism with its ideal—the "calling"—a control over the forms of everyday life that privileges the individual's fulfillment of the obligations imposed on him by his position in the world. This satisfaction of worldly duties was considered "the highest form which the moral activity of the individual could assume," as Baxter's talk of morals and Stowe's talk of sin readily indicate (Weber, *Protestant Ethic*, 80). Through the aphoristic accents of Benjamin Franklin's "Poor Richard," Protestantism weds a pious restraint to a rational ethos, will to accumulate and profit seeking of, in Weber's words, "a peculiarly calculating sort" (55). "Remember," Franklin's Poor Richard counsels, "the good paymaster is lord of another man's purse. . . . After industry and frugality, nothing contributes more to the raising of a young man in the world than punctuality and justice in all his dealings" (49). It is this philosophy of avarice that contributes most to the objectives of "the honest man of recognized credit"—that golden objective of "the increase of his capital" (51). And moral philosophy begets economic pedagogy the more thoroughly those restraints of the pious life serve as the "ideal foundations" to capitalist economic action, which Weber defines as "the expectation of profit by the utilization of opportunities for exchange, that is . . . (formally) peaceful chances of profit" (17–18, 157, 169). In essence, restraint becomes rationality through sundry turns of phrase. Hence, Poor Richard's infamous counsel: "Remember, that time is money . . . that credit is money . . . [and] that money is of the prolific, generating nature. Money can beget money, and its offspring can beget more, and so on" (Weber, *Protestant Ethic*, 49); "If time be of all things the most precious, wasting time must be . . . the greatest prodigality [since] lost time is never found again; and what we call time enough always proves little enough" (Franklin, *The Way to Wealth*, 453–68).

133. George Fitzhugh, "Freedmen and Free Men," *DeBow's Review* 1 (1866): 416–20, 416. Political economy shall always have the inducement to labor at its ethical core, Fitzhugh adds elsewhere, for "to punish idleness is the first and most incumbent duty of government" (see "What's to Be Done with the Negroes?" *DeBow's Review* 1 [1866]: 577–81).

134. The riddle of Reconstruction—Will the free Negro work?—could be reduced neither to a dispute over whether blacks would work in the everyday meaning of the word nor to the question of whether the free Negro would continue to work like a slave. On the first matter, Gerald Jaynes has argued, nearly everyone agreed that the freedman would choose work when the only other alternative was starvation. Furthermore, the second matter could just as easily be resolved through recognition that it was slavery's discipline that made the slave (as one overseer put it, "no Nigger, nor anybody else, will work like a slave works with the whip behind him"). The disputed question, in Jaynes's estimation, "was whether or not the freed black would soon respond to market incentives with the work discipline of an acquisitive agricultural proletary striving to gain entry into the landowning class" (*Branches without Roots: Genesis of the Black Working Class in the American South, 1862–1882* [Oxford: Oxford University Press, 1986], 57).

135. It is not too hard to imagine that Dinah's revered yet forever remote "clarin' up times" would resonate, in the ears of a less refined readership, with T. D. Rice's famous mid-1830s version of "Clar de Kitchen," itself a comedic reprise of the animal tales of African-American folklore:

A jay bird sot on a hickory limb,
He wink'd at me and I wink'd at him;
I pick'd up a stone and I hit his shin,
Says he you better not do dat agin.

A Bull frog dress'd sogers close,
Went in de field to shoot some crows;
De crows smell powder and fly away,
De Bull frog might mad dat day.

("Clar de Kitchen," in S. Foster Damon, *Series of Old American Songs* [Providence, R.I.: Brown University Library, 1936], no. 16)

136. Julius Caesar Hanibal, *Black Diamonds; or, Humor, Satire and Sentiment, Treated Scientifically by Professor Julius Caesar Hanibal in a Series of Burlesque Lectures Darkly Colored* (New York: A. Ranney, 1855), reprinted in Sterling A. Brown, Arthur P. Davis, and Ullysses Lee, *The Negro Caravan* (New York: Dryden Press, 1941), 574.

137. Byron Christy, *Christy's New Songster and Black Jester . . .* (New York: Dick & Fitzgerald, 1863), 6, 38. Houston A. Baker, Jr., discusses a similar minstrel oration in *Modernism and the Harlem Renaissance* (Chicago: University of Chicago Press, 1987), 22.

138. *Antistoecon* is defined as a "type of metaplasm; substituting one letter or sound for another within a word: [e.g.] 'strond' for 'strand.'" *Barbarismus* (Gr. "foreign mode of speech") originally referred to any error of grammar, pronunciation, or usage committed by *barbaroi*, foreigners, but now refers to mispronunciations arrived at through ignorance. See Richard A. Lanham, *A Handlist of Rhetorical Terms*, 2d. ed. (Berkeley: University of California Press, 1991), 16, 28 – 29.

139. Sam's citation of the old English proverb "An ill wind that bloweth no man to good" (John Heywood, *Proverbs* [1546]) was picked up, most famously, by William Shakespeare in *Henry IV, Part II* (1597 – 98), 5.3.87:

> Falstaff: WHAT WIND BLEW YOU HITHER, PISTOL?
> Pistol: NOT THE ILL WIND WHICH BLOWS NO MAN TO GOOD.

140. Houston Baker writes: "Rather than concealing or disguising in the manner of the *cryptic* mask (a colorful mastery of codes), the phaneric mask is meant to advertise. . . . It secures territorial advantage and heightens a group's survival possibilities" See Baker, *Modernism and the Harlem Renaissance*, 51.

141. Stowe, *Uncle Tom's Cabin*, 375. *Acyrologia* (Gr. "incorrect in phraseology") signifies the use of an inexact or illogical word. It is sometimes called "malapropism," but the latter is distinctly any "vulgar error through an attempt to seem learned" (Lanham, *Handlist of Rhetorical Terms*, 2, 97).

I deliberately echo here Michael Fried's insight into the ubiquity of writing in the literary work of Stephen Crane (*Realism, Writing, Disfiguration: On Thomas Eakins and Stephen Crane* [Chicago: University of Chicago Press, 1988]).

142. J. C. Furnas, *Goodbye to Uncle Tom* (New York: Williams Sloan Associates, 1956), 262.

143. The reference to the novel's "ghastly" scenes appears in a letter from Asa Hutchinson to Harriet Beecher Stowe, quoted in "George L. Aiken's Dramatization of *Uncle Tom's Cabin*," in *Representative Plays by American Dramatists: From 1765 to the Present Day*, ed. Montrose J. Moses (1925; reprint, New York: Benjamin Blom, 1964), 606.

144. Stephen Foster, "Old Folks at Home: Ethiopian Melody," in *Minstrel Show Songs*, ed. H. Wiley Hitchcock (New York: Da Capo Press, 1980).

145. Phinneas T. Barnum, *Uncle Tom's Cabin*, advertisement, November 7, 1853, reprinted in Thomas Gossett, *Uncle Tom's Cabin and American Culture* (Dallas: Southern Methodist University Press, 1985), 275.

146. George L. Aiken, *Uncle Tom's Cabin* (1852), in *Representative Plays*, ed. Moses, 672.

147. The central issue in the paper money debate (and, specifically, the greenback crisis) of the nineteenth century was "how, if at all, paper money and coined money represent substantial things such as gold." Whether paper was an appropriate symbol (the position of

the "paper money men") or an inappropriate and misleading one (the position of the "gold bugs," advocates of gold against paper money, and of a gold against a silver standard), the sign or inscription making money money was "'insubstantial' insofar as the paper counted for nothing as a commodity and was thus 'insensible' in the economic system of exchange [predicated on traffic in goods]" (Marc Shell, "The Gold Bug," *Genre* 13 [1980]: 11–30, 15, 20). See also Walter Benn Michaels, *Gold Standard*, 139–56.

148. Marc Shell provides, to my knowledge, the most thorough discussion of the monetary *diabolus,* citing the following congressional analogy between governmental inscription and God's impression in Cain's forehead: "You send these notes out into the world stamped with irredeemability. You put on them the mark of Cain, and, like Cain, they will go forth to be vagabonds and fugitives on the earth" (Representative George Pendleton [Ohio], January 29, 1862, *Congressional Globe,* 37th Cong., 2d sess. 1:549 ff., quoted in Shell, *Money, Language, and Thought,* 7n. 8). Shell notes, further, that it is political cartooning and popular pamphleteering spawned by the South Sea Bubble that first directs public discussion to paper money as "the devil in specie," as a "nothing" pretending to be a "something." See *Money, Language, and Thought,* 7–15.

Why the *diabolus?* Interest was equivalent to making time pay, and time (unlike space) was considered, in Catholic theology, God's domain.

149. *Heteroglossia:* the notion that competing languages and discourses apply equally to "text" and "context"; that languages may be " juxtaposed to one another, mutually supplement one another, contradict one another and be inter-related dialogically" (Mikhail Bahktin, *The Dialogical Imagination,* ed. Caryl Emerson and Michael Holquist, trans. Michael Holquist [Austin: University of Texas Press, 1981], 292).

150. See Zora Neale Hurston's "Characteristics of Negro Expression" for a discussion of the tension within black English to aspire, on the one hand, toward a "will to adorn" (to embellish, to bring an "angularity" and "asymmetry" to language), while, on the other, insisting that the terms of "negro expression" remain "close fitting" (words for things necessarily embroiled with use, with illustration, a "hieroglyphics"). "Characteristics" first appeared in *Negro: An Anthology,* ed. Nancy Cunard (New York: Continuum, 1934), 24–31. This tension between a close fit and adornment echoes the oscillation in Topsy's speech between literalization and usury; a tension resolved, argues Henry Louis Gates, Jr., in the consideration that the "masking function of dialect" is its "self-conscious switch of linguistic codes from white to black or, more properly, from standard English to the black vernacular"—i.e., from verbal exactitude to loose poetic embellishment (*Figures in Black: Words, Signs, and the "Racial" Self* [New York: Oxford University Press, 1987], 171). See also Michael North, *The Dialect of Modernism: Race, Language and Twentieth-Century Literature* (New York: Oxford University Press, 1994), 75–76.

151. Ralph Waldo Emerson, "Nature," in *Selections from Ralph Waldo Emerson,* ed. Stephen E. Whicher (Boston: Houghton Mifflin Co., 1957), 33, quoted in *Money, Language, and Thought,* 18–19, emphasis mine.

152. Henry Louis Gates, Jr., *The Signifying Monkey: A Theory of Afro-American Literary Criticism* (New York: Oxford University Press, 1988), 53.

153. Jacques Derrida, "Structure, Sign and Play in the Discourse of the Human Sciences," in *Writing and Difference,* trans. Alan Bass (Chicago: University of Chicago Press, 1978), 278–93, 278, 289.

154. Georges Bataille, "The Notion of Expenditure," in *Visions of Excess: Selected Writings, 1927–1939,* ed. and trans. Allan Stoekl (Minneapolis: University of Minnesota Press, 1985), 116–29. On the notion of "general economy," see Bataille, *The Accursed Share: An Essay on General Economy,* vol. 1, *Consumption,* trans. Robert Hurley (New York: Zone Books,

1991), originally published as *La part maudite: Essai d'economie generale* (Paris: Editions de Minuit, 1949).

155. Derrida, *Given Time*, 6–7. For one of Derrida's early attempts to refigure economy, one that pays particular attention to the ways in which the Hegelian *Aufhebung* ("to surpass while maintaining") preserves the principles of restricted economy, see "From Restricted to General Economy: A Hegelianism without Reserve," in *Writing and Difference*, 251–77.

156. Marcel Mauss, *The Gift: Forms and Functions of Exchange in Archaic Societies*, trans. Ian Cunnison (1925; reprint, New York: W. W. Norton & Co., 1967), 45, originally published as "Essai sur le don," in *Sociologie et anthropologie* (1923; reprint, Paris: Presses Universitaires de France, 1950), 145–279.

157. Here is Bourdieu on the matter of gifts: "The most ordinary and even the seemingly most routine exchanges of ordinary life, like the 'little gifts' that 'bind friendship,' presuppose an improvisation, and therefore a constant uncertainty, which, as we say, make all their *charm*, and hence all their social efficacy. . . . To reintroduce uncertainty is to reintroduce time, with its rhythm, its orientation and its irreversibility, substituting the dialectic of strategies for the mechanics of the model, but without falling over into the imaginary anthropology of 'rational actor' theories" ("The Work of Time," in *The Logic of Practice*, trans. Richard Nice [Stanford, Calif.: Stanford University Press, 1990], 98–111, 99).

158. Ralph Ellison, "Change the Joke and Slip the Yoke," in *Shadow and Act* (New York: Vintage, 1972), 45–59, 49, originally published in *Partisan Review* (spring 1958).

159. See Gates, *Signifying Monkey*, 44–60. It is Roger D. Abrahams, however, who notes early on the gestural and perfomative dimensions of signifyin(g), for in his early work *Deep Down in the Jungle* he includes as one of its definitions "speaking with the hands and eyes" (*Deep Down in the Jungle: Negro Narrative Folklore from the Streets of Philadelphia* [Chicago: Aldine Publishing, 1970]).

160. Robert Stam, Robert Burgoyne, and Sandy Flitterman-Lewis, *New Vocabularies in Film Semiotics: Structuralism, Post-Structuralism, and Beyond* (New York: Routledge, 1992), 38.

161. Ibid., 103. I thank D. A. Miller for suggesting to me the connections between Porter's *Uncle Tom's Cabin* and the Hollywood musical. It was that implied relation that urged this narrative to its long-awaited yet forever deferred close.

CHAPTER THREE

1. Margaret Fuller, "Entertainments of the Past Winter," *Dial* 3, no. 1 (1842): 46–72; *Century Dictionary and Cyclopedia* (New York: Century Co., 1904), 4:3233; Hugh H. Smythe, "The Concept of 'Jim Crow,'" *Social Forces* 27, no. 1 (1948): 45–48, 45.

For a sustained and provocative analysis of the relationship between blackface and blackness that is deeply psychoanalytic, see Eric Lott, *Love and Theft: Blackface Minstrelsy and the American Working Class* (New York: Oxford University Press, 1993), 15–37.

2. European visitors to America have witnessed this passion since at least the time of Tocqueville (circa 1830). See Michel Chevalier, *Society, Manners, and Politics in the United States: Letters on North America* (Glouchester, Mass: Peter Smith, 1967), 71–76. On American mobility and "industry," see also Alexis de Tocqueville, "What Causes Almost All Americans to Follow Industrial Callings," chap. 19 of *Democracy in America* (New York: Alfred Knopf, 1980), 163–67.

3. On "machine culture," see Mark Seltzer, *Bodies and Machines* (New York: Routledge, 1992).

4. Charles Dickens, *Dombey and Son* (1848), ed. Peter Fairclough (New York: Penguin Books, 1981), 120–21.

5. The figure of the railway as history is, as I have said, a venerable one and, as an expression of historical determinism, drives everyone from Leo Tolstoy's *Anna Karenina* to Robert Musil's "man without qualities" to flee its fated confines, either from suicidal impulse or philosophical inclination, respectively. See Raymond Williams's reading of Dickens, "People of the City," in *The Country and the City* (New York: Oxford University Press, 1975), 153-64; see also Leo Marx's brilliant and still-relevant treatment of the metaphor, "The Machine," in *The Machine in the Garden: Technology and the Pastoral Ideal in America* (New York: Oxford University Press, 1964), 145-226.

6. Paul Hastings, *Railroads: An International History* (New York: Praeger, 1972), 50-51.

7. The emancipation amendments passed between the years 1863 and 1877, the official era of Reconstruction, read as follows:

Thirteenth: "Neither slavery nor *involuntary servitude,* except as a punishment for crime whereof the party shall have been duly convicted, shall exist within the United States, or any place subject to their jurisdiction."

Fourteenth: "No state shall make or enforce any law which shall abridge the *privileges and immunities* of citizens of the United States; nor shall any state deprive any person of life, liberty, or property, without *due process of law;* nor deny to any person within its jurisdiction *the equal protection of the laws.*"

Fifteenth: "The right of citizens of the United States to vote shall not be denied or abridged by the United States or by any state on account of race, color, or previous condition of servitude."

8. George Washington Cable, "The Freedman's Case in Equity," *Century Illustrated Monthly Magazine* 39 (January 1885): 94 ff., reprinted in George Washington Cable, *The Negro Question: A Selection of Writings on Civil Rights in the South* (Garden City, N.Y.: Doubleday Anchor Books, 1958), 54-82, 57-58.

9. Henry W. Grady, "In Plain Black and White," *Century Illustrated Monthly Magazine* 29 (November 1884-April 1885): 909-917, 910.

10. Ibid., 912, 916. For a sustained discussion of Cable's call for a "just assortment of persons" based on "the decency or indecency of appearance or manners," a call that allows elements of the social (e.g., intimacy, association, and need) to intrude on the legal and private feelings to encroach on matters of public policy, see Saidiya Hartman, "Instinct and Injury: Bodily Integrity, Natural Affinities, and the Constitution of Equality," in *Scenes of Subjection: Terror, Slavery, and Self-Making in Nineteenth-Century America* (New York: Oxford University Press, 1997), 164-206, esp. 164-71.

11. Ralph Ellison, "What America Would Be Like without Blacks," in *Going to the Territory* (New York: Random House, 1986), 104-12, originally published in *Time* (April 6, 1970), 54-55.

12. I have Catherine Gallagher to thank for this and many other insights concerning counterfactuals. Gallagher's own work on "undoing history"—and, specifically, on the pertinence of the counterfactual to twentieth-century civil rights law's "remedial" vision of justice—has revealed to me the difference between a cynical social imaginary of the pre-*Plessy* era, which sees the present in question as the only possible present, and a more optimistic post-*Brown v. Board of Education* (1954) jurisprudence, in which the ability to imagine an alternative and parallel universe (an essentially post-Einsteinian achievement) is prerequisite to the law's application of a logic of remedy, remediation, and, in certain instances, reparations; prerequisite, i.e., to such acts of judicial intervention as affirmative action. Another

way of making this distinction—which Gallagher herself does—would be to say that the architects of Reconstruction were not motivated by an idea of equitable remedy and that the Supreme Court would not have to contend with the issue of "restitution" for segregation in public accommodations until the latter half of the twentieth century, because it was only following the passage of the Civil Rights Act of 1964 that "remedy" for the present effects of past discrimination became a legitimate legal concern. Catherine Gallagher, "Undoing," in *Time and the Literary,* ed. Karen Newman, Jay Clayton, and Marianne Hirsch (New York: Routledge, 2002), 11-29.

Conscious, no doubt, of the primacy of remediation in current civil rights law, Derrick Bell structures his pathbreaking meditation on racial justice, *And We Are Not Saved: The Elusive Quest for Racial Justice* (New York: Basic Books, 1987), around plots of backward time travel very similar to the plots Gallagher observes in such films as *Back to the Future* (1985) and *Terminator* (1984) and in the case of *Regents of the University of California v. Bakke* (1978). In ten allegories of the law he calls "Chronicles," Bell has his fictional protagonist, Geneva Crenshaw, participate in a series of visitations to deliberative junctures in the history of American jurisprudence, to events that have a direct bearing on the black experience under (and of) the law. The structure of these visitations—their plots as well as their purposes—echo Croce's sketch of history's reconfiguration into "necessary" and "accidental" events, and what Gallagher designates the Y-shaped plot of backward time-travel narratives. Geneva's first words to the delegates to the Constitutional Convention of 1787 reveal as much: "Gentlemen, my name is Geneva Crenshaw, and I appear here to you as a representation of the late twentieth century *to test* whether the decisions you are making today *might be altered* if you were to know their future disastrous effect on the nation's people, both white and black" (26, emphasis mine). Bell explains that his choice of a format more suited to literature than to law was motivated by his need to find "a method of expression adequate to the phenomenon of rights gained, then lost, then gained again" (xi). The chronicles reflect this method, drawing on the tools "not only of reason but of unreason, of fantasy" (5). The chronicles employ "stories that are *not true*"— or, what are, in essence, counterfactuals—"to explore situations that are *real enough* but, in their many and contradictory dimensions, defy understanding" (7, emphases mine).

13. The tone of the protasis is subjunctive—i.e., designating a mood "the forms of which are employed to denote an action or a state as conceived (and not as a fact) and therefore used to express a wish, command, exhortation, or a contingent, hypothetical, or prospective event" (*Oxford English Dictionary,* 2d ed.).

14. E. D. Hirsch, "Counterfactuals in Interpretation," in *Interpreting Law and Literature,* ed. Sandford Levinson and Stephen Mailloux (Evanston, Ill.: Northwestern University Press, 1988), 55-68, 65. For a different account of counterfactuals (in history and the social sciences), see Geoffrey Hawthorn, "Counterfactuals, Explanation, and Understanding," in *Plausible Worlds: Possibility and Understanding in History and the Social Sciences* (Cambridge: Cambridge University Press, 1991), 1-37.

15. H. L. A. Hart and A. M. Honoré, *Causation in the Law* (Oxford: Clarendon Press, 1959), 15. See also Richard B. Brathwaite, *Scientific Explanation: A Study of the Function of Theory, Probability and Law in Science* (Cambridge: Cambridge University Press, 1953).

16. What I mean to say here is that any relationship of causality can be deconstructed into a metonymy—so, e.g., while there is truth in the observation that "bees sting!" it does not follow that when one finds a drone perched menacingly on one's forearm pain imminently will follow. Causality is a function of the metaphor sustained (e.g., chain of causation, web of causation); so my assertion might be translated, less complexly, as "a metaphor can be deconstructed into a metonymy." On the distinction of "chain" and "web" as metaphors

of causation, as "pure fabrication[s] of the mind," see Nicholas St. John Green, "Proximate and Remote Cause," *American Law Review* 4 (1870): 201-16, 211; see also, Morton J. Horwitz, "The Progressive Attack on Freedom of Contract and Objective Causation," in *The Transformation of American Law, 1870 -1960: The Crisis of Legal Orthodoxy* (New York: Oxford University Press, 1992), 33-63; and Brook Thomas, "Narratives of Responsibility and Blame in Nineteenth-Century United States Law and Literature," *Narrative* 5, no. 1 (1997): 3-19.

17.   Hume's claim protects the fundamentally determinist idea that causal statements can only be predicated on laws—also known as the "covering law" model of causation—that a causal link between two phenomena X_1 and Y_1 could only be posited if a "series of cases in which events $X_1, X_2, X_3, X_4 \ldots$ had been followed by $Y_1, Y_2, Y_3, Y_4 \ldots$ had been observed—a series sufficiently long to justify the inference that Xs are always (or very likely to be) followed by Ys." See Niall Ferguson, "Virtual History: Toward a 'Chaotic' Theory of the Past," in *Virtual History: Alternatives and Counterfactuals,* ed. Niall Ferguson (London: Macmillan, 1997), 1-90, 79. See also, David Hume, *A Treatise on Human Nature* (1739, 1740), ed. Ernest C. Mossner (New York: Penguin, 1985), bk. 1, pt. 3, chap. 14, 205-23, 216.

18.   Joel Fineman terms this law "narrative." He queries: "How, in principle, does one identify an event within an historical frame, first, as an event, second, as an event that is, in fact, historically significant? . . . How do singular events warrant or call out for the contextualizing, narrative frame within which they will individually play their collectively intelligible parts, i.e., how does one arrive, from a multiplicity of occurrences, first, at a single and coordinating story, second, at an historically significant story, for, again, these are stories that are not, as such, historically significant" ("The History of the Anecdote," in *The New Historicism,* ed. H. Aram Veeser [New York: Routledge, 1989], 49-76, 54). See also Jacques Derrida, "Signature Event Context," in *Limited Inc.* (Evanston, Ill.: Northwestern University Press, 1988), 1-23.

19.   In John Rawls's assessment of Kant, the categorical imperative represents a "principle of conduct that applies to a person in virtue of his nature as a free and equal rational being" and ranks as valid precisely to the extent that it does not presuppose that one has a particular desire or aim. See John Rawls, *A Theory of Justice* (1971; reprint, Cambridge, Mass.: Belknap Press, Harvard University Press, 1999), 222-23.

20.   For a sustained critique of the notion of "neutral principles," see Stanley Fish, *The Trouble with Principle* (Cambridge, Mass.: Harvard University Press, 1999), 1-15.

21.   These questions form the crux of Robert W. Fogel's work on the railroads and slavery: *Railroads and American Economic Growth: Essays in Interpretative Econometric History* (Baltimore: Johns Hopkins University Press, 1964), and *Without Consent or Contract: The Rise and Fall of American Slavery* (New York: W. W. Norton, 1989); and R. W. Fogel and Stanley L. Engerman, *Time on the Cross: The Economics of American Negro Slavery* (Boston: Little, Brown, 1974).

22.   Isaac D'Israeli, "Of a History of Events Which Have Not Happened," in *Curiosities of Literature* (1791-93; reprint, New York: Garland, 1971).

23.   On counterhistory, see Catherine Gallagher and Stephen Greenblatt, "Counterhistory and the Anecdote," in *Practicing New Historicism* (Chicago: University of Chicago Press, 2000), 49-74.

24.   Benedetto Croce, "'Necessity' in History," in *Philosophy, Poetry, History: An Anthology of Essays,* trans. Cecil Sprigge (London: Oxford University Press, 1966), 557-61, 557, originally published as *Filosofia, Poesia, Storia* (Milan and Naples: Riccardo Riccarddi, 1951).

25.   To object to causality on the grounds of its alleged disciplinary origins is, from the

vantage of a currently influential interdisciplinarity, an astonishingly weak claim but one that, for all its weakness, here deserves our attention.

26. Hume had himself observed this implicit connection: "[When] I turn my eye to two objects suppos'd to be plac'd in that relation [of cause and effect] . . . I immediately perceive, that they are *contiguous* in time and place, and that the object we call cause *precedes* the other we call effect . . . After a frequent repetition, I find, that upon the appearance of one of the objects, the mind is *determin'd* by custom to consider its usual attendant, and to consider it in a stronger light upon account of its relation to the first object.'Tis this impression, then, or *determination*, which affords me the idea of necessity" (*Human Nature*, 205-6).

27. I have attempted to lay out, in an admittedly condensed form, some of the central concerns raised by counterfactual history. For a more sustained discussion of counterfactualism and alternative histories, see Ferguson, "Virtual History," 1-90.

28. For an account of this transformation in nineteenth-century America, see Thomas, "Narratives of Responsibility," 3-19.

29. *Plessy* v. *Ferguson*, 163 U.S. 537 (1896), 551.

30. John Hart Ely has done much to clarify the precise error in the majority's claim. The claim here is that if blacks are insulted by segregation they have found harm in merely being classified as "black"; and, as the law often sorts people out for differential treatment (e.g., classifying "burglars" as a class to be discouraged from thievery), sting at the insult is a matter of blacks' own choosing, and not "a legally cognizable injury." The current version of this argument asserts that "homosexuals" choose not to correct our stereotype of them and, thus, given that refusal, skeptics ask, "Why should we let them seek salvation in the courts when we ask [*sic*] on the basis of it?" Both arguments concern the "mutability" of a classification and will be associated in twentieth-century American jurisprudence (esp. under the Court of Chief Justice Earl Warren) with "suspect classifications" doctrine. The doctrine of suspect classifications permits judges to analyze the goals legislators had in mind when they passed a law; and if the law turns out "directly to pursue a substantial goal (other than the impermissible one of simply disadvantaging those it disadvantages), it will survive." Therein lies the error of the Brown Court's ways. See Ely's "Facilitating the Representation of Minorities," chap. 6 of *Democracy and Distrust: A Theory of Judicial Review* (Cambridge, Mass.: Harvard University Press, 1980), 145-70, 163.

31. On the Hayes-Tilden Compromise of the 1876 presidential election, the Progress of the Age Centennial Exposition in Philadelphia, and the ways in which they together mark the failure of republican (and Republican) promises of civic virtue, see Eric Foner, *Reconstruction: America's Unfinished Revolution, 1863-1877* (New York: Harper & Row, 1988), 564-87.

32. Albion W. Tourgée, *Pactolus Prime* (1890; reprint, Upper Saddle River, N.J.: Gregg Press, 1968), 310.

33. For more on Posner and White's value-neutral view of the law, see the discussion at n. 98, chap. 1, above.

34. Wai Chee Dimock, *Residues of Justice: Literature, Law, and Philosophy* (Berkeley: University of California Press, 1996), 23. Dimock takes the term "frugality" from Bentham's *Principles of Morals and Legislation,* I assume. There, Bentham describes "frugality" as the sixth property of punishment (after [1] "variability," [2] "equability," [3] "commensurability," [4] "characteristicalness," and [5] "exemplarity," and before [7] "subservience to reformation," [8] "efficacy in disabling," [9] "subserviency to compensation," [10] "popularity," and, finally [11] "remissability"). By "frugality," Bentham means punishment absent a superfluity of pain, free from the production of "any particle of pain . . . which contributes nothing to the effect proposed." He explains: "Now if any mode of punishment is more apt

than another to produce any such superfluous and needless pain, it may be styled *unfrugal;* if less, it may be styled *frugal. Frugality,* therefore, is a sixth property to be wished for in a mode of punishment" ("Of the Properties to Be Given to a Lot of Punishment," in *An Introduction to the Principles of Morals and Legislation* (1780), ed. Wilfrid Harrison [New York: Macmillan, 1948], 299-311, esp. 303-4).

The phrase "uneven development" properly belongs, of course, to Karl Marx, who in the *Grundrisse* describes an "uneven development of material production relative to artistic development," which can be discovered as well in an assessment of "how relations of production develop unevenly as legal relations" (*Grundrisse: Foundations of the Critique of Political Economy (Rough Draft),* trans. Martin Nicolaus [New York: Penguin, 1993], 109, originally published as *Grundrisse der Kritik der Politischen Ökonomie (Rohentwurf)* [1857-58]). What is more, regarding the uneven development between law and literature, or jurisprudence and rhetoric, Dimock certainly has cause for concern, as Holmes himself intimates that it is this "unevenness" that lends law its own discrete purposes (though I will argue against even this forcefully ascetic self-fashioning):

> The process [of predicting the force of the law] is one, from a lawyer's statement of a case, eliminating as it does all the dramatic elements with which his client's story has clothed it, and retaining only the facts of legal import, up to the final analyses and abstract universals of theoretic jurisprudence. The reason why a lawyer does not mention that his client wore a white hat when he made a contract, while Mrs. Quickly would be sure to dwell upon it along with the parcel gilt goblet and the sea-coal fire, is that he foresees that the public force will act in the same way whatever his client had upon his head. ("The Path of the Law," in *Collected Legal Papers* [New York: Harcourt, Brace & Co., 1920], 168, originally published in *Harvard Law Review* 10 [1897]: 457)

Shakespeare's garrulous matron need not worry, for, as Holmes makes clear, lush signification and what we might call "thick description" (following Geertz) are together the province of literature, not law.

35. Immanuel Kant, *The Philosophy of Law,* trans. W. Hastie (Edinburgh: T. & T. Clark, 1887), 197, originally published as *Metaphysische Anfangsgrunde der Rechslehre* (1796). Jeremy Bentham, *A Fragment on Government and an Introduction to the Principles of Morals and Legislation* (1789), ed. Wilfrid Harrison (New York: Macmillan Co., 1948), 3. Holmes, "Path of the Law," 171 and passim.

36. Dimock, *Residues of Justice,* 33. Guyora Binder and Robert Weisberg hold a position in relation to this literary sensibility to law that is very much in sympathy with my own. They note that when this sensibility is expressed in terms of the profit to be derived from reading imaginative literature (as in the case of *Residues of Justice* it is), "it is too easily inferred that the literary imagination can have no place in the actual practice, critique, and reform of law." What can result, they add, is "a reductive view of law and an uncritical acceptance of imaginative literature's hardly impartial self-portrayals" (*Literary Criticisms of the Law* [Princeton, N.J.: Princeton University Press, 2000], 4).

37. Jeremy Bentham, *A Fragment on Ontology,* in *The Works of Jeremy Bentham,* ed. John Bowring, 11 volumes (Edinburgh: W. Tait, 1838-43), 8:197-99. A "legal fiction" was, of course, for both Bentham and his mentor Cesare Beccaria, a quite specific thing, a fallacious derivation of legal conclusions from assumptions that were far from legal in origin. Thus, in the *Theory of Legislation,* e.g., Bentham chastises rules derived from the fiction that a traitor's blood is corrupt—specifically, the consequence under law that, for reasons of the convicted traitor's sanguineal impurity, his property cannot be inherited by his descen-

dants and must be forfeited to the state. Beccaria, similarly, in *On Crimes and Punishments*, mocks the rule that warrants the exclusion of a condemned criminal's testimony, the rule that views him as "civilly dead" and, thus, as a dead man, incapable of any action. See Bentham, *Theory of Legislation*, trans. Richard Hildreth (London: Trübner, 1874), 71. See also Beccaria, *On Crimes and Punishments*, trans. H. Paolucci (Indianapolis: Library of Liberal Arts, 1963), 23, originally published as *Dei delitti e delle pene* (1764).

Logical fictions, on the contrary, were quite distinct from legal fictions in the minds of both and proved the first step in Bentham's construction of a general theory of obligation. H. L. A. Hart finds a simple modern example of a logical fiction in the concept of "the average man."

> There are in our language many expressions which at first sight look as if they were the names of real things in the world but are not such names; yet none the less they are used in making statements about real things in the world which are perfectly meaningful and often true. . . . The expression "the average man" does not name or refer to stand for any particular body or any thing, yet the sentence "In America the average man is 5 feet 6 in height and weighs 135 lb." has certainly a meaning and it may be true; and we can say perfectly well what this meaning is in sentences that dispense with the expression "the average man." . . . So for Bentham "the average man" would be the name of a fiction: and it is in this sense that "obligation" and "duty" are fictitious entities. ("Legal Duty and Obligation," in *Essays on Bentham: Studies in Jurisprudence and Political Theory* [Oxford: Clarendon Press, 1982], 127–61, 128–29)

38. Hence, we might consider that the speaker meant to say (or said, yet more efficiently), "I am bound to serve this obligation," where the material image is said to be "the image of a cord or any other tie or bond (from the Latin *ligo* to bind) by which the object in question is *bound* or fastened to any other, the person in question bound to a certain course of practice." See Bentham, *Chrestomathia* (1816), in *The Works of Jeremy Bentham*, ed. Bowring, 8:126.

39. Albion W. Tourgée, "Brief for Plaintiff in Error," in *Ex parte Homer A. Plessy* (October term, 1895), 35–36, in *Landmark Briefs and Arguments of the Supreme Court of the United States: Constitutional Law*, ed. Philip B. Kurland and Gerhard Casper (Washington, D.C.: University Publications of America, 1975), 13:27–63, 62–63.

40. Harry Berger, "Metaphor and Metonymy and the End of the Middle Ages" (Literature Board, University of California, Santa Cruz, photocopy), 5.

41. William Empson quoted in ibid., 5.

42. Adam Smith, *The Theory of Moral Sentiments* (1759), ed. D. D. Raphael and A. L. Macfie (Indianapolis: Liberty Fund, 1984), 7.3.1.4.

43. James Chandler has recently proposed that this promise of sympathy to allow us to put ourselves in another's "case" makes up part of the genealogy of the shot/reverse shot structure of Frank Capra's sentimental dramas ("Remediated Sentiments: Theater, Print, Cinema" [paper delivered in the Department of English, University of California, Berkeley, November 6, 2000]). For a dazzling account of the fetishistic residues of antislavery sentimentality, see Saidiya Hartman, "Innocent Amusements: The Stage of Sufferance," in *Scenes of Subjection*, 17–23 and passim.

44. Karl Marx, *Das Kapital: Kritik der politischen Ökonomie*, in Karl Marx and Friedrich Engels, *Werke* (1890; reprint, Berlin: Dietz, 1984]), 23:52.

45. George Puttenham, *The Arte of English Poesie* (1589; reprint, Cambridge: Cambridge University Press, 1936), 180.

46. I take this narrative from Thomas Keenan's "The Point Is to (Ex)change It: Reading *Capital*, Rhetorically," in *Fetishism as Cultural Discourse*, ed. Emily Apter and William Pietz (Ithaca, N.Y.: Cornell University Press, 1993), 152–85, 183.

47. I attribute counterfactual logic as a "fuzzy logic" inspired, in part, by Richard Posner's use of the phrase "fuzzy analysis" to describe the competing contentions, commonsense assumptions, and conspiratorial suspicions that, in his words, were "once used to justify the separate but equal doctrine of *Plessy v. Ferguson*" ("The *Bakke* Case and the Future of 'Affirmative Action,'" *California Law Review* 67, no. 1 [1979]: 171–89, 176). Of course, over the course of the twentieth century, constitutional law would develop two more rigorous (and less fuzzy) standards of equal protection—the "rationality" test and the "strict scrutiny" test (a.k.a., "special scrutiny" or "suspect classifications" doctrine)—about which I will have a great deal more to say in the coming pages.

48. The proposition that a history of segregation might be written absent an account of slavery as its causal precursor is not as outlandish as it seems, especially when we consider that, in the wake of *Plessy's* passage, adherents to the school of historical relativism would essentially (though only analogously) attempt to do just that. I have in mind here Charles A. Beard's *The Discussion of Human Affairs* (New York: Macmillan, 1936), a speculative attempt to write a history without causes; which attempt, notes Brook Thomas, "run[s] the risk of writing histories without agents either to praise or to blame" ("Narratives of Responsibility," 10–11).

49. Geoffrey Chaucer, *The Canterbury Tales*, ed. V. A. Kolve and Glending Olsen (New York: W. W. Norton & Co., 1989), 75–104. The description of these tales' "joke of malice in the dark" is taken from "The Cook's Prologue," 105.

50. André Gaudrault, "Temporality and Narrativity in Early Cinema, 1895–1908," in *Film before Griffith*, ed. John Fell (Berkeley: University of California Press, 1983), 311–29, 324.

51. Tom Gunning, "The Cinema of Attraction: Early Film, Its Spectator and the Avant-Garde," *Wide Angle* 8, nos. 3/4 (1986): 63–70, 64.

52. Georges Méliès, "Importance du Scénario," in *Georges Méliès*, ed. Georges Sadoul (Paris: Seghers, 1961), 118, quoted in Gunning, "The Cinema of Attractions," 64. For further elaborations of the "cinema of attractions" thesis, see also, Tom Gunning's "Heard over the Phone: *The Lonely Villa* and the De Lorde Tradition of the Terrors of Technology," *Screen* 32, no. 2 (1991): 184–96, and "Weaving a Narrative: Style and Economic Background in Griffith's Biograph Films," *Quarterly Review of Film Studies* 6 (1981): 12–25.

53. Saint Augustine, *The Confessions*, trans. Rex Warner (New York: New American Library, 1963), 245–47, quoted in Tom Gunning, "An Aesthetic of Astonishment: Early Film and the (In)Credulous Spectator," in *Viewing Positions: Ways of Seeing Film*, ed. Linda Williams (New Brunswick, N.J.: Rutgers University Press, 1995), 114–33, 124. See also Jacques Lacan's "Of the Subject Who Is Supposed to Know, of the First Dyad, and of the Good," for a discussion of the *unlust* as that which remains unassimilable, "irreducible to the pleasure principle" (in *The Four Fundamental Concepts of Psycho-Analysis*, ed. Jacques-Alain Miller [New York: W. W. Norton, 1981], 230–43, 241).

54. Gunning, "Cinema of Attraction[s]," 66.

55. Sigmund Freud, *Beyond the Pleasure Principle* (1920–22), vol. 18 of *Standard Edition of the Complete Psychological Works of Sigmund Freud,*, gen. ed. James Strachey, in collaboration with Anna Freud, and with the assistance of Alix Strachey and Alan Tyson, 24 vols. (London: Hogarth Press, 1953–74), 35, vol. 18 originally published as *Jenseits des Lustprinzips* (Leipzig: Internationaler Psychoanalytischer Verlag, 1920).

56. Gunning, "Aesthetic of Astonishment," 119.

57. Some of the most brilliant and "perceptive" work on the aesthetics of trompe l'oeil

can be found in the field of art history. On trompe l'oeil and the realist project, see Michael Fried, *Courbet's Realism* (Chicago: University of Chicago Press, 1990), and *Realism, Writing, and Disfiguration: On Thomas Eakins and Stephen Crane* (Chicago: University of Chicago Press, 1987), 42–56. See also, Norman Bryson's "The Natural Attitude" and "The Essential Copy," chaps. 1 and 2, respectively, of *Vision and Painting: The Logic of the Gaze* (New Haven, Conn.: Yale University Press, 1983), 1–35. On the origins of modern trompe l'oeil, see Svetlana Alpers, *The Art of Describing: Dutch Art in the Seventeenth Century* (Chicago: University of Chicago Press, 1983), 72–118; and Madlyn Millner Kahr, *Dutch Painting in the Seventeenth Century* (New York: Harper & Row, 1978), 189–203. On trompe l'oeil and the illusionist fundaments of turn-of-the-century theories of paper money, see Walter Benn Michaels, *The Gold Standard and the Logic of Naturalism* (Berkeley: University of California Press, 1987), 161–66.

58. Mary Ann Doane, *Femmes Fatales: Feminism, Film Theory, Psychoanalysis* (New York: Routledge, 1991), 193.

59. Jean-Louis Comolli cited in ibid., 193; see Comolli, "Technique and Ideology: Camera, Perspective, Depth of Field," *Film Reader* 2 (1977): 136.

60. Robert Sklar, *Movie-Made America: A Cultural History of American Movies* (New York: Random House, 1976), 21.

61. Lynne Kirby, *Parallel Tracks: The Railroad and Silent Cinema* (Durham, N.C.: Duke University Press, 1997), 94.

62. Sigmund Freud, *Jokes and Their Relation to the Unconscious*, ed. and trans. James Strachey (New York: Norton, 1963), 97.

63. The space Kirby describes is akin to what Margaret Morse terms the "nonspace" of postmodernity, which describes the experience of televisual, mall, and freeway space. Morse designates nonspace as a type of "mobile privatization," as the "ground within which communication as a flow of values among and between two and three dimensions and between virtuality and actuality . . . can 'take place'" ("An Ontology of Everyday Distraction: The Freeway, the Mall, and Television," in *Logics of Television: Essays in Cultural Criticism*, ed. Patricia Mellencamp [Bloomington: Indiana University Press, 1990], 196). Anne Freidberg's *Window Shopping: Cinema and the Postmodern* (Berkeley: University of California Press, 1993) follows a line of argument similar to Morse's. I thank Manthia Diawara for bringing this work to my attention.

64. D. A. Miller makes a trenchant (and persuasive) case for the hermeneutic and narrative import of the fade to black in his "Anal *Rope*," *Representations* 32 (fall 1990): 114–33.

65. On the concept of *Erwartungshorizont*, see Hans Robert Jauss, "Literatur als Provokation der Literatur-Wissenschaft," in *Literaturegeschichte als Provokation* (Frankfurt a.M.: Suhrkamp, 1970).

66. Aristotle, *Physics*, trans. Hippocrates G. Apostle and Lloyd P. Gerson (Grinnell, Iowa: Peripatetic Press, 1982), 2.5.189–91, 197a20. Hereafter cited by line number in parenthesis in the text.

For Aristotle, time is characterized by its alleged "nonbeing," which poses particular phenomenological difficulties: "One part of it has come to be but no longer exists; the other part will be but does not yet exist; and it is of these two parts that . . . any time one might take, is composed" (4.10. 217b35–37). He continues: "The prior and the posterior are attributes primarily of a place, and in virtue of position. . . . We also know the time when we limit a motion by specifying in it a prior and a posterior as its limits; and it is then that we say that time has elapsed, that is, when we perceive the prior and the posterior *in a motion*" (219a15–25, emphasis mine).

67. Michel Foucault, "Of Other Spaces," *Diacritics* 16, no. 1 (1986): 22–27, 26.

68. Jacques Lacan, "*Tuché* and Automaton," in *The Four Fundamental Concepts of Psycho-analysis*, ed. Jacques-Alain Miller, trans. Alan Sheridan (New York: W. W. Norton, 1978), 53-64, 52, originally published as *Le Séminaire de Jacques Lacan, Livre XI, "Les quatre concepts fondamentaux de la psychanalyse"* (Paris: Éditions du Seuil, 1973).

69. The clearest elaboration of the concept of *Wiederholungszwang* is in *Beyond the Pleasure Principle*, though Freud makes reference to the concept in "Recollecting, Repeating and Working-Through" (1914), published in German as, "Erinnern, Wiederholen, und Durcharbeiten," in *Studienausgabe*, ed. A. Mitscherlich, A. Richards, and J. Strachey (Frankfurt am Main: S. Fisher, 1969-), *Ergänzungsband: Schriften zur Behandlungstechnik*, 210-11. For a meditation on repetition and history engaged with an intellectual lineage leading back to Vico's *Sciencia Nuovo*, see Edward Said's "On Repetition," in *The World, the Text, and the Critic* (Cambridge, Mass.: Harvard University Press, 1983), 111-25.

70. *Ob-* (pref.), toward, before, about, near; *sceaena*, ~*ae*, background against which a play is performed. Most dictionaries and lexicons admit that the term *obscene* is of "doubtful etymology." See *A Concise Etymological Dictionary of the English Language*, ed. Walter W. Skeat (New York: Pedigree, 1980); *Oxford Latin Dictionary*, ed. P. G. W. Glare (Oxford: Clarendon, 1996).

71. Charles A. Lofgren, *The Plessy Case: A Legal-Historical Interpretation* (New York: Oxford University Press, 1987), 28-29.

72. *Slaughter-House Cases*, 16 Wallace 36 (1873), 68-72.

73. *United States v. Cruikshank*, 92 U.S. 542 (1876); *United States v. Harris*, 106 U.S. 629 (1883); *Civil Rights Cases*, 109 U.S. 3 (1883), 22. See John Hope Franklin, *From Slavery to Freedom: A History of Negro Americans* (New York: Alfred A. Knopf, 1974), 266-67, for a discussion of the *U.S. v. Harris* and *U.S. v. Cruikshank* Supreme Court decisions.

74. *State ex rel. Abbott v. Hicks*, 44 La. Ann. 583, 11 So. 74 (1892); *Louisville, New Orleans and Texas Railway Company v. Mississippi*, 133 U.S. 587 (1890); *State v. Desdunes* (Crim. Dist. Ct., Parish of Orleans, 1892).

75. *State v. Plessy*, Crim. Dist. Ct., Parish of Orleans, 1892-97; *Ex parte Homer A. Plessy*, 45 La. Ann. 80, 11 So. 949 (1892).

76. *Ex parte Homer A. Plessy*, quoted in *The Thin Disguise: Turning Point in Negro History, Plessy v. Ferguson, a Documentary Presentation (1864-1896)*, ed. Otto H. Olsen (New York: Humanities Press, 1967), 71.

77. *Roberts v. City of Boston*, 5 Cushing 198 (1849); *West Chester and Philadelphia Railroad Company v. Miles*, 55 Pa. 209 (1867).

78. A "writ of error *coram nobis*" is a civil action. A higher court will make a writ of error available to an aggrieved party who feels that an inferior court has committed an error. The writ of error is a request issuing from a superior court "commanding an inferior court of record to send up the entire record of a contested procedure" and is called *coram nobis* because "the record and process upon which it is founded are stated in the writ to remain 'before us.'" A writ of error is neither intended to correct any perceived faults in the judgment of the court nor "to contradict or put in issue any fact already adjudicated." The writ simply intends "to correct an error of law committed in the course of the proceedings" (e.g., evidence, requests, rulings on motions, instructions to lawyers or jury) ("Writs of Error," in *American and English Encyclopedia of Law*, ed. John Houston Merrill [Northport, N.Y.: Edward Thompson Co., 1888], 6:810-83, 811, 812). See also Calvin W. Chesnut, "Assignment of Errors," in *Encyclopedia of Pleading and Practice*, comp. William. M. McKinney (Northport, N.Y.: Edward Thompson Co., 1895), 926-39.

79. "Assignment of Errors," *Ex parte Homer A. Plessy*, January 5, 1893, in *Landmark Briefs*, ed. Kurland and Casper, 30.

80. Samuel Warren and Louis Brandeis, "The Right to Privacy," *Harvard Law Review* 4, no. 5 (1890): 193–220, 194, 205. For another set of reflections from the time on the topic of reputation, see E. L. Godkin, "The Rights of the Citizen: IV. To His Own Reputation," *Scribner's Magazine* 8 (1890): 66. See also Cheryl Harris's "Whiteness as Property" for a more sustained discussion of how Homer Plessy's claim to a property right in his whiteness intersects with concurrent conceptualizations of the privacy tort. Harris's investigations into Plessy's assertions of his property right in himself qua reputation provide a touchstone in her argument that racial identity and property are deeply interrelated concepts ("Whiteness as Property," *Harvard Law Review* 106, no. 8 [1993]: 1709–91).

81. In the debate over the language of the Fourteenth Amendment, Representative John A. Bingham held that under the amendment's remedy "the powers of the States have been limited and the powers of Congress extended" (quoted in Foner, *Reconstruction*, 258).

82. *Strauder v. West Virginia*, 110 U.S. 303 (1880), 308; in Tourgée, "Brief for Plaintiff in Error," 23.

83. As an unremarked irony in these deliberations over separate-but-equal doctrine, an anticipation of that phrase appears in embryo, in the text of American law, in the Declaration of Independence itself. The first lines of the Declaration read, familiarly: "When, in the course of human events, it becomes necessary for one people to dissolve the political bands which have connected them with another, and to assume among the powers of the earth the *separate and equal* station to which the laws of nature and of nature's God entitle them, a decent respect to the opinions of mankind requires that they should declare the causes which impel them to the separation." The irony, of course, is that where the claim to "separate and equal station" founds the claims of the American colonies to revolutionary sovereignty, invoked as a metaphor for racial segregation separate-but-equal doctrine will protect southern cultural sovereignty. One need only recall here Grady's appeal for regional independence: "The South must be allowed to settle the social relations of the races according to her own views of what is right and best."

84. The relevant passage from the Declaration of Independence reads: "We hold these truths to be self-evident; that all men are created equal; that they are endowed by their creator with certain unalienable rights." The phrase is frequently misquoted as "inalienable," as occurs in *Cruikshank*.

85. Much early privacy case law protected a right against intrusion and to seclusion, which together made up a general privilege to withdraw from public life. But the transformation to which Tourgée's defense of Plessy's "reputation" pointed, the transformation of a right to privacy into a right to publicity, presented both a manifest contradiction ("How can a person insist, at one and the same time, on a right to be left alone and a right to stake out a claim to a public persona?") and one that would take decades to work itself out in the courts. The property rights Tourgée described—a right to "the reputation of being a white man," a "right of action or inheritance," a right to a property with "actual pecuniary value"—essentially add up to a right to stake out a claim to a public persona. This right, similar in many regards to a trademark in one's persona, lends the latter commercial viability, affords it a pecuniary value, and entitles the right-bearer to either transfer the right or leave it to his or her heirs. It is a right to publicity born once courts turned inside out the older right to be let alone. The right to publicity entered common law with the judgment in *Haelan Laboratories, Inc. v. Topps Chewing Gum, Inc.* (202 F. 2d 866 [2d Cir. 1953]) and was limned doctrinally to the right to privacy in *Lugosi v. Universal Pictures, Inc.* (172 U.S. P. Q. 541 [1972], rev'd, 70 Cal. App. 3d 552 [1977], aff'd, 25 Cal. 3d 813 [1979]). On the transformation of privacy into publicity, see Jane Gaines, *Contested Culture: The Image, the Voice, and the Law* (Chapel Hill: University of North Carolina Press, 1991), 175–207, 178.

86. See Foner, *Reconstruction,* 257–58; and Ronald Dworkin, *Taking Rights Seriously* (Cambridge, Mass.: Harvard University Press, 1977), 133.

87. In the debate over the language of the Fourteenth Amendment, Democrats charged that the Amendment was "open to ambiguity and . . . conflicting constructions" (Foner, *Reconstruction,* 257). The Fifth, Sixth and similar restrictive amendments are essentially "statutes" writ large, where we would take a statute to deal with narrow, immediate concerns. These sorts of amendments, Foner notes, alter "one aspect of national life, . . . leav[ing] the larger structure intact" (*Reconstruction,* 257). Other amendments, such as the Fourteenth, are "broad statements of principle, giving constitutional form to the resolution of national crises, and permanently altering American nationality" (*Reconstruction,* 257). See also Edward S. Corwin, "The Supreme Court and the Fourteenth Amendment," *Michigan Law Review* 7, no. 8 (1909): 643–72; Daniel A. Farber and John E. Muench, "The Ideological Origins of the Fourteenth Amendment," *Constitutional Commentary* 1 (1984): 235–79; and Robert J. Kaczorowski, "Searching for the Intent of the Framers of the Fourteenth Amendment," *Connecticut Law Review* 5 (1972–73): 368–98.

88. Cheryl Harris offers a trenchant critique of the Supreme Court's recent reduction of equal protection to the narrowed contours of equal treatment in "Equal Treatment and the Reproduction of Inequality" (Symposium on the Constitution of Equal Citizenship for a Good Society), *Fordham Law Review* 69 (April 2001): 1753 ff.

89. The provision of the Fourteenth Amendment concerned with "property," specifically, is addressed to myriad patterns of "distribution" generally. The amendment has been taken, over the course of its judicial interpretation, to cover both immunity from hurts (punishments, taxes, regulations) and benefits (rights, entitlements).

90. Bentham, *Anarchical Fallacies,* in *The Works of Jeremy Bentham,* ed. Bowring, 2:501. Bentham's caricature is directed at the doctrine of natural rights enshrined in the French Declaration of the Rights of Man and the Citizen (1791) and the American Declaration of Independence (1776)—the belief, specifically, that there are rights anterior to positive law, that there are essentially "antilegal" rights. The argument of Dworkin's *Taking Rights Seriously* is that there are important conceptual connections between law and morality obscured by the positivist, utilitarian tradition identified with Bentham; and, to the extent that Dworkin's theory of "equality" fits within this argument, its corresponding implicit notion of justice extends a doctrine of the "unalienable rights of man" of long and esteemed provenance. For a critique of Dworkin, see H. L. A. Hart's "Between Utility and Rights," *Columbia Law Review* 79, no. 5 (1979): 828–46.

91. See John Austin, *The Province of Jurisprudence Determined* (London: J. Murray, 1832); Nicholas St. John Green, "Proximate and Remote Cause," *American Law Review* 4 (1870): 201–16; Charles Sanders Pierce, *Pragmatism and Pragmaticism,* in *Collected Papers of Charles Sanders Peirce,* ed. Charles Hartshorne and Paul Weiss (Cambridge, Mass.: Harvard University Press, 1960), 5:1–455, esp. the section titled "Normative Judgements," 69–73; and Holmes, "Path of the Law."

92. Alexander Bickel, *The Least Dangerous Branch* (Indianapolis: Bobbs-Merrill, 1962), 55.

93. John Rawls, *A Theory of Justice* (Cambridge, Mass.: Harvard University Press, 1971), 72.

94. Bickel, *Least Dangerous Branch,* 103.

95. Ely, *Democracy and Distrust,* 32.

96. *United States v. Carolene Products Co.,* 304 U.S. 144 (1938).

97. I thank Tobias B. Wolff for bringing the *Carolene* footnote to my attention.

98. The rationality standard rarely suffices, and gives rise in the *Carolene* footnote to a

"more searching judicial inquiry," for two reasons. First, rationality, when used as a constitutional standard, often dampens the spirit of the equal protection clause—perhaps no less
so than when Justice Brown responds to the plaintiff's assertion in *Plessy* that separate-but-
equal doctrine might also authorize legislatures to pass laws requiring "white men's houses
to be painted white, and colored men's black" with the disclaimer that "every exercise of the
police power must be reasonable, and extend only to such laws as are enacted in good faith
for the promotion for [*sic*] the public good, and not for the annoyance or oppression of a particular class" (*Plessy*, 549, 550). Second, and most important, a rationality standard is
difficult to defend in theory, since when one takes into account all the many legislative coun-
terexamples and cross-purposes the classification at issue is bound to relate at least "ration-
ally." Richard Posner has come to something of the same conclusion: "A good deal of racially
discriminatory state action could probably be justified under a broad 'rationality' standard.
For example, since blacks are disproportionately responsible for crimes of violence, it might
be rational . . . to require blacks, but not whites, to carry identification. Or, since the educational performance of blacks is on average below that of whites, it might be rational to seg-
regate blacks in separate school, just as second graders are 'segregated' from third graders"
("The *Bakke* Case," 173).

The first case to test "strict scrutiny" as a de jure doctrine involved the matter of Japanese internment during World War II—the matter, as it would figure in the terms of the doctrine, of classifying persons and then incarcerating them for reason of advancing the constitutionally protected larger goal of maintaining peace in time of war. In *Korematsu v. United
States,* the Court's expression of the standard reads as follows: "All legal restrictions which
curtail the civil rights of a single racial group are immediately suspect. . . . Courts must subject them to the most rigid scrutiny. . . . Although pressing public necessity may sometimes
justify the existence of such restrictions, racial antagonism never can." Needless to say, the
Court found "pressing public necessity" in its belief that "persons of Japanese ancestry may
have a dangerous tendency to commit sabotage and espionage and to aid our Japanese enemy in other ways" (*Korematsu v. United States,* 323 U.S. 214, 216, 235 [1944]). The "strict
scrutiny" standard receives an important strengthening in the pivotal affirmative action case
of *Regents of the University of California v. Bakke* (1978): "A State must show that its purpose or interest is both constitutionally permissible and substantial, and that its use of the
classification is 'necessary . . . to the accomplishment' of its purpose or the safe-guarding of
its interest" (*Regents v. Bakke*, 98 S. Ct. 2733, at 2756-57, quoting *In re Griffiths,* 413 U.S.
717, at 722-23 [1973]). "Strict scrutiny" is also known as "suspect classifications" doctrine
and grants to the Supreme Court a means of analyzing the goals legislators had in mind, an
assessment of whether those goals were unconstitutional. See n. 30 above, this chap., on the
more specific goals of "suspect classifications" doctrine.

99. See n. 13 above, this chap. *Protasis* (Late L., a. Gr. πρότασις, a stretching forward,
a proposition): "The first or introductory clause in a sentence, *esp.* the clause which expresses the condition in a conditional sentence; opposed to the *apodosis*" (*Oxford English
Dictionary,* 2d ed.).

100. Robert Nozick, *Anarchy, State, and Utopia* (New York: Basic Books, 1974), 154.

101. Ibid., 154. Of structural identity, Nozick observes: "Two distributions are structurally identical if they present the same profile, but perhaps have different persons occupy-
ing the particular slots. My having ten and your having five, and my having five and your having ten are structurally identical distributions" (154).

Many early antimiscegenation cases (the word was only coined in 1864) applied "end-
result" standards to discern the constitutionality of prohibitions against racial mixture.
These laws proved so amenable to the standard's structural measure of equivalence, and so

aversive to the inclusion of history into the law, as to make of equal protection law a reductio ad absurdum. For example, in the case of *Pace v. Alabama*, the U.S. Supreme Court affirmed as constitutional an Alabama law limiting to a maximum penalty of two years imprisonment at hard labor acts of adultery or fornication between a man and a woman of the same race, a law that increased those penalties to seven years when parties of different races were involved. Justice Stephen A. Field, who wrote for the majority in that case, conceding that the Fourteenth Amendment intended equal protection to guard citizens from state legislation based on race, held that the Alabama law did not discriminate. The law's two disputed sections punished different offenses, he averred, one involving persons of the same race, the other involving persons of different races. The penalties in the former would apply whether the parties were both white or both black, as there are no "persons" subject to this law: "Whatever discrimination is made in the punishment prescribed in the two sections is directed against the offense designated and not against the person of any particular color or race" (*Pace v. Alabama*, 106 U.S. 583 [1883]).

102. Conceding a place for history (even counterfactual history) in the delivery of justice, but correcting for Nozick's undifferentiated "law" and differentiated principles of equity, John Hart Ely argues that constitutional law bears a necessary antipathy to history — presumably history of both the hypothetical and the actual kind. In *Democracy and Distrust*, Ely distinguishes the constitutionally guaranteed, which proves anathema to history, from the "constitutionally gratuitous." The Constitution grants entitlements that are presumptive — such as the right to the freedom of speech, the right peaceably to assemble, the right to redress, the right to be secure against unreasonable searches and seizures. The foundation of citizenship, the Constitution's rights, Ely cautions, can be approached intelligibly only by attending to all patent imbalances in their distribution. In short, a law withholding rights that are constitutionally presumptive should not be approached historically: "The Court's job in such cases is to look at the world as it exists and ask whether such a right is in fact being abridged, and if it is, to consider what reasons might be adduced in support of the deprivation, without regard to what actually occasioned it" (136). To the extent that these rights prove uneven in their dispersal, to the extent that there is a stoppage in their distribution, "the system is malfunctioning, and the Court should unblock it without caring about how it got that way" (136). At the same time, where matters turn to the "constitutionally gratuitous"—to those goods, benefits, rights, and exemptions that are "not essential to political participation or explicitly guaranteed by the language of the Constitution"—malfunction in their distribution "can intelligibly inhere only in the way the distribution was arrived at" (145). Ely's distinction seems accurate, since it might be taken to explain the turn in equal protection law toward a "rationality" and a "strict scrutiny" standard—both of which, with the exception the latter makes for legislators' intent, brook no quarter for historical information. Nothing in the text of the *Plessy* case or ancillary documents suggests that either the Court or Plessy's defenders found this distinction or anything analogous to it legally efficacious. See Ely, *Democracy and Distrust*, 135-45.

103. On Juba, see Eric Lott, *Love and Theft*, 113; and on "pattin' juba" see Hartman, *Scenes of Subjection*, 70-76.

104. "The 'grain' is the body in the voice as it sings, the hand as it writes, the limb as it performs" (Roland Barthes, *Image/Music/Text* [New York: Hill & Wang, 1987], 188, quoted in Lott, *Love, and Theft* 122).

105. "Zip Coon" (circa 1834), reprinted in Constance Rourke, *American Humor: A Study of the National Character* (New York: Harcourt, Brace & Co., 1931), 97.

106. Mary Ann Doane, "The Voice in Cinema: The Articulation of Body and Space," *Yale French Studies*, no. 60 (1980): 33-50, 33.

107. Jane Gaines, *Fire and Desire: Mixed-Race Movies in the Silent Era* (Chicago: University of Chicago Press, 2001), 190.

108. When I first began my research for this chapter at the Library of Congress's Motion Picture, Broadcasting and Recorded Sound Division, I was presented with a rather banal set of instructions for viewing works from the Library's Paper Print Collection. The most important directive instructed me not to rewind the films at high speed, for to do so could potentially damage the films beyond repair. At a pragmatic level, this meant that I had two options if I wanted to see a film again. Either I could return the viewed film to the librarian and have him or her rewind it for me or I could rewind it myself at normal playing speed and watch it as it rewound. I had lots of time, so I chose the latter option.

109. Charles Musser, *Before the Nickelodeon: Edwin S. Porter and the Edison Manufacturing Company* (Berkeley: University of California Press, 1991), 84. "Vitascoplcy" is an adverbial reference to Edison's "Vitascope." And we should note alternatively that Tom Gunning takes these films' primitive, nonnarrative qualities to be indicative of their place in an emergent "cinema of attractions," which he distinguishes from the current theoretical emphasis on voyeurism ("The Cinema of Attraction[s]," 63–70). And Miriam Hansen has argued that the films' crude, "primitive," and unpredictable organization marks them as the building blocks of cinema's organization as an alternative public sphere — an alternative, i.e., to other, more common amusements such as the theater, vaudeville, and the music hall (*Babel and Babylon: Spectatorship in American Silent Film* [Cambridge, Mass: Harvard University Press, 1991], 90–101).

110. I earlier emphasize the centrality of white men in this rudimentary construction of cinematic narrative, for, as Carol Clover reminds me, white women were frequently clothed and laden with props while white men strutted about in Edenic nakedness. Linda Williams (*Hard Core: Power, Pleasure, and the "Frenzy of the Visible"* [Berkeley: University of California Press, 1989]) demonstrates further that this fetishization of the white woman's body transforms Eadweard Muybridge's prototypical cinema (with all its scientific pretensions) into something of a "pornographic girlie show" (45). In her words, "the very invention of cinema develops, to a certain extent, from the desire to place the clocked and measured bodies produced by the first machines into narratives that naturalize their movements" (36), and the assumption of women's bodies into a quasi-pornographic economy of concealment and disclosure makes them (and not men) the primary sites in the early narrativization of scientific cinema. Combining Williams's insights and my own arguments regarding race in early cinema, it seems clear that women and blacks (and, in particular, the figure of the black woman) function as foils in the narrativization of cinematic expression.

111. James Snead, "On Repetition in Black Culture," in *Black Literature and Literary Theory*, ed. Henry Louis Gates, Jr. (New York: Methuen, 1984): 59–79, 60.

112. G. W. F. Hegel, *Philosophy of History*, trans. J. Sibree (New York: Collier & Son, 1902), 148–57, also published as *Die Vernunft in der Geshichte*, 5th rev. ed. (Hamburg: Felix Meiner, 1955), 216–18, quoted in Snead, "On Repetition in Black Culture," 62.

113. For more on the nonconformist, "metacultural" aspects of black musical forms, see LeRoi Jones (Imamu Amiri Baraka), *Blues People* (New York: Morrow Quill, 1963), 1–10, 175–236. See also Ingrid Monson, "Doubleness and Jazz Improvisation: Irony, Parody, and Ethnomusicology," *Critical Inquiry* 20 (winter 1994): 284–313; and Gary Tomlinson, "Cultural Dialogics and Jazz: A White Historian Signifies," in *Disciplining Music: Musicology and Its Canons* ed. Katherine Bergeron and Philip V. Bohlman (Chicago: University of Chicago Press, 1992), 64–94.

114. J. G. A. Pocock, *Virtue, Commerce, and History: Essays on Political Thought and History, Chiefly in the Eighteenth Century* (Cambridge: Cambridge University Press, 1985), 112.

115. Frederick Douglass, *Narrative of the Life of Frederick Douglass, an American Slave* (1845), ed. Houston A. Baker, Jr. (New York: Penguin, 1986), 47.

116. *Anaphora* (Gr. "carrying back"): Repetition of the same word at the beginning of successive clauses or verses (Richard A. Lanham, *A Handlist of Rhetorical Terms* [Berkeley: University of California Press, 1991]). Though both *anaphora* and *epistrophe* are related by their "continued repetition of the same word in one or diuers sentences," the former is distinguished by "a bringing back of the same soūd . . . when the same sound is iterated in the beginning of the sentence" (Abraham Fraunce, *The Arcadian Rhetorike*, ed. Ethel Seaton [Oxford: Basil Blackwell, 1588], 40.

117. Bishop E. E. Cleveland, "He Wants Your Life: The Search for the Religion of Christ," app. 1, lines 35-41, reprinted in Gerald L. Davis, *I Got the Word in Me and I Can Sing It, You Know: A Study of the Performed African-American Sermon* (Philadelphia: University of Pennsylvania Press, 1987), 121-30.

118. Snead, "On Repetition in Black Culture," 67. Snead also notes the correspondence between this musical notion of the "cut" and the cinematic notion of "cutting, editing, or montage," which "changes the picture all at once from one view to another" (Ralph Stephenson and J. R. Debrix, *The Cinema as Art* [Harmondsworth: Penguin, 1965], 238, cited in Snead, 77n. 21).

119. Richard Middleton, "In the Groove, or Blowing Your Mind? The Pleasures of Musical Repetition," in *Popular Culture and Social Relations*, ed. Tony Bennett et al. (Milton Keynes: Open University Press, 1986), 159-75, 163.

120. Ibid., 164.

121. Snead, "On Repetition in Black Culture," 148. The repression of the contributions of blacks to the sphere of invention during and after the era of slavery only adds eloquent testimony to this fractured temporality. On the historical repression of black "inventive genius," see Portia P. James, *The Real McCoy: African-American Invention and Innovation, 1619-1930* (Washington, D.C.: Smithsonian Institution Press, 1989), 47-83.

CONCLUSION

1. The higher law tradition was at ebb in the first half of the century, reinvigorated in antislavery debates (for writers such as Emerson and Douglass, and legislators such as William Seward and William Graham Sumner kept it alive), under attack by a conservative counterrevolution, and mildly ascendant in the early twentieth century with writers such as Charles Chesnutt and lawyers such as Moorfield Storey (see the latter's opinion in *Buchanan v. Worley* [1917]).

2. This closing provocation—this claim to a hermeneutic identity between the law of property and the law of equal protection—extends the insight of the mainstream of critical legal studies thought, specifically that there is no qualitative difference between the "private" rules of contract, property, and tort law and the "public" rules of environmental, administrative, and civil rights law, for "both kinds of rules had to be chosen; they were not natural or neutral. Both had distributive consequences; both were politically contentious" (Peter Boyle, introduction to *Critical Legal Studies* [New York: New York University Press, 1992], xv).

3. Eric Foner, "Blacks and the U.S. Constitution, 1789-1989," *New Left Review* 183 [1990]: 63-74, 68.

4. Robert Cover's *Justice Accused: Antislavery and the Judicial Process* (New Haven, Conn.: Yale University Press, 1975) is arguably the best exploration of the philosophical and psychological tensions between law and morality in antebellum jurisprudence. Politically (if not quite methodologically), I have taken my cue from both Cover and Foner.

5. Louis Menand, *The Metaphysical Club: A Story of Ideas in America* (New York: Farrar, Straus, & Giroux, 2001), 432.

6. Stanley Fish, *The Trouble with Principle* (Cambridge, Mass.: Harvard University Press, 1999), 4.

7. Reification in legal thought, according to Peter Gabel—the turning of concepts or social roles into things—makes us perceive our achieved structure of legal rights as a description of the way things are rather than a moral and political choice ("Reification in Legal Reasoning," *Research in Law and Sociology* 3 [1980]: 25-51).

8. Boyle, introduction, xvii-xviii.

9. The idea that all liberties flow from the principle of equality is the view of Ronald Dworkin in *Taking Rights Seriously* (Cambridge, Mass.: Harvard University Press, 1977), 273-74.

10. This is the central fracture in American jurisprudence that motivates Peter Westen's critique of the idea of equality in his essay "The Empty Idea of Equality"—and much of what I have to say in this paragraph is taken from that pathbreaking essay. See "The Empty Idea of Equality," *Harvard Law Review* 95, no. 3 (January 1982): 537-96, 538.

11. Charles Sanders Pierce, "How to Make Our Ideas Clear" (1878), reprinted in *Pragmatism: A Contemporary Reader,* ed. Russell B. Goodman (New York: Routledge, 1995), 44.

INDEX